This book focuses on conceptualizing the process of economic adjustment and growth, and testing it with empirical methods. The critical components of a successful economic growth strategy include physical, financial, and educational infrastructures supported by macro-financial stabilization policies and structural reforms. With this in mind, the authors begin with a review of the neoclassical growth model, before delving into more specialized topics such as endogenous growth, adaptive inflationary expectations, learning by doing, optimal saving, and sustainable foreign debt. The final chapter presents Philippines as a case study, and narrates the evolution of a successful strategy of adjustment and growth practiced by an emerging market economy that had shown stellar pre-pandemic growth performance, low and stable inflation, and a sustainable external current account position.

Economic Adjustment and Growth

Theory and Practice

Other Titles by Delano S Villanueva

Macroeconomic Policies for Stable Growth
Macroeconomics of Adjustment and Growth

Other Titles by Roberto S Mariano

Simulation-based Inference in Econometrics
Econometric Forecasting and High-Frequency Data Analysis

Other Titles by Diwa C Guinigundo

Trauma to Triumph: Rising from the Ashes of the Asian Financial Crisis
Redefining Strategic Routes to Financial Resilience in ASEAN+3

Economic Adjustment and Growth

Theory and Practice

Delano S Villanueva

Roberto S Mariano
University of Pennsylvania, USA &
Singapore Management University, Singapore

Diwa C Guinigundo
AIA Philippines Investment Management Corporation,
Philippines & Singapore Management University, Singapore

Foreword by

Abbas Mirakhor

EW JERSEY • LONDON • SINGAPORE • BEIJING • SHANGHAI • HONG KONG • TAIPEI • CHENNAI • TOKYO

Published by

World Scientific Publishing Co. Pte. Ltd.
5 Toh Tuck Link, Singapore 596224
USA office: 27 Warren Street, Suite 401-402, Hackensack, NJ 07601
UK office: 57 Shelton Street, Covent Garden, London WC2H 9HE

Library of Congress Cataloging-in-Publication Data
Names: Villanueva, Delano, author. | Mariano, Roberto S, author. | Guinigundo, Diwa C, author.
Title: Economic adjustment and growth : theory and practice / Delano S Villanueva, Roberto S Mariano, Diwa C Guinigundo.
Description: Hackensack, NJ : World Scientific, 2023. | Includes bibliographical references and index.
Identifiers: LCCN 2022021781 | ISBN 9789811258770 (hardcover) | ISBN 9789811258787 (ebook) | ISBN 9789811258794 (ebook other)
Subjects: LCSH: Economic stabilization. | Economic development. | Neoclassical school of economics.
Classification: LCC HB3732 .V84 2023 | DDC 338.9--dc23/eng/20220516
LC record available at https://lccn.loc.gov/2022021781

British Library Cataloguing-in-Publication Data
A catalogue record for this book is available from the British Library.

For any available supplementary material, please visit
https://www.worldscientific.com/worldscibooks/10.1142/12903#t=suppl

Desk Editor: Shaun Tan Yi Jie

Typeset by Stallion Press
Email: enquiries@stallionpress.com

Printed in Singapore

Foreword

Here is a book that has been missing from the library shelves of policy makers, policy advisers, teachers and students of economics and anyone who is seriously concerned with economic growth and policies addressed to the processes, infrastructure, and institutions needed to achieve prosperity and economic development without experiencing recurrent bouts with instability and crises. The Publisher, World Scientific, deserves commendation for its acute sense of relevance on display in this book. Authors deserve congratulations for this product of their unique intellectual and practical ability to bring their lifetime of experience, consisting of a total of more than a century of efforts on theory and policy, to bear on a vital subject of economic adjustment and growth and to do so in a readable style. This is a remarkable team of experts, innovators and highly respected thinkers. Their contributions to the field, which is the subject of the book, are well known (think of Villanueva's contributions to the theory and application of endogenous growth, Mariano's inputs to econometrics theory and application (like the famous and most useful Diebold-Mariano test for accuracy of econometric forecasts), and Guinigundo's long-time experience as a central banker).

Readers are in for a treat. Here are three brilliant minds that lived — as researchers, policy advisers and policy makers — through intellectually and practically unprecedented challenging times. The period of their contributions, spanning the 1970s to the present, represents a time of shifting theoretical and policy grounds; a time when a new economic paradigm was emerging, forged by Mont Pelerin ideology; and a time of Chicago school's triumph, liberalism,

Washington Consensus, and Reagan-Thatcher policy commitment to individualism. This was also a time of emergence for a new paradigm of adjustment and growth, with the main objective of making developing countries debt worthy and capable of producing enough fiscal room to service their debt to the international banking community, with little or no concern for the infrastructural, educational and health needs of these countries.

The authors of this book are not armchair theoreticians. They have had an eye wide open to the problems of adjustment and growth programs, externally designed and domestically applied, in developing countries leading to recurrent cycles of instability consequent of big-bang liberalization. At the present challenging time for emerging market economies facing instability and debt crises, this book could not be timelier as it focuses on conceptualizing an alternative process of adjustment and growth, testing it empirically, and applying it to an emerging market economy. The critical components of a successful economic growth strategy include physical, financial, and educational infrastructures supported by macroeconomic and financial stabilization policies and structural reforms. The authors begin the book with a review of the neoclassical growth model before delving into more specialized topics such as endogenous growth theory, adaptive inflationary expectations, learning by doing, optimal saving, and sustainable external debt. Guided by the principles enunciated in these chapters, the authors illustrate the interplay between economic adjustment strategy and growth, culminating in a case study of the Philippines.

The book's wide-ranging and rich collection of analytical papers on transitory and permanent growth effects of monetary, financial, fiscal, external trade and debt policies, labor participation and capital accumulation provide an original and valuable overview of diverse aspects of modern growth economics. Simple mathematical models of economic growth often neglect key factors critical in the growth process, while larger and more complex models often mire in minutia of details, thus missing the forest for the trees. Thanks to the efforts of Villanueva, Mariano, and Guinigundo, the book manages to correct the shortcomings of simple models without losing sight of core policy issues. Hence, it has achieved the status of an effective guide for policy makers and policy advisers in developing and emerging market economies facing the challenges of adjustment and growth. It is a remarkably challenging alternative to the traditional and naive models of adjustment and growth. The authors deserve our thanks and congratulations.

Abbas Mirakhor*
Former Executive Director and Dean of the Executive Board
International Monetary Fund
September 2022

*Dr. Abbas Mirakhor is an alumnus of Kansas State University, USA, where he received his Bachelor, Master and PhD degrees in Economics. From 1968–1984, he was a Professor of Economics at the University of Alabama, Alabama A&M University, and the Florida Institute of Technology. In 1984 he joined the International Monetary Fund, spending 24 years with the organization and serving as its Executive Director and Dean of the Executive Board, before retiring in 2008. He has published books and papers on a wide range of areas including microeconomic theory, mathematical economics and Islamic economics. For his contributions, he was conferred the "Quaid-e Azam" star for service to Pakistan by the President of Pakistan in 1997, and the "Order of Companion of Volta" for service to Ghana by the President of Ghana in 2005.

Acknowledgments

Delano S. Villanueva owes a great deal of his academic training to the late John Conlisk, who retired as Distinguished Professor in 1999, University of California, San Diego (UCSD, 1969–1999). Villanueva's initial exposure to aggregate growth theory began from a course at the University of Wisconsin–Madison taught by Professor Conlisk in the late 60s, who suggested Villanueva's doctoral thesis, *Monetary and Fiscal Policies in Aggregate Growth Models with Endogenous Technical Change*, a set of essays that formed the only requirement for the course. When John Conlisk left Madison for UCSD, his research continued to influence Villanueva, particularly the former's seminal contributions to bounded rationality, acknowledged by Nobel Laureate Herbert Simon. Professor Conlisk passed away on October 22, 2021. This book is dedicated to his memory.

Villanueva wishes to thank many colleagues at the International Monetary Fund (IMF), as well as those outside, who read and commented on **Chapters 1–11** of this book, namely, Pierre-Richard Agénor, Jose de Gregorio, Dean DeRosa, Joshua Greene, Thorvaldur Gylfason, Graham Hacche, Mohsin Khan, Deena Khatkhate, Malcolm Knight, Manmohan Kumar, Jong-Wha Lee, Guillermo Le Fort, Donald Mathieson, Gian Maria Milesi-Ferretti, Abbas Mirakhor, Peter Montiel, Alexandros Mourmouras, Kent Osband, Ichiro Otani, Ratna Sahay, Julio Santaella, and Sunil Sharma.

Outside the IMF, Villanueva is indebted to Jose Balmaceda, Gary Chamberlain, Jose Encarnacion, Jr., Lee Endress, Zvi Griliches, Diwa Guinigundo, Takatoshi Ito, Gonzalo Jurado, Vincent Lim Choon-Seng, Norman Loayza, Francis Lui, Roberto Mariano, Manuel

Montes, Andrew Rose, Partha Sen, Gerardo Sicat, Hoon Hian Teck, Amando Tetangco, Jr., and anonymous referees.

Special appreciation goes to Roberto S. Mariano, the founding Dean of the School of Economics and Social Sciences, Singapore Management University, who invited and welcomed Villanueva as Visiting Professor in 2005–06. **Chapters 9 and 10** of this volume were co-written by Mariano and Villanueva during that academic year.

Roberto S. Mariano and Delano S. Villanueva acknowledge the excellent research facilities at Singapore Management University and many useful discussions with Hoon Hian Teck on the growth models presented in **Chapters 9 and 10**.

Diwa C. Guinigundo acknowledges his interest in macroeconomics and growth theory started during his undergraduate course at the University of the Philippines School of Economics. It was also during this time that he was engaged in student political movement at the height of martial law in the Philippines. Alternative modalities of economic growth were the most preferred point of both academic and policy discussions then. While his graduate study at The London School of Economics and Political Science focused on both international and monetary economics under Willem Buiter and Charles Bean, he was also preoccupied with sitting in on Michio Morishima's lectures elaborating on his own theories of economic growth and modern society. His sprinkling of his own take of Walras and Marx during those lectures was most inspiring.

In writing the volume's last chapter on the case study of the Philippines, Guinigundo recognizes his over 40-year career at the Bangko Sentral ng Pilipinas (BSP) in shaping his own appreciation of and his own contribution to how the Philippines evolved from a so-called basket case in Asia to a strong emerging market with now an investment grade credit rating. He owes a great deal to Dr. Benito Legarda Jr., Edgardo P. Zialcita, Escolastica Bince, and Amando M. Tetangco Jr. His colleagues at the Monetary and Economics Sector helped him with the data, and they include Francis Dakila Jr., Iluminada Sicat, Zeno Abenoja, Paolo Alegre and Justin Fernandez.

Guinigundo's international and regional perspectives derive from his long engagement with the meetings organized by the International Monetary Fund, Bank for International Settlements, Asian Development Bank, ASEAN+3 and ASEAN Governors and Finance Ministers, and Executive Meetings of East Asia and the Pacific.

Finally, Delano S. Villanueva and Roberto S. Mariano are grateful to the International Monetary Fund, Bulletin of Monetary Economics and Banking, World Scientific Publishing Company, National Bureau of Economic Research and University of Chicago Press, Southeast Asian Central Banks (SEACEN) Research and Training Centre, Singapore Management University, and the Philippine Review of Economics for permitting materials to be reprinted or published in this volume. Complete identification of source and specific acknowledgments are found at the beginning of each chapter. Last but not least, Villanueva acknowledges the emotional support he has received through all the years, and still does, from his wife Hyeon-Sook, to whom this book is dedicated as well.

About the Authors

Delano S. Villanueva is Former Advisor, International Monetary Fund (IMF), where he worked in the functional, area (geographic), and capacity development departments. In 1982–86, he was the IMF Resident Representative in Seoul, Republic of Korea. In 1997–98, the IMF assigned him as Research Director, Southeast Asian Central Banks Research and Training Centre, Malaysia. After his IMF career, he served as Consultant to the IMF Institute for Capacity Development, World Bank, Asian Development Bank, and the Monetary Authority of Singapore. He was also Visiting Professor of Economics at Singapore Management University, and Distinguished Visiting Professor at De La Salle University. His research is public policy-oriented, focusing on Asian macroeconomic and financial sector policies, and economic growth and development. He has published extensively in international journals such as *The Quarterly Journal of Economics*, *Journal of Money, Credit and Banking*, *IMF Economic Review* (previously *IMF Staff Papers*) and *Economic Development and Cultural Change*, and wrote the books *Macroeconomic Policies for Stable Growth* (2008) and *Macroeconomics of Adjustment and Growth* (2017). He holds a Ph.D. in Economics from the University of Wisconsin, USA.

Roberto S. Mariano is Professor Emeritus of Economics at the University of Pennsylvania, USA, where he has been on the faculty since 1971. He is also Professor Emeritus at Singapore Management University, Singapore, where he served as Founding Dean of the School of Economics, Vice Provost for Research, and Founding Director of the Sim Kee Boon Institute for Financial Economics. He is an Elected Fellow of the Econometric Society. In 2022, the Holy Father Pope Francis appointed him as member of the Board of the Vatican Financial Authority for Supervision and Information (Autorita di Supervisioine e Informazione Financiara, ASIF). His research activity — centered on econometric theory, methods, and applications — spans various areas including analytical finite-sample econometrics as well as mixed-frequency forecasting and nowcasting. He co-edited the books *Simulation-based Inference in Econometrics* (2000) and *Econometric Forecasting and High-Frequency Data Analysis* (2008), and published many important journal articles. In statistical forecasting, his highly cited co-authored paper "Comparing Predictive Accuracy" introduces the Diebold-Mariano test — that has become one of the standard statistical procedures widely used in studies in economics and other disciplines to assess the relative accuracy of competing forecasting methods. He holds a Ph.D. in Statistics from Stanford University, USA.

Diwa C. Guinigundo is Former Deputy Governor of the Central Bank of Philippines (BSP), handling economic research and statistics, monetary policy, international operations, and currency management. He led the efforts in pioneering inflation targeting and interest rate corridor system for monetary management at the BSP. He championed the establishment of Credit Surety Fund to empower small business and Economic and Financial Learning Center to promote financial inclusion. He also participated in various banking rehabilitation workouts. Previously, he was Alternate Executive Director at the International Monetary Fund in 2001–2003, and Head of Research at the Southeast Asian Central Banks Research and Training Centre in 1992–1994. Currently, he is a member of the advisory boards of Sim Kee Boon Institute for Financial Economics of the Singapore Management University and the International Care Ministries Philippines, as well as an independent director of AIA Investment Management Philippines. He also writes weekly columns for the *Manila Bulletin* and *Business World.* He is co-editor of ASEAN+3's *Trauma to Triumph: Rising from the Ashes of the Asian Financial Crisis* (2021) and ADB's *Redefining Strategic Routes to Financial Resilience in ASEAN+3* (2021). He holds an M.Sc. in Economics from the London School of Economics, UK.

Contents

Introduction and Overview*

> *In my graduate courses in growth theory in the early 1960s, I liked macro better than micro. The reason had nothing to do with level of aggregation, but rather with a difference in approach. In macro at the time, we would write down plausible behavioral relations, phrased as a difference (differential) equation system, and let the adaptive dynamics play out. What would happen? What would we learn? The macro approach seemed closer to behavior and more open to novelty and imagination (word in parentheses added).*
>
> — John Conlisk (2004) in a *Festschrift* for Nobel Laureate Herbert Simon

This book is about conceptualizing the process of economic adjustment and growth and testing it with empirical methods, supported by a case study of an emerging market economy. Economic growth is measured as rates of increase in per capita real *GDP* (Gross Domestic Product) in a closed economy and in per capita real *GNI* (Gross National Income) in an open economy. The critical components of a successful economic growth strategy include physical, financial, and educational infrastructures supported by macro financial stabilization policies to moderate aggregate demand and structural reforms to boost aggregate supply.

Economic development is a much broader concept covering economic growth and the "quality" of life, encompassing life expectancy,

*Written by Delano S. Villanueva.

literacy rates, and poverty rates.[1] However, there can be no lasting and permanent improvement in economic development without sustained and high growth rates of per capita real *GDP* and *GNI*. Critical variables driving such growth rates are investments in physical, human, and intellectual capital, and payments on foreign debt.[2]

This volume consists of 12 chapters, covers both closed and open economies, and discusses the neoclassical theory of economic adjustment and growth and its econometric testing, as well as its practice in a country case study (the Philippines). It provides theoretical and practical support to the International Monetary Fund (IMF) approach to economic stabilization.

Figure 0.1 is a chart classifying models according to whether they refer to a closed or open economy, or whether the saving rate, technical change, or labor participation, respectively, is exogenous or endogenous. Table 0.1 places each growth model in the classificatory format of Figure 0.1.[3]

The narrative on theory begins with the closed economy models of Harrod (1939) and Domar (1946), henceforth H-D, and Solow (1956) and Swan (1956), henceforth S-S. The critical difference between the H-D and S-S models is the behavior of the *warranted rate* (saving-investment as a ratio to the capital stock, or capital growth). The H-D model assumes that the warranted rate is an exogenously fixed constant (constant saving-income ratio divided by constant capital-output ratio minus constant depreciation rate). With the *natural rate* (labor growth) fixed at a constant rate of

[1]One popular metric is the UN Human Development Index (HDI), comprising three elements: (1) life expectancy; (2) educational attainment; and (3) per capita real *GNI*.

[2]Including principal and interest payments, net of principal and interest received. Also included are profits and dividends repatriated by foreign owners of domestic companies, net of profits and dividends received.

[3]Notes to Table 0.1 contain definitions of the three levels and related terminologies of Figure 0.1. All models, except one, assume exogenous labor participation. The only growth model with endogenous labor participation is the closed-economy model of Villanueva (2020, **Chapter 3**), with exogenous saving rate and exogenous technical change à la Solow (1956)-Swan (1956) (**Chapter 1**).

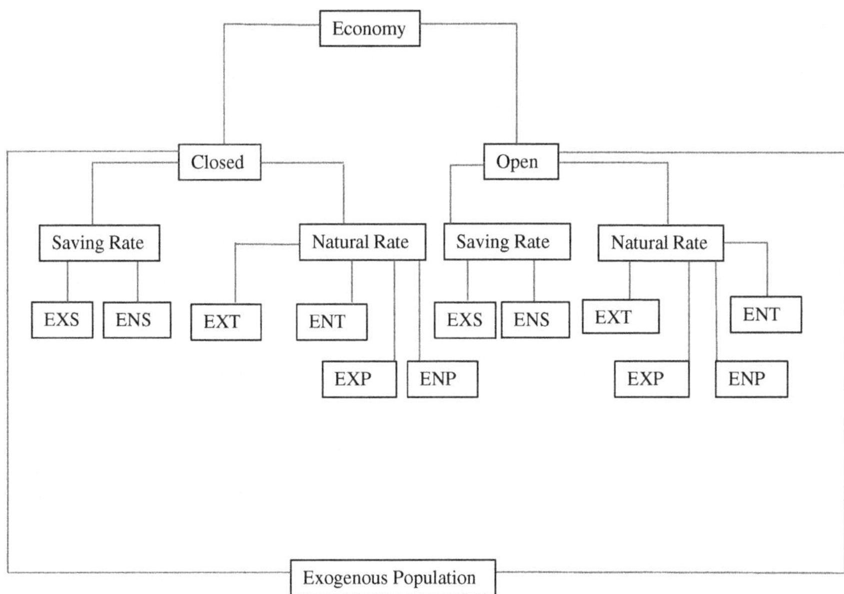

Figure 0.1. Aggregate growth models. EXS = Exogenous Saving; ENS = Endogenous Saving; EXT = Exogenous Technical Change; ENT = Endogenous Technical Change; EXP = Exogenous Labor Participation; ENP = Endogenous Labor Participation.

exogenous Harrod-neutral technical change plus a constant rate of exogenous working population growth, the H-D model has a "knife-edge" dilemma — only by accident does the constant warranted rate match the constant natural rate to achieve full employment on a balanced and stable growth path.

The S-S model provides an elegant solution to the H-D "knife-edge" problem. **Chapter 1** reviews the S-S model's standard neoclassical assumptions and simple structure. With a single homogeneous good produced by a well-behaved neoclassical production that is subject to diminishing returns to capital and labor separately and constant returns jointly, the warranted rate is a negative function of the capital-labor ratio. Along with wage-price flexibility in perfect markets, this ensures the attainment of a full-employment equilibrium growth path that equates the endogenously determined warranted rate to the exogenously fixed natural rate (Hacche, 1979).

Table 0.1. Aggregate growth models: summary features. C = Closed, O = Open, EXS = Exogenous Saving, ENS = Endogenous Saving, EXT = Exogenous Natural Rate *via* Exogenous Technical Change, ENT = Endogenous Natural Rate *via* Endogenous Technical Change, EXP = Exogenous Natural Rate *via* Exogenous Labor Participation, ENP = Endogenous Natural Rate *via* Endogenous Labor Participation.

	C	**O**	**EXS**	**ENS**	**EXT**	**ENT**	**EXP**	**ENP**
Ramsey (1928)	*			*	*		*	
Harrod (1939)	*		*		*		*	
Domar (1946)	*		*		*		*	
Solow (1956)	*		*		*		*	
Swan (1956)	*		*		*		*	
Arrow (1962)	*		*		*		*	
Cass (1965)	*			*	*		*	
Koopmans (1965)	*			*	*		*	
Phelps (1966)	*		*		*		*	
Conlisk (1967)	*		*			*	*	
Romer (1986)	*			*		*	*	
Lucas (1988)	*			*		*	*	
Romer (1990)	*			*		*	*	
Grossman & Helpman (1991)	*			*		*	*	
Rivera-Batiz & Romer (1991)	*			*		*	*	
Rebelo (1991)	*		*		*		*	
Mankiw, Romer & Weil (1992)	*		*		*		*	
Barro & Sala-i-Martin (1992)	*		*		*		*	
Knight, Loayza & Villanueva (1993)	*		*		*		*	
Villanueva (1994)	*		*			*	*	
Barro & Sala-i-Martin (1995)	*			*		*	*	
Aghion & Howitt (1997)	*			*		*	*	
Villanueva (1997)		*	*			*	*	
Villanueva & Mariano (2007)		*	*			*	*	
Villanueva (2008)		*	*			*	*	
Villanueva (2020)	*		*		*			*
Villanueva (2021)	*		*			*	*	
Villanueva & Mariano (2021)		*		*		*	*	
Villanueva (2022)	*		*			*	*	

The S-S model is a closed economy with an exogenously fixed saving rate and exogenous technical change. The Ramsey (1928), Cass (1965), and Koopmans (1965), henceforth R-C-K, model is a closed economy with an optimally derived saving rate, and exogenous technical change. The Arrow (1962) model is a closed economy that links learning by doing to either the growth rate of the capital stock or to the capital-labor ratio, making technical change potentially endogenous. The S-S and Arrow models are followed by the closed-economy, fixed saving rate, endogenous technical change model of Conlisk (1967), a neglected first attempt at making labor-augmenting technical change (a component of the natural rate) a positive function of the capital-labor ratio. The Conlisk model makes both warranted and natural rates adjust toward equality, leading to an endogenously determined equilibrium growth of per capita income. A variant of the Conlisk model is Villanueva (1994, **Chapter 6**).[4]

During the 1980s and 1990s, S-S was under attack by the new endogenous growth models (discussed below), alleging that it failed to explain observed differences in per capita income across countries. By augmenting the S-S model to include human capital and using a cross-sectional approach, Mankiw, Romer and Weil (1992, or M-R-W) found that the S-S model's predictions were indeed consistent with the empirical evidence.

Chapter 2 (Knight *et al.*, 1993) extends the M-R-W model in two directions: First, a panel of time-series, cross-sectional data is used to determine the significance of country-specific effects assumed away in the cross-sectional approach used by M-R-W, Barro and Sala-i-Martin (1992), and nearly all other studies. In order to exploit the additional information contained in these panel data, the econometric analysis is extended by applying an estimation procedure outlined by Chamberlain (1982, 1984).[5] Second, labor-augmenting technical change is influenced by two factors: outward-oriented trade policies and the stock of public infrastructure. The empirical results support the view that both country-specific and time-varying factors such as human capital, public investment and outward-oriented trade policies exert positive and significant influence on growth.

Enter the closed-economy, optimally derived saving rate, endogenous technical change models of Romer (1986, 1990), Lucas (1988), Grossman and Helpman (1990, 1991), Rivera-Batiz and Romer

[4]Villanueva's reference to the Conlisk model is acknowledged by Agénor (2004, footnote 4, p. 466).

[5]**Chapter 2** uses a panel data approach to estimate an augmented S-S model covering 98 countries (22 industrial and 76 developing) over the period 1960–85, taken from the Penn World Tables in Summers and Heston (1991).

(1991), Barro and Sala-i-Martin (1995), and Aghion and Howitt (1997). These new endogenous growth models conclude that the economy's long-run output can grow at least as fast as, or faster than, the capital stock, and public policies on saving and investment affect long-run economic growth. In the AK model (Rebelo, 1991), output grows at the same rate as capital stock K, equal to sA, where s (larger than the saving rate of the S-S model by the amount of investment in human capital) is the fraction of income saved and invested, and A is a technological constant.[6] In the R&D models of Romer (1986), Grossman and Helpman (1991), Barro and Sala-i-Martin (1995), and Aghion and Howitt (1997), firms operate in imperfectly competitive markets and undertake R&D investments that yield increasing returns, which are ultimately the source of long-run per capita income growth.[7] On the other hand, the closed-economy, exogenous saving rate, endogenous technical change models of Conlisk (1967) and Villanueva (1994, **Chapter 6**), and the open-economy, endogenous saving rate, endogenous technical change models of Villanueva and Mariano (2007, **Chapter 9**; 2021, **Chapter 10**) were developed under the neoclassical model assumptions of diminishing returns to capital and labor separately and constant returns jointly, operating in perfectly competitive markets with complete wage-price flexibility. Villanueva (1994, **Chapter 6**) and Villanueva and Mariano (2021, **Chapter 10**) are modified versions of the Arrow (1962) learning-by-doing model, wherein experience on the job raises labor productivity.[8] The equilibrium properties of the

---

[6]The AK model has no transitional growth dynamics. Output growth always equals the steady state level, sA.

[7]On increasing returns, Solow (1991, p. 12) comments: "As I have emphasized, the key assumptions all seem to require that some economic activity be exempt from diminishing returns. That is hard enough to test for a single industry or process, and even then might not settle the relevant question." Conlisk (1967) argues that increasing returns to capital yield explosive growth.

[8]Agénor (2004, pp. 466–471) refers to the 1994 Villanueva (**Chapter 6**) model as "An extension of Arrow's (1962) learning by doing model... (wherein) the productivity of workers increases when the relative availability of capital goods (for instance, the stock of high-performance computers) rises," leading to enhanced long-run growth effects of saving and investment rates.

new endogenous growth models and of the exogenous saving rate, endogenous technical change models of Conlisk (1967) and Villanueva (1994, **Chapter 6**; 2021, **Chapter 4**), and of the endogenous saving rate, endogenous technical change model of Villanueva and Mariano (2021, **Chapter 10**), are similar.[9]

As Table 0.1 shows, all growth models assume exogenous labor participation. In light of robust econometric results on the determinants of labor participation in 36 advanced economies reported by Grigoli *et al.* (2018) and independently by CBO (2018), **Chapter 3** (Villanueva, 2020) modifies the S-S model by introducing endogenous labor participation that responds to the real wage, among other factors, and thus to the ratio of capital to effective labor, making the natural rate fully flexible, much like what the S-S model does for the warranted rate. By allowing a fully adjusting natural rate, both warranted and natural rates adjust to changes in the capital-labor ratio. Thus, the positive growth effects of the saving rate hold in the transition to and in the steady state (a generalization of the S-S model).[10]

Chapter 4 (Villanueva, 2021) presents a closed-economy, neoclassical growth (henceforth, DV) model with two reproducible inputs: physical capital stock and combined stock of human and intellectual capital. In flow terms, these correspond to Solow's (1991) physical (capital), and human and intellectual investments (technology). The production process is subject to diminishing returns to capital in perfect markets, in sharp contrast to endogenous growth models that assume increasing returns to capital in imperfect markets. The DV model's predictions are similar to those of new endogenous growth models emphasizing R&D investments. What

[9]Lucas (1988) specifies effective labor $L = uhN$, where h is the skill level, and u is the fraction of non-leisure time devoted to current production. The uh variable is T in Villanueva (1994, **Chapter 6**), defined as labor productivity multiplier or technical-change multiplier, and $uhN = K_h$ in Villanueva (2021, **Chapter 4**), defined as combined human and intellectual capital.

[10]**Chapter 1** shows that, in the steady state, the S-S model yields an endogenously determined *level* of per capita income and an exogenously determined *growth rate* of per capita income.

is different is that the new endogenous growth models assume constant or increasing returns to capital — incompatible with balanced growth — and imperfect markets, while the DV model assumes diminishing returns to capital and perfect markets (standard neoclassical assumptions). The DV model's transitional dynamics is consistent with the empirical findings reported in **Chapter 2**. The DV model concludes that a high saving rate raises both transitional and steady state growth rates of output through increases in physical, human, and intellectual investments that augment labor productivity — a key extension of the S-S model. Additionally, the DV model derives an optimal rule for choosing the saving rate that maximizes consumer welfare.

Chapter 5 (Villanueva, 2022a) discusses a simple growth model with a financial sector and endogenous technical change. In a two-class growth model of Pasinetti (1962), there is no financial intermediary that mobilizes bank deposits loaned out to the capitalist class for physical investment. The absence of a capital market also precludes workers from buying capitalists' new issues of stocks and bonds to finance investment.[11] Thus, the equilibrium rate of return to capital is independent of the saving rate of the working class — what Samuelson and Modigliani (1966) referred to as the Pasinetti paradox. In this chapter's modified Pasinetti model with endogenous growth, the equilibrium rate of return to capital is shown to be a function of all structural parameters, including both saving rates of the capitalist and working classes. Additionally, the modified model explains the recessionary dynamics of the 2007–08 global and regional financial crises.

The next five chapters examine the roles of fiscal, monetary, trade, and external debt management policies in the short-run

[11]There are, of course, studies linking finance to output growth. For example, the Atje-Jovanovic (1993) model uses an augmented M-R-W (Mankiw, Romer and Weil, 1992) growth format, introducing finance in the form of a stock market as the third input in the aggregate production function, additional to capital and labor. In a more conventional manner, the model of **Chapter 5** views the banking sector as an intermediary that mobilizes workers' deposits on-lent to the capitalists for investments in the capital stock, thus retaining the S-S model's traditional two-input (capital and labor) aggregate production function.

and long-run behavior of per capita income growth. **Chapter 6** (Villanueva, 1994) analyses the effects of fiscal policies on economic growth and speed of adjustment. It postulates that learning through experience raises labor productivity with three major consequences. First, the equilibrium growth rate of per capita income becomes endogenous and is influenced by government policies. Second, the speed of adjustment to equilibrium per capita income growth increases, and enhanced learning further reduces adjustment time. Third, the optimal net rate of return to capital is higher than the sum of the exogenous rates of technical change and working population growth, or alternatively the optimal saving rate is only a fraction of capital's income share because of endogenous growth and the induced learning associated with increases in the capital stock. Simulation results confirm the model's faster speed of adjustment, and cross-country regression analysis finds that a large part of divergent growth patterns is related to the extent of economic openness, depth of human development and quality of fiscal policies, particularly growth of real expenditures on education and health and avoidance of high fiscal deficits as ratio to *GDP*.[12]

Chapter 7 (Villanueva, 2008) is an open economy model that modifies and extends the modern macroeconomic model of economic fluctuations presented in the macroeconomics textbook by Hall and Taylor (1997), and links it formally to the S-S model (reviewed in Chapter 1).[13] The integrated model answers the question of whether monetary policy matters for long-run growth, arguing that both levels *and* growth rates of potential output and real *GDP* change in economically sensible ways when monetary policy changes. The effects of monetary policy on stabilization and growth are analyzed and simulated.

Chapter 8 (Villanueva, 1997) discusses the role of outward-oriented trade policies, particularly export policies, in the behavior of per capita output growth. Because of the central role of exports in the absorption of modern technology, and the interdependence

[12]See **Chapter 2** (Knight *et al.*, 1993) for panel data evidence.

[13]Otani and Villanueva (1989) is an earlier attempt at open-economy growth modeling with endogenous technical change.

of investment, technical change and the size of the export sector, a successful growth-oriented strategy should begin with exporting manufactured goods in early stages of economic development. Trade policies should avoid high protective tariffs because they result in an inefficient industrial sector, prevent the adoption of modern techniques, and stunt factor productivity. In this regard, a crucial policy instrument is a competitive, market-determined exchange rate, complemented by low, non-discriminatory tariffs and elimination of non-tariff import barriers.

Chapter 9 (Villanueva and Mariano, 2007) explores the joint dynamics of external debt, capital accumulation, and growth. Reliance on foreign saving has limits, particularly in the current global environment of rising interest rates and risk spreads. The optimal domestic saving rate is derived and estimated using Phelps' (1966) *Golden Rule* maximization criterion. On the balanced growth path, if consumption per unit of effective labor (or any monotonically increasing function of it) is taken as a measure of the social welfare of society, the domestic saving rate that maximizes consumption per unit of effective labor is chosen. Consistent with this optimal outcome is a sustainable ratio of net external debt to total output.[14] Using parameters for the Philippines to calibrate the model, the growth model's steady state solution is characterized by a constant capital-effective labor ratio, an optimal domestic saving rate, and a unique external debt-capital ratio. The latter ratio interacts with long-run growth and domestic adjustment, and is determined jointly with other macroeconomic variables, including a country's set of structural parameters. A weakness of the above growth model is its unrealistically high estimate of the optimal saving rate associated with a lack of micro-foundation, a criticism leveled by Lui (2007).

In response to Lui (2007), **Chapter 10** (Villanueva and Mariano, 2021) incorporates consumer preferences explicitly in the optimization process, and presents an open-economy growth model with

[14]For research on the sustainability of external debt using various statistical procedures, see Manasse and Schimmelpfenning (2003), Reinhart *et al.* (2003), Kraay and Nehru (2004), Patillo *et al.* (2004), and Manasse and Roubini (2005). For an excellent survey, see Kraay and Nehru (2004).

endogenous technical change and optimally derived saving rate. More importantly, it incorporates a modified Arrow (1962) learning-by-doing feature. Imports of capital goods with embodied advanced technology allow learning by doing to raise labor productivity and long-run growth. An RCK optimal control setup derives sustainable ratios of foreign debt to *GDP* and saving rates that maximize the discounted stream of intertemporal consumption. The model generates a feasible range of optimal domestic saving rates corresponding to an estimated range of intertemporal substitution elasticities.[15]

Chapter 11 reviews the IMF approach to economic adjustment and sums up the analysis of economic adjustment and growth covered in previous chapters. Following an external current account deficit, and in response to tight fiscal and monetary policies, the open economy model of **Chapter 7** (Villanueva, 2008) clearly shows a short-term improvement and eventual balance in the external current account. In the medium- and long-term, the supply side effects are favorable owing to investment accelerating in response to expected inflation successfully anchored to a stable low rate. The resulting larger capital stock with embodied advanced technology enhances labor productivity via learning by doing. The higher potential output matches the larger aggregate demand. Similarly, the higher investment rate (warranted rate) matches the larger natural rate, strengthening the growth impact ignored in traditional macroeconomics. The IMF approach to economic adjustment and growth (Mussa and Savastano, 1999) is consistent with this chapter's summing up.

Using cross-country and panel data, the narrative on growth empirics includes, besides Knight *et al.* (1993, **Chapter 2**), studies by Conlisk (1967), Otani and Villanueva (1990), Villanueva (1994, **Chapter 6**), and Barro and Sala-i-Martin (1995). Specific country studies of developing and emerging market economies include,

[15]Recall Lui's (2007) comment that the high domestic saving rate estimated by Villanueva and Mariano (2007, **Chapter 9**) owes to the failure to consider the elasticity of intertemporal substitution in the optimization process inherent in the Phelps' (1966) Golden Rule criterion.

among others, Villanueva and Mariano (2007, **Chapter 9** and 2021, **Chapter 10**).

Guided by the principles covered in **Chapters 1–11**, **Chapter 12** (Guinigundo, 2022) narrates the evolution of a successful strategy of adjustment and growth practiced by an emerging market economy that had shown stellar pre-COVID-19 pandemic growth performance, low and stable inflation, and a sustainable external current account position. In this regard, Peter Wallace's[16] (2022) 12-point policy agenda for the incoming Philippine administration is well-placed and logically flows from this volume's analytic and empirical chapters, particularly the emphasis on upgrading the educational and health sectors of the economy; expansion and modernization of the public infrastructure; increased investments in physical, human and intellectual capital, including education-training-experience of workers; and, in both public and private sectors, widespread adoption of blueprints, methods, and processes to efficiently produce goods and services, including IT, R&D, applied software development, Internet, Internet of Things, 5G technology, AI, Business Management Software and similar high-tech, intellectual activities.[17]

[16]Peter Wallace is a successful and influential businessman in the Philippines. Read proposals 1–5 and 7–9 in his column at https://opinion.inquirer.net/153885/if-it-were-me.

[17]See the model of **Chapter 4** and its extension in Villanueva (2022b) to include the overarching role of government and economic institutions in long-run economic growth. The World Bank regularly publishes six Worldwide Governance Indicators (WGI): (1) Voice and Accountability, (2) Political Stability and Absence of Violence/Terrorism, (3) Government Effectiveness, (4) Regulatory Quality, (5) Rule of Law, and (6) Control of Corruption. For an explanation of these indicators, read Kaufmann *et al.* (2010). For regularly published data, see https://databank.worldbank.org/reports.aspx?Report_Name=WGI-Table&Id=ceea4d8b. The effectiveness of growth policies and the speed of adjustment to steady-state growth are determined by individual country values of the six WGI. Improvements in the WGI are political decisions made by government officials and the body politic in a democracy. The stellar pre-COVID19 pandemic growth performance of the Philippines was supported by improvements in four out of the six WGI since 2010, namely (2), (3), (4), and (6).

References

Agénor, P.-R. (2004). *The Economics of Adjustment and Growth.* Cambridge, MA: Harvard University Press.

Aghion, P. and P. Howitt (1997). *Endogenous Growth Theory.* Cambridge, MA: MIT Press.

Arrow, K. (1962). The economic implications of learning by doing. *Review of Economic Studies*, 29, 155–173.

Atje, R. and B. Jovanovic (1993). Stock markets and development. *European Economic Review*, 37, 632–640.

Barro, R. and X. Sala-i-Martin (1992). Convergence. *Journal of Political Economy*, 100, 223–251.

Barro, R. and X. Sala-i-Martin (1995). *Economic Growth.* NY: McGraw Hill.

Cass, D. (1965). Optimum growth in an aggregative model of capital accumulation. *Review of Economic Studies,* 32, 233–240.

Chamberlain, G. (1982). Multivariate regression models for panel data. *Journal of Econometrics*, 18, 5–46.

Chamberlain, G. (1984). Panel data. In Z. Griliches and M. Intriligator (eds), *Handbook of Econometrics*, Vol. II, pp. 1247–1318. Amsterdam: North-Holland Publishing.

Congressional Budget Office (2018). CBO's Projection of Labor Force Participation Rates.

Conlisk, J. (1967). A modified neoclassical growth model with endogenous technical change. *The Southern Economic Journal,* 34, 199–208.

Conlisk, J. (2004). Herbert Simon as friend to economists out of fashion. In M. Augier and J. March (eds), *Models of a Man: Essays in Memory of Herbert A. Simon*, pp. 191–197. Cambridge, MA: MIT Press.

Domar, E. (1946). Capital expansion, rate of growth, and employment. *Econometrica*, 14, 137–147.

Grigoli, F., Z. Koczan, and P. Tapalova (2018). Drivers of labor participation: macro and micro evidence. *IMF Working Paper WP/18/150.*

Grossman, G. and E. Helpman (1990). Comparative advantage and long-run growth. *American Economic Review*, 80, 796–815.

Grossman, G. and E. Helpman (1991). *Innovation and Growth in the Global Economy.* Cambridge, MA: MIT Press.

Guinigundo, D. (2022, **Chapter 12**). Stabilization policies and structural reforms: the Philippine case. In D. Villanueva, R. Mariano, and D. Guinigundo, *Economic Adjustment and Growth: Theory and Practice*, pp. 289–317. Singapore: World Scientific.

Hacche, G. (1979). *The Theory of Economic Growth: An Introduction.* NY: St Martin's Press.

Hall, R. and J. Taylor (1997). *Macroeconomics.* NY: WW Norton & Company.

Harrod, R. (1939). An essay in dynamic theory. *The Economic Journal*, 49, 14–33.

Ito, T. and A. Rose, eds (2007). *Fiscal Policy and Management in East Asia.* Chicago: NBER, University of Chicago Press.

Kaufmann, D., A. Kraay, and M. Mastruzzi (2010). The worldwide governance indicators: methodology and analytical issues. *Policy Research Working Paper No. 5430.* Washington, D.C.: World Bank.

Knight, M., N. Loayza, and D. Villanueva (1993, **Chapter 2**). Testing the neoclassical theory of economic growth: a panel data approach. *IMF Staff Papers*, 40, 512–541.

Koopmans, T. (1965). On the concept of optimal economic growth. In J. Johansen (ed), *The Econometric Approach to Development Planning*, Chapter 4. Amsterdam: North-Holland Publishing.

Kraay, A. and V. Nehru (2004). When is external debt sustainable? *World Bank Policy Research Working Paper 3200.*

Lucas, R. (1988). On the mechanics of economic development. *Journal of Monetary Economics*, 22, 3–42.

Lui, F. (2007). Comment on external debt, adjustment and growth, by D Villanueva and R Mariano. In T. Ito and A. Rose (eds), *Fiscal Policy and Management in East Asia*, pp. 221–222. Chicago: NBER, University of Chicago Press.

Manasse, P. and N. Roubini (2005). Rules of thumb for sovereign debt crises. *IMF Working Paper 05/42.*

Manasse, P. and A. Schimmelpfenning (2003). Predicting sovereign debt crises. *University of Bologna, IMF, and New York University Working Paper.*

Mankiw, N. G., D. Romer, and D. Weil (1992). A contribution to the empirics of economic growth. *The Quarterly Journal of Economics*, 107, 407–437.

Mussa, M. and M. Savastano (1999). The IMF approach to economic stabilization. *IMF Working Paper 99/104.*

Otani, I. and D. Villanueva (1989). Theoretical aspects of growth in developing countries: external debt dynamics and the role of human capital. *IMF Staff Papers*, 36, 307–342.

Otani, I. and D. Villanueva (1990). Long-term growth in developing countries and its determinants: an empirical analysis. *World Development*, 18, 769–783.

Pasinetti, L. (1962). Rate of profit and income distribution in relation to the rate of economic growth. *Review of Economic Studies*, 29, 267–279.

Patillo, C., H. Poirson, and L. Ricci (2004). What are the channels through which external debt affects growth?. *IMF Working Paper 04/15.*

Phelps, E. (1966). *Golden Rules of Economic Growth.* NY: WW Norton & Company.

Ramsey, F. (1928). A mathematical theory of saving. *Economic Journal*, 38, 543–559.

Rebelo, S. (1991). Long-run policy analysis and long-run growth. *Journal of Political Economy*, 99, 500–521.

Reinhart, C., K. Rogoff, and M. Savastano (2003). Debt intolerance. *Brookings Papers on Economic Activity.*

Rivera-Batiz, L. and P. Romer (1991). International trade with endogenous technical change. *NBER Working Paper 3594.*

Romer, P. (1986). Increasing returns and long-run growth. *Journal of Political Economy*, 94, 1002–1037.

Romer, P. (1990). Endogenous technical change. *Journal of Political Economy*, 98, S71–S102.

Samuelson, P. and F. Modigliani (1966). The Pasinetti paradox in neoclassical and more general models. *Review of Economic Studies*, 33, 269–301.

Solow, R. (1956). A contribution to the theory of economic growth. *The Quarterly Journal of Economics*, 70, 65–94.

Solow, R. (1991). *Policies for Economic Growth.* Sturc Memorial Lecture, Johns Hopkins University School of Advanced International Studies.

Summers, R. and A. Heston (1991). The Penn World table (Mark 5): an expanded set of international comparisons, 1950–1988. *The Quarterly Journal of Economics*, 106, 327–361.

Swan, T. (1956). Economic growth and capital accumulation. *Economic Record*, 32, 334–362.

Villanueva, D. (1994, **Chapter 6**). Openness, human development, and fiscal policies: effects on economic growth and speed of adjustment. *IMF Staff Papers*, 41, 1–29.

Villanueva, D. (1997, **Chapter 8**). Exports and economic development. *SEACEN Staff Papers 58.*

Villanueva, D. (2008, **Chapter 7**). Does monetary policy matter for long-run growth? In D. Villanueva, *Macroeconomic Policies for Stable Growth*, pp. 211–236. Singapore: World Scientific.

Villanueva, D. (2020, **Chapter 3**). A modified neoclassical growth model with endogenous labor participation. *Bulletin of Monetary Economics and Banking*, 23, 83–100.

Villanueva, D. (2021, **Chapter 4**). Capital and growth. *Bulletin of Monetary Economics and Banking*, 24, 285–312.

Villanueva, D. (2022a, **Chapter 5**). Finance and endogenous growth. *Bulletin of Monetary Economics and Banking*, 25, 55–72.

Villanueva, D. (2022b). Institutions and growth: a macroeconomic framework. *DLSU Business and Economics Review*, 32, 1–13.

Villanueva, D. and R. Mariano (2007, **Chapter 9**). External debt, adjustment, and growth. In T. Ito and A. Rose (eds), *Fiscal Policy and Management in East Asia*, pp. 199–221. Chicago: NBER, University of Chicago Press.

Villanueva, D. and R. Mariano (2021, **Chapter 10**). Optimal saving and sustainable foreign debt. *The Philippine Review of Economics*, 57, 170–199.

Wallace, P (2022). If it were me. *Philippine Daily Enquirer*, June 13.

Chapter 1

The Basic Neoclassical Growth Model: A Review*

The basic neoclassical growth model of Solow (1956) and Swan (1956), henceforth S-S, has been the workhorse for economic growth theorists for the past six and a half decades.[1] Earlier, the growth frameworks of Harrod (1939) and Domar (1946), henceforth H-D, had assumed a constant capital-output ratio v (or a constant output-capital ratio $1/v$). Saving S is a constant fraction s of income Y. Gross investment I equals saving S, less depreciation δK, where K = capital stock and δ = constant depreciation rate. Thus, capital growth $\dot{K}/K$ (the warranted rate) equals $s/v - \delta$. (A dot over a variable denotes time derivative, $\dot{K} = \frac{d(K)}{dt}$). Labor growth $\dot{L}/L$ (the natural rate) $= \lambda + n$, where $L = AN$, L = effective labor, A = labor-augmenting technology/productivity multiplier, N = working population, and $\lambda + n$ = constant growth rates of A and N, respectively. Long-run, full employment equilibrium with price stability requires that the warranted rate (S = I) matches the full employment natural rate, or $s/v - \delta = \lambda + n$. Since this equality happens only by accident, the economy is on a "knife-edge." An inequality between the warranted and natural rates implies either

---

*Written by Delano S. Villanueva and adapted from *Bulletin of Monetary Economics and Banking*, 24, 304-308, by the permission of the Bulletin of Monetary Economics and Banking. Copyright 2021 by the Bulletin of Monetary Economics and Banking.

[1]1956–2022.

a deflationary (unemployment) or inflationary spiral. There is no assurance of full employment with price stability.

Enter the S-S model. Its simple assumptions and structure — a single homogeneous good, a well-behaved neoclassical production function subject to diminishing returns to capital and exogenous labor-augmenting technical progress and working population growth — provide an elegant solution to the "knife-edge" problem posed by H-D, and ensure the attainment of a balanced equilibrium growth path (Hacche, 1979).

The S-S model consists of the following relationships:

$$Y = K^{\alpha}L^{(1-\alpha)} \tag{1.1}$$

$$L = AN \tag{1.2}$$

$$I = S = sY \tag{1.3}$$

$$\dot{K} = I - \delta K \tag{1.4}$$

$$\frac{\dot{A}}{A} = \lambda \tag{1.5}$$

$$\frac{\dot{N}}{N} = n \tag{1.6}$$

$$k = \frac{K}{L} \tag{1.7}$$

Y = GDP, K = capital, L = effective labor, A = Harrod-neutral technical change/productivity multiplier, N = working population, k = capital intensity, α = output elasticity with respect to capital, $1 - \alpha$ = output elasticity with respect to effective labor,[2] s = gross fixed saving to income ratio, δ = depreciation rate, λ = constant, exogenous technical change parameter, and n = exogenous population growth rate. Y is produced according to a Cobb-Douglas production in Equation (1.1), using

[2]In Equation (1.1), under assumed marginal factor productivity pricing and wage-price flexibility, the parameters α and $(1-\alpha)$ represent the income shares of capital and labor, respectively.

K and L as inputs.[3] Equation (1.2) defines L as the product AN.[4]

Equation (1.3) expresses the warranted rate in which investment is equal to saving, the latter being a fixed proportion s of income Y. Equations (1.4)–(1.6) are dynamic equations for the state variables K and L. Dividing Equation (1.4) by K, and using Equations (1.1), (1.3) and (1.7),

$$\frac{\dot{K}}{K} = s\frac{Y}{K} - \delta = sk^{(\alpha-1)} - \delta. \tag{1.8}$$

Equation (1.8) is termed the warranted rate. Time differentiating Equation (1.2) and substituting Equations (1.5) and (1.6) yield

$$\frac{\dot{L}}{L} = \lambda + n. \tag{1.9}$$

Equation (1.9) is termed the natural rate.

Time differentiating Equation (1.7) and substituting Equations (1.8) and (1.9) yield the proportionate change in the capital intensity k,

$$\frac{\dot{k}}{k} = \frac{\dot{K}}{K} = \frac{\dot{L}}{L} = sk^{(\alpha-1)} - (\lambda + n + \delta). \tag{1.10}$$

From Equations (1.1) and (1.7), output in intensive form is:

$$\frac{Y}{L} = k^{\alpha}. \tag{1.11}$$

---

[3]Any unit-homogeneous function $Y = F(K, L)$ satisfying the Inada (1963) conditions will suffice. Given $F(K, L) = Lf(k)$, where K is capital, L is effective labor, and k is the ratio of K to L, these conditions can be summarized as follows: $\lim \frac{\partial F}{\partial K} = \infty\, as\, K \to 0$; $\lim \frac{\partial F}{\partial K} = 0\, as\, K \to \infty$; $f(0) \geq 0$; $f'(k) > 0, f''(k) < 0$ for all $k > 0$. The Cobb-Douglas production function Equation (1.1) satisfies these conditions.

[4]Generally, the definition of L should be $L = APN$, where P is the labor participation rate, $0 < P \leq 1$. The working population is PN. When $P = 1$, $L = AN$. Whatever P is, it is usually assumed as an exogenous constant, whose rate of change is zero. For an endogenous and variable P, see Villanueva (2020, **Chapter 3**).

Time differentiating Equation (1.11) and substituting Equation (1.9) yield the *transitional*[5] growth rate of output,

$$\frac{\dot{Y}}{Y} = (\lambda + n) + \alpha\frac{\dot{k}}{k}. \tag{1.12}$$

Substituting Equation (1.10),

$$\frac{\dot{Y}}{Y} = \alpha[sk^{(\alpha-1)} - \delta] + (1-\alpha)(\lambda + n). \tag{1.13}$$

Equation (1.13) expresses the growth rate of Y during time t as the sum of capital and labor growth rates weighted by the income shares of capital α and labor $(1-\alpha)$.[6]

In the steady state, k is constant at $k^*(\frac{\dot{k}}{k} = 0)$,[7] and by the constant-returns assumption,

$$\frac{\dot{K}^*}{K} = \frac{\dot{L}^*}{L} = \frac{\dot{Y}^*}{Y} = g^* = \lambda + n. \tag{1.14}$$

Equation (1.14) is the *steady state*[8] output growth rate, at which the warranted and natural rates are equal, and the economy is on a full-employment, balanced growth path.[9]

---

[5] *Temporary*, *transitory*, or *short run*.

[6] Alternatively, Equation (1.13) may be derived by time differentiating Equation (1.1) and substituting Equations (1.8) and (1.9) into the result.

[7] The Inada (1963) conditions enumerated in footnote 3 ensure a unique and globally stable k^*.

[8] *Permanent*, *equilibrium*, or *long run*.

[9] This is the S-S solution to the knife-edge problem posed by H-D, whose assumed *constant*, *exogenous* capital-output ratio or its reciprocal *constant*, *exogenous* output-capital ratio, implies that balanced growth, macroeconomic stability, and full employment are not assured and may happen only by accident. S-S offers a *variable*, *endogenous* output-capital ratio linked to the capital-labor ratio Equation (1.8) — a fully adjusting warranted rate — as a solution. Another solution is found in Villanueva (2020, **Chapter 3**) via a fully adjusting natural rate through endogenous labor participation linked to the real wage (a function of the capital-labor ratio), or through endogenous investments in human and intellectual capital Equation (4.12) of the DV model in Villanueva (2021, **Chapter 4**), complementing a fully adjusting S-S warranted rate.

Substituting Equation (1.8) into Equation (1.14), and setting $k = k^*$,

$$sk^{*(\alpha-1)} = \lambda + n + \delta. \tag{1.15}$$

Solving for the equilibrium capital intensity,

$$k^* = \left[\frac{s}{(\lambda + n + \delta)}\right]^{\frac{1}{(1-\alpha)}}. \tag{1.16}$$

Equation (1.16) states that the equilibrium capital-labor ratio, k^*, is a positive function of the saving rate s, and a negative function of λ, n, δ. From Equations (1.1), (1.2), (1.5), (1.7), and (1.16), steady state per capita output is given by:

$$\frac{Y}{N}^* = A(0)e^{\lambda t}\frac{s}{(\lambda + n + \delta)}^{\frac{\alpha}{(1-\alpha)}}. \tag{1.17}$$

In the S-S model, even though the steady state output *growth rate* is exogenously fixed by effective labor growth $\lambda + n$, independent of the saving rate s, the steady state *level* of per capita output $\frac{Y^*}{N}$ is a positive function of s.

Figure 1.1 is the phase diagram showing the S-S model's equilibrium behavior and growth dynamics. It illustrates the transitional and steady state growth effects of an increase in the saving rate. The vertical axis graphs the rates of change in output $= \frac{\dot{Y}}{Y}$ Equation (1.12), warranted rate $= \frac{\dot{K}}{K}$ Equation (1.8), natural rate $= \frac{\dot{L}}{L}$ Equation (1.9), and capital intensity $= \frac{\dot{k}}{k}$ Equation (1.10). The horizontal axis measures the level of the capital-labor ratio $= k$ Equation (1.7).[10]

The steady state solution of the S-S model occurs at points $A(k^*, 0)$ and $C(k^*, g^*)$, at which the warranted and natural rates are equal (warranted rate line intersects natural rate line at point C), k^* is steady state capital intensity (the $\frac{\dot{k}}{k}$ line intersects the k-axis at point A), and $g^* = \lambda + n$ is steady state output growth rate (reading

[10]The $\frac{\dot{K}}{K}$ line and $\frac{\dot{k}}{k}$ line are downward-sloping and parallel to each other because they have a common slope $s(\alpha - 1)k^{(\alpha-2)}$. Both lines are steeper than the $\frac{\dot{Y}}{Y}$ line, whose slope is equal to $\alpha s(\alpha - 1)k^{(\alpha-2)}$, where α is a positive fraction.

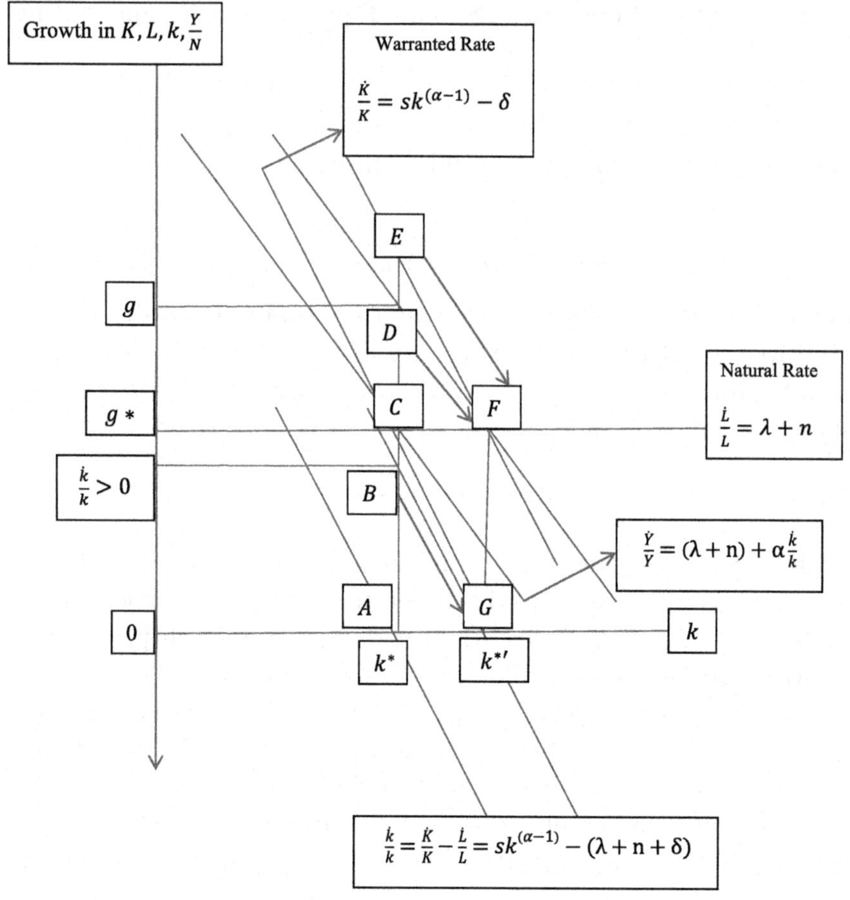

Figure 1.1. Equilibrium and growth dynamics, S-S Model: Effects of an increase in s.

off the $\frac{\dot{Y}}{Y}$ or $\frac{\dot{L}}{L}$ line). Equilibrium at point $A(k^*, 0)$ is unique and globally stable, ensured by the Inada (1963) conditions enumerated in footnote 3. Any capital intensity k different from k^* will bring k back to k^* because of the adjustments of the output-capital ratio and, hence, of the saving-capital ratio $\frac{Y}{K}$, as capital's marginal and average products deviate from their equilibrium values at k^*. The warranted rate adjusts to the natural rate to bring balanced growth back to points $A(k^*, 0)$ and $C(k^*, g^*)$.

Assume an increase in the saving rate s, say through a higher fiscal surplus. The warranted rate, output growth, and capital intensity growth lines will shift upward to the right, while the natural rate remains stationary. The new steady state occurs at points $G(k^{*\prime}, 0)$ and $F(k^{*\prime}, g^*)$, characterized by a higher equilibrium capital-labor ratio and the same equilibrium output growth rate, equal to the constant natural rate $g^* = \lambda + n$. More interesting is the transition to the new steady state. At the starting capital intensity k^*, a higher saving rate temporarily raises the warranted rate to point E (segment k^*E), which is larger than the natural rate (segment k^*C). Capital intensity growth turns positive (segment k^*B). Consequently, output growth goes up to g (segment k^*D) (reading off the new output growth line), that is temporarily higher than g^*. As the capital-labor ratio increases, the marginal returns on investment decline. The output-capital ratio falls, decreasing the saving-capital ratio and, hence, the warranted rate. This downward adjustment of the warranted rate (along segment $E - F$) continues until it equals the natural rate at F, at which point the growth rate of output g reverts back to its original rate g^* (traced by the segment $D - F$).[11] Meanwhile, the growth rate of capital intensity turns less and less positive until it is zero at point G (traced by the segment $B - G$), characterized by a higher level at $k^{*\prime}$.

Figure 1.1 shows that, although the steady state output growth rate is fixed at $\lambda + n$, invariant with respect to the saving rate s, the output growth at any time is a function of s and all the other structural parameters of the model λ, δ, n. From Equations (1.10) and (1.13) and Figure 1.1, an increase in the saving rate s will raise the growth rate of capital intensity $\frac{\dot{k}}{k}$ and the transitional output growth rate $\frac{\dot{Y}}{Y}$. This rich dynamics is a major strength of the S-S model.[12]

---

[11]Segment C-D-F traces the output growth adjustment. Solow's (1991) *temporary* growth is $g(> g^*)$, then back to $g^* = \lambda + n$.

[12]This transitional dynamics is absent in the endogenous AK growth model of Rebelo (1991). Output growth always equals the steady state level sA, where s is the constant saving to income ratio (sum of investments in physical *and* human capital) and A is a technological constant. In contrast to the S-S model, the AK

Solow's (1991) thought experiment on the *temporary* growth effects of an increase in productivity (invention of a computer) is an example.

During the 1980s and 1990s, the S-S model was under attack by the new growth theorists,[13] alleging that it failed to explain observed differences in per capita income across countries. By augmenting the S-S model to include human capital and using a cross-sectional approach, Mankiw, Romer and Weil (1992, or M-R-W) found that the S-S model's predictions were indeed consistent with the empirical evidence. Knight *et al.* (1993, **Chapter 2**) has validated the S-S growth model using an innovative panel data approach. They extend the M-R-W model in two directions: first, a panel of time-series cross-sectional data is used to determine the significance of country-specific effects assumed away in the cross-sectional approach used by M-R-W, Barro and Sala-i-Martin (1992), as well as nearly all other studies. In order to exploit the additional information contained in these panel data, the econometric analysis is extended by applying an estimation procedure outlined by Chamberlain (1982, 1984).[14] Second, labor-augmenting technical change is influenced by two factors: outward-oriented trade policies and the stock of public infrastructure. The empirical results support the view that both country-specific and time-varying factors such as human capital, public investment, and outward-oriented trade policies exert positive and significant influence on growth.

Villanueva (2020, **Chapter 3** and 2021, **Chapter 4**) discusses neoclassical growth models that preserve the S-S short-run (*transitional*) dynamics, while simultaneously pointing to higher long-run (*steady state*) growth effects of saving and investment rates, a generalization of the S-S model.

---

model shows that both saving rate and technology influence the steady state rate of output growth.

[13]For details, see ***Introduction and Overview*** and Knight *et al.* (1993, **Chapter 2**).

[14]**Chapter 2** uses a panel data approach to estimate an augmented S-S model covering 98 countries (22 industrial and 76 developing over the period 1960–85), taken from the Penn World Tables in Summers and Heston (1991).

References

Barro, R. and X. Sala-i-Martin (1992). Convergence. *Journal of Political Economy*, 100, 223–225.

Chamberlain, G. (1982). Multivariate regression models for panel data. *Journal of Econometrics*, 18, 5–46.

Chamberlain, G. (1984). Panel data. In Z Griliches and M Intriligator (eds), *Handbook of Econometrics*, Vol. II, pp. 1247-1318. Amsterdam: North-Holland Publishing.

Domar, E. (1946). Capital expansion, rate of growth, and employment. *Econometrica*, 14, 137–147.

Hacche, G. (1979). *The Theory of Economic Growth: An Introduction.* NY: St Martin's Press.

Harrod, R. (1939). An essay in dynamic theory. *The Economic Journal*, 49, 14–33.

Inada, K. (1963). On a two-sector model of economic growth: comments and generalization. *Review of Economic Studies*, 30, 119–127.

Knight, M., N. Loayza, and D. Villanueva (1993, **Chapter 2**). Testing the neoclassical theory of economic growth: a panel data approach. *IMF Staff Papers*, 40, 512–541.

Mankiw, N., D. Romer, and D. Weil (1992). A contribution to the empirics of economic growth. *The Quarterly Journal of Economics*, 107, 407–437.

Rebelo, S. (1991). Long-run policy analysis and long-run growth. *Journal of Political Economy*, 99, 500–21.

Solow, R. (1956). A contribution to the theory of economic growth. *Quarterly Journal of Economics*, 70, 65–94.

Solow, R. (1991). *Policies for Economic Growth.* Sturc Memorial Lecture, Johns Hopkins University School of Advanced International Studies.

Summers, R. and A. Heston (1991). The Penn world table (mark 5): an expanded set of international comparisons, 1950–1988. *The Quarterly Journal of Economics*, 106, 27–361.

Swan, T. (1956). Economic growth and capital accumulation. *Economic Record*, 32, 334–61.

Villanueva, D. (2020, **Chapter 3**). A modified neoclassical growth model with endogenous labor participation. *Bulletin of Monetary Economics and Banking*, 23, 83–100.

Villanueva, D. (2021, **Chapter 4**). Capital and growth. *Bulletin of Monetary Economics and Banking*, 24, 285–312.

Chapter 2

Testing the Neoclassical Theory of Economic Growth: A Panel Data Approach*

The basic neoclassical model of Solow (1956) and Swan (1956) has been the workhorse of economic growth theorists for the past three and a half decades. Its simple assumptions and structure — a single homogenous good, a well-behaved neoclassical production function, exogenous labor-augmenting technical progress, full employment, and exogenous labor force growth — provide an elegant solution to the "knife-edge" problem posed by Harrod (1939) and Domar (1946) and ensure the attainment of a balanced equilibrium growth path (Hacche (1979)).

The Solow-Swan growth model predicts that in steady-state equilibrium the level of per capita income will be determined by the prevailing technology, as embodied in the production function, and by the rates of saving, population growth, and technical progress, all three of which are assumed exogenous. Since these rates differ across countries, the Solow-Swan model yields testable predictions about how differing saving rates and population growth rates, for example, might affect different countries' steady-state levels of per capita income: other things being equal, countries that have higher saving rates tend to have higher levels of per capita income, and countries with higher population growth rates tend to have lower levels of per capita income.

---

*Written by Delano Villanueva with Malcolm Knight and Norman Loayza and adapted from *IMF Staff Papers*, 40, 512–541, by the permission of the International Monetary Fund.

Recently, the Solow-Swan model has come under attack by the new growth theorists, who dismiss it in favor of "endogenous growth" models that assume constant or increasing returns to capital. These critics allege that the standard neoclassical model fails to explain observed differences in per capita income across countries. The different implications of the two growth models have led to renewed empirical work in recent years. A major concern of this work has been whether one should see a long-run tendency toward convergence of per capita income levels across countries. "Unconditional convergence" implies that in a cross-country sample the simple correlation between the growth rate of real per capita GDP and the initial level of real per capita GDP is negative. In other words, the lower the starting level of real per capita income, the higher is its subsequent rate of growth. In a recent cross-section study, however, Barro and Sala-i-Martin (1992) find that this simple correlation is positive rather than negative, albeit statistically insignificant.

In itself, the empirical evidence against unconditional convergence is not inconsistent with the implications of the neoclassical growth model. The Solow-Swan model does not predict unconditional convergence of per capita income across countries; rather, it predicts convergence only after controlling for the determinants of the steady state (that is, it predicts "conditional convergence"). Recent work by Mankiw, Romer, and Weil (1992) contends, using a cross-sectional approach, that the Solow-Swan model's predictions are indeed consistent with the empirical evidence. They also find, however, that if human capital is not accounted for in the model the quantitative implications of different saving and population growth rates are biased upward (in absolute value), since human capital is positively correlated with both saving and population growth.

Accordingly, in an effort to understand the quantitative relationships among saving, population growth, and income, Mankiw, Romer, and Weil augment the Solow-Swan model to include human capital accumulation. They find that this variable is indeed correlated positively with saving and population growth. Relative to estimates based on the text-book model, this augmented Solow-Swan model implies smaller effects of saving and population growth on per capita income growth and explains about 80 percent of the cross-country variation in per capita income.

Despite the evidence on the failure of per capita income to converge across countries — the failure of the "unconditional convergence" hypothesis — Mankiw, Romer, and Weil find evidence of conditional convergence at about the rate predicted by the Solow-Swan model once cross-country differences in saving and population growth rates are taken into account. Moreover, they interpret the available evidence on cross-country variations in the rates of return to capital as being consistent with the Solow-Swan growth model. Thus, their work provides empirical support for the model and casts doubt on the new endogenous growth models that invoke constant or increasing returns to capital.

This paper extends the Mankiw, Romer, and Weil analysis in two directions. First, a panel of time series cross-sectional data is used to determine the significance of country-specific effects that are assumed away in the cross-sectional approach employed by Barro and Sala-i-Martin (1992) and Mankiw, Romer, and Weil (1992), as well as nearly all other studies. In order to exploit the additional information contained in these panel data, we extend the econometric analysis by applying an estimation procedure outlined in Chamberlain (1984). Second, we assume that labor-augmenting technical change is influenced by two potentially important factors: (1) the extent to which a country's trade policies are outward-oriented — whether they increase or decrease its openness to international trade (see Edwards (1992)); and (2) the stock of public infrastructure in the domestic economy.

As already noted, our first extension of the Mankiw, Romer, and Weil analysis refers to the econometric treatment of the data. In the empirical part of their paper, they use cross-sectional data for various groups of countries. Essentially, they take averages of the relevant variables over the whole period, 1960–85. Since only one cross-section of countries is used for the entire time period, they are obliged to make some restrictive assumptions about the nature of the shift parameter (technology) in the neoclassical production function and its relation to other variables. Specifically, all unobservable factors that characterize each economy (and are contained in the shift parameter) are assumed to be uncorrelated with the available information. Econometrically, this means that "country-specific" effects are ruled out by assumption. Our procedure, on the other hand, allows for a more general econometric specification of the model by appropriately using panel data to account for important country-specific effects. This approach yields a number of interesting extensions to the empirical results of Mankiw, Romer, and Weil, particularly when the estimates for the full sample of both industrial and developing countries are compared with those for developing countries only.[1] Provided the assumptions required for using the panel data hold, our approach also improves the efficiency of the estimates by using more information.[2]

Our second, related, extension of Mankiw, Romer, and Weil's empirical analysis refers to the country-specific variables — trade policies, human capital, and government fixed investment — that we include in the model. Policies that foster more openness in a country's international trade regime help to stimulate labor-augmenting technological change in two ways.[3] First, the import-export sector serves as a vehicle for technology transfer through the importation of technologically advanced capital goods, as elucidated by Bardhan and Lewis (1970), Chen (1979), and Khang (1987), and as a channel for intersectoral external economies through the development of efficient and internationally competitive management, the training of skilled workers, and the spillover consequences of scale expansion (Keesing (1967) and Feder (1983)). Second, rising exports help to relieve the foreign exchange constraint — that is, a country's ability to import technologically superior capital goods is augmented directly by rising export receipts and indirectly by the higher flows

[1]Our sample of industrial countries consists of the 21 developed countries that are members of the OECD; our sample of developing countries consists of 76 non-OECD developing countries. See Appendix 2.A.

[2]The panel data set increases the number of observations from 98 to 490 — that is, 98 countries multiplied by five time periods of five years each.

[3]See the discussion on the production linkage summarized by Khan and Villanueva (1991). See also Edwards (1992), Roubini and Sala-i-Martin (1992), and Villanueva (1993, **Chapter 8**).

of foreign credits and direct investment caused by the country's increased ability to service debt and equity held by foreigners.[4]

As regards government fixed investment, it is reasonable to assume that an expansion in the amount of public goods concentrated in physical infrastructure (such as transport and telecommunications) will be associated with greater economic efficiency. Empirical studies that emphasize other productive public expenditures, such as education and health spending, include Diamond (1989), Otani and Villanueva (1990), and Barro (1991); those that focus on fixed investment include Diamond (1989), Orsmond (1990), and Barro (1991).

2.1 The Model

The Mankiw, Romer, and Weil model is an augmented neoclassical Solow-Swan model that accounts for human capital in the production function and saving decisions of the economy.

Consider the following Cobb-Douglas production function:

$$Y_t = K_t^{\alpha} H_t^{\beta} (A_t L_t)^{1-\alpha-\beta}, \tag{2.1}$$

where Y is real output, K is the stock of physical capital, H is the stock of human capital, L is raw labor, A is a labor-augmenting factor reflecting the level of technology and efficiency in the economy, and t refers to time in years. We assume that $\alpha + \beta < 1$, so that there are constant returns to factor inputs jointly and decreasing returns separately.

Raw labor and labor-augmenting technology are assumed to grow according to the following functions,

$$L_t = L_0 e^{nt}, \tag{2.2}$$

$$A_t = A_0 e^{gt\,F^{\theta_f} P^{\theta_p}}, \tag{2.3}$$

where n is the exogenous rate of growth of the labor force, g is the exogenous rate of technological progress, F is the degree of

[4]The transfer of efficient technologies and the availability of foreign exchange have featured in recent experiences of rapid economic growth (Thirlwall (1979)).

openness of the domestic economy to foreign trade, and P is the level of government fixed investment in the economy. (For simplicity, we normalize L_0 to unity.) Thus, our efficiency variable A differs from that used by Mankiw, Romer, and Weil in that it depends not only on exogenous technological improvements but also on the degree of openness of the economy (with elasticity θ_f) and on the level of government fixed investment (with elasticity θ_p). We believe that this modification is particularly relevant to the empirical study of economic growth in developing countries, where technological improvements tend to be absorbed domestically through imports of capital goods and where the productive sector's efficiency may depend heavily on the level of fixed investment undertaken by the government.

As in the Solow-Swan model, the savings ratios are assumed to be exogenously determined either by savers' preferences or by government policy. Thus, physical and human capital are accumulated according to the following functions,

$$\frac{dK_t}{dt} = s_k Y_t - \delta K, \tag{2.4}$$

$$\frac{dH_t}{dt} = s_h Y_t - \delta H, \tag{2.5}$$

where s_k and s_h are the fractions of income invested in physical capital and human capital and δ is the depreciation rate (assumed, for simplicity, to be the same for both types of capital).

To facilitate analysis of the steady state and the behavior around it, we redefine each variable in terms of its value *per effective unit of labor*, by dividing each variable by the efficiency-adjusted labor supply. Lower-case letters with a hat represent quantities per effective worker: for instance, output per effective unit of labor ($\hat{y}$) is equal to Y/AL.

We now rewrite the production and accumulation functions in terms of quantities per effective worker:

$$\hat{y}_t = \hat{k}_t^{\alpha} \hat{h}_t^{\beta}, \tag{2.1$'$}$$

$$\frac{d\hat{k}_t}{dt} = s_k \hat{y}_t - (n + g + \delta)\hat{k}_t, \tag{2.4$'$}$$

and

$$\frac{d\hat{h}_t}{dt} = s_h \hat{y}_t - (n + g + \delta)\hat{h}_t. \tag{2.5'}$$

2.1.1 *The Steady State*

In the steady state, the levels of physical and human capital per effective worker are constant. (Variables in the steady state are represented by a star superscript.) From Equations (2.4′) and (2.5′), this assumption implies

$$\hat{k}^* = \left(\frac{s_k^{l-\beta} s_h^{\beta}}{n+g+\delta}\right)^{1/l-\alpha-\beta},$$

$$\hat{h}^* = \left(\frac{s_k^{\alpha} s_h^{1-\alpha}}{n+g+\delta}\right)^{1/1-\alpha-\beta}, \tag{2.6}$$

and

$$\ln \hat{y}^* = -\left(-\frac{\alpha+\beta}{1-\alpha-\beta}\right)\ln(n+g+\delta) + \left(\frac{\alpha}{1-\alpha-\beta}\right)\ln(s_k) + \left(\frac{\beta}{1-\alpha-\beta}\right)\ln(s_h).$$

Furthermore, in the steady state, output per worker (y) grows at the constant rate g (the exogenous component of the growth rate of the efficiency variable A). This result can be obtained directly from the definition of output per effective worker:

$$\begin{aligned} \ln \hat{y}_t &= \ln Y_t - \ln L_t - \ln A_t \\ &= \ln y_t - \ln A_0 - gt - \theta_f \ln F - \theta_p \ln P. \end{aligned} \tag{2.7}$$

Taking time derivatives of both sides of the equation gives

$$\frac{d \ln \hat{y}_t}{dt} = \frac{d \ln y_t}{dt} - g.$$

Therefore, in the steady state, when the growth rate of output per effective worker is zero, the growth rate of output per worker is equal to g:

$$\frac{d \ln y_t^*}{dt} = g.$$

2.1.2 *Dynamics Around the Steady State*

Following Mankiw, Romer, and Weil, we do not impose the restriction that the economy is continuously in the steady state. However, we do assume that the economy is sufficiently close to its steady state that a linearization of the transition path around it is appropriate. Such a linearization produces the following result[5]:

$$\frac{d \ln \hat{y}_t}{dt} = \eta(\ln \hat{y}^* - \ln \hat{y}_t), \tag{2.8}$$

where $\eta = (n + g + \delta)(1 - \alpha - \beta)$.

The parameter η defines the speed of convergence: how fast output per effective worker reaches its steady state. We want to obtain an expression that can be treated as a regression equation for our empirical study. Accordingly, we integrate Equation (2.8) from $t = t_0$ to $t = t_0 + r$:

$$\ln \hat{y}_{t_0+r} = (1 - e^{-\eta r}) \ln \hat{y}^* + e^{-\eta r} \ln \hat{y}_{t_0}.$$

Next, we substitute for $\ln \hat{y}^*$,

$$\begin{aligned} \ln \hat{y}_{t_0+r} = &- (1 - e^{-\eta r}) \left(\frac{\alpha + \beta}{1 - \alpha - \beta}\right) \ln(n + g + \delta) \\ &+ (1 - e^{-\eta r}) \left(\frac{\alpha}{1 - \alpha - \beta}\right) \ln s_k \\ &+ (1 - e^{-\eta r}) \left(\frac{\beta}{1 - \alpha - \beta}\right) \ln s_h + e^{-\eta r} \ln \hat{y}_{t_0}. \end{aligned}$$

For purposes of estimation, we need an expression in terms of output per worker rather than output per effective worker. Accordingly, following Mankiw, Romer, and Weil, we substitute for

[5]The linearization of the transition path around the steady state is derived in Appendix I of our original working paper (Knight, Loayza, and Villanueva (1992)).

$\ln \hat{y}_t$ using Equation (2.7). Finally, we rearrange terms to get the change in the natural logarithm of output as the left-hand variable:

$$\begin{aligned}\ln y_{t0+r} - \ln y_{t0} = &-(1-e^{-\eta r})\left(\frac{\alpha+\beta}{1-\alpha-\beta}\right)\ln(n+g+\delta)\\ &+(1-e^{-\eta r})\left(\frac{\alpha}{1-\alpha-\beta}\right)\ln s_k\\ &+(1-e^{-\eta r})\left(\frac{\beta}{1-\alpha-\beta}\right)\ln s_h\\ &+(1-e^{\eta r})\theta_f\ln F+(1-e^{\eta r})\theta_p\ln P\\ &-(1-e^{-\eta r})\ln y_{t_0}+\left[(1-e^{-\eta r})(t_0+r)g\right.\\ &\left.+e^{-\eta r}rg\right]+(1-e^{-\eta r})\ln A_0. \qquad (2.9)\end{aligned}$$

Equation (2.9) provides a useful specification for our empirical study.[6] We will use it as a guide but not apply it literally.

The growth effects that we next discuss apply to the transition to the steady state. As noted earlier, in the steady state, output per capita grows at the exogenous rate g. If the speed of convergence η is positive (as we expect), we can predict the sign of the coefficients in Equation (2.9). The first coefficient indicates that for given α, β, δ, and g the rate of growth of per capita output is negatively related to the growth of the working-age population. The second and third coefficients indicate that the more a country saves and invests in physical and human capital, the more rapidly it grows. The fourth coefficient is positive if θ_f is positive, meaning that greater openness to international trade — by contributing to the efficiency of production — raises the rate of economic growth. A similar analysis holds for the fifth coefficient, which applies to the level of government fixed investment. The sixth term indicates that countries grow faster if they are initially below their steady-state growth path, what is known as "conditional convergence" in the growth literature (Barro

[6]Note that as t_0 goes to infinity, both sides of Equation (2.9) go to the value rg. This is so because in the limit (steady state), the growth of per capita output is equal to g, the exogenous growth rate of technology.

and Sala-i-Martin (1992), Mankiw, Romer, and Weil (1992), and Loayza (1992)). Next, the term in brackets suggests the presence of a time-specific effect on growth. The last term contains A_0, which represents all the unobserved elements that determine the efficiency with which the factors of production and the available technology are used to create wealth. Of course, the greater is such efficiency, the higher the growth rate of the economy. This last term suggests the presence of a country-specific effect, which may well be correlated with the other explanatory variables considered in the model.

The above interpretation of Equation (2.9) suggests a natural specification for the regression that can be used to study output growth and its determinants using panel data for a sample of different countries and time periods. Let us write a more general form of Equation (2.9) for a given country i:

$$\begin{aligned}\ln y_{i,t} - \ln y_{i,t-1} = {} & \theta_1 \ln(n_{j,t} + g + \delta) + \theta_2 \ln s_{ki,t} + \theta_3 \ln s_{h_i} \\ & + \theta_4 \ln F_i + \theta_5 \ln P_i \\ & + \gamma \ln y_{i,t-1} + \xi_t + \mu_i + \epsilon_{i,t}, \end{aligned} \tag{2.10}$$

where ξ_t and μ_i represent time-specific and country-specific effects and where $\theta_1, \ldots, \theta_5$ and γ are parameters to be estimated.

The use of the time index requires some explanation. First, we have normalized the "time length" between the first and last observations for each period to equal unity (in Equation (2.9), $r = 1$). Second, we are indexing the physical capital investment rate s_k by time to allow it to change from period to period. Notice that the rate of human capital investment s_h, the level of openness F, and the stock of government fixed investment P may differ from country to country, but owing to the limited availability of data their levels in each country are assumed to remain unchanged for all time periods in the sample.[7] Notice also that neither the value for g nor that for δ is specific to each country. In essence, we assume that, conditional on

[7]This refers to those data in our study for which only cross-sectional data are available.

the other variables in the model, the exogenous rate of technological change and the rate of depreciation are equal across countries.[8]

The disturbance term $\epsilon_{i,t}$ is not assumed to be identically and independently distributed. Thus, the model does not impose either conditional homoskedasticity across countries or independence over time on the disturbances within each country. We want to allow for serial correlation in the error term because there may be some excluded variables that result in short-run persistence. The μ_i component accounts for long-run persistence in excluded variables that are correlated with the independent regressors.

2.2 Panel Data Estimation

As we have noted, previous empirical studies of long-run growth have made use of cross-sectional data. This practice forced the use of some rather restrictive assumptions in the econometric specifications. For instance, Mankiw, Romer, and Weil, who take averages of the relevant variables over the period 1960 to 1985, assume that $\ln A0$ is independent of the investment ratios and growth rates of the working-age population. This amounts to ignoring country-specific effects. For example, their assumption implies that government policies regarding taxation and international trade do not affect domestic investment and that the endowment of natural resources does not influence fertility. Furthermore, since only one cross-section is considered, the time-specific effect becomes irrelevant. Fortunately, panel data are available for most variables of interest. Thus, we exploit the additional information contained in the panel data to analyze regression Equation (2.10), using a technique suggested by Chamberlain (1984).

We rewrite Equation (2.10) as follows:

$$z_{i,t} - z_{i,t-1} = \boldsymbol{\theta}'\boldsymbol{v}_{i,t} + \gamma z_{i,t-1} + \xi_t + \mu_i + \epsilon_{i,t} \tag{2.10$'$}$$

[8]This assumption corresponds to that in Mankiw, Romer, and Weil. The value for $g + \delta$ that is used in the estimation procedure actually matched the available data.

where $z_{i,t} = \ln(y_{i,t}); \boldsymbol{v}_{i,t} = [\ln(n_{i,t} + g + \delta), \ln(s_{k_{t,t}}), \ln(s_{h_{i,t}}), \ln F_i, \ln P_i]'$; and $\boldsymbol{\theta} = (\theta_i, \ldots, \theta_5)'$. First, we need to process the data to eliminate the time effects, which we do by removing the time means from each variable. The ξ_t's can then be ignored, and the regression can be estimated without constants (McCurdy (1982)).

Taking account of the country-specific effects is not so simple. If the μ_i's are treated as fixed (as in a fixed-effects model), we may be tempted to use the "within" estimator procedure, which is obtained by removing the country means prior to least-squares estimation.[9] However, this procedure would result in inconsistent estimators because of the presence of a lagged dependent variable in the right-hand side of the regression equation. The inconsistency comes from the fact that the error term obtained after removing the country means is correlated with lagged output.

Our chosen estimation method is the $\boldsymbol{\Pi}$ matrix approach outlined in Chamberlain (1984). Chamberlain's $\boldsymbol{\Pi}$ matrix procedure consists of two steps. In the first step, we estimate the parameters of the reduced-form regressions for the endogenous variable in each period in terms of the exogenous variables in all periods. Thus, we estimate a multi-variate regression system with as many regressions as periods for the endogenous variables we consider. Since we allow for heteroskedasticity and correlation between the errors of all regressions, we use the seemingly unrelated regression (SUR) estimator. As a result of this first step, we obtain estimates of the parameters of the reduced-form regressions (the elements of the $\boldsymbol{\Pi}$ matrix) and the robust (White's (1980) heteroskedasticity-consistent) variance-covariance matrix of such parameters.

The specific model we are working with implies some restrictions on the elements of the $\boldsymbol{\Pi}$ matrix: the parameters of interest are functions of the $\boldsymbol{\Pi}$ matrix. This takes us to the second step in the procedure: we estimate the parameters of interest by means of a minimum-distance estimator using the robust variance-covariance of

[9]References on the "within" estimator include Mundlak (1978) and Greene (1990, chapter 16).

the estimated $\mathbf{\Pi}$ as the weighting matrix:

$$\min[\text{vec}\,\mathbf{\Pi} - f(\mathbf{\Psi})]'\mathbf{\Omega}[\text{vec}\,\mathbf{\Pi} - f(\mathbf{\Psi})],$$

where $\mathbf{\Psi}$ is the set of parameters of interest and $\mathbf{\Omega}$ is the robust variance-covariance of the $\mathbf{\Pi}$ matrix. Chamberlain (1982) shows that this procedure obtains asymptotically efficient estimates.

In order to use this method, we need to make explicit the restrictions that our model imposes on the $\mathbf{\Pi}$ matrix. After removing the time means, our basic model in Equation (2.10′) can be written as

$$z_{i,t} - z_{i,t-1} = \boldsymbol{\theta}'\boldsymbol{v}_{i,t} + \gamma_{z_{i,t-1}} + \mu_i + \epsilon_{i,t}. \tag{2.11}$$

At this point it is necessary that we distinguish the two kinds of variables contained in the vector $\boldsymbol{v}_{i,t}$: those that are both country and time specific ($\ln[n_{i,t} + g + \delta]$ and $\ln[s_{k_{i,t}}]$) and those that are only country specific ($\ln[s_{hi}], \ln[F_i]$ and $\ln[P_i]$). Then we rewrite Equation (2.11) as follows:

$$z_{i,t} - z_{i,t-1} = \boldsymbol{\theta}_{\boldsymbol{a}}'\mathbf{x}_{i,t} + \boldsymbol{\theta}_{\boldsymbol{b}}'\mathbf{w}_i + \gamma z_{i,t-1} + \mu_i + \epsilon_{i,t}, \tag{2.12}$$

where $\mathbf{x}_{i,t} = [\ln(n_{i,t} + g + \delta), \ln(s_{k_{i,t}})]', \mathbf{w}_i = [\ln(s_{h_i}), \ln F_i, \ln P_i]'$, $\boldsymbol{\theta}_{\boldsymbol{a}} = (\theta_1, \theta_2)'$, and $\boldsymbol{\theta}_b = (\theta_3, \theta_4, \theta_5)'$.

By recursive substitution of the z_{t-1} term in each regression equation, we have[10]

$$\begin{aligned}
z_{i,1} - z_{i,0} &= \boldsymbol{\theta}_{\boldsymbol{a}}'\,\mathbf{x}_{i,1} + \boldsymbol{\theta}_{\boldsymbol{b}}'\,\mathbf{w}_i + \gamma_{z_{i,0}} + \mu_i + \omega_{i,1},\\
z_{i,2} - z_{i,1} &= \gamma\boldsymbol{\theta}_{\boldsymbol{a}}'\mathbf{x}_{i,l} + \boldsymbol{\theta}_{\boldsymbol{a}}'\mathbf{x}_{\boldsymbol{i},\mathbf{2}} + (1+\gamma)\boldsymbol{\theta}_{\boldsymbol{b}}'\mathbf{w}_i + \gamma(1+\gamma)z_{i,0}\\
&\quad + (1+\gamma)\mu_i + \omega_{i,2},\\
z_{i,3} - z_{i,2} &= \gamma(1+\gamma)\boldsymbol{\theta}_{\boldsymbol{a}}'\mathbf{x}_{i,1} + \gamma\boldsymbol{\theta}_{\boldsymbol{a}}'\mathbf{x}_{i,2} + \boldsymbol{\theta}_{\boldsymbol{a}}'\mathbf{x}_{i,3} + (1+\gamma)^2\boldsymbol{\theta}_{\boldsymbol{b}}'\mathbf{w}_i\\
&\quad + \gamma(1+\gamma)^2 z_{i,0} + (1+\gamma)^2\mu_i + \omega_{i,3},\\
&\;\;\vdots
\end{aligned}$$

[10]In the term z_{t-1} the index "1" refers to five years.

$$\begin{aligned} z_{i,T} - z_{i,T-1} &= \gamma(1+\gamma)^{T-2}\boldsymbol{\theta}_{\boldsymbol{a}}'\mathbf{x}_{i,1} + \gamma(1+\gamma)^{T-3}\boldsymbol{\theta}_{\boldsymbol{a}}'\mathbf{x}_{i,2} + \cdots \\ &\quad + \gamma(1+\gamma)\boldsymbol{\theta}_{\boldsymbol{a}}'\mathbf{x}_{i,T-2} + \gamma\boldsymbol{\theta}_{\boldsymbol{a}}'\mathbf{x}_{i,T-1} \\ &\quad + \boldsymbol{\theta}_{\boldsymbol{a}}'\mathbf{x}_T + (1+\gamma)^{T-1}\boldsymbol{\theta}_{\boldsymbol{b}}'\mathbf{w}_i + \gamma(1+\gamma)^{T-1}z_{i,0} \\ &\quad + (1+\gamma)^{T-1}\mu_i + \omega_{i,T}, \end{aligned}$$

$$E^*(\omega_{i,r}|\mathbf{x}_{i,1},\ldots,\mathbf{x}_{i,T},\mathbf{w}_i) = 0, \quad \text{for } t = 1,\ldots,T.$$

Chamberlain (1984) proposes to deal with the correlated country-specific effect μ_i and the initial condition $z_{i,0}$ by replacing them by their linear predictors:

$$\begin{aligned} E^*(\mu_i|\mathbf{x}_{i,1},\mathbf{x}_{i,2},\ldots,\mathbf{x}_i,T,\mathbf{w}_i) &= \boldsymbol{\tau}_1'\mathbf{x}_{i,1} + \boldsymbol{\tau}_2'\mathbf{x}_{i,2} + \cdots \\ &\quad + \boldsymbol{\tau}_T'\mathbf{x}_{i,T} + \boldsymbol{\tau}_w'\mathbf{w}_i; \\ E^*(z_{i,0}|\mathbf{x}_{i,1},\mathbf{x}_{i,2},\ldots,\mathbf{x}_{i,T},\mathbf{w}_i) &= \boldsymbol{\lambda}_1'\mathbf{x}_{i,1} + \boldsymbol{\lambda}_2'\mathbf{x}_{i,2} + \cdots \\ &\quad + \boldsymbol{\lambda}_T'\mathbf{x}_{i,T} + \boldsymbol{\lambda}_w'\mathbf{w}_i. \end{aligned}$$

In order to identify the coefficients of the variables for which we have only cross-sectional data ($s_{h_i}, F_i,$ and P_i), it is necessary to assume that $\boldsymbol{\tau}'\mathbf{w} = 0$. This assumption is not very restrictive if one believes that the partial correlation between $\mathbf{w}_i$ and μ_i is low, given that the panel data variables $\mathbf{x}_{i,t}$ are accounted for.

As Chamberlain points out, assuming that the variances are finite and that the distribution of $(\mathbf{x}_{i,1},\ldots,\mathbf{x}_{i,T},\mathbf{w}_i,\mu_i)$ does not depend on i, then the use of the linear predictors does not impose any additional restrictions. However, using the linear predictors does not account completely for the presence of country-specific effects when the correct specification includes interactive terms (that is, non-linear terms including products of the observed variables and the country-specific factors). Of course, we assumed away such a possibility when we declared that Equation (2.10) represented our maintained model.

We now write the $\mathbf{\Pi}$ matrix implied by our model. As will be seen in the next section, our panel data consist of five cross-sections for the variables $(z_{i,t} - z_{i,t-1})$ and $\mathbf{x}_{i,t}$, six cross-sections for the variable $z_{i,t}$ (the additional cross-section being the initial condition $z_{i,0}$), and one cross-section for the variables $\mathbf{w}_i$. Thus, the multivariate regression implied by our model is

$$\begin{bmatrix} Z_{i,0} \\ Z_{i,1} - Z_{i,0} \\ Z_{i,2} - Z_{i,1} \\ Z_{i,3} - Z_{1,2} \\ Z_{i,4} - Z_{i,3} \\ Z_{i,5} - Z_{i,4} \end{bmatrix} = \mathbf{\Pi} \begin{bmatrix} \mathbf{x}_{i,1} \\ \mathbf{x}_{i,2} \\ \mathbf{x}_{i,3} \\ \mathbf{x}_{i,4} \\ \mathbf{x}_{i,5} \\ \mathbf{w}_i \end{bmatrix} \tag{2.13}$$

$$\mathbf{\Pi} = [\mathbf{B} + \boldsymbol{\Psi}\boldsymbol{\lambda}' + \boldsymbol{\phi}\boldsymbol{\tau}'],$$

$$\mathbf{B} = \begin{bmatrix} 0 & 0 & 0 & 0 & 0 & 0 \\ \boldsymbol{\theta}'_{\mathbf{a}} & 0 & 0 & 0 & 0 & \boldsymbol{\theta}'_{\mathbf{b}} \\ \gamma\boldsymbol{\theta}'_{\mathbf{a}} & \boldsymbol{\theta}'_{\mathbf{a}} & 0 & 0 & 0 & (1+\gamma)\boldsymbol{\theta}'_{\mathbf{b}} \\ \gamma(1+\gamma)\boldsymbol{\theta}'_{\mathbf{a}} & \gamma\boldsymbol{\theta}'_{\mathbf{a}} & \boldsymbol{\theta}'_{\mathbf{a}} & 0 & 0 & (1+\gamma)^2\boldsymbol{\theta}'_{\mathbf{b}} \\ \gamma(1+\gamma)^2\boldsymbol{\theta}'_{\mathbf{a}} & \gamma(1+\gamma)\boldsymbol{\theta}'_{\mathbf{a}} & \gamma\boldsymbol{\theta}'_{\mathbf{a}} & \boldsymbol{\theta}'_{\mathbf{a}} & 0 & (1+\gamma)^3\boldsymbol{\theta}'_{\mathbf{b}} \\ \gamma(1+\gamma)^3\boldsymbol{\theta}'_{\mathbf{a}} & \gamma(1+\gamma)^2\boldsymbol{\theta}'_{\mathbf{a}} & \gamma(1+\gamma)\boldsymbol{\theta}'_{\mathbf{a}} & \gamma\boldsymbol{\theta}'_{\mathbf{a}} & \boldsymbol{\theta}'_{\mathbf{a}} & (1+\gamma)^4\boldsymbol{\theta}'_{\mathbf{b}} \end{bmatrix}$$

$$\boldsymbol{\Psi}\boldsymbol{\lambda}' = \begin{bmatrix} 1 \\ \gamma \\ \gamma(1+\gamma) \\ \gamma(1+\gamma)^2 \\ \gamma(1+\gamma)^3 \\ \gamma(1+\gamma)^4 \end{bmatrix} [\boldsymbol{\lambda}'_1\ \boldsymbol{\lambda}'_2\ \boldsymbol{\lambda}'_3\ \boldsymbol{\lambda}'_4\ \boldsymbol{\lambda}'_5\ \boldsymbol{\lambda}'_{\mathbf{w}}],$$

$$\boldsymbol{\phi}\boldsymbol{\tau}' = \begin{bmatrix} 0 \\ 1 \\ (1+\gamma) \\ (1+\gamma)^2 \\ (1+\gamma)^3 \\ (1+\gamma)^4 \end{bmatrix} [\boldsymbol{\tau}'_1\ \boldsymbol{\tau}'_2\ \boldsymbol{\tau}'_3\ \boldsymbol{\tau}'_4\ \boldsymbol{\tau}'_5\ \boldsymbol{\tau}'_{\mathbf{w}}],$$

2.3 Data and Results

We consider three different specifications of the growth model in our econometric analysis. The first is a simple Solow-Swan model; the second is a version of the Solow-Swan model that includes investment in human capital; and the third, which was presented in Section 2.1, is a version that includes human capital investment, openness to foreign trade, and the stock of public infrastructure. The first two models can be obtained by applying appropriate exclusion restrictions to the third model. Thus, the basic Solow-Swan model is obtained from Equation (2.9) by setting $\beta = \theta_f = \theta_p = 0$. Its corresponding regression equation is

$$\ln y_{i,t} - \ln y_{i,t-1} = \theta_1 \ln(n_{i,t} + g + \delta) + \theta_2 \ln s_{k_{i,t}} + \gamma \ln y_{i,t-1} + \xi_t + \mu_i + \epsilon_{i,t}. \tag{2.10$''$}$$

The second model can also be obtained from Equation (2.9) by setting $\theta_f = \theta_p = 0$. Its regression equation is

$$\ln y_{i,t} - \ln y_{i,t-1} = \theta_1 \ln(n_{i,t} + g + \delta) + \theta_2 \ln s_{k_{i,t}} + \theta_3 \ln s_{h_i} + \gamma \ln y_{i,t-1} + \xi_r + \mu_i + \epsilon_{i,t}. \tag{2.10$'''$}$$

We will consider an alternative specification for this second model in which panel data rather than cross-sectional data are used as a proxy for the ratio of human capital investment to GDP. The regression equation for this alternative model is the same as Equation (2.10$'''$), except that the investment ratio for human capital is also indexed by time.

The definitions and sources of the data used for estimation are described in Appendix 2.A. Our sample extends over the period from 1960 to 1985. We work with regular non-overlapping intervals of five years. Thus, our five cross-sections correspond to the years 1965, 1970, 1975, 1980, and 1985. For the variables y_t, and s_{h_t}, the observations for each cross-section correspond exactly to the year of the cross-section. For others — such as n_t, and s_{k_t} — such observations correspond to averages over the previous five years. For the variables s_h and P, the observations correspond to averages over the whole period 1960 to 1985. For the openness variable, F, the observation for each country is taken from various years in the first part of the 1980s.

Each of the variables under consideration is now explained in more detail. The dependent variable is the five-year difference in the natural logarithm of real GDP per worker — that is, $\ln(y_{i,65}) - \ln(y_{i,60}), \ldots, \ln(y_{i,85}) - \ln(y_{i,80})$. As noted above, the most general model considers six explanatory variables. The first is the natural logarithm of the average growth rate of the working-age population, plus $(g+\delta)$; we follow Mankiw, Romer, and Weil in assuming that $(g+\delta) = 0.05$. The average growth rate of the working-age population is taken over the preceding five-year interval. Thus, we also have five observations of this variable for each country — that is, $\ln(n_{i,65}+0.05), \ldots, \ln(n_{i,85}+0.05)$.

The second explanatory variable is the natural logarithm of the average ratio of real investment (including government investment) to real GDP. These averages are also taken over the preceding five-year intervals, so that we have five observations for each country — that is, $\log(s_{k_i,65}), \ldots, \log(s_{k_i,85})$.

The third explanatory variable is a proxy for the ratio of human capital investment to GDP. Specifically, following Mankiw, Romer, and Weil (1992), we use the percentage of the working-age population that is enrolled in secondary school, a measure that is approximated by the product of the gross secondary-school enrollment ratio times the fraction of the working-age population that is of secondary-school age (aged 15 to 19).[11] In the main specifications of the second and third models, we use cross-sectional data for this variable: its average over the whole period from 1960 to 1985. In the alternative specification of the second model, we use panel data for the proxy of the human capital investment ratio — that is, for each country we have five observations, namely $\ln(s_{h_i,65}), \ldots, \ln(s_{h_i,85})$.

The fourth variable, $\ln F$, is a proxy for the restrictiveness of the economy's foreign trade regime: it is a weighted average of tariff rates on intermediate and capital goods. The weights are the

[11]For a discussion of the appropriateness of this proxy, see Mankiw, Romer, and Weil (1992).

respective import shares, and each tariff rate is calculated as the percentage ad valorem import charge. Thus, the larger the value of this variable, the *less open* is the domestic economy. We obtain the data from Lee (1993). This measure of openness to trade is used because we are interested in the relation between the availability of foreign technology (embodied in intermediate and capital goods) and the efficiency parameter in the production function. Lee points out that there are some problems with this measure of the weighted-average tariff rate, the most important of which is that the data refer to various years in the first part of the 1980s and thus may not be representative of our entire sample period (1960 to 1985). Nevertheless, we believe that this simple proxy is likely to be inversely correlated with openness for the majority of countries under consideration during our sample period.

The fifth variable, $\ln P$, is a proxy for the level of the public capital stock; it is defined as the average level of the ratio of general government fixed investment (central government plus public enterprises) to GDP in each five-year period. There are obvious problems in using this flow variable as a proxy for the stock of public capital. It does not account for the initial level of public capital (in our case the 1960 level). Nor does it allow for country-specific differences in depreciation rates or in the quality of investment expenditures. Nevertheless, it is likely that our proxy is positively correlated with the level of public capital, and the omitted factors discussed above will be reflected in the country-specific constants.

The sixth explanatory variable is the natural logarithm of real GDP per worker, lagged one "period" (that is, five years back). The observations for each country are therefore $\ln(y_{i,60}), \ldots, \ln(y_{i,80})$.

Appendix 2.A lists the countries used to obtain the empirical estimates for each of the three models of interest. The sample includes all industrial and developing countries for which data are available and for which petroleum production is not the primary economic activity.[12] Excluding the countries for which data are not available

[12]It is well known that standard growth models do not account for growth in economies that specialize in the extraction of depletable resources (see Sala-i-Martin (1990)).

may create sample selectivity problems, particularly since these countries are frequently the poorest ones. Thus, it is not appropriate to assume that the results could be extrapolated to those economies that had to be excluded from the sample owing to data problems, most of which are also in the lowest-income category. We estimate each of the models using two samples of countries. The first is the full sample of 98 countries (22 industrial OECD-member countries and 76 developing countries), and the second consists of the 76 developing countries only. Hence, a second aspect of the empirical work is a comparison of the estimated coefficients obtained from the two samples. Our main results are presented in Tables 2.1–2.3. In all models, time-specific and country-specific effects are dealt with using the methodology outlined in Section 2.2 above.

Before presenting the results, we need to clarify the meaning of the "country-specific effects" in each of the estimated models. All empirical growth models implicitly assume that the excluded variables can be grouped into a single factor that affects the included variables in a given uniform way. This is rather restrictive, since each unobserved variable may affect the included variables in a different way. Thus, grouping them together introduces biases and inefficiencies. Much is gained by identifying and obtaining information on the different components of the country-specific factor. This is precisely our intention when we go from the first to the second and third models. In a sense, adding information on human capital, public capital, and openness to the simple Solow-Swan model may be viewed as an attempt to disaggregate the components of the all-inclusive country-specific factor assumed in the first model. Specifically, in the second model we identify the human capital component of the country-specific factor, while in the third model we add proxies for public capital and openness to disaggregate the country-specific effects further.

We begin with the simple Solow-Swan model (regression Equation (2.10″)). Results for this specification are reported in Table 2.1 using a Cobb-Douglas production function in the Solow growth model, we expect the estimated values of γ to be negative, those for θ_1 to be negative, and those for θ_2 to be positive; furthermore, we

Table 2.1. Two versions of the Solow-Swan model.

Variable[a]	Simple Solow-Swan model		Simple restricted Solow-Swan model[b]	
	All countries ($n = 98$)	Developing countries ($n = 76$)	All countries ($n = 98$)	Developing countries ($n = 76$)
$\ln(y_{t-1})$	−0.2686	−0.2707	−0.2782	−0.2660
	(−5.90)	(−6.47)	(−6.37)	(−6.63)
$\ln(n_r + 0.05)$	−0.1220	−0.1474	−0.1401	−0.1285
	(−4.90)	(−6.64)	(−9.52)	(−9.55)
$\ln(s_{k_r})$	0.1489	0.1184	0.1401	0.1285
	(8.36)	(7.03)	(9.52)	(9.55)
Implied η	0.0626	0.0631	0.0652	0.0619
	(5.03)	(5.50)	(5.39)	(5.66)
Implied α	...	...	0.335	0.326
Wald test for uncorrelated effects	164.53	167.21	...	...
(P-value)	0.0000	0.0000		
Wald test for $\theta_1 = -\theta_2$ in Equation (10*)	0.798	1.093	...	...
(P-value)	0.3718	0.2959		

Notes: [a]$\ln(y_{t-1})$ is the logarithm of real GDP per worker lagged one period (five years). $\ln(n_r + 0.05)$ is the logarithm of the average growth rate of the working-age population plus the sum of technological progress and depreciation. $\ln(s_{k_i})$ is the logarithm of the average ratio of real investment to real GDP. Implied η is the speed of convergence per year. T-ratios are in parentheses. Implied α is the income share accruing to non-human capital.

[b]These estimates are obtained by imposing the restriction implied by the Cobb-Douglas assumption — namely, that $-\theta_1 = \theta_2$.

Table 2.2. Solow-Swan model augmented to include human capital investment.

	Using cross-sectional data for human capital investment		Using panel data for human capital investment	
Variable[a]	All countries ($n = 98$)	Developing countries ($n = 76$)	All countries ($n = 96$)	Developing countries ($n = 75$)
$\ln(y_{t-1})$	−0.1775	−0.2095	−1.0383	−1.2961
	(−3.41)	(−4.27)	(−34.55)	(−95.73)
$\ln(n_t + 0.05)$	−0.0873	−0.1007	−0.0389	−0.0114
	(−3.02)	(−3.86)	(−5.25)	(1.45)
$\ln(s_{k_i})$	0.1061	0.0844	0.0233	0.1048
	(6.60)	(5.54)	(1.61)	(10.16)
$\ln(s_h)$	0.1064	0.0995		
	(4.91)	(5.38)		
$\ln(s_{h_t})$			−0.0652	−0.1108
			(−5.09)	(−13.26)
Implied η	0.0391	0.0470		
	(3.09)	(3.79)		
Wald test for uncorrelated effects	87.91	178.85	3249.00	60274.42
(P-value)	0.0000	0.0000	0.0000	0.0000
Wald test for $\theta_1 = -(\theta_2 + \theta_3)$ in equation (10‴)	12.31	5.16	12.23	0.07
(P-value)	0.0000	0.02317	0.0000	0.7974

Notes: [a]$\ln(y_{t-1})$ is the logarithm of real GDP per worker lagged one period (five years). $\ln(n_r + 0.05)$ is the logarithm of the average growth rate of the working-age population plus the sum of technological progress and depreciation. $\ln(s_{k_t})$ is the logarithm of the average ratio of real investment to real GDP. $\ln(s_{h_t})$ is the logarithm of the ratio of human capital investment to GDP, proxied by the product of gross secondary-school enrollment ratio times the fraction of the working-age population aged 15 to 19. T-ratios are in parentheses.

expect θ_1 and θ_2 to have approximately the same absolute value. As can be seen from Table 2.1 all these predictions of the Solow-Swan model hold true for the sample that includes all countries, as well as for that including developing countries only.

Moreover, our estimated values for the speed of convergence η are 0.0626 a year for the sample containing all 98 countries and 0.0631 for that containing developing countries, implying that the economy moves halfway to the steady state in about 11 years.[13] These estimates are much larger than those reported in Barro (1991) and Mankiw, Romer, and Weil (1992), but similar to the predicted value of the simple Solow-Swan model (see the formula for η in Equation (2.8), setting $\beta = 0$ and using sensible values for n, g, and δ). Mankiw, Romer, and Weil find that the implied estimate for the speed of convergence to its steady-state growth path is 0.0137 a year. Barro (1991), using variables such as school enrollment ratios, the government consumption expenditure ratio, proxies for political stability, and a measure of market distortions, finds an estimated speed of convergence equal to 0.0184 a year. These estimates correspond to a half-life for the logarithm of output per effective worker of between 37 and 50 years.[14] We believe that the large difference between their estimates and ours can be explained by the fact that their studies do not account for the correlation between the country-specific effects and the independent variables in the model, thus producing biased coefficients. Specifically, when country-specific effects are ignored, the coefficient on lagged output is biased toward zero because there is a positive correlation between country-specific effects (defined to be positive) and the initial levels of income in every interval (lagged output).

We can test for the presence of such a correlation. Consider the null hypothesis of "uncorrelated effects," which means that the country-specific effects have no correlation with the independent variables. From the equation for the linear predictor of μ_i and

---

[13]Note that in the estimating Equation (2.9) the parameters η and r appear on both sides; we set $r = 5$ years in our panel data regressions.

[14]The half-life formula is $T = \ln(2)/\eta$, where T is number of years.

Equation (2.13), it is evident that the null hypothesis of uncorrelated effects in the framework of our maintained model, is equivalent to $H_0 : \boldsymbol{\lambda}_1' = \cdots = \boldsymbol{\lambda}_5' = 0$. As can be seen in Table 2.1 the Wald test strongly rejects the null hypothesis of uncorrelated effects.

In Table 2.1 we also report the results of an estimation that assumes the coefficients on $\ln(n_t+0.05)$ and $\ln(s_{k_t-1})$ are the same in absolute value but opposite in sign ($\theta_1 = -\theta_2$). We do this in order to obtain estimates for the implied capital share, α, in the Cobb-Douglas production function. The estimates for α are 0.335 for all countries and 0.326 for developing countries.[15] These estimated capital shares are very close to the value of 0.350 that Maddison (1987) obtains for the share of non-human capital in production. Our estimated non-human capital shares imply that diminishing returns set in quickly, which explains the rapid convergence predicted by the model.

Table 2.1 also allows us to examine the differences in the estimated coefficients obtained using the two samples. For the sample of developing countries, the absolute value of the coefficient on population growth is larger than that for the sample of all countries. This can be explained by the fact that the developed industrial countries have tended to show relatively steady per capita growth over the sample period while experiencing relatively low population growth. Accordingly, when they are excluded from the sample the estimated effect of population growth is larger. Our estimates also suggest that investment in physical capital is less productive for developing countries than for developed countries. The fact that we do not obtain the same parameter estimates using the two different samples has to do with sampling error and with the inability to control completely for the country-specific effects.[16]

[15]Somehow contradicting our finding that the capital share in production is approximately the same for both industrial and developing countries, De Gregorio (1992) finds an estimate for the capital share of about 0.5 for a sample of Latin American economies.

[16]There are two basic reasons for this imperfection. The first has to do with the fact that we are grouping together all unobservable factors into the country-specific effects; thus, if an unobserved variable affects the two samples differently, we obtain sharper estimates by separating the two samples. The second reason

Table 2.2 presents the econometric estimates for the second version of the Solow-Swan model (regression Equation (2.10‴)). As might be expected, the inclusion of a proxy for the ratio of human capital investment to GDP has the effect of lowering the absolute value of the estimated coefficients on the other variables in both the full sample and the developing country subsample. However, the changes are relatively small, apparently because most of the effect of human capital investment has already been captured by the country-specific effects in the estimates of the first model. As also expected, the coefficient on the proxy for the human capital investment ratio is significantly positive. In this second model, a Cobb-Douglas production function implies that $-\theta_1 = \theta_2 + \theta_3$ in Equation (2.10‴). This restriction, however, is rejected by the data on the basis of the Wald test. This result may be due to the fact that education is more closely related to the efficiency variable than to human capital proper as an accumulatable factor of production. The reason why this assumption does not appear to be consistent with the sample data could be that the aggregate production function is more complex than the Cobb-Douglas form allows. It is also interesting to note that for both samples the speed of convergence is now estimated to be lower than in the first model. We believe this is due to higher returns to capital broadly defined to include human capital. In fact, when only physical capital is accumulated its marginal productivity decreases rapidly. Thus, the steady state is achieved more quickly but at a lower per capita output level (see the definition of η in Equation (2.8) and set the share of human capital β at a positive level).

Table 2.2 also reports the results of the second model when panel data for the human capital proxy, rather than only cross-sectional data, are used. We find that the estimated coefficient on this proxy is now significantly negative for both samples.[17] This result is at first

may be the presence of non-linear interactions between physical capital investment and the variables that are left out of the first model, such as education, public infrastructure, and openness to trade (linear interactions are accounted for by our methodology).

[17]De Gregorio (1992) reports similar results for a sample of Latin American countries.

surprising. Why does the addition of the time series dimension to the proxy for human capital change the sign of its effect on growth? Our explanation for this result is that when we incorporate time series data on education for each country we use not only the cross-country differences in the relation between education and growth but also the effect of *changes* in the human capital proxy over time in each country. This temporal relationship has been negative over the years, especially in developing countries (see Tilak (1989) and Fredriksen (1991)). In other words, adjusted secondary-school enrollment ratios rose steadily in most developing countries during 1960–85, sometimes by large amounts, while output growth remained stable or fell. Apparently, this time series relation is strong enough to override the cross-sectional effects in the estimation.

This empirical result points to the possibility that the adjusted secondary-school enrollment ratio may not be a good proxy for the ratio of human capital investment to GDP when relatively short intervals (in our case, five-year intervals) are compared. The length of the interval is important for the quality of such a proxy because there is a considerable lag between the completion of education and its appropriate use as a factor of production (see Psacharopoulos and Ariagada (1986)). Therefore, cross-sectional data (data where the observation for each country is an average of its respective time series observations) may be the preferred proxy in estimating the growth effects of human capital investment. The implication is that when the secondary-school enrollment ratio is used as the proxy, we can obtain good estimates of cross-country differences in human capital investment but not of *changes* in the rate of human capital investment within a country over time.

Table 2.3 reports the results for the third augmented version of the Solow-Swan model. Its corresponding regression is represented by Equation (2.10). Considerations of data availability obliged us to restrict the sample of countries used in this last estimation (see Appendix 2.A). Therefore, one would have to be particularly cautious about extrapolating the results described below to countries that are not included in the sample. The negative sign of the coefficient on lagged output indicates "conditional convergence," which means

Table 2.3. Solow-Swan model augmented to include human capital investment, openness to foreign trade, and public infrastructure.

Variable[a]	All countries ($n = 81$)	Developing countries ($n = 59$)
$\ln(y_{t-1})$	−0.2208	−0.6836
	(−9.45)	(−17.75)
$\ln(n_t + 0.05)$	−0.1470	−0.1760
	(−12.52)	(−9.01)
$\ln(s_{k_t})$	0.2013	0.2057
	(18.17)	(14.24)
$\ln(s_{h_t})$	0.0945	0.3197
	(8.18)	(18.15)
$\ln(F)$	−0.0650	−0.0820
	(−11.76)	(−15.97)
$\ln(P)$	0.0128	0.0978
	(0.78)	(6.47)
Implied η	0.0499	0.2301
	(8.32)	(9.45)
Wald test for uncorrelated effects	526.03	5596.77
(P-value)	0.0000	0.0000
Wald test for $\theta_1 = -(\theta_2 + \theta_3)$ in Equation (2.10)	61.76	238.19
(P-value)	0.0000	0.0000

Notes: [a]$\ln(y_{t-1})$ is the logarithm of real GDP per worker lagged one period (five years). $\ln(n_t + 0.05)$ is the logarithm of the average growth rate of the working-age population plus the sum of technological progress and depreciation. $\ln(s_{k_t})$ is the logarithm of the average ratio of real investment to real GDP. $\ln(s_{h_t})$ is the logarithm of the ratio of human capital investment to GDP, proxied by the product of gross secondary-school enrollment ratio times the fraction of the working-age population aged 15 to 19. $\ln(F)$ is the logarithm of the "closedness" of the economy, proxied by the weighted average of tariff rates on imported intermediate and capital goods. $\ln(P)$ is the logarithm of the ratio of public infrastructure to GDP, proxied by the average ratio of general government fixed investment (central government plus public enterprises) to GDP. T-ratios are in parentheses.

that — controlling for the determinants of the steady state across countries — poor countries would tend to grow faster than rich ones (see Barro and Sala-i-Martin (1992)). By including the investment ratios as well as the proxies for openness and public infrastructure in the regression equation, we appropriately condition for different preferences and technologies.

The growth rate of the labor force is estimated to be negatively related to per capita output growth, especially when the estimates come from the sample that includes only developing countries. Investments in both physical capital and human capital are strongly and positively correlated with growth. When proxies for openness and public capital are included in the model, the coefficient on the rate of investment in physical capital becomes twice as large as it was in the second model, for both samples. This seems to indicate that the quality of physical investment increases when the international transfer of technology is allowed and when better public capital is provided. We believe that this has to do with the fact that greater openness and better public services create a market environment where allocative efficiency is enhanced. In addition, the rate of investment in human capital becomes much stronger in the case of the developing country sample when the aforementioned proxies are included.

The variable F, defined as the weighted average of tariffs on intermediate and capital goods, has a significant negative effect on output growth. This measure of openness ("closedness" may be a better term given how this variable is defined) affects growth not only through the investment ratios, as indicated above, but also through the efficiency term, which accounts for technological improvement. The evidence of such an independent role for openness, combined with the fact that the absolute value of the coefficient's point estimate is larger for the developing countries, lends support to the view that for many countries, particularly developing ones, liberal trade regimes provide a source of technological progress via the freedom to import sophisticated goods from the most technologically advanced nations. At a broader level, this result provides a measure of empirical confirmation for the familiar argument that outward-oriented trade strategies tend to promote economic growth in developing countries.

The ratio of government fixed investment to GDP (the variable P) has a positive coefficient for both samples, but this coefficient is statistically significant at the 95 percent level only for the developing country sample. The statistical insignificance of this coefficient in the full sample may be due to the fact that our proxy for public capital is based on flow data that do not account for the initial level of the associated stock. This is especially important for the industrial countries, which by 1960 had accumulated substantial stocks of public capital, relative to those in developing countries. In that sense, our proxy is better suited to developing countries, which may explain why we find a much larger and highly significant coefficient in the sample for the latter group. As in the case of the openness variable, it is interesting to note that, at least for the latter sample, the proxy for public capital has an independent role in economic growth, even when physical and human capital are already included.

2.4 Concluding Remarks

This paper has extended the work of Mankiw, Romer, and Weil (1992) in two directions. Unlike their analysis, which relies exclusively on cross-sectional data, we find evidence of significant country-specific effects, which our panel data estimation procedure is able to detect. One important consequence of this result is the faster rate of conditional convergence that we find in our model, relative to that estimated by Mankiw, Romer, and Weil and by Barro (1991). We surmise that this difference occurs because the latter studies do not take into account the correlation between country-specific effects and the independent variables in the growth equation. The other new result is that overall economic efficiency is influenced significantly and positively by the extent of openness to international trade and by the level of government fixed investment in the domestic economy.

Like Mankiw, Romer, and Weil, we find that the Solow-Swan model's predictions are consistent with the evidence. These include the positive effects of saving ratios and the negative effects of population growth on the steady-state level and on the transitional growth path of per capita GDP. We also find (conditional) convergence to be approximately the rate predicted by the Solow-Swan model. We estimate the share of capital at about one-third, which is close to the value estimated by Maddison (1987) for the share of non-human capital in GDP. Our estimated capital shares imply that diminishing returns to physical capital set in quickly, explaining the rapid convergence predicted by our model.

Comparing the results between the two samples of industrial and developing countries, we find that the absolute value of the estimated coefficient on population growth is larger for our sample of developing countries alone, reflecting the fact that many countries in this group have tended to exhibit slow growth in per capita terms while experiencing rapid rates of population growth. Moreover, there is evidence that investment in physical capital has been less productive for those developing countries that have had lower initial stocks of human capital and of government fixed investment as well as higher rates of effective protection, all of which have tended to reduce the overall efficiency of physical investment.

Our results on the growth effects of a country's openness to international trade and on government fixed investment deserve some elaboration. When openness and the level of public infrastructure are taken into account, physical investment becomes quantitatively more important in the growth process, implying that a better quality of investment is encouraged by a more liberal international trade regime and by more government fixed investment. Particularly for the developing countries, investment in human capital also becomes more quantitatively important when a more open trading environment and a better public infrastructure are in place.

There are two channels through which the negative impact on growth of a restrictive trade system (proxied by the weighted average of tariffs on intermediate and capital goods) is transmitted, particularly in developing countries where the capital goods industries are in their infancy or nonexistent: through the rate of investment and through its efficiency. A high tariff structure discourages imports of capital goods and leads to less technology transfer, and thus to less technological improvement. The strong statistical significance of the proxy for "closedness" provides evidence that outward-oriented development strategies have a positive impact on economic growth.

The government fixed investment variable is statistically and positively significant only in the developing countries, and appropriately so. This can be explained by the failure of our proxy for public infrastructure to account for its initial level. Among the industrial country group, the level of public infrastructure in 1960 was a large multiple of the level in the developing country group. As in the case of the outward orientation of development strategies, better provision of public infrastructure exerts an independent influence on the rate of economic growth. This may mean that the government is in a better position to provide infrastructure than the private sector. In other words, either the private sector, if it had the resources, would tend to underinvest in infrastructure or the marginal productivity of public sector resources devoted to infrastructure is higher than that of private sector resources (presumably owing to significant externalities).

Appendix 2.A: Data Sources, Definitions, and the Sample of Countries

The basic data used in this study are annual observations for the period 1960 to 1985. The following variables were taken from Penn World Tables in Summers and Heston (1991):

y = real GDP per worker;

s_k = real investment to GDP ratio (five-year average);

n = growth rate of the number of workers (five-year average).

The following variable was taken from Mankiw, Romer, and Weil (1992):

s_h = percent of working-age population enrolled in secondary school (average for the 1960-85 period).

Panel data for the proxy of human capital investment were obtained from the UNESCO *Statistical Yearbook* 1991 and were adjusted for age using population data from UN Population Division (1991). Data on tariffs were taken from Lee (1992):

F = import-share weighted average of tariffs on intermediate and capital goods (from various years in the early 1980s).

The DEC Analytical data base from the World Bank (1991) was used to obtain a proxy for public infrastructure:

P = average ratio of general government fixed investment to GDP. The sample of countries was as follows.

Industrial countries

1. Australia
2. Austria
3. Belgium
4. Canada
5. Denmark
6. Finland
7. France
8. Germany (West)
9. Greece
10. Ireland
11. Italy
12. Japan
13. Netherlands
14. New Zealand
15. Norway
16. Portugal
17. Spain
18. Sweden
19. Switzerland
20. Turkey
21. United Kingdom
22. United States

Developing countries

1. Algeria
2. Angola
3. Argentina
4. Bangladesh
5. Benin
6. Bolivia
7. Botswana
8. Brazil
9. Burkina Faso
10. Burundi
11. Cameroon
12. Central African Republic
13. Chad
14. Chile
15. Colombia
16. Congo
17. Costa Rica
18. Côte d'Jvoire
19. Dominican Republic
20. Ecuador
21. Egypt
22. El Salvador
23. Ethiopia
24. Ghana
25. Guatemala
26. Haiti
27. Honduras
28. Hong Kong
29. India
30. Indonesia
31. Israel
32. Jamaica
33. Jordan
34. Kenya
35. Liberia
36. Madagascar
37. Malawi
38. Malaysia
39. Mali
40. Mauritania
41. Mauritius
42. Mexico
43. Morocco
44. Mozambique

45. Myanmar
46. Nepal
47. Nicaragua
48. Niger
49. Nigeria
50. Pakistan
51. Panama
52. Papua New Guinea
53. Paraguay
54. Peru
55. Philippines
56. Republic of Korea
57. Rwanda
58. Senegal
59. Sierra Leone
60. Singapore
61. Somalia
62. South Africa
63. Sri Lanka
64. Sudan
65. Syrian Arab Republic
66. Tanzania
67. Thailand
68. Togo
69. Trinidad and Tobago
70. Tunisia
71. Uganda
72. Uruguay
73. Venezuela
74. Zaire
75. Zambia
76. Zimbabwe

References

Bardhan, P. and S. Lewis (1970). Models of growth with imported inputs. *Economica*, 37, 373–385.

Barro, R. J. (1991). Economic growth in a cross section of countries. *The Quarterly Journal of Economics*, 106, 407–443.

Barro, R. J. and X. Sala-i-Martin (1992). Convergence. *Journal of Political Economy*, 100, 223-225.

Chamberlain, G. (1982). Multivariate regression models for panel data. *Journal of Econometrics*, 18, 5–46.

Chamberlain, G. (1984). Panel data. In Z Griliches and M Intriligator (eds), *Handbook of Econometrics*, Vol. II, pp. 1248–1318. Amsterdam: North-Holland Publishing.

Chen, E. K. Y. (1979). *Hyper-Growth in Asian Economies: A Comparative Study of Hong Kong, Japan, Korea, Singapore, and Taiwan.* NY: Harper Hall.

De Gregorio, J. (1992). Economic growth in Latin America. *Journal of Development Economics*, 39, 59–84.

Diamond, J. (1989). Government expenditure and economic growth: an empirical investigation. *IMF Working Paper 89/45.*

Domar, E. D. (1946). Capital expansion, rate of growth, and employment. *Econometrica*, 14, 137–147.

Edwards, S. (1992). Trade orientation, distortions and growth in developing countries. *Journal of Development Economics*, 39, 31–57.

Feder, G. (1983). On exports and economic growth. *Journal of Development Economics*, 12, 59–73.

Fredriksen, B. J. (1991). An introduction to the analysis of student enrollment and flow statistics. *Report No. PHREE/91/39.*

Greene, W. H. (1990). *Econometric Analysis.* NY: Macmillan Publishing Company.

Hacche, G. (1979). *The Theory of Economic Growth: An Introduction.* NY: St. Martins Press.

Harrod, R. F. (1939). An essay in dynamic theory. *Economic Journal*, 49, 14–33.

Keesing, D. B. (1967). Outward-looking policies and economic development. *Economic Journal*, 78, 303–320.

Khan, M. and D. Villanueva (1991). Macroeconomic policies and Long-Term growth. *Special Paper 13, Nairobi: African Economic Research Consortium.*

Khang, C. (1987). Export-led economic growth: the case of technology transfer. *Economic Studies Quarterly*, 38, 131–147.

Knight, M., N. Loayza, and D. Villanueva (1992). Testing the neoclassical theory of economic growth. *IMF Working Paper 92/106.*

Lee, J.-W. (1993). International trade, distortions, and long-run economic growth. *IMF Staff Papers*, 40, 299–328.

Loayza, N. (1992). A test of the convergence hypothesis using panel data. Unpublished; Harvard University.

Maddison, A. (1987). Growth and slowdown in advanced capitalist economies: techniques of quantitative assessment. *Journal of Economic Literature*, 25, 649–698.

Mankiw, N. G., D. Romer, and D. N. Weil (1992). A contribution to the empirics of economic growth. *The Quarterly Journal of Economics*, 107, 407–437.

McCurdy, T. E. (1982). The use of time series processes to model the error structure of earnings in a longitudinal data analysis. *Journal of Econometrics*, 18, 83–114.

Mundlak, Y. (1978). On the pooling of time series and cross section data. *Econometrica*, 46, 69–85.

Orsmond, D. W. H. (1990). The size and composition of the public sector and economic growth: a theoretical and empirical review. Unpublished; International Monetary Fund.

Otani, I. and D. Villanueva (1990). Long-term growth in developing countries and its determinants: an empirical analysis. *World Development*, 18, 769–783.

Psacharopoulos, G. and A.-M. Ariagada (1986). The educational composition of the labor force: an international comparison. *International Labor Review*, 125, 561–574.

Roubini, N. and X. J. Sala-i-Martin (1992). Financial repression and economic growth. *Journal of Development Economics*, 39, 5–30.

Sala-i-Martin, X. J. (1990). Lecture notes on economic growth (I). *NBER Working Paper No. 3563.*

Solow, R. M. (1956). A contribution to the theory of economic growth. *The Quarterly Journal of Economics*, 50, 65–94.

Summers, R. and A. Heston (1991). The Penn world table (mark 5): an expanded set of international comparisons, 1950–1988. *The Quarterly Journal of Economics*, 106, 327–361.

Swan, T. W. (1956). Economic growth and capital accumulation. *Economic Record*, 32, 334–361.

Thirlwall, A. P. (1979). The balance of payments constraint as an explanation of international growth rate differences. *Banca Nazionale del Lavoro Quarterly Review*, 128, 45–53.

Tilak, T. B. G. (1989). Education and its relation to economic growth, poverty, and income distribution: past evidence and further analysis. *Discussion Paper 46, Washington: World Bank.*

UNESCO (1992). *Statistical Yearbook 1991.* Paris: UNESCO.

United Nations Population Division (1991). *Global Estimates and Projections of Population by Sex and Age: The 1990 Revision.* NY: United Nations.

Villanueva, D. (1993). Exports and economic development. *IMF Working Paper 93/41.*

White, H. (1980). A heteroskedasticity-consistent covariance matrix estimator and a direct test for heteroskedasticity. *American Economic Review*, 48, 817–838.

World Bank (1991). *DEC Analytical Database.* Washington: World Bank.

Chapter 3

A Modified Neoclassical Growth Model with Endogenous Labor Participation*

3.1 Introduction

Assume an aggregate Cobb-Douglas production function,

$$Y = K^{\alpha} L^{(1-\alpha)} \tag{3.1}$$

where Y is output, K is capital stock, $L = APN$ is effective labor (in efficiency units), A = a labor-augmenting (or Harrod-neutral) technology multiplier, P = labor participation (a positive fraction), N = total population, α = elasticity of output with respect to capital, and $1 - \alpha$ = output elasticity with respect to labor. Output growth is equal to the weighted sum of capital growth and labor growth, the weights being α and $1 - \alpha$, respectively. Capital growth is the warranted rate and labor growth is the natural rate. The warranted rate is:

$$\frac{\dot{K}}{K} = s\frac{Y}{K} - \delta \tag{3.2}$$

where s is the fixed gross saving/income ratio and δ is a constant depreciation rate.

*Written by Delano S. Villanueva and adapted from the *Bulletin of Monetary Economics and Banking*, 23, 83–100, by the permission of the Bulletin of Monetary Economics and Banking.

From the definition $L = APN$, labor growth is given by

$$\frac{\dot{L}}{L} = \frac{\dot{A}}{A} + \frac{\dot{P}}{P} + \frac{\dot{N}}{N}. \tag{3.3}$$

Let $k = K/L$ be the level of capital intensity. In the steady state, if it exists, k is constant at k^*, which means that

$$\frac{\dot{K}}{K} = s\frac{Y}{K} - \delta = \frac{\dot{L}}{L} = \frac{\dot{A}}{A} + \frac{\dot{P}}{P} + \frac{\dot{N}}{N}. \tag{3.4}$$

And by the constant-returns assumption,

$$\frac{\dot{K}}{K} = \frac{\dot{L}}{L} = \frac{\dot{Y}}{Y}, \tag{3.5}$$

which defines the steady-state growth rate of output Y, or the balanced growth path.

The knife-edge H-D (Harrod (1939), Domar (1946)) problem (**Chapter 1**) is expressed by the condition

$$\frac{\dot{K}}{K} = \frac{s}{v} - \delta \gtreqless \frac{\dot{L}}{L} = \frac{\dot{A}}{A} + \frac{\dot{P}}{P} + \frac{\dot{N}}{N} \gtreqless \lambda + n, \tag{3.6}$$

where $v = K/Y$ is the fixed capital-output ratio, $\frac{\dot{A}}{A} = \lambda$, $\frac{\dot{P}}{P} = 0$, and $\frac{\dot{N}}{N} = n$, where λ and n are constants. Balanced growth, macroeconomic stability, and full employment are not assured.

As **Chapter 1** points out, S-S (Solow (1956), Swan (1956)) solved the knife-edge H-D problem by employing a neoclassical production function with smooth substitutability between capital and labor, i.e., $1/v$ is a monotonically decreasing function of the capital-labor ratio, k, such that the warranted rate (saving-investment) fully adjusts from any initial level of capital intensity, making balanced growth possible.

However, the steady state remains exogenous because the natural rate (effective labor growth), which is fixed at $\lambda + n$ by assumption, remains the bottleneck in the growth process, with the result that the positive growth effect of a higher saving rate s during the transition[1] disappears in the steady state.

---

[1] *Temporary* growth as Solow (1991, p. 4) calls it.

The 1960s through 1990s saw attempts to solve the S-S model's exogeneity of the natural rate, $\frac{\dot{A}}{A} + \frac{\dot{P}}{P} + \frac{\dot{N}}{N}$, by making technical change $\frac{\dot{A}}{A}$ endogenous.[2] An early learning-by-doing model by Arrow (1962) found that learning has a positive effect on the steady-state growth of output, but the latter is independent of the saving rate, depending on whether learning is a function of capital growth or of the stock of capital per capita. Nelson and Phelps (1966), Conlisk (1967), and Villanueva (1994, **Chapter 6**)[3] advanced early models with endogenous labor-augmenting technical change, deriving the key result that the growth effect of an increased saving rate does not vanish in the steady state.

Subsequent contributions constructed increasingly complex models. Romer (1986, 1990) posited a knowledge-producing sector, alongside a goods-producing sector. The stock of knowledge is a non-rival good — its use in one sector does not preclude its use in the other sector. Lucas (1988) proposed models emphasizing human capital accumulation through schooling and learning-by-doing, but he abstracted from the economics of demography.[4] Grossman and Helpman (1991) focused on innovation financed by investments in industrial research. Rebelo's (1991) AK model assumed that all productive inputs, including human capital, are reproducible capital.[5] Aghion and Howitt (1998) highlighted imperfect markets in the R&D sector and Schumpeterian creative destruction. The knowledge-innovation-R&D

[2]For an engaging history of endogenous growth theory, see Warsh (2007). Solow (1991) has been critical of endogenous growth models with their emphasis on endogenous technical change and increasing returns.

[3]Agénor (2004, pp. 466–471) refers to Villanueva's (1994, **Chapter 6**) model as "An extension of Arrow's (1962) learning by doing model,...(wherein) the productivity of workers increases when the relative availability of capital goods (for instance, the stock of high-performance computers) rises," leading to enhanced long-run growth effects of saving and investment rates.

[4]Lucas (1988, p. 6) admits that this is a serious omission.

[5]Output $Y = AK$, where Y is constant returns to capital K, implying that Y always grows at the same rate as K, and is equal to $s * A$, where $s*$ is the fraction of income saved for investment in physical *and* human capital ($s* > s$, where s is income saved for investment in physical capital) and A is a technological constant. This property is in sharp contrast to the transitional growth dynamics in the S-S model.

sector is assumed to be subject to increasing returns, so that growth does not vanish in the long run. Conlisk (1967) has shown that increasing returns to capital yield explosive growth, which rarely happens in the real world. He has demonstrated that a growth model with endogenous labor-augmenting technical change and an aggregate production function that is subject to diminishing returns to capital is consistent with the proposition that the positive growth effects of an increased saving rate (or of any change in the other model parameters) do not cease in the steady state.

In all the above growth models, the labor participation rate, P, is an exogenous constant fraction by assumption.[6] Another solution to the knife-edge problem, besides the S-S model's variable capital-output ratio implicit in a well-behaved neoclassical production function with smooth factor substitution and wage-rice flexibility, is a fully adjusting natural rate via an endogenously determined labor participation rate, P. In a carefully researched IMF empirical study, Grigoli *et al.* (2018, Table 3.1, p. 18) found robust results indicating that, among others, an increasingly educated[7] labor force influenced significantly and positively labor participation rates in 36 advanced economies. Referring to the U.S., in particular, the Congressional Budget Office (CBO, 2018) issued a working paper on labor participation, containing similar explanatory variables included in the IMF study and arriving at similar statistical results. The study noted that the U.S. labor participation rate began an uninterrupted decline in the latter half of the 1990s, coinciding with the aging and retirement of baby boomers. In 2007, the labor participation rate stood at 66%. A decade later, in 2017 Q4, it fell to 63.2%. CBO projects that the U.S. labor participation rate will continue to decline and will be 60.2% in 2028 Q4. The projected increase in educational attainment, which has a positive effect on the labor participation

[6]Whether it is 70% or any other percentage, the rate of change in P is assumed to be zero. The labor participation rate and unemployment rate are metrics used to gauge the health of the labor market. The key difference between the two indicators is that the participation rate measures the percentage of the population who are in the labor force, while the unemployment rate measures the percentage within the labor force that is currently unemployed.

[7]Workers with secondary and tertiary degrees.

rate, will not be enough to offset the continued decline attributed to aging and retirements, and to the stagnation in real wages, among other factors.

Motivated by the empirical findings of Grigoli *et al.* (2018) and CBO (2018), this chapter postulates that the proportionate change in labor participation consists of exogenous components including aging and retirements, and endogenous components including aggregate income per man-hour and real wages. The objective and hence novelty of this chapter is to generalize the steady state property of the S-S model by making the natural rate fully adjusting through endogenous labor participation, P, i.e., a non-zero variable $\frac{\dot{P}}{P}$, while retaining the twin assumptions of $\frac{\dot{A}}{A} = \lambda$ and $\frac{\dot{N}}{N} = n$. To elaborate, in the effective labor definition $L = APN$, the S-S model assumes that P is a constant fraction of population N, and thus, $\frac{\dot{P}}{P} = 0$. It also assumes that A and N are exogenous variables growing at constant rates λ and n, respectively. The natural rate can be made fully adjusting by assuming that either A, P, or N is endogenously determined. Some endogenous growth models [Nelson and Phelps (1966), Conlisk (1967), and Villanueva (1994, **Chapter 6**)] make the case for an endogenous A. This chapter, considering the work of Grigoli *et al.* (2018) and CBO (2018), makes the case for an endogenous P.

3.2 The Modified Growth Model

I retain the S-S model's assumption of fully exogenous rates of labor-augmenting technical change, A, and population growth, N. The only modification I make is to rely on the IMF and CBO empirical studies to justify that the labor participation rate, P, is not a constant but a variable that is partly endogenous and partly exogenous (for explanation, see Section 3.2.1 below). Figure 3.1 is a schematic presentation of the model.

Capital intensity, measured by the capital-labor ratio, has short-run (transitional) and long-run (steady state) effects on output growth through changes in labor participation. The first channel works through an expansion in aggregate income per man-hour

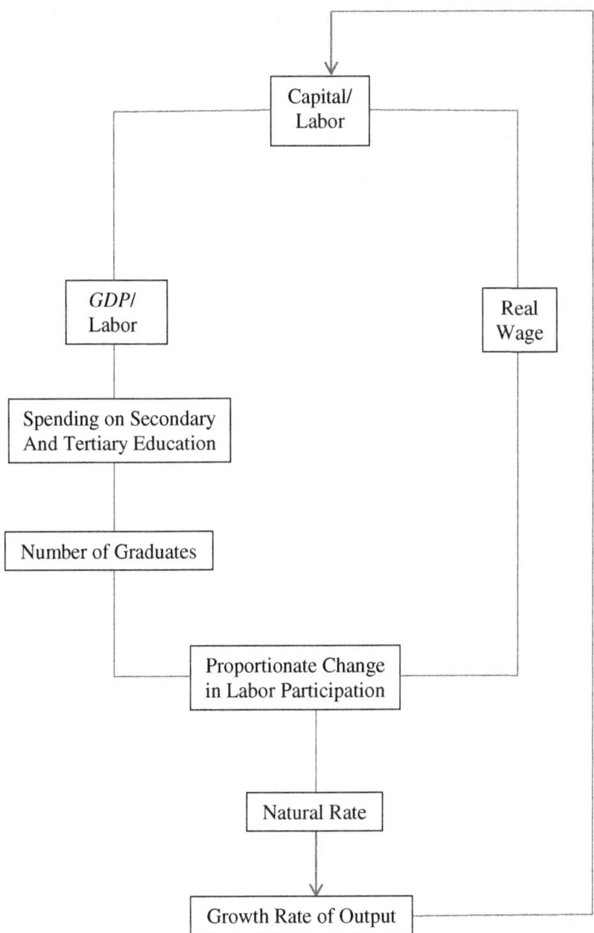

Figure 3.1. Links in the modified model. Y = output (GDP); K = capital stock; L = effective labor (man-hours), A = technology-productivity multiplier; P = labor participation rate (fraction); N = population; RW = real wage; k = capital-labor ratio; t = time (suppressed); α, s, δ, λ, n, β, ρ, and ω = fixed parameters, with ρ, $\omega > 0$. A dot over a variable denotes time derivative, i.e., $\dot{A} = dA/dt$.

resulting from a higher capital-labor ratio, with consequent higher spending on secondary and tertiary education that produces higher number of graduates who enter the labor force. The second channel works through movements in real wage that enter labor supply decisions. A higher capital-labor ratio raises labor's marginal product and hence the real wage, inducing increased labor supply and output growth. The model is closed loop. There is feedback effect of output growth on the capital-labor ratio. Changes in the capital-labor ratio are triggered by discrepancies in the warranted and natural rates, whose weighted average determines the instantaneous output growth rate.

The structural model is as follows:

$$Y = K^{\alpha} L^{(1-\alpha)} \quad \text{Aggregate Production Function} \tag{3.7}$$

$$\dot{K} = sY - \delta K \quad \text{Growth in Capital Stock} \tag{3.8}$$

$$\mathrm{L} = \mathrm{APN} \quad \text{Labor (Efficiency Units)} \tag{3.9}$$

$$\dot{N}/N = n \quad \text{Population Growth} \tag{3.10}$$

$$\frac{\dot{A}}{A} = \lambda \quad \text{Productivity/Technical Change} \tag{3.11}$$

$$\frac{\dot{P}}{P} = \beta + \rho\left(\frac{Y}{L}\right) + \omega RW \quad \text{Change in Labor Participation} \tag{3.12}$$

$$RW = \frac{\partial Y}{\partial L} \quad \text{Profit Maximization} \tag{3.13}$$

$$k = K/L \quad \text{Capital Intensity} \tag{3.14}$$

3.2.1 *Discussion*

Equation (3.7) is the aggregate production function, identical to Equation (3.1). Using capital and labor, aggregate output is produced according to the Cobb-Douglas function satisfying the Inada (1963) conditions.[8] Equation (3.8), which is identical to Equation (3.2), states that the increment in the capital stock equals gross domestic saving less capital depreciation.

[8]With reference to any production function $F(K, L) = Lf(k)$, where K is capital, L is labor, and k is the ratio of K to L, these conditions can be summarized as follows: $\lim \partial F/\partial K = \infty$ as $K \to 0$; $\lim \partial F/\partial K = 0$ as $K \to \infty; f(0) \geq 0$; $f'(k) > 0$, and $f''(k) < 0$ for all $k > 0$.

Equation (3.9) defines effective labor L as the product of a technology/productivity multiplier, A, labor participation P, and population N.[9] Equation (3.10) is the conventional assumption that population grows exogenously at rate n. Equation (3.11) states that technical change grows at a constant rate λ. Solow (1987) refers to an increase in λ as an upward shift in the production function, i.e., more output is produced with the same amounts of capital and labor.

Reflecting the empirical findings of Grigoli *et al.* (2018) and CBO (2018), Equation (3.12) postulates that the proportionate change in labor participation P consists of exogenous component β and endogenous components $\rho(\frac{Y}{L})$ and ωRW. The exogenous term β includes aging and retirements, changes in labor market policies and institutions, e.g., tax benefits (tax credits and unemployment benefits), and a host of non-economic variables identified in the aforementioned empirical studies. The endogenous terms are: (a) the portion of aggregate income per man-hour $(\frac{Y}{L})$ spent on secondary and tertiary education and its effect on the number of graduates, and the latter's effect on the labor participation rate;[10] and (b) the real wage RW that, under profit maximization, is equal to labor's marginal product $\frac{\partial Y}{\partial L} = (1 - \alpha)k^{\alpha}$ as specified in Equation (3.13), where k is capital intensity, defined as the ratio of K to L in Equation (3.14). An increase in the real wage is expected to raise the rate of labor participation ($\omega > 0$).

3.2.2 *Reduced Model*

Dividing Equations (3.7) and (3.8) by K and using Equation (3.14) yield

$$\frac{\dot{K}}{K} = sk^{(\alpha-1)} - \delta. \tag{3.15}$$

---

[9]Its time derivative is given by Equation (3.3).

[10]The coefficient $\rho > 0$ is a composite parameter reflecting the fraction of aggregate income spent on secondary and tertiary education and its effect on the number of graduates, and the latter's effect on labor participation.

Time differentiating Equation (3.9) and substituting Equations (3.10)–(3.14) into the result yield

$$\frac{\dot{L}}{L} = [\rho + \omega(1-\alpha)]k^{\alpha} + \lambda + n + \beta. \tag{3.16}$$

Time differentiating Equation (3.14) and substituting equations (3.15) and (3.16) into the result yield the rate of change of capital intensity

$$\frac{\dot{k}}{k} = sk^{(\alpha-1)} - [\rho + \omega(1-\alpha)]k^{\alpha} - (\lambda + n + \beta + \delta). \tag{3.17}$$

Time differentiating Equation (3.7) and substituting Equations (3.15) and (3.16) into the result yield the growth rate of output at any moment of time

$$\frac{\dot{Y}}{Y} = g = \alpha s k^{(\alpha-1)} + (1-\alpha)[\rho + \omega(1-\alpha)]k^{\alpha} + (1-\alpha)(\lambda + n + \beta) - \alpha\delta. \tag{3.18}$$

The reduced models in $\frac{\dot{k}}{k}$, $\frac{\dot{K}}{K}$, and $\frac{\dot{L}}{L}$ in the S-S (denoted by s) and modified (denoted by m) models are shown in Figure 3.2. The upper part shows the proportionate rate of change in the capital-labor ratio, k, and the lower part shows the growth rate of output, Y. Given the Inada (1963) conditions, the $\frac{\dot{k}}{k}$ line in either model is downward-sloping and intersects the k-axis at some finite, positive k, such as k_s^* or k_m^*. In either model, for $k < k^*$, $\frac{\dot{k}}{k} > 0$, and k increases until it reaches k^* at which it becomes constant. For $k > k^*$, $\frac{\dot{k}}{k} < 0$, and k decreases until it goes back to k^* at which it becomes constant. As capital intensity changes, diminishing marginal and average productivity of capital and positive dependence of labor participation on capital intensity provide the economic rationale behind the proportionate changes in capital intensity and in the warranted and natural rates. Specifically, with reference to the lower part of Figure 3.2, the downward-sloping warranted rate line in either model owes to diminishing marginal and average capital productivities as K/L increases. The horizontal natural rate line in the S-S model reflects the full exogeneity of technical change.

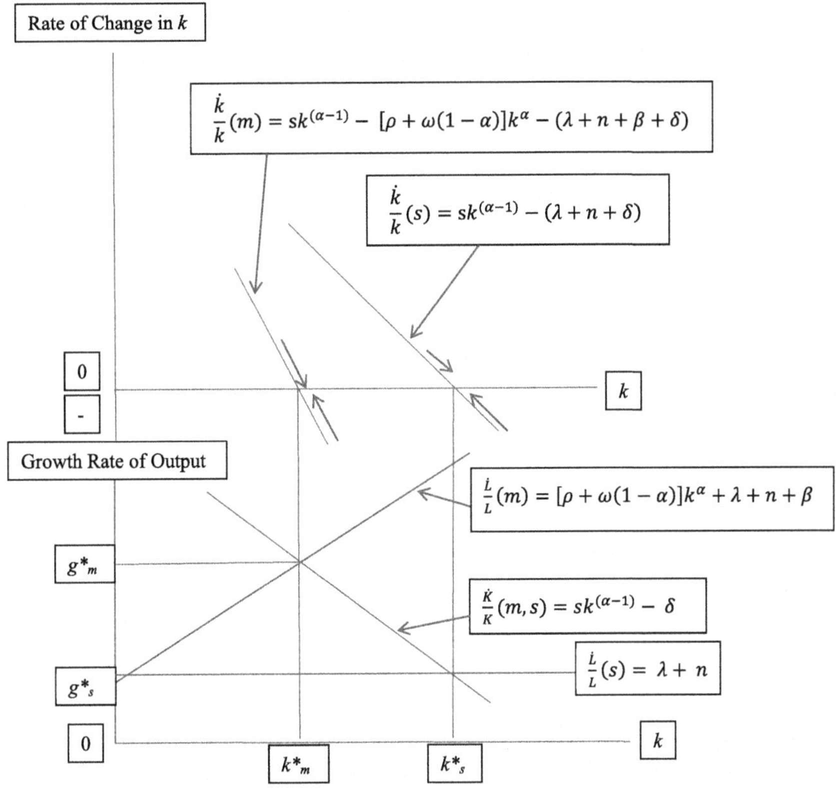

Figure 3.2. Modified (m) and Solow-Swan (s) models.

The upward-sloping natural rate line in the modified model reflects the positive dependence of labor participation on K/L, i.e., as K/L rises, higher aggregate income per man-hour translates into higher spending on secondary and tertiary education, higher number of graduates, and increased labor participation. Additionally, as K/L rises, labor's marginal product goes up and, hence, the real wage increases, encouraging higher labor participation.

Notice that the $\frac{\dot{k}}{k}(m)$ line is drawn steeper than the $\frac{\dot{k}}{k}(s)$ because of the negative term representing labor participation in the $\frac{\dot{k}}{k}(m)$ line. The lower panel of Figure 3.2 shows the equilibrium capital intensity, k^*, and equilibrium output growth, g^*, in either model — k_s^* and g_s^*, and k_m^* and g_m^*, respectively, in the S-S model and in the modified model.[11] The equilibrium capital-labor ratio is lesser in the modified model. The intuitive reason is that effective labor in the modified model is larger because of a variable labor participation rate (as opposed to a constant rate in the S-S model). The equilibrium output growth is larger in the modified model because its natural rate is greater for a similar reason. Finally, if labor participation rate is a constant number, such that $\frac{\dot{P}}{P} = 0$ $(\beta = \rho = \omega = 0)$, then $\frac{\dot{k}}{k} = \text{s}k^{(\alpha-1)} - (\lambda + n + \delta)$ and $\frac{\dot{L}}{L} = \lambda + n$, and the modified model collapses into the S-S model.

3.3 Comparative Dynamics

Table 3.1 shows the steady-state effects of changes in the modified model's parameters on the equilibrium capital intensity and the equilibrium growth rate of per capita output. A higher saving rate and a higher income share going to capital have positive effects on equilibrium capital intensity. Higher values for labor participation, population growth, technical change and physical capital depreciation impact negatively on equilibrium capital intensity.

Higher values for the saving rate, labor participation and technical change have positive effects on equilibrium per capita output growth. Rapid population growth, higher capital income share, and an increase in capital depreciation lower equilibrium per capita output growth.[12]

In the long run, on the balanced growth path, a (constant) equilibrium capital/labor ratio $k^* = (K/L)^*$ means that the warranted and natural rates are equal to each other, and by the constant returns

---

[11] See Equations (3.17) and (3.18).

[12] The $\frac{\dot{k}}{k}(m) = 0$ [Equation (3.17)] is the steady-state condition with an implicit solution for k^*. The reader can easily check the signs of Table 3.1 by implicit differentiation of k^* in the equation $\frac{\dot{k}}{k}(m) = 0$ with respect to the parameters. Substituting such changes in k^* into the partial derivatives of $\frac{\dot{K}}{K} * (m)$ and $\frac{\dot{L}}{L} * (m)$ [Equations (3.15) and (3.16), evaluated at k^*] with respect to the parameters determines the signs of the partial derivatives of $g^* - n$ with respect to the parameters shown in Table 3.1.

Table 3.1. Sensitivity of k^* and $g^* - n$ to parameter changes. This table reports the sensitivity of k^* = equilibrium capital-labor ratio and of $g^* - n$ = equilibrium growth rate of per capita GDP to parameter changes to all-else-equal increase in s = saving rate, ρ = response coefficient of labor participation to aggregate spending on secondary and tertiary education, on-the-job training, and skills upgrade, ρ = response coefficient of labor participation to the real wage, n = exogenous population growth, λ = exogenous rate of labor-augmenting technical change, β = exogenous rate of labor participation, δ = rate of depreciation of capital, and α = capital share of income.

Description	s	ρ	ω	n	λ	β	δ	α
Change in k^*	+	−	−	−	−	−	−	+
Change in $g^* - n$	+	+	+	−	+	+	−	−

assumption, to the growth rate of output as well:

$$\frac{\dot{K}}{K}* = \frac{\dot{L}}{L}* = \frac{\dot{Y}}{Y}* = g^* = sk^{*(\alpha-1)} - \delta$$
$$= [\rho + \omega(1-\alpha)]\mathrm{k}^{*\alpha} + \lambda + n + \beta.$$

In the short run, the output growth rate is a weighted average of the warranted and the natural rates, $\frac{\dot{Y}}{Y} = \alpha\frac{\dot{K}}{K} + (1-\alpha)\frac{\dot{L}}{L}$, derived by time differentiating Equation (3.7). There is a divergence between the warranted and natural rates in the short-run transition to the next equilibrium. In the S-S model, the natural rate is equal to a constant term: $\frac{\dot{L}}{L}(s) = \lambda + n$; the short-run output growth adjustment falls only on the warranted rate as the capital/labor ratio adjusts to its next equilibrium value. In the modified model, the natural rate adjusts as well to a moving capital/labor ratio, i.e., $\frac{\dot{L}}{L}(m) = [\rho + \omega(1-\alpha)]k^{\alpha} + \lambda + n + \beta$.

3.3.1 *The Growth Effects of a Higher Saving Rate*

Figure 3.3 reproduces the lower part of Figure 3.2, showing the effects of an increased saving rate on equilibrium capital intensity and equilibrium output growth in the S-S and modified models. The starting equilibrium positions are points $B(k_s^*, g_s^*)$ for the S-S model and $A(k_m^*, g_m^*)$ for the modified model. A higher saving rate shifts the warranted rate line to the right in either model. The new equilibrium

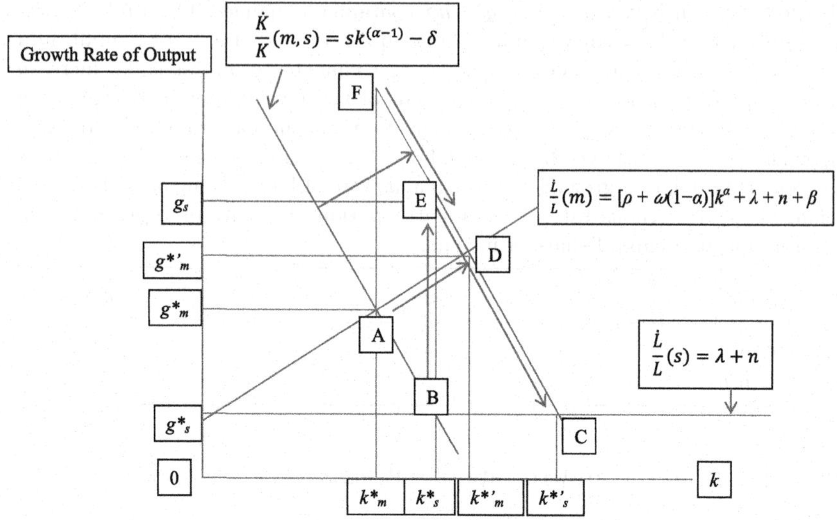

Figure 3.3. Short-run and long-run growth effects of a higher saving rate.

positions are indicated by point C in the S-S model and point D in the modified model. In both models, the capital/labor ratio goes up, albeit the new ratio remains lower in the modified model than in the S-S model, owing to positive labor participation in the modified model. The key difference is that the new equilibrium output growth increases in the modified model but remains unchanged in the S-S model.

The short-run dynamics of the S-S model is taken up first, followed by that of the modified model. During the steady-state transition between equilibrium points B and C, the S-S output growth rate is momentarily higher than the natural rate g_s^* at point E because of a higher warranted rate owing to a higher saving rate.[13] As noted, Figure 3.3 repeats the lower panel of Figure 3.2 [see Equations (3.15) and (3.16)]. The capital/labor ratio begins to rise from k_s^* to $k_s^{*\prime}$, which slows the warranted rate. Since the natural rate is independent of the capital/labor ratio, only the warranted rate

[13]The output growth rate at $E = \alpha g_s + (1-\alpha)g_s^*$.

adjusts downward along the segment EC.[14] Over time, labor becomes a bottleneck, and the output growth rate slows to the constant natural rate $g_s^* = \lambda + n$ at C. At this point, the capital/labor ratio stops rising and stabilizes at a new and higher level $k_s^{*\prime}$. Thus, the output growth rate effect of a higher saving rate vanishes in the long run, and a higher equilibrium capital/labor ratio is the only long-run effect.

In the modified model, following the increase in the saving rate, equilibrium shifts from A to $D(k_m^{*\prime}, g_m^{*\prime})$. At the starting position A, capital grows faster than labor (by the segment AF), and the capital/labor ratio rises from k_m^* to $k_m^{*\prime}$. The marginal and average products of capital fall, lowering the level of saving per unit of capital, thus slowing the warranted rate downward along the segment FD. On the other hand, the natural rate, instead of remaining constant as in the S-S model, accelerates from A to D along the $\frac{\dot{L}}{L}(m)$ line because of a higher labor participation rate associated with a rising capital/labor ratio.[15] This process continues until the warranted and natural rates are again equal via a continuous increase in the capital/labor ratio at the new long-run equilibrium, D, at which point the warranted rate would have fallen to the new and higher value of the natural rate, equal to the new and higher equilibrium output growth rate $g_m^{*\prime}$ ($> g_m^*$). Thus, unlike in the S-S model, the output growth effect of a higher saving rate does not peter out in the long run, because of the existence of endogenous labor participation, which makes the natural rate respond positively to an increase in the capital/labor ratio.[16]

[14]The output growth rate adjustment is traced by the segment BEC in terms of the weighted average of the warranted and natural rates.

[15]Through (a) higher Y/L and associated higher spending on secondary and tertiary education that increases the size of the educated labor force, and (b) increase in the real wage.

[16]The output growth rate adjustment is traced by the weighted average of segments $F - D$ and $A - D$ as the capital-labor ratio moves from k_m^* to $k_m^{*\prime}$ (weighted by α and $1 - \alpha$, respectively).

3.3.2 *The Growth Effects of an Increase in Technical Change*

Figure 3.4 shows the effects of a higher exogenous rate of technical change λ on equilibrium capital intensity and equilibrium output growth in the S-S and modified models. The starting equilibrium positions are points $D(k_s^*, g_s^*)$ for the S-S model and $A\ (k_m^*, g_m^*)$ for the modified model. A higher λ shifts the natural rate of the S-S model upward to the $\frac{\dot{L}}{L}(s) = \lambda_1 + n$ line, a parallel shift from the previous line. The modified model's natural rate shifts upward to the left. The new equilibrium positions are indicated by points F in the S-S model and C in the modified model. In either model, the capital/labor ratio goes down, albeit the new ratio remains lower in the modified model than in the S-S model, owing to positive labor participation in the former. The key difference is that, while the new equilibrium output growth increases to the higher rate of $g_s^{*\prime} = \lambda_1 + n$ in the S-S model, in the modified model the new equilibrium output growth increases to an even higher rate equal to $g_m^{*\prime} = g_s^{*\prime} + [\rho + \omega(1 - \alpha)]k_{m}^{*\prime}{}^{\alpha} + \beta$.

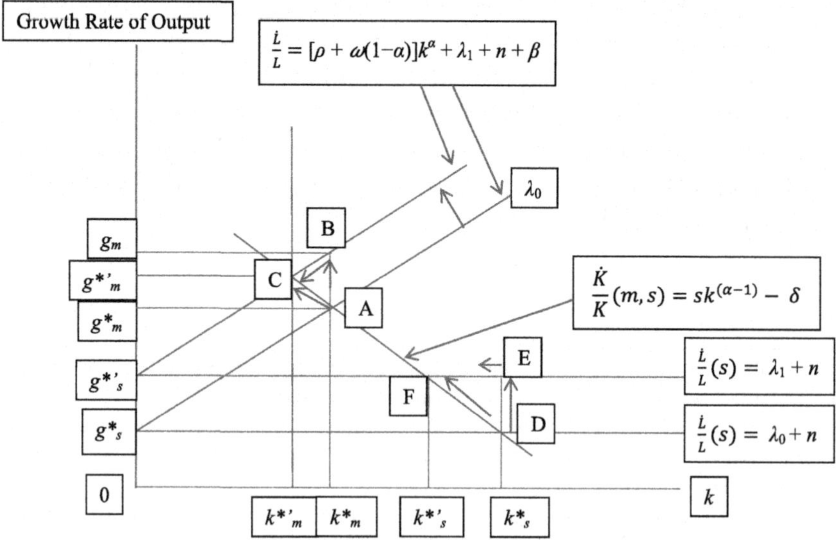

Figure 3.4. Short-run and long-run growth effects of an increase in technical change.

The short-run dynamics of the S-S model is taken up first, followed by that of the modified model. Before the steady-state transition between equilibrium points D and F begins, the natural rate jumps to $\lambda_1 + n = g_s^{*\prime}$ (higher than the warranted rate by the segment DE), after which the capital/labor ratio begins to fall, raising the warranted rate. Since the natural rate is independent of the capital/labor ratio, the natural rate slides horizontally along the segment EF, and only the warranted rate adjusts upward along the segment DF as capital intensity contracts from k_s^* to $k_s^{*\prime}$. Over time, as before, labor becomes a bottleneck, and the output growth rate slows to the constant natural rate $g_s^{*\prime} = \lambda_1 + n$ at F. At this point, the capital/labor ratio stops falling and stabilizes at a new and lower level $k_s^{*\prime}$. Thus, the output growth rate effect of a higher technical change λ_1 vanishes in the long run, and a lower equilibrium capital/labor ratio is the only long-run effect.

In the modified model, following the increase in technical change, equilibrium shifts from A to C $(k_m^{*\prime}, g_m^{*\prime})$. At the starting position, A, labor grows faster than capital (by the segment $A - B$), and the capital/labor ratio declines from k_m^* toward $k_m^{*\prime}$.[17] The marginal and average products of capital rise, raising the level of saving per unit of capital, accelerating the warranted rate upward along the segment $A - C$. On the other hand, the natural rate, instead of remaining constant at $\lambda_1 + n$ as in the S-S model, slows from B to C along the $\frac{\dot{L}}{L}(m)$ line because of a lower labor participation rate associated with a declining capital/labor ratio.[18] This process continues until the warranted and natural rates are again equal via a continuous fall in the capital/labor ratio at the new long-run equilibrium, C, at which point the warranted rate would have risen to the new value of the natural rate, equal to the new and *higher* equilibrium output growth rate $g_m^{*\prime}$ $(> g_m^*)$ owing to a *higher* rate of technical change. Thus, unlike in the S-S model, the output growth effect of a higher

[17] The modified model's output growth rate adjustment is traced by the weighted average of segments BC and AC, as capital intensity falls from k_m^* to $k_m^{*\prime}$.

[18] Through the two channels noted in footnote 16, but in opposite directions.

rate of technical change does not peter out in the long run, because of the existence of endogenous labor participation.[19]

3.3.3 *The Growth Effects of a Decline in Labor Participation*

Figure 3.5 illustrates the effects of a decline in labor participation as predicted by the CBO (2018) — a lower ρ, ω, or β. The initial equilibrium is at point A, with capital/labor ratio k_m^* and output growth g_m^*. Following the fall in labor participation, the natural rate line shifts downward to the right. Equilibrium shifts from A

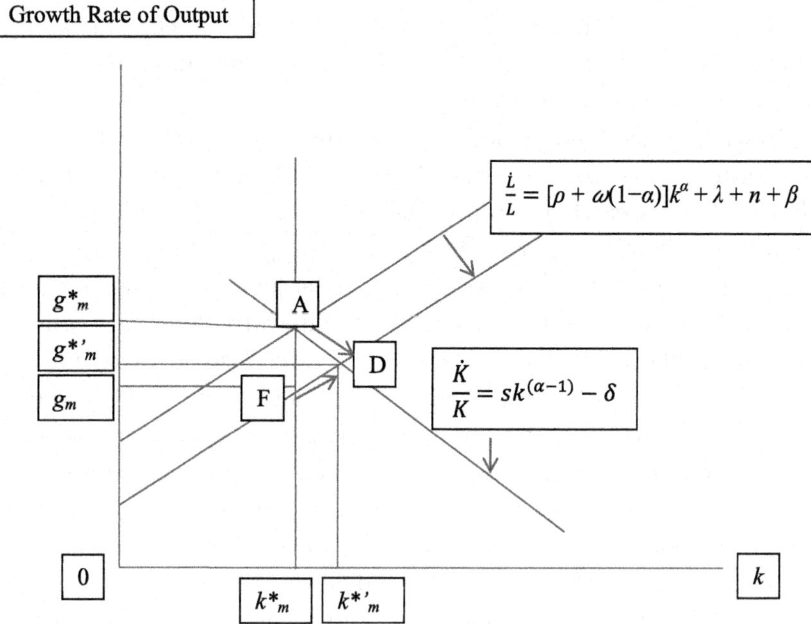

Figure 3.5. Short-run and long-run growth effects of a decline in labor participation (lower ρ, ω, or β).

[19]In Figure 3.4, before k has time to adjust, the output growth rate jumps to $g_m = \alpha[sk_m^{*(\alpha-1)} - \delta] + (1-\alpha)\{[\rho + (1-\alpha)]k_m^{*\alpha} + \lambda_1 + n + \beta\}$. Thus, an exogenous increase in technical change results in a short-term *expansionary* overshooting (a burst of short-run output growth, temporarily higher than the next steady state output growth at $g_m^{*\prime}$).

to D. The capital/labor ratio goes up from k_m^* to $k_m^{*\prime}$, and the equilibrium output growth goes down from g_m^* to $g_{\prime m}^*$. The increase in the equilibrium capital/labor ratio owes to lower effective labor induced by a lower rate of labor participation. The fall in equilibrium output growth is the result of a lower natural rate line in the face of an unchanged warranted rate line.

Notice that there is an overshooting of the lower output growth rate at F in the short run (in relation to the new long-run growth rate at D). At the starting capital intensity k_m^* the natural rate has a precipitous drop to $g_m\,(< g_{\prime m}^*)$ at F, following the decline in labor participation.[20] As the capital-labor ratio begins to rise from k_m^* to $k_m^{*\prime}$, the natural rate recovers along the segment $F - D$, while the warranted rate falls along the segment $A - D$ because of diminishing marginal and average products of capital. This process continues until the warranted and natural rates are again equal via a continuous increase in the capital/labor ratio at the new long-run equilibrium D, where the equilibrium output growth $g_m^{*\prime}$ is lower than the initial equilibrium rate g_m^*. One way to restore or even to improve macroeconomic performance is to prevent the decline in, and to encourage higher, labor participation through vigorous implementation of public policies on education, on-the-job training, upgrading skills for a digital economy, real wage increases in line with labor productivity, and other labor market participation initiatives identified by Grigoli *et al.* (2018) and CBO (2018).[21]

3.4 Related Issues

Econometric evidence pointing to positive growth effects of the saving rate may be consistent with the transitional dynamics of the Solow-Swan model, in view of the absence of substantially long-run data on a large sample of countries. Thus, even on empirical grounds, the

---

[20]In Figure 3.5, before k has time to adjust, the output growth rate falls to $g_m = \alpha[sk_m^{*(\alpha-1)} - \delta] + (1-\alpha)\{[\rho + (1-\alpha)]k_m^{*\alpha} + \lambda + n + \beta\}$. Thus, a decline in labor participation results in a short-term contractionary overshooting (lower short-run output growth, temporarily less than the next steady state output growth at $g_m^{*\prime}$).

[21]Working through calibrated changes in the parameters ρ, ω, and β.

issue is far from settled. On the S-S transitional growth dynamics, Solow (1991, p. 4) remarks: "Imagine an economy that has a constant, unchanging level of productivity. Then something happens — the invention of a computer, for instance — and productivity begins to rise. We know it will reach a new plateau and level off there. Then it will become constant again, higher than it was before but no longer changing. Such a process might take thirty years or even longer for a major invention. If you look at the annual growth rate, it will start at zero, build up to a positive value, perhaps quite suddenly, then start to fall back and reach zero again after thirty years have passed. Should we classify it as an episode of temporary growth or as something else? It is not surely a steady state. Such one-time gains in productivity are very valuable achievements." Solow (1991), in describing the "new growth" theory (Romer, 1986, 1990; Lucas, 1988, among others) vs. the "older S-S growth" theory, observes, "The theory differentiated sharply between policies that could *lift* the potential trend curve from those that could *tilt* the curve, i.e., change the rate of growth." The modified S-S model of this chapter not only *lifts* the potential (natural rate) curve but also *tilts* the curve in Figure 3.3 because of endogenous labor participation.

Another issue relates to the empirical validation of the modified model. Table 3.1 and Figures 3.3 and 3.5 show the dynamics of the growth effects of the saving rate and labor participation rate. The signs and magnitudes of such predictions can be empirically tested. All explanatory variables are observables, except for the technical change parameter λ, which can be impounded in the constant term of the growth regressions. This is a subject for future research.[22]

3.5 Conclusion

This chapter's main conclusion is that endogenous labor participation ensures a fully adjusting natural rate together with a fully adjusting warranted rate of the S-S model. Thus, the steady-state

[22]Panel data regressions (temporal and cross-country) would be appropriate to use in order to draw out the short-run and long-run growth effects of the independent variables. See Knight *et al.* (1993, **Chapter 2**).

growth rate of output and the steady-state level of the capital-labor ratio are functions of all the structural parameters, including the saving rate. The growth effects of an increased saving rate do not disappear in the long run, even when technical change and population growth are fully exogenous. One by-product is a new result: The CBO (2018) projected decline in labor participation over the next decade will result in a lower *long-run* per capita output growth path, with *short-run* recessionary overshooting.

This chapter also derives the simple analytics of the short-run and long-run output growth effects of a decline in labor participation, as projected by the CBO (2018). In the short run, there is a *temporary overshooting* of *recessionary* growth. In the long run, there is an eventual return to a *permanently lower* growth path.[23] Policies to restore the previous growth path or to achieve a higher growth path involve avoiding the projected fall in labor participation by aggressive and calibrated spending on secondary and tertiary education, on-the-job training, and skills upgrade to a full-fledged digital economy (a higher ρ), steady increases in real wages in line with labor productivity (a higher β), vigorous labor market participation activities and more generous tax benefits (higher β), in order to offset the negative effects of aging and retirements (lower β).

References

Agenor, P. (1994). *The Economics of Adjustment and Growth.* Cambridge, MA: Harvard University Press.

Aghion, P. and P. Howitt (1998). *Endogenous Growth Theory.* Cambridge, MA: MIT Press.

Arrow, K. (1962). The economic implications of learning by doing. *Review of Economic Studies*, 29, 155–173.

Congressional Budget Office (2018). CBO's projection of labor force participation rates. *Working Paper No. 2018–04.*

[23]Section 3.3.2 discusses the opposite scenario showing the growth effects of an increase in exogenous technical change. In the short run, there is a *temporary overshooting of expansionary* growth, followed by a *permanently higher* growth path in the long run (in relation to the initial growth equilibrium).

Conlisk, J. (1967). A modified neoclassical growth model with endogenous technical change. *Southern Economic Journal*, 34, 199–208.

Domar, E. (1946). Capital expansion, rate of growth, and employment. *Econometrica*, 14, 137–147.

Grigoli, F., Z. Koczan, and P. Tapalova (2018). Drivers of labor participation: macro and micro evidence. *International Monetary Fund Working Paper 18/150.*

Grossman, G. and E. Helpman (1991). *Innovation and Growth in the Global Economy.* Cambridge, MA: MIT Press.

Harrod, R. (1939). An essay in dynamic theory. *The Economic Journal*, 49, 14–33.

Inada, K.-I. (1963). On a two-sector model of economic growth: comments and generalization. *Review of Economic Studies*, 30, 119–127.

Lucas, R. (1988). On the mechanics of economic development. *Journal of Monetary Economics*, 22, 3–42.

Nelson, R. and E. Phelps (1966). Investment in humans, technological diffusion, and economic growth. *American Economic Review*, 56, 69–75.

North, D. (1990). *Institutions, Institutional Change, and Economic Performance.* Cambridge: Cambridge University Press.

Rebelo, S. (1991). Long-run policy analysis and long-run growth. *Journal of Political Economy*, 99, 500–521.

Romer, P. (1986). Increasing returns and long-run growth. *Journal of Political Economy*, 94, 1002–1037.

Romer, P. (1990). Endogenous technical change. *Journal of Political Economy*, 98, s71–s102.

Solow, R. (1956). A contribution to the theory of economic growth. *Quarterly Journal of Economics*, 70, 65–94.

Solow, R. (1987). Growth theory and after. *Nobel Prize Lecture*, December 8.

Solow, R. (1991). Policies for economic growth. *Ernest Sturc Memorial Lecture.* SAIS, Johns Hopkins University. November 12.

Swan, T. (1956). Economic growth and capital accumulation. *Economic Record*, 32, 334–362.

Villanueva, D. (1994, **Chapter 6**). Openness, human development and fiscal policies. *IMF Staff Papers*, 41, 1–29.

Warsh, D. (2007). *Knowledge and the Wealth of Nations: A Story of Economic Discovery.* NY: W.W. Norton and Company.

Chapter 4

Capital and Growth*

4.1 Introduction

A key proposition of the basic neoclassical growth S-S model Solow (1956)–Swan (1956) (**Chapter 1**) is that the saving rate drives economic growth during the transition to the steady state, but owing to diminishing returns to capital, does not affect the steady state growth rate of per capita output, which is fixed by the rate of exogenous Harrod-neutral technical change.[1] On the latter, Solow (1991, p. 4) says: "Imagine an economy that has a constant, unchanging level of productivity. Then something happens — the invention of a computer, for instance — and productivity begins to rise. We know it will reach a new plateau and level off there. Then it will become constant again, higher than it was before but no longer changing. Such a process might take thirty years or even longer for a major invention. If you look at the annual growth rate, it will start at zero, build up to a positive value, perhaps quite suddenly, then start to fall back and reach zero again after thirty years have passed. I do

---

*Written by Delano S. Villanueva and adapted from the *Bulletin of Monetary Economics and Banking*, 24, 285–312, by the permission of the Bulletin of Monetary Economics and Banking. Copyright 2021 by the Bulletin of Monetary Economics and Banking.

[1]Generally, output growth comes from two sources: capital growth and labor growth. Owing to diminishing returns to capital, ultimately the only other source of output growth is labor growth. In the S-S model, labor growth is equal to the sum of exogenous population growth and exogenous labor-augmenting technical change. Since the latter is exogenously fixed, no amount of saving can affect output growth in the steady state.

not object to classifying this story as an interval of temporary growth. Such one-time gains in productivity are very valuable achievements."

The S-S growth model motivates, and is nested in, this chapter's (henceforth, DV) model, summarized as follows.

The sources of economic growth in the S-S model (**Chapter 1**) are endogenous investments in physical capital during the transition to the steady state, and exogenous labor-augmenting technical change (exogenous investments in human and intellectual capital in the model of Section 4.2) in the steady state.[2] The broader sources of growth in the DV model are endogenous and exogenous investments in all types of capital — physical, human, and intellectual — during the transition and in the steady state. In Section 4.2, the DV model shows that large exogenous investments in human and intellectual capital — as in the S-S model — and high saving rates raise the steady-state per capita output growth rate.[3]

The DV growth model captures the S-S model's rich transitional dynamics — absent in new endogenous growth theories and models (see additional comments below). Increases in physical, human, and intellectual investments result in a burst of transitional output growth, overshooting the new and higher steady state per capita output growth rate.[4] Another contribution of the model concerns the optimal choice of the saving rate, so that a unique value of the saving rate is obtained. The model employs the Golden Rule

[2]For proof, see **Chapter 1**, Equation (1.12) for the transitional, and Equation (1.14) for the steady-state, growth rate of per capita output. Although in the S-S model the saving rate does not affect the steady state "growth" of per capita output, a high saving rate nevertheless raises the steady state "level" of per capita output — see Equation (1.17). In the absence of panel data with sufficiently long time series, econometric evidence pointing to positive growth effects of the saving rate is consistent with the transitional dynamics of the S-S model. See Knight *et al.* (1993, **Chapter 2**).

[3]Moreover, the DV model predicts that high rates of population growth and depreciation of physical capital lower the steady state per capita output growth rate — unlike in the S-S model where the steady state per capita output growth rate is determined exclusively by exogenous labor-augmenting technical change.

[4]The latter steady state result is a major extension of the S-S model, owing to the DV model's endogenous human and intellectual investments that are positive functions of the ratio of physical to human and intellectual capital (Section 4.2).

criterion suggested by Phelps (1966), based on maximization of real consumption per unit of human capital.

The model's predictions are similar to those of endogenous growth models emphasizing R&D investments. What is different is that endogenous growth models assume increasing returns to capital — incompatible with balanced growth — and imperfect markets, while the DV model assumes diminishing returns to capital and perfect markets (standard neoclassical assumptions).[5] The model's transitional dynamics is consistent with the empirical findings reported by Knight *et al.* (1993, **Chapter 2**), using a novel panel data methodology. The empirical testing of the model's steady state predictions would have to await availability of very long-run data on a very large sample of countries.

The new endogenous growth theory [Romer (1986); Rebelo (1991), among others] questions the neoclassical S-S proposition that the saving rate does not affect the steady state output growth rate. By assuming constant or increasing returns to capital (broadly defined to include human capital), the new endogenous growth theory concludes that the economy's steady state output can grow as fast (or as slow) as the capital stock, and public policies with regard to saving affect steady state economic growth. In the AK model of Rebelo (1991), output Y is constant returns to capital K, implying that Y grows at the same rate as K, equal to sA (s multiplied by A), where s (larger than the saving rate in the S-S model by the amount of investment in human capital) is the fraction of income saved and invested, and A is a technological constant. In contrast to the S-S model, the AK model shows that both saving rate and technology determine the steady-state rate of output growth.[6] Aghion and Howitt (1998) analyze a growth model with imperfect markets in the R&D sector characterized by Schumpeterian creative destruction. Along with Romer (1986), the knowledge-innovation-R&D production sector is

[5]Among endogenous growth models, the AK model of Rebelo (1991) assumes constant returns to capital (see next paragraph).

[6]The AK model has no transitional growth dynamics. Output growth always equals the steady state level, sA.

subject to increasing returns to capital, so that economic growth does not fade away in the steady state.[7]

This chapter presents and discusses the DV model, addressing the following research questions. Retaining the neoclassical assumption of diminishing returns to capital, does the rate of saving, among other parameters, affect the steady state output growth rate? If the answer is yes, how does the former influence the latter? Using the Golden Rule criterion suggested by Phelps (1966), what is the optimal rule for choosing the saving rate that maximizes consumer welfare? Below is a summary of brief answers, explained and elaborated in the remainder of this chapter.

First, the model finds that a high saving rate raises both the steady state and transitional per capita output growth rates through increases in physical, human, and intellectual investments that raise labor productivity (Section 4.2). An optimal choice of the saving rate can be made using the Golden Rule criterion (Phelps, 1966) or the Golden Utility criterion (Ramsey, 1928). The Phelps criterion is used in this chapter (Section 4.3).[8]

Second, the DV model is neoclassical, in the tradition of old S-S growth theory. Thus, it captures the S-S model's rich transitional dynamics — absent in new growth models of the AK variety. The policy implications of the S-S model are made wide-ranging by the DV model. Not only are saving policies effective in influencing the growth rate of per capita output at any point in time, but they can be used in "tilting" — to borrow Solow's word[9] — the steady state per capita output growth to a higher path. Increases in physical, human, and intellectual investments result in a burst of transitional output growth, overshooting the new and higher steady state growth rate — a key extension of the S-S model.

[7]On increasing returns, Solow (1991, p. 12) comments: "As I have emphasized, the key assumptions all seem to require that some economic activity be exempt from diminishing returns. That is hard enough to test for a single industry or process, and even then might not settle the relevant question." Conlisk (1967) argues that increasing returns to capital yield explosive growth.

[8]The Ramsey criterion is used in Villanueva and Mariano (2021, **Chapter 10**).

[9]Solow (1991, p. 17).

Third, to maximize social welfare, the net rate of return on capital should be greater than the sum of exogenous Harrod-neutral technical change and population growth, in order to compensate capital for magnified output growth generated by physical, human, and intellectual investments.[10] Equivalently stated, capital's income share should exceed the saving rate to compensate capital for raising labor productivity and enhancing growth.[11]

The rest of the chapter is organized as follows. Section 4.2 introduces the model, solves for and analyzes the uniqueness and stability of the steady state, and discusses its steady state and transitional growth dynamics. Section 4.3 derives the saving rate that maximizes consumer welfare using Phelps' (1966) Golden Rule. Section 4.4 concludes with a summary and some implications for growth policy. Appendix 4.A provides the derivation and economic explanation of the DV growth model's key innovation regarding the dynamic equation for the stock of human and intellectual capital.

4.2 A Neoclassical Model of Capital and Growth

Output Y is produced using as inputs physical capital K_p, human capital, and intellectual capital. For tractability, human capital and intellectual capital are combined in one capital input K_h. The stock of physical capital is the result of accumulated physical investment I. The stock of human and intellectual capital consists of accumulated human and intellectual investments V.[12]

Output I includes advanced capital goods (e.g., high-speed computers and modern industrial equipment). Output V includes

[10]In the S-S model (**Chapter 1**), for maximum consumer welfare the net rate of return on capital should be equal to the sum of exogenous Harrod-neutral technical change and population growth. In Equation (4.21) of Section 4.3, set $gw(k^*) = 0$ and $gw'(k^*) = 0$.

[11]In the S-S model, capital's income share should equal the saving rate. In Equation (4.22) of Section 4.3, set $\frac{I}{G(I,V)} = 1, gw(k^*) = 0$ and $gw'(k^*) = 0$.

[12]Solow's physical investment (Solow, 1991, p. 15) is I as in the S-S model, and human-intellectual investments are captured by V (DV model's key innovation; for derivation, see Appendix 4.A). The accumulated stocks of I and V are, respectively, K_p and K_h.

education-training-experience of workers (gained at Harvard, MIT, Caltech, Silicon Valley and elsewhere), blueprints, methods, and processes to produce goods and services, including IT, R&D, applied software development, Internet, Internet of Things, 5G technology,[13] AI, Business Management Software and similar high-tech, intellectual activities.

The structural model of the paper is as follows, beginning with a unit-homogeneous neoclassical production function satisfying the Inada (1963) conditions (Cobb-Douglas).[14] Aggregate output Y is produced using two inputs K_p and K_h:

$$Y = K_p^{\alpha} K_h^{(1-\alpha)}. \tag{4.1}$$

K_h is defined as

$$K_h = AN. \tag{4.2}$$

A constant fraction $(1 - s)$ of Y is consumed

$$C = (1 - s)Y \quad 0 < s < 1, \tag{4.3}$$

Y = aggregate output or income, K_p = stock of physical capital, K_h = stock of human and intellectual capital, A = K_h-augmenting productivity multiplier, N = working population,[15] C = consumption, α = output elasticity with respect to K_p, $(1 - \alpha)$ =

[13]See IHS Markit (2019) report on the importance of 5G technology to the global economy through 2035.

[14]With reference to the production function, $F(K_p, K_h) = K_h f(k)$, where K_p = physical capital, K_h = combined human and intellectual capital, and $k = \frac{K_p}{K_h}$, these conditions can be summarized as follows: $\lim \frac{\partial F}{\partial K_p} = \infty$ as $K_p \to 0$; $\lim \frac{\partial F}{\partial K_p} = 0$ as $K_p \to \infty$; $f(0) \geq 0$; $f'(k) > 0, f''(k) < 0$ for all $k > 0$. The Cobb-Douglas production function, Equation (4.1), satisfies these conditions.

[15]Equation (4.2) is analogous to the S-S definition $L = AN$, where $L = K_h$, except that A in the S-S model is entirely exogenous and excludes saving-dependent investment in human and intellectual capital; see Equation (1.5), **Chapter 1**. Generally, the definition of L should be $L = APN$, where P is the labor participation rate, $0 < P \leq 1$. The working population is PN. When $P = 1$, $L = AN$. Whatever P is, it is usually assumed as an exogenous constant, whose rate of change is zero. For an endogenous and variable P, see Villanueva (2020, **Chapter 3**).

output elasticity with respect to K_h, s = saving rate and t = time (suppressed). Saved resources are used in the production of outputs I = physical investment (goods) and V = combined human and intellectual investments (services).

Substituting Equation (4.1) for Y,

$$G(I, V) = sY = sK_p^{\alpha} K_h^{(1-\alpha)}. \tag{4.4}$$

$G(I, V)$ is assumed to be a unit-homogeneous joint index of I and V, with $\frac{\partial G}{\partial I} = G_1 > 0$ and $\frac{\partial G}{\partial V} = G_2 > 0$. Economic growth requires a high rate of saving s, so that more resources are made available to produce outputs I and V, in a proportion that depends on the ratio $\frac{K_p}{K_h}$.[16]

$$\frac{I}{V} = \emptyset\left(\frac{K_p}{K_h}\right) \quad \emptyset' < 0 \tag{4.5}$$

The assumption $\emptyset' < 0$ is reasonable. When the ratio of physical capital K_p to human and intellectual capital K_h rises (falls), the marginal product of K_p falls (rises) relative to the marginal product of K_h, and the economy produces less (more) I and more (less) V; thus $\frac{I}{V}$ falls (rises).

Finally, k is the ratio of K_p to K_h:

$$k = \frac{K_p}{K_h}. \tag{4.6}$$

The model consists of 6 equations in 6 variables (Y, K_p, K_h, I, V, and k). The variable C is determined by Equation (4.3) once the saving rate s is assigned an arbitrary value or an optimal value (Section 4.3), or through the accounting definition $C = Y - G(I, V)$.

[16]The saving parameter s needs a broader interpretation. It partly reflects the consumption-saving choice of society. It is also partly a production parameter since it determines factor intensity in the production of outputs I and V, relative to the production of C.

4.2.1 *Reduced Model*

The dynamic equations for the state variables K_p and K_h are given by:

$$\dot{K}_p = I - \delta K_p \tag{4.7}$$

$$\dot{K}_h = V + \lambda K_h + nK_h. \tag{4.8}$$

Equation (4.7) states that the increment in the physical capital stock $\dot{K}_p$ equals gross fixed investment I less depreciation δK_p. Owing to the assumed unit-homogeneity of the output index $G(I, V)$, and using Equations (4.4) and (4.6), Equation (4.5) can be rewritten to show that gross fixed investment is equal to a fraction, $\frac{s}{G[1, \frac{1}{\varnothing(k)}]} = \frac{sI}{G(I,V)}$ of income Y,

$$I = \frac{sY}{G\left[1, \frac{1}{\varnothing(k)}\right]}.^{17} \tag{4.9}$$

Substituting Equation (4.9) into Equation (4.7) and using $\frac{Y}{K_p} = k^{(\alpha-1)}$ [from Equations (4.1) and (4.6)],

$$\frac{\dot{K}_p}{K_p} = \frac{sk^{(\alpha-1)}}{\mathrm{G}\left[1, \frac{1}{\varnothing(k)}\right]} - \delta. \tag{4.10}$$

Equation (4.10) is the equation of motion for the physical capital stock.

Next is the derivation of the equation of motion for the combined stock of human and intellectual capital [Equation (4.12) below]. Equation (4.8) is the major innovation of the DV model and is the basis for Equation (4.12) using the relation $\frac{Y}{K_h} = k^{\alpha}$ [from Equations (4.1) and (4.6)]. Its derivation and economic explanation are detailed in Appendix 4.A. Owing to the assumed unit-homogeneity of the output index $G(I, V)$, and using Equations (4.4) and (4.6), Equation (4.5) can be rewritten to show that the sum of human and intellectual investments V is equal to a fraction $\frac{s}{G[\varnothing(k),1]} = \frac{sV}{G(I,V)}$ of

[17] $G[1, \frac{1}{\varnothing(k)}] = \frac{G(I,V)}{I}$. Thus, $\frac{sY}{G[1,\frac{1}{\varnothing(k)}]} = \frac{sI}{G(I,V)}Y, 0 < \frac{I}{G(I,V)} < 1$.

income Y,

$$V = \frac{sY}{G[\varnothing(k), 1]}.^{18} \tag{4.11}$$

Substituting Equation (4.11) into Equation (4.8) and using $\frac{Y}{K_h} = k^{\alpha}$ [from Equations (4.1) and (4.6)],

$$\frac{\dot{K}_h}{K_h} = \frac{sk^{\alpha}}{\mathrm{G}[\varnothing(k), 1]} + \lambda + n. \tag{4.12}$$

If $V = 0$ (all saving is invested in physical capital), the model collapses to the S-S model, and the steady-state per capita output growth rate equals λ.[19] Generally, however, saving is invested partly in physical capital I and partly in human and intellectual capital V, and both investments drive economic growth.[20]

Time differentiating Equation (4.6), and substituting Equations (4.10) and (4.12)

$$\frac{\dot{k}}{k} = \frac{\dot{K}_p}{K_p} - \frac{\dot{K}_h}{K_h} = \frac{sk^{(\alpha-1)}}{\mathrm{G}[1, \frac{1}{\varnothing(k)}]} - \frac{sk^{\alpha}}{\mathrm{G}[\varnothing(k), 1]} - (\lambda + n + \delta). \tag{4.13}$$

At any point in time, the growth rate of output is given by time differentiating $\frac{Y}{K_h} = k^{\alpha}$ [from Equations (4.1) and (4.6)],

$$\frac{\dot{Y}}{Y} = \frac{\dot{K}_h^*}{K_h} + \alpha\frac{\dot{k}}{k}. \tag{4.14}$$

---

[18] $G[\varnothing(k), 1] = \frac{G(I,V)}{V}$. Thus, $\frac{sY}{G[\varnothing(k),1]} = \frac{sV}{G(I,V)}Y, 0 < \frac{V}{G(I,V)} < 1$.

[19] Set Equation (4.11) to zero, $V = \frac{sY}{G[\varnothing(k),1]} = 0$, so that Equation (4.12) becomes $\frac{\dot{K}_h}{K_h}^* = \frac{\dot{Y}}{Y}^* - n = \lambda$ (asterisk denotes steady state value). In the steady state, $k = \frac{K_p}{K_h}$ is constant at $k^*(\frac{\dot{k}}{k} = 0)$, and $\frac{\dot{K}_p}{K_p}^* = \frac{\dot{K}_h}{K_h}^* = \frac{\dot{Y}}{Y}^*$. The latter equality to the steady state growth rate of output Y follows from the constant returns assumption on the production function, Equation (4.1).

[20] Solow (1991) affirms that all physical, human and intellectual investments matter for growth.

$\frac{\dot{K_h}}{K_h}^*$ is given by Equation (4.12) evaluated at the steady state value of k at k^*, and $\frac{\dot{k}}{k}$ is given by Equation (4.13). Thus,

$$\frac{\dot{Y}}{Y} - n = \frac{sk*^{\alpha}}{\mathrm{G}[\varnothing(k*), 1]|} + \lambda + \alpha\frac{\dot{k}}{k}. \tag{4.15}$$

Equation (4.15) states that the transitional growth rate of per capita output $\frac{\dot{Y}}{Y} - n$ will be above (below) the steady state level $\frac{sk*^{\alpha}}{\mathrm{G}[\varnothing(k*),1]} + \lambda$ for a rising (falling) k, or whenever k is smaller (larger) than k^*.[21] The phase diagram of the DV model is shown in Figure 4.1, containing plots of Equations (4.13) and (4.15). The vertical axis measures the growth rates of K_p, K_h, k and $\frac{Y}{N}$ (transitional and steady state), and the horizontal axis measures $k = \frac{K_p}{K_h}$. Note that the $\frac{\dot{k}}{k}$ line is steeper than the $\frac{\dot{Y}}{Y} - n$ line, because in the latter, the slope of the first term on the RHS is positive (at a single value of k at k^*) and subtracts from the negative slope of the third term on the RHS (at all values of k).[22]

The steady state value k^* of k is obtained at the intersection of the $\frac{\dot{k}}{k}$ line with the k-axis at point B. At this steady-state equilibrium, balanced growth in physical capital $\frac{sk*^{(\alpha-1)}}{\mathrm{G}\left[1, \frac{1}{\varnothing(k*)}\right]} - \delta$, and in human-intellectual capital $\frac{sk*^{\alpha}}{\mathrm{G}[\varnothing(k*0),1]} + \lambda + n$, prevails at point A, and by the constant-returns assumption on the production function, the steady state growth rate of per capita output is $\frac{\dot{Y}}{Y}^* - n = g^* - n = \frac{sk*^{\alpha}}{[G[\varnothing(k*).1]} + \lambda$. In Figure 4.1, it can be seen that at $k = k^*, \frac{\dot{k}}{k} = 0$ and the economy is on its balanced per capita output growth path at point $A(k^*, g^* - n)$. When k exceeds k^*, e.g., at k^2, $\frac{\dot{k}}{k} < 0$ (point D), the per capita output growth rate $\frac{\dot{Y}}{Y} - n = g^2 - n$ (point F) is temporarily less than its steady state rate $g^* - n$. On the other hand, when k falls short of k^*, e.g., at k^1, $\frac{\dot{k}}{k} > 0$ (point C), the per capita

[21]It can also be seen from Equation (4.15) that the steady state growth rate of per capita output, evaluated at $k = k^*$, is equal to $\frac{\dot{Y}}{Y} * -n = \frac{sk*^{\alpha}}{\mathrm{G}[\varnothing(k*),1]} + \lambda$, since the third term on the right-hand side (RHS) disappears when the economy reaches the steady state at $\frac{\dot{k}}{k} = 0$. See equilibrium points A and B in Figure 4.1.

[22]The third term on the RHS is $\alpha\frac{\dot{k}}{k}$ and α is a fraction.

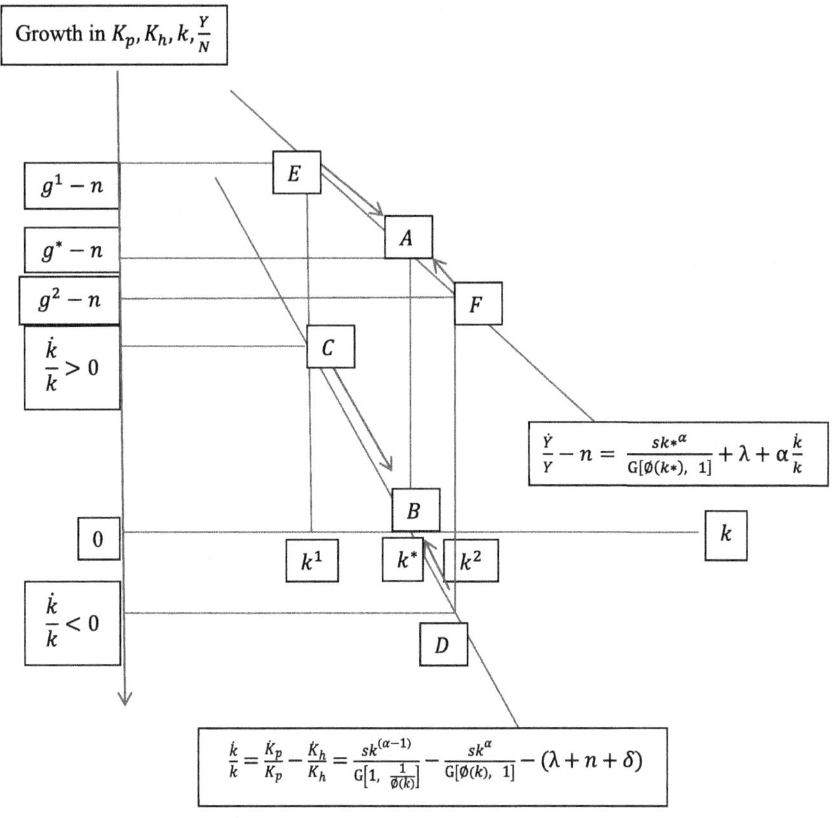

Figure 4.1. Equilibrium and growth dynamics.

output growth rate $\frac{\dot{Y}}{Y} - n = g^1 - n$ (point E) is temporarily higher than the steady state rate $g^* - n$. The next paragraphs elaborate on the economics of the DV model's equilibrium behavior and growth dynamics both in the transition to and in the steady state.

4.2.2 *Stability of Equilibrium and Growth Dynamics*

In Figure 4.1, the equilibrium points A and B, characterized by the steady state k^* and steady state per capita output growth rate $g^* - n$, are not only unique but they are also globally stable.[23] Consider any

[23]The Inada (1963) conditions — refer back to footnote 13 — and the slope conditions [Equations (4.A.10)–(4.A.11), Appendix 4.A] — ensure an intersection

level of k to the left of k^*, such as k^1, at which K_p grows faster than K_h ($\frac{\dot{k}}{k} > 0$ at point C) owing to a larger marginal product of K_p relative to that of K_h. As k rises from k^1 to k^*, the marginal returns on physical investment I fall and the marginal returns on human-intellectual investment V rise. Consequently, less I and more V are produced, and $\frac{I}{V}$ falls. Thus, $\dot{K}_p$ slows, while $\dot{K}_h$ accelerates, i.e., $\frac{\dot{k}}{k}$ becomes less and less positive until it falls to zero at the original equilibrium point B, or until k^1 has risen to k^*, traced by segment CB, to restore balanced growth. The opposite sequence of events unfolds for any initial value of k to the right of k^*, such as k^2. At k^2, K_h grows faster than K_p($\frac{\dot{k}}{k} < 0$ at point D) owing to a smaller marginal product of K_p relative to that of K_h. As k^2 falls, the marginal returns on physical investment I rise and the marginal returns on human-intellectual investment V decline; thus, $\frac{I}{V}$ goes up, and $\dot{K}_p$ accelerates while $\dot{K}_h$ decelerates, i.e., $\frac{\dot{k}}{k}$ becomes less and less negative until it is zero at the original equilibrium point B (until k^2 has fallen to k^*, traced by segment DB).

The dynamics of the transitional per capita output growth rate is the following. At k^1, output growth rate is $g^1 - n$ at point E, temporarily higher than the steady state growth rate $g^* - n$ because the third term $\alpha\frac{\dot{k}}{k}$ on the RHS of the per capita output growth equation $\frac{\dot{Y}}{Y} - n$ in Figure 4.1 is positive ($\frac{\dot{k}}{k} > 0$) at point C. As k^1 rises towards k^*, the marginal returns on physical investment I decline and the marginal returns on human-intellectual investment V rise; $\frac{\dot{k}}{k}$ while still positive, decelerates, so that $\frac{\dot{Y}}{Y}$ falls from $g^1 - n$ to $g^* - n$. The adjustment process continues until the original equilibrium at point A is restored when k^1 settles at k^*, and the per capita output growth rate has fallen to the original equilibrium level $g^* - n$, traced by segment EA. The opposite sequence of events occurs when k is temporarily higher than k^* at k^2. At k^2, per capita output growth is $g^2 - n$ at point F, temporarily lower than the steady-state growth

between the downward-sloping $\frac{\dot{k}}{k}$ line and the k-axis at some positive k, such as k^* at point $B(\frac{\dot{k}}{k} = 0)$ in Figure 4.1.

rate $g^* - n$, because the third term $\alpha\frac{\dot{k}}{k}$ on the RHS of the output growth equation $\frac{\dot{Y}}{Y} - n$ at point D is negative ($\frac{\dot{k}}{k} < 0$). As k^2 falls towards k^*, the marginal returns on physical investment I go up and the marginal returns on human-intellectual investment V go down; $\frac{\dot{k}}{k}$ while still negative accelerates, so that $\frac{\dot{Y}}{Y} - n$ rises from $g^2 - n$ to $g^* - n$, traced by segment FA. The adjustment process continues until point A is reached, where k^2 stops falling and settles at k^*, and the per capita output growth rate has risen to the original equilibrium level $g^* - n$.

4.2.3 *Comparative Dynamics*

Recall that in the S-S model (**Chapter 1**), with identical assumption on the production function (diminishing returns to inputs separately and constant returns jointly), the steady state growth rate of per capita output is invariant to changes in the saving rate (and in the other structural parameters except λ). For comparison, Table 4.1 and Figures 4.2–4.4. show the equilibrium growth effects of the saving rate and the other structural parameters of the DV model.

Table 4.1 shows the sensitivity of k^* and $g^* - n$ to parameter changes. The signs can be determined either algebraically or with reference to Figures 4.2–4.4. The solution to k^* is derived when Equation (4.11) is equated to zero, solving for k^* as an implicit function of s, λ, n and δ: $k^* = \vartheta(s, \lambda, n, \delta)$, with signs of the partial derivatives shown on the second row of Table 4.1. A higher k^* is associated with a higher saving rate, lower productivity of human-intellectual capital, lower population growth, and lower depreciation of physical capital. Evaluated at k^*, $g^* - n$ is given by either Equation (4.10) or (4.12), either one as a function of k^*, s, λ, n and δ, or $g^* - n = \varphi(k^*; s, \lambda, n, \delta)$. The signs of $g^* - n$ with respect to s, λ, n and δ can be derived by differentiation of $g^* - n = \varphi[\vartheta(s, \lambda, n, \delta); s, \lambda, n, \delta]$ with respect to each parameter. The signs are given by the third row of Table 4.1.

A higher $g^* - n$ is associated with a higher saving rate, higher productivity of human-intellectual capital, lower population growth, and lower depreciation of physical capital.

Table 4.1. Sensitivity of k^* and $g^* - n$ to parameter changes. This table reports the sensitivity of $\boldsymbol{k^*}$ = equilibrium ratio of K_p to K_h, $\boldsymbol{g^* - n}$ = equilibrium growth rate of per capita *GDP* to all-else-equal increase in s = saving rate, λ = exogenous rate of human-intellectual investment, n = exogenous working population growth, δ = rate of depreciation of the capital stock K_p, K_p = physical capital, and K_h = combined human and intellectual capital.

Description	s	λ	n	δ
Change in $\boldsymbol{k^*}$	+	−	−	−
Change in $\boldsymbol{g^* - n}$	+	+	−	−

The signs and magnitudes of growth predictions in Table 4.1 can be empirically tested and estimated. All independent variables are observables, except for the exogenous K_h-augmenting productivity parameter λ, which can be impounded in the constant term of the growth regressions.[24] Panel data regressions would be appropriate to use in order to draw out the transitional growth effects of the independent variables. Knight *et al.* (1993, **Chapter 2**) pioneered a panel data methodology that has been successfully used in estimating the transitional dynamics of growth models. As noted earlier, the DV — as well as the S-S — model's transitional growth dynamics is consistent with the findings of Knight *et al.* However, averages of very long time series on a fairly large sample of countries are needed to test the DV model's steady-state predictions shown in Table 4.1.

The signs in the second and third rows of Table 4.1 can also be determined through inspection of Figures 4.2–4.4. Figure 4.2 illustrates the transitional and steady-state growth effects of a higher saving rate s. The original equilibrium occurs at points $A(k^*, 0)$ and $B(k^*, g^* - n)$ Appendix Equations (4.A.17)–(4.A.19), Table 4.A.1, and related discussion demonstrate that the $\frac{\dot{k}}{k}$ equation shifts upward under the impact of a higher saving rate. The new $\frac{\dot{k}}{k}$ line intersects the k-axis at $k^{*\prime}$ (point C), higher than k^*. Meanwhile, the $\frac{\dot{Y}}{Y} - n$ line shifts upward because the RHS is larger (involving a higher s),

[24]As noted earlier, K_h is analogous to effective labor L in the S-S model–see **Chapter 1**, Equation (1.2).

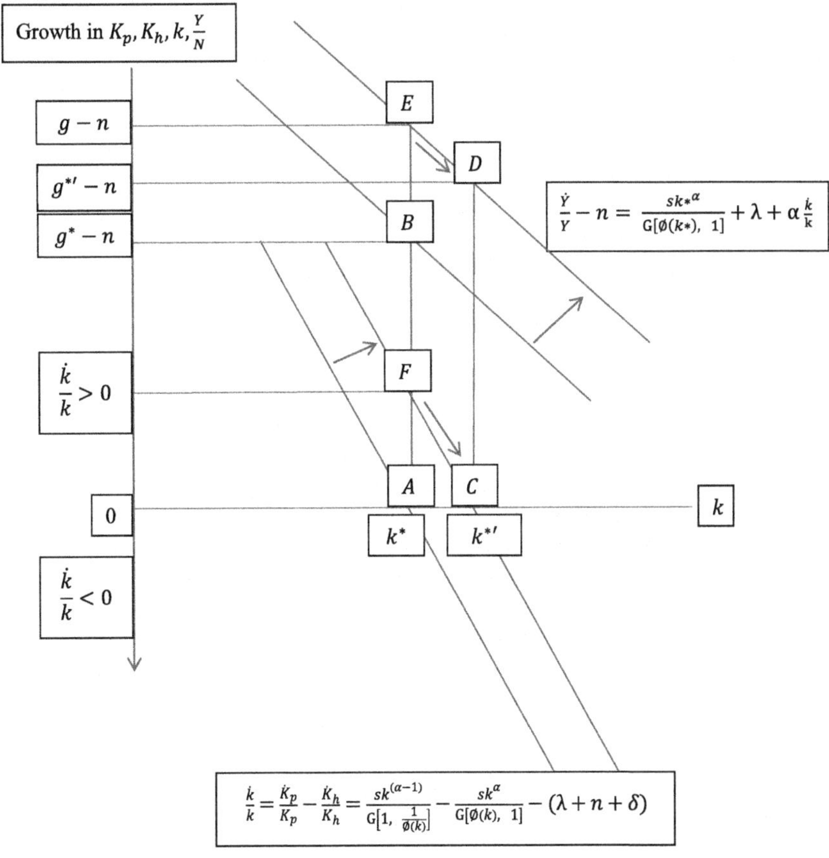

Figure 4.2. Equilibrium and growth dynamics: Effects of an increase in s.

resulting in a higher steady state per capita output growth rate $g^{*\prime} - n$ at point D.

The economics of the transitional effects of a higher saving rate is the following. Immediately after the saving rate is raised through, for instance a higher fiscal surplus, at the initial k^* per capita output growth rate jumps to $g - n$ (segment k^*E), reflecting positive growth in k ($\frac{\dot{k}}{k} > 0$) at point F, feeding into a positive value for $\alpha\frac{\dot{k}}{k}$ in the $\frac{\dot{Y}}{Y} - n$ line. This outcome is a short-run expansionary overshooting of the next and higher steady state output growth $g^{*\prime} - n$ at point D. As k rises from k^* to $k^{*\prime}$, the marginal returns on physical investment

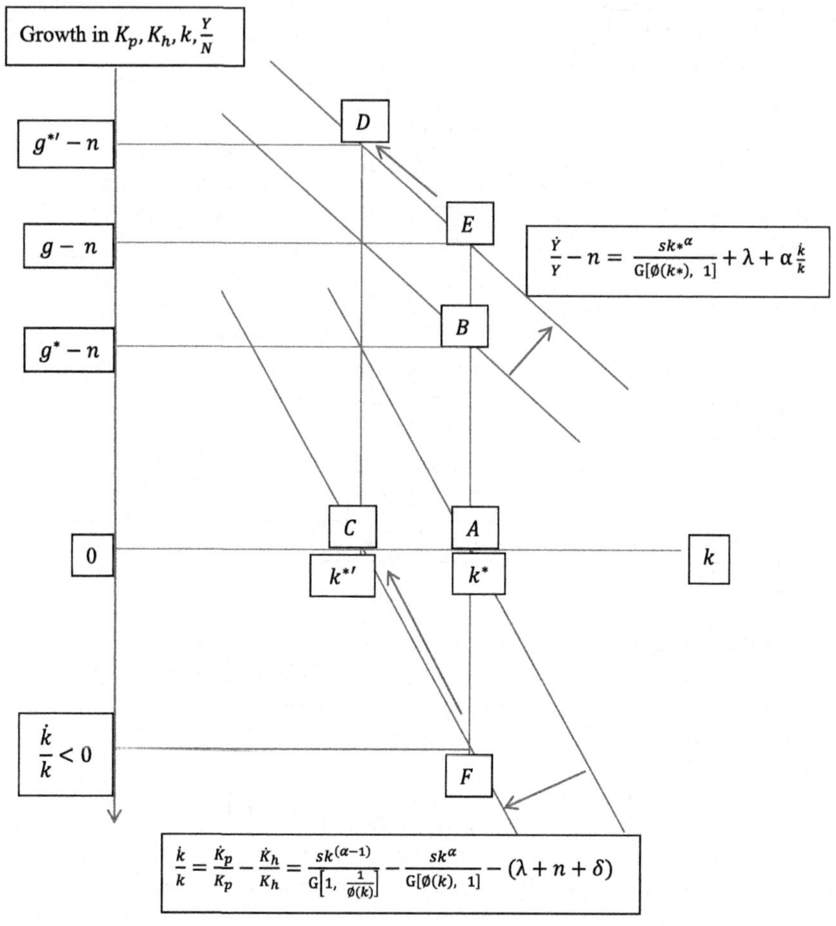

Figure 4.3. Equilibrium and growth dynamics: effects of an increase in λ.

fall, and the marginal returns on human-intellectual investment rise. The third term on the RHS of the $\frac{\dot{Y}}{Y} - n$ line, $\alpha\frac{\dot{k}}{k}$ becomes less and less positive, leading to a deceleration of per capita output growth (adjustment from $g - n$ to $g^{*\prime} - n$ is traced by segment ED). This process continues until the next steady state at $D(k^{*\prime}, g^{*\prime} - n)$, when $\alpha\frac{\dot{k}}{k} = 0$, $\left(\frac{\dot{Y}}{Y}\right)^* - n = g^{*\prime} - n > g^* - n$, and $k^{*\prime} > k^*$.

The new result is a higher steady state growth rate of per capita output, compared with no change in the S-S model [see Equation (1.14) and Figure 1.1 in **Chapter 1**]. The reason can be

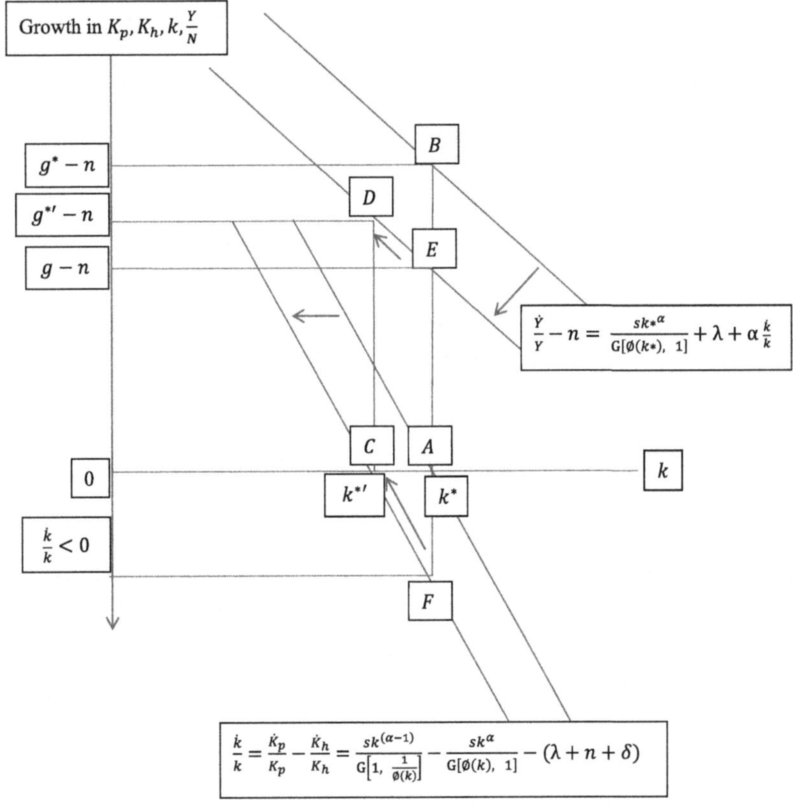

Figure 4.4. Equilibrium and growth dynamics: Effects of an increase in n, δ.

seen by comparing Figure 4.2 with Figure 1.1 of the S-S model. The $\frac{\dot{Y}}{Y} - n$ line of the S-S model is $\frac{\dot{Y}}{Y} - n = \lambda + \alpha\frac{\dot{k}}{k}$, while the $\frac{\dot{Y}}{Y} - n$ line of the DV model is $\frac{\dot{Y}}{Y} - n = \frac{sk*\prime^{\alpha}}{G[\emptyset(k*\prime), 1]} + \alpha\frac{\dot{k}}{k}$. When the saving rate goes up, the S-S steady state per capita output growth rate is unchanged at λ, whereas the DV model's steady state per capita output growth rate goes up because of a higher growth rate of K_h productivity $\frac{sk*\prime^{\alpha}}{G[\emptyset(k*\prime), 1]}$ where $k^{*\prime} > k^*$, resulting from higher saving-induced human and intellectual investments.[25]

[25]Set $\alpha\frac{\dot{k}}{k} = 0$ in the expression for $\frac{\dot{Y}}{Y} - n$ in either S-S [Equation (1.12), **Chapter 1**] or DV Equation (4.15) model to obtain the steady-state per capita output growth rate.

Next, consider the growth effects of changes in the other structural parameters λ, δ, and n. Figure 4.3 shows the growth dynamics following an increase in the exogenous K_h productivity rate λ. The starting equilibrium occurs at $A(k^*, 0)$ and $B(k^*, g^* - n)$. The higher K_h productivity λ shifts the $\frac{\dot{k}}{k}$ line downward, and the $\frac{\dot{Y}}{Y} - n$ line upward,[26] leading to a new steady state equilibrium at points $C(k^{*\prime}, 0)D(k^{*\prime}, g^{*\prime} - n)$, characterized by a higher steady state per capita output growth rate and a higher steady state ratio of human-intellectual capital to physical capital, reflecting higher endogenous human and intellectual investments. What happens to k and $g - n$ during the transition from initial steady state points A and B to new steady state points C and D?

At the starting level k^* and relative to its new steady state lower level $k^{*\prime}$, physical capital's marginal product is less than that of human-intellectual capital following the rise in K_h productivity. Physical investment goes down, and human and intellectual investments go up. The proportionate rate of change in k turns negative at point $F(\frac{\dot{k}}{k} < 0)$. As k^* contracts to its new steady state level $k^{*\prime}$, the marginal returns on physical investment rise and the marginal returns on human and intellectual investments fall. The proportionate rate of change in k turns less and less negative until it becomes zero at point C (adjustment is traced by segment FC in Figure 4.3). The growth effects of a higher exogenous productivity rate λ take place in two stages. At the initial k^*, the per capita output growth rate increases from $g^* - n$ at B to $g - n$ at E. As k^* shrinks to $k^{*\prime}$, higher returns on physical investment translate into higher income per unit of physical capital and higher saving-investment, i.e., higher warranted rate. When k^* has fallen to $k^{*\prime}$, per capita output growth settles at the new steady state rate $g^{*\prime} - n$ at D, still higher than the previous rate $g - n$.[27] Owing to endogenous human and intellectual investments, the higher productivity parameter λ

[26] $\frac{\partial(\frac{\dot{Y}}{Y} - n)}{\partial\lambda} = (1 - \alpha) > 0$.

[27] The two-stage upward growth adjustment is traced by the path $B - E - D$.

leads to higher transitional growth, and eventually to higher steady state per capita output growth.[28]

Finally, Figure 4.4 illustrates the steady state and transitional growth effects of higher population growth and larger depreciation rate. The initial equilibrium occurs at points $A(k^*, 0)$ and $B(k^*, g^* - n)$. A higher rate of population growth lowers both $\frac{\dot{k}}{k}$ and $\frac{\dot{Y}}{Y} - n$ lines.[29] The new equilibrium occurs at points $C(k^{*\prime})$, and $D(k^{*\prime}, g^{*\prime} - n)$, characterized by lower steady state per capita output growth rate and lower steady state ratio of physical to human-intellectual capital.

The transitional growth dynamics is as follows. In Figure 4.4, a higher population growth rate n lowers both $\frac{\dot{k}}{k}$ and $\frac{\dot{Y}}{Y} - n$ lines (the latter through a drop in $\alpha\frac{\dot{k}}{k}$). Reading off the new and lower $\frac{\dot{k}}{k}$ line, at the starting k^* physical capital's marginal product is less than that of human-intellectual capital. Physical investment goes down, and human and intellectual investments go up. The proportionate rate of change in k turns negative at point F. As k^* contracts to its new steady state value $k^{*\prime}$, the marginal returns on physical investment rise and those on human and intellectual investments fall, and the proportionate rate of change in k turns less and less negative until it is zero at point C (adjustment is traced by segment FC). Meanwhile, at the starting k^*, the per capita output growth rate, which starts at $g^* - n$ at B, and drops sharply to $g - n$ at E. As k^* contracts to $k^{*\prime}$, higher returns on physical investment translate into higher income per unit of physical capital and thus, higher saving-investment, i.e., higher warranted rate. Growth recovers from $g - n$ to $g^{*\prime} - n$. Note that this new steady state output growth is lower than the starting steady state growth rate $g^* - n$, a plausible prediction of the DV

[28]Recall the Solow quote on the temporary growth effect of the invention of a computer in the first paragraph of Section 4.1. Instead of the λ-effect dissipating in the steady state as in the S-S model, the DV model yields a permanently higher steady-state warranted rate $g^{*\prime} - n$, reflecting larger investments in physical capital because of higher returns on a smaller $k^{*\prime}$.

[29]$\frac{\dot{Y}}{Y} - n$ line shifts downward because the third term on the RHS ($\alpha\frac{\dot{k}}{k}$) goes down as n increases.

model.[30] The economics of the steady state and transitional growth dynamics of a higher rate of depreciation δ (Figure 4.4) follows similar arguments.

4.3 Optimal Saving Rate

In intensive form (as ratio to K_h) total output in the steady state is $y^* = k^{*\alpha}$ [from Equations (4.1) and (4.6)]. If the level of y^* is considered a measure of the standard of living, and since $\frac{dy^*}{dk^*} = \alpha k^{*(\alpha-1)} > 0$, it is possible to raise living standards by increasing k^*. This can be done by adjusting the saving rate s. If consumption $c^* = \frac{C}{K_h}^*$ (or any monotonically increasing function of it) is taken as a measure of the social welfare of society, the saving rate that will maximize social welfare by maximizing steady state c^* can be determined. Phelps (1966) refers to this criterion as the Golden Rule of Accumulation.

Consumption is $c^* = \frac{C^*}{K_h} = \frac{Y^*}{K_h} - \frac{S^*}{K_h}$, where $S = I + V =$ saved output. $\frac{Y}{K_h} = y^* = k^{*\alpha}$ and $S = I + V = \dot{K}_p + \delta K_p + \dot{K}_h - (\lambda + n)K_h$ [from Equations (4.7)–(4.8)]. Thus,

$$c^* = k^{*\alpha} - \left(\left(\frac{\dot{K}_p}{K_p}\right)^* + \delta\right) k^* - \left(\frac{\dot{K}_h}{K_h}\right)^* - (\lambda + n). \tag{4.16}$$

[30] The adjustment of per capita income growth is traced by a sharp fall from B to E, followed by a recovery from E to D. However, the new steady state per capita growth at point D remains lower than the initial one at point B — there is a permanent reduction in steady state per capita output growth resulting from higher population growth. Arrow (1962) discusses a learning-by-doing growth model with a prediction that higher population growth increases the per capita output growth rate. Available empirical evidence does not support such a hypothesis. Among other empirical studies, Conlisk (1967), Knight *et al.* (1993, **Chapter 2**), and Villanueva (1994, **Chapter 6**) find the opposite result, i.e., that higher population growth decreases the per capita output growth rate. However, if Arrow's learning by doing is interpreted as being positively influenced by the stock of capital per worker and not by the growth rate of the capital stock, Arrow (1962) predicts that a higher population growth rate depresses per capita output growth, consistent with empirical evidence. For further discussion, see Villanueva (2022, **Chapter 5**, Section 5.2, Equation 5.11).

On the balanced growth path $(\frac{\dot{K}_p}{K_p})^* = (\frac{\dot{K}_h}{K_h})^*$, so that

$$c^* = k^{*\alpha} - \left(\frac{\dot{K}_h}{K_h}\right)^* (1 + k^*) - \delta k^* - (\lambda + n). \tag{4.17}$$

Now, evaluating Equation (4.12) at $k = k^*$,

$$\left(\frac{\dot{K}_h}{K_h}\right)^* = gw(k^*) + \lambda + n = \frac{\mathrm{s}k^{*\alpha}}{\mathrm{G}[\text{Ø}(k^*),\, 1]} + \lambda + n,$$

$$gw(k^*) = \frac{\mathrm{s}k^{*\alpha}}{\mathrm{G}[\text{Ø}(k^*),\, 1]}. \tag{4.18}$$

Substituting Equation (4.18) into Equation (4.17) yields,

$$c^* = k^{*\alpha} - [gw(k^*) + \lambda + n](1 + k^*) - \delta k^* - (\lambda + n). \tag{4.19}$$

Maximizing c^* with respect to s and equating to zero,

$$\partial c^*/\partial s = [\alpha k^{*(\alpha-1)} - \delta - gw(k^*) - \lambda - n - gw'(k^*)(1 + k*)]\frac{\partial k^*}{\partial s} = 0. \tag{4.20}$$

Since $\frac{\partial k^*}{\partial s} > 0$,[31] the Golden Rule condition for maximum social welfare is

$$\alpha k^{*(\alpha-1)} - \delta = gw(k^*) + \lambda + n + gw'(k^*)(1 + k^*). \tag{4.21}$$

Here, $gw(k^*) + \lambda + n + \delta + gw'(k^*)(1 + k^*)$ is the gross social marginal product of capital, inclusive of higher K_h productivity through human and intellectual investments induced by a higher k^* that is in turn triggered by a higher saving rate.[32]

---

[31]For empirical support of this inequality, see Appendix 4.A, Equations (4.A.17)–(4.A.19), Table 4.A.1, and related discussion.

[32]The first term on the RHS of Equation (4.21) $gw(k^*)$ is investment in new human and intellectual capital, and the fourth term $gw'(k^*)(1 + k^*)$ is the investment response to a higher k^* induced by a higher saving rate. The higher k^* lowers physical capital's marginal product and raises human-intellectual capital's marginal product, raising investments in the latter, and leading to higher steady state per capita output growth $g* - \mathrm{n} = \frac{\dot{K}_h}{K_h}* = \frac{\mathrm{s}k^{*\alpha}}{\mathrm{G}[\text{Ø}(k^*),\, 1]} + \lambda$ Equation (4.18).

If there are no endogenous human and intellectual investments, the first-order condition reduces to $\alpha k^{*(\alpha-1)} - \delta = \lambda + n$, which is the S-S model's optimal rule for maximum consumer welfare.[33] It is evident that the optimal net rate of return to capital should be higher than $\lambda + n$ when there are human and intellectual investments, i.e., $V^* > 0$ or $gw(k^*) > 0$, and $gw'(k^*) > 0$ or V^* responds positively to k^*; see Equation (4.21).[34] An alternative interpretation of the above Golden Rule can be given. A standard neoclassical (S-S) result is that the optimal saving rate s should be set equal to the income share of capital α — see discussion below. When there are endogenous human and intellectual investments V, the optimal saving rate should be set as a fraction of α, the fraction being equal to:

$$\frac{s}{\alpha} = \left\{[gw(k^*) + \lambda + n + \delta]\left[\frac{I}{G(I,V)}\right]\right\} / \{[gw(k^*) + \lambda + n + \delta] \\ + gw'(k^*)(1 + k^*)]\} < 1. \tag{4.22}$$

The ratio $\frac{s}{\alpha}$ is less than unity because the ratio $0 < [gw(k^*) + \lambda + n + \delta] / \{[gw(k^*) + \lambda + n + \delta + [gw'(k^*)(1 + k^*)]\} < 1$ and $0 < \frac{I}{G(I,V)} < 1$. Equations (4.18) and (4.21) are used to derive Equation (4.22). In the S-S model, (a) $I = G(I, V) = sY$, i.e., all saving is invested in new physical capital, so that $\frac{I}{G(I,V)} = 1$ and (b) $gw(k^*) = 0, gw'(k^*) = 0$ (no saving-induced human and intellectual investments, or $V = 0$). Statements (a) and (b) together yield the S-S result, $\frac{s}{\alpha} = \frac{(\lambda+n+\delta)}{(\lambda+n+\delta)} = 1$.

The inequality Equation (4.22) can be restated as $\frac{\alpha}{s} > 1$. Equivalently stated, the income share of capital should exceed[35] the saving rate to compensate capital for the additional output generated

[33]Set $gw(k^*) = 0, gw'(k^*) = 0$ in Equation (4.21).

[34]Recall the discussion of Figure 4.2 on the growth effects of a higher k^* triggered by an increase in the saving rate. A higher k^* implies smaller returns on physical investment I^* and larger returns on human-intellectual investments V^*, resulting in less production of I^* and more of V^*.

[35]By the factor $\{[gw(k^*) + \lambda + n + \delta] + gw'(k^*)(1 + \text{k}*)]\}/\{[gw(k^*) + \lambda + n + \delta][\frac{I}{G(I,V)}]\}$.

by k^*-induced human and intellectual investments that augment labor productivity.

4.4 Summary and Conclusion

This chapter has presented and discussed a growth model consisting of two inputs: stock of physical capital; and stock of human and intellectual capital. The production process is subject to diminishing marginal returns to the two inputs separately and constant returns jointly in the context of perfect markets, in contrast to increasing returns to capital in imperfect markets assumed by endogenous growth models. Three major theoretical results are: (1) A higher saving rate raises both the steady state and transitional output growth rate through increases in physical, human, and intellectual investments that augment labor productivity; (2) The DV model captures the S-S model's rich and stable transitional dynamics — absent in endogenous growth models. Large physical, human, and intellectual investments result in a burst of transitional output growth, overshooting the new and higher steady state per capita output growth rate (the latter is a new result from the DV model, a major extension of the S-S model), owing to endogenous human and intellectual investments (positive function of the ratio of physical to human-intellectual capital k); and (3) To maximize social welfare, the net rate of return on capital should be greater than the sum of exogenous Harrod-neutral technical change and population growth in order to compensate capital for the positive growth generated by physical, human and intellectual investments. Equivalently stated, the income share of capital should exceed the saving rate in order to compensate capital for the output generated by a higher level of k, leading to higher K_h productivity. The implications for growth policy are straightforward. Public policies that raise public sector saving for physical, human, and intellectual investments have magnified positive effects on the growth rate of per capita *GDP*. Strong incentives for private saving are essential for similar investments because of their positive growth effects in both the short run (transition) and the long run (steady state). The

COVID-19 pandemic complicates the execution and implementation of public policies on saving and investments in physical, human, and intellectual capital. For countries with fiscal difficulties, such policies may have to await the resolution of the pandemic and restoration of sufficient fiscal space in order to create maximum growth effects. Meanwhile, the international lending community has an important role to play. Loans to purchase, distribute, and vaccinate the public should be made available to countries with sustainable foreign debt.[36]

Appendix 4.A: Derivation of the Key Innovation of DV Model

Take the time derivative of the main text Equation (4.2):

$$\dot{K}_h = \dot{A}N + A\dot{N}. \tag{4.A.1}$$

The increment in the human-intellectual capital stock $\dot{K}_h$ is the sum of the increment in the K_h-augmenting productivity multiplier $\dot{A}N$ and the increment in the working population $A\dot{N}$. The increment in the K_h-augmenting productivity multiplier is

$$\dot{A}N = V + \lambda K_h. \tag{4.A.2}$$

Incremental changes in K_h productivity $\dot{A}N$ result from human and intellectual investments (e.g., in education and R&D) captured by the variable V plus an exogenous component λK_h [analogous, but not identical, to Solow's λL; see **Chapter 1**, Equations (1.A.2), (1.A.5), (1.A.6)].

[36]Extending the Ramsey (1928) optimal control procedure to an open economy and using a CRRA form of the utility function, Villanueva and Mariano (2021, **Chapter 10**) estimates sustainable gross foreign debt in range of 39 ∼ 50% of GDP and domestic saving rates of 18 ∼ 22% of GDP, depending on estimated elasticities of intertemporal substitution. These are feasible targets in developing and emerging market economies.

The increment in the working population $A\dot{N}$ is given by

$$A\dot{N} = nK_h. \tag{4.A.3}$$

Equations (4.A.1)–(4.A.3) imply that the increment in human and intellectual capital $\dot{K}_h$ is the sum of three elements: V, λK_h, and nK_h, explained below.

Repeating the main text Equation (4.11),

$$V = \frac{sY}{G[\text{Ø}(k), 1]}, \tag{4.A.4}$$

$$G[\text{Ø}(k), 1] = \frac{G(I, V)}{V}. \text{ Thus, } \frac{sY}{G[\text{Ø}(k), 1]} = \frac{sV}{G(I, V)}Y,$$

$$0 < \frac{V}{G(I, V)} < 1.$$

Combining Equations (4.A.1)–(4.A.4),

$$\dot{K}_h = \frac{sY}{G[\text{Ø}(k), 1]} + \lambda K_h + nK_h. \tag{4.A.5}$$

Equation (4.A.5) shows how V, the first element comprising the increment in the human and intellectual capital $\dot{K}_h$, is determined. V is equal to a fraction, $\frac{s}{G[\text{Ø}(k),1]} = \frac{sV}{G(I,V)}$ of income Y. The second element of $\dot{K}_h$ is exogenous change in K_h productivity λK_h, roughly corresponding to the S-S model's rate of exogenous Harrod-neutral technical change λL. The third and final element of $\dot{K}_h$ is an exogenous increase in the population of workers nK_h.

Using main text Equation (4.6), main text Equation (4.1) can be rewritten in intensive form as:

$$\frac{Y}{K_p} = k^{(\alpha-1)} \tag{4.A.6}$$

$$\frac{Y}{K_h} = k^{\alpha}. \tag{4.A.7}$$

Repeating main text Equation (4.A.10),

$$\frac{\dot{K}_p}{K_p} = \frac{sk^{(\alpha-1)}}{G\left[1, \frac{1}{\text{Ø}(k)}\right]} - \delta. \tag{4.A.8}$$

Dividing Equation (4.A.5) by K_h, using Equation (4.A.7),

$$\frac{\dot{K}_h}{K_h} = \frac{sk^{\alpha}}{G[\text{Ø(k)}, 1]} + \lambda + n. \tag{4.A.9}$$

The slopes are given by:

$$\frac{d}{\text{dk}}\left(\frac{\dot{K}_p}{K_p}\right) = G\left[1, \frac{1}{\text{Ø}(k)}\right]^{-1}\left[s(\alpha-1)k^{(\alpha-2)}\right]$$
$$+ sk^{(\alpha-1)})\text{Ø}'(k)G_2\left[1, \frac{1}{\text{Ø}(k)}\right]\text{Ø}(k)^{-2}G\left[1, \frac{1}{\text{Ø}(k)}\right]^{-2} < 0 \tag{4.A.10}$$

$$\frac{d}{\text{dk}}\left(\frac{\dot{K}_h}{K_h}\right) = G[\text{Ø}(k), 1]^{-1}\text{s}\alpha k^{(\alpha-1)}$$
$$-\text{s}k^{\alpha}G_1[\text{Ø}(k), 1]\text{Ø}'(k)G[\text{Ø}(k), 1]^{-2} > 0. \tag{4.A.11}$$

The inequalities (4.A.10) and (4.A.11) imply that physical capital growth is a monotonically decreasing function of k, and human-intellectual capital growth is a monotonically increasing function of k.

Time differentiating the main text Equation (4.6) and substituting Equations (4.A.8) and (4.A.9) yield

$$\frac{\dot{k}}{k} = \frac{\dot{K}_p}{K_p} - \frac{\dot{K}_h}{K_h} = \frac{sk^{(\alpha-1)}}{\text{G}\left[1, \frac{1}{\text{Ø}(k)}\right]} - \frac{sk^{\alpha}}{\text{G}[\text{Ø}(k), 1]} - (\lambda + n + \delta), \tag{4.A.12}$$

whose slope, given inequalities (4.A.10)–(4.A.11), is

$$\frac{d(\frac{\dot{k}}{k})}{\text{dk}} = \frac{d}{\text{dk}}\left(\frac{\dot{K}_p}{K_p}\right) - \frac{d}{\text{dk}}\left(\frac{\dot{K}_h}{K_h}\right) < 0. \tag{4.A.13}$$

The steady-state k^* is the root of Equation (4.A.12) equated to zero:

$$\frac{\dot{k}}{k} = \frac{sk^{*(\alpha-1)}}{\mathrm{G}\left[1, \frac{1}{\emptyset(k^*)}\right]} - \frac{sk^{*\alpha}}{\mathrm{G}[\emptyset(k^*), 1]} - (\lambda + n + \delta) = 0. \qquad (4.\mathrm{A}.14)$$

Evaluated at k^*, the steady state growth rate of per capita output $g^* - n$ is given by either Equation (4.A.8),

$$g^* - n = \frac{\dot{K}_p}{K_p} = \frac{sk^{*(\alpha-1)}}{\mathrm{G}\left[1, \frac{1}{\emptyset(k^*)}\right]} - \delta - n, \qquad (4.\mathrm{A}.15)$$

or Equation (4.A.9),

$$g^* - n = \frac{\dot{K}_h}{K_h} = \frac{sk^*}{\mathrm{G}[\emptyset(k^*), 1]} + \lambda. \qquad (4.\mathrm{A}.16)$$

From Equations (4.A.14)–(4.A.16), a sensitivity matrix (signs indicated on the k^* and $g^* - n$ rows of Table 4.1 in the main text) can be derived either algebraically or with the help of Figures 4.2–4.4 in the main text — see discussion in Section 4.2.3.

Figure 4.2 in the main text reproduces Figure 4.1 without reference to k^1 or k^2 on the k-axis, showing the steady state and transitional growth effects of an increase in the saving rate s. The initial steady state occurs at points $A(k^*, 0)$ and $B(k^*, g^* - n)$. When the saving rate increases, the first term on the RHS of the $\frac{\dot{Y}}{Y} - n$ line is larger, shifting this line upward. Whether the $\frac{\dot{k}}{k}$ line shifts upward as shown in Figure 4.2 is not obvious because the saving rate s enters in the first and second terms on the RHS of the $\frac{\dot{k}}{k}$ line symmetrically with opposite signs. For $\frac{\partial k^*}{\partial s} > 0$, i.e., for k^* at point A to increase to $k^{*\prime}$ at point C, it must be demonstrated that the $\frac{\dot{k}}{k}$ line shifts upward.

For the $\frac{\dot{k}}{k}$ line to shift upward, it must be shown that the upward shift of the $\frac{\dot{K}_p}{K_p}$ line is larger than the upward shift of the $\frac{\dot{K}_h}{K_h}$ line. Owing to the assumed unit-homogeneity of the joint output index $G(I, V)$, and noting that $\frac{Y}{K_p} = k^{(\alpha-1)}$ and $\frac{Y}{K_h} = k^{\alpha}$,

Equations (4.A.8)–(4.A.9) can be rewritten as

$$\frac{\dot{K}_p}{K_p} = \frac{sk^{(\alpha-1)}}{G\left[1, \frac{1}{Ø(k)}\right]} - \delta = \frac{sY\left(\frac{I}{K_p}\right)}{G(I,V)} - \delta \tag{4.A.17}$$

$$\frac{\dot{K}_h}{K_h} = \frac{sk^{\alpha}}{G[Ø(k),\, 1]} + \lambda + n = \frac{sY(\frac{V}{K_h})}{G(I,V)} + \lambda + n. \tag{4.A.18}$$

Repeating Equation (4.A.14), after substituting Equations (4.A.17)–(4.A.18),

$$\frac{\dot{k}}{k} = \frac{sY(\frac{I}{K_p})}{G(I,V)} - \frac{sY\left(\frac{V}{K_h}\right)}{G(I,V)} - (\lambda + n + \delta). \tag{4.A.19}$$

From Equations (4.A.17)–(4.A.19), when s is raised, for the $\frac{\dot{K}_p}{K_p}$ line to have an upward shift larger than the upward shift of the $\frac{\dot{K}_h}{K_h}$ line, or for the $\frac{\dot{k}}{k}$ line to shift upward, $\frac{I}{K_p}$ must be larger than $\frac{V}{K_h}$ for all k. Then the RHS of Equation (4.A.19) is positive ($\frac{\dot{k}}{k} > 0$) when s increases, and for Equation (4.A.12) to be zero (an implicit solution for k^*), k^* must increase since $\frac{d}{dk}(\frac{\dot{k}}{k}) = \frac{d}{dk}\left(\frac{\dot{K}_p}{K_p}\right) - \frac{d}{dk}(\frac{\dot{K}_h}{K_h}) < 0$ Equation (4.A.13). Therefore, if $\frac{I}{K_p} > \frac{V}{K_h}$ in the neighborhood of the steady state, then $\frac{\partial k^*}{\partial s} > 0$ as shown in Figure 4.2 in the main text.

The inequality $\frac{I}{K_p} > \frac{V}{K_h}$ can be roughly checked around the neighborhood of the steady state. This inequality can be restated as $\frac{[\frac{I}{Y}]}{[\frac{V}{Y}]} > [\frac{K_p}{Y}]/[\frac{K_h}{Y}]$, where $\frac{K_p}{Y} = k^{(1-\alpha)}$, $\frac{K_h}{Y} = k^{\alpha}$, so that $\frac{\left[\frac{K_p}{Y}\right]}{\left[\frac{K_h}{Y}\right]} = k^{(1-2\alpha)}$. Thus, the condition for $\frac{\partial k^*}{\partial s} > 0$ is that

$$\frac{I^*}{Y} > \{[k^{*(1-2\alpha)}]\,\text{multiplied by}\left(\frac{V^*}{Y}\right)\}.$$

Table 4.A.1 reports the data to evaluate the above inequality. The data inputs are:

$$\frac{I^*}{Y} = 0.225;\, k^* = 2.5;\, \frac{V^*}{Y} = 0.077.$$

Table 4.A.1. Data on $k, \frac{I}{Y}, \frac{V}{Y}$. This table reports the data on $k = \frac{K_p}{K_h}$, measured as capital services per hour for all private business during 1987–2018 (BLS, 2020), $\frac{I}{Y}$ = ratio of gross domestic capital formation to *GDP* (CEIC, 2020), $\frac{EDU}{Y}$ = ratio of total public and private expenditures on education to *GDP* (World Bank, 2020), $\frac{R\&D}{Y}$ = ratio of expenditures on research and development to *GDP* (OECD, 2020), and $\frac{V}{Y} = \frac{EDU}{Y} + \frac{R\&D}{Y}$. CEIC Notes on $\frac{I}{Y}$: United States Investment accounted for 20.4% of its Nominal *GDP* in March 2020, compared with a ratio of 20.5% in the previous quarter. United States investment share of Nominal *GDP* data is updated quarterly, available from March 1947 to March 2020, with an average ratio of 22.5%. The data reached an all-time high of 25.4% in December 1978 and a record low of 16.1% in June 1947. CEIC calculates Investment as % of Nominal *GDP* from quarterly Nominal Gross Capital Formation and quarterly Nominal *GDP*. The Bureau of Economic Analysis provides Nominal Gross Capital Formation in *USD* and Nominal *GDP* in *USD*. Seasonally adjusted auxiliary series is used.

Description	1987–2018	1987–1990	1990–1995	1995–2000	2000–2007	2007–2018	2016–2017	2017–2018
k	2.5	2.1	2.1	3.7	3.4	1.7	1.3	0.7
$\frac{I}{Y}$ (average) (March 1947–March 2020)	0.225							
$\frac{EDU}{Y}$ (2014)	0.050							
$\frac{R\&D}{Y}$ (2018)	0.027							
$\frac{V}{Y}$	0.077							

Two alternative values for α are used: 0.3 and 0.4. The results are:
For $\alpha = 0.3$:

$$\frac{I^*}{Y} = 0.225 > 0.1334.$$

For $\alpha = 0.4$:

$$\frac{I^*}{Y} = 0.225 > 0.0924.$$

The inequality $\frac{\partial k^*}{\partial s} > 0$ is supported by the data in Table 4.A.1.

References

Aghion, P. and P. Howitt (1998). *Endogenous Growth Theory.* Cambridge, MA: MIT Press.

Arrow, K. (1962). The economic implications of learning by doing. *Review of Economic Studies*, 29, 155–173.

Bureau of Labor Statistics (2020). *Multifactor Productivity Trends, 1987–2019.* Washington, DC: U.S. Department of Labor.

CEIC (2020). *Ratio of Nominal Gross Capital Formation to Nominal GDP, Seasonally Adjusted Auxiliary Series.* Washington, DC: U.S. Department of Commerce. https://www.ceicdata.com/en/indicator/united-states/investment--nominal-gdp.

Conlisk, J. (1967). A modified neoclassical growth model with endogenous technical change. *Southern Economic Journal*, 34, 199–208.

IHS Markit (2019). *The 5G Economy, How 5G Will Contribute to the Global Economy.*

Inada, K. (1963). On a two-sector model of economic growth: comments and generalization. *Review of Economic Studies*, 30, 119–127.

Knight, M., N. Loayza, and D. Villanueva (1993, **Chapter 2**). Testing the neoclassical theory of economic growth: a panel data approach. *IMF Staff Papers*, 40, 512–541.

Organization for Economic Cooperation and Development (2020). https://data.oecd.org/united-states.htm#profile-innovationandtechnology.

Phelps, E. (1966). *Golden Rules of Economic Growth.* NY: W.W. Norton & Company.

Ramsey, F. (1928). A mathematical theory of saving. *Economic Journal*, 38, 543–559.

Rebelo, S. (1991). Long-run policy analysis and long-run growth. *Journal of Political Economy*, 99, 500–521.

Romer, P. (1986). Increasing returns and long-run growth. *Journal of Political Economy*, 94, 1002–1037.

Solow, R. (1956). A contribution to the theory of economic growth. *Quarterly Journal of Economics*, 70, 65–94.

Solow, R. (1991). *Policies for Economic Growth.* Sturc Memorial Lecture, Johns Hopkins University School of Advanced International Studies.

Swan, T. (1956). Economic growth and capital accumulation. *Economic Record*, 32, 334–61.

Villanueva, D. (1994, **Chapter 6**). Openness, human development, and fiscal policies: effects on economic growth and speed of adjustment. *IMF Staff Papers*, 41, 1–29.

Villanueva, D. (2020, **Chapter 3**). A modified neoclassical growth model with endogenous labor participation. *Bulletin of Monetary Economics and Banking*, 23, 83–100.

Villanueva, D. and R. Mariano (2021, **Chapter 10**). Optimal saving and sustainable foreign debt. *Philippine Review of Economics*, 57, 170–199.

World Bank (2020). *Government Expenditure on Education, Total — United States*. https://data.worldbank.org/indicator/SE.XPD.TOTL.GD.ZS?locations=US.

Chapter 5

Finance and Endogenous Growth*

5.1 Introduction

The Solow (1956)-Swan (1956), or S-S, model (**Chapter 1**) has been, and still is, the workhorse of basic neoclassical growth theory. It has two distinguishing features: (a) it is a "real" model, i.e., it has no financial sector; and (b) all technical change is exogenous. In this chapter, I relax both features in a two-class neoclassical growth model with a highly simplified financial sector. The other innovation is to incorporate the learning-by-doing model in Villanueva (1994, **Chapter 6**) to make Harrod-neutral technical change endogenous.[1]

Luigi Pasinetti (1962) developed a two-class model of income distribution involving the capitalist and working classes that led to what Samuelson and Modigliani (1966) referred to as the Pasinetti paradox, which says that the equilibrium rate of return to capital (capital's marginal product) is given by the ratio $\frac{n}{s_c}$ where n = the growth rate of labor adjusted for Harrod-neutral technical change and s_c = saving rate of the capitalist class. Thus, the equilibrium rate of return to capital is independent of the saving rate s_w of the

*Written by Delano S. Villanueva and adapted from the *Bulletin of Monetary Economics and Banking*, 25, 55–72, by the permission of the Bulletin of Monetary Economics and Banking.

[1]Although it incorporates rudimentary finance, this chapter's model is a special, deterministic version of the more general evolutionary real growth model of Conlisk (1989). See Conlisk (1996) for a closely related contribution to bounded rationality.

working class. The Pasinetti model has neither financial sector nor capital market. Investment in the capital stock K is financed by the internal saving of the capitalist class, i.e., $\frac{\dot{K}}{K} = s_c r$ (ignoring depreciation), where s_c is the ratio of capitalist saving S_c to capitalist income rK, and r is the rate of return to capital (rentals rate = marginal product of capital), which is a function of the capital-labor ratio $k = K/L$, given unit-homogeneity of the production function. In equilibrium, the capital-labor ratio is constant at k^*, so that $\frac{\dot{K}}{K}* = s_c r^* = \frac{\dot{L}}{L}* = n$, or $r^* = \frac{n}{s_c}$ (Pasinetti paradox, absence of s_w). There is no financial intermediary mobilizing bank deposits that can be lent to the capitalist class for investment in K. The absence of a capital market also precludes workers from buying the capitalist new issues of stocks and bonds to finance investment.

This chapter's model is a neoclassical version of the Pasinetti two-class model that includes a rudimentary financial sector and endogenous learning-by-doing à la Villanueva (1994, **Chapter 6**). It generalizes the S-S growth model by introducing a financial intermediary sector and endogenizing labor-augmenting technical change. There are, of course, studies linking finance to output growth. For example, the Atje-Jovanovic (1993) model used an augmented MRW (Mankiw, Romer and Weil, 1992) growth format, introducing finance in the form of a stock market as the third input in the aggregate production function, additional to physical capital and effective labor. In a more conventional manner, the model of this chapter views the financial sector as a banking intermediary that mobilizes workers' financial savings to be on-lent to the capitalists for investments in the physical capital stock, thus retaining the S-S model's traditional two-input aggregate production function (capital and labor).

A new theoretical result is that the equilibrium rate of return to capital is a function of all the structural parameters of the growth model, including both saving rates of the capitalist and working classes. Another major result is that a financial crisis, such as happened in 2007–08 globally and regionally in Asia, produces a temporary, recessionary overshooting of a permanently lower equilibrium growth rate of per capita income.

Table 5.1. Group incomes and expenditures.

	Capitalists (c)	Workers (w)
Income (GDP)	$Y_c = rK$	$Y_w = wL$
Investment in K	$I = s_c Y_c + \dot{B}$	
Increment in B		$\dot{B} = \dot{D}$
Increment in D		$\dot{D} = s_w Y_w$

K = capital owned by the capitalist class, L (efficiency units) = labor = AN, A = technology or labor productivity multiplier, N = working population, Y_c = income of the capitalist class, Y_w = income of the working class, r = rentals rate, w = real wage rate, I = gross investment, B = bank credit, D = bank deposits, s_c = saving rate of the capitalist class, s_w = saving rate of the working class, and L in efficiency units means that if a 2018 man-hour is equivalent as an input in the production function to two man-hours in the base period, say, 2000, then the ratio K/L is the amount of capital per half-hour 2018 or per man-hour 2000.

Table 5.2. Balance sheets.

ASSETS	*LIABILITIES*	*NET WORTH*
	A. Capitalists	
K	B	$K - B$
	B. Banks	
B	D	$B - D$
	C. Capitalists/Banks	
K	D	$K - D$
	D. Workers	
D	0	D
	E. Economy	
K	0	K

Table 5.1 organizes the closed economy model, showing group incomes and expenditures (summary income statements). Table 5.2 shows the summary sectoral and national balance sheets. The model economy comprises two groups: the capitalist class (c) and the

working class (w). Capitalists own the entire capital stock K. Their income is rK where r = rate of return (Table 5.1, Row 1). I assume that the only financial institution in the model economy is a banking system, and for simplicity, there is no capital market. The capitalist class owns all banks, and the only financial asset available to the working class is a bank deposit. There is no central bank — thus, no currency and no reserve requirements.[2] Total income of workers is wL where w = real wage (Table 5.1, Row 1), of which a portion s_w is set aside as financial saving in the form of bank deposits (Table 5.1, Row 4). Investment undertaken by capitalists is financed by internal saving s_cY_c and bank credit B (Table 5.1, Row 2; Table 5.2, Balance Sheet A). Banks extend credit B and accept bank deposits D (Table 5.1, Row 3; Table 5.2, Balance Sheet B). The consolidated balance sheet of the capitalists and banks is shown in Balance Sheet C. When consolidated, net financial flows going to the capitalist class are assumed to be demand-determined by workers' demand for bank deposits D (Table 5.1, Row 4; Table 5.2, Balance Sheet D). Losses on bank credit suffered by banks are absorbed by the capitalist class. Workers are assumed to rent houses or apartments from the capitalists, who hire workers, pay competitive wages, and credit their bank accounts on payday. Bank deposits, insured by banks, are used to write checks or to honor debit cards used as payments for current expenditures. Check-writing and use of debit cards are free of charge and, as offsets, bank deposits pay no interest. For the economy as a whole, the asset (net worth) is the capital stock K (Table 5.2, Balance Sheet E).

[2]Although there is no currency, I allow debit cards issued by banks. Bank deposits are necessary to pay credit card charges. In Villanueva (2008, **Chapter 7**), I include an inflation-targeting, currency-issuing central bank that employs all the traditional monetary policy tools. Fiscal policy and borrowing from global capital markets are covered by Otani and Villanueva (1989) and Villanueva and Mariano (2007, **Chapter 9**). An endogenous saving rate in a closed economy Ramsey (1928) optimal control set-up is derived by Villanueva (1994, **Chapter 6**, Appendix 6.B) and in an open economy by Villanueva and Mariano (2021, **Chapter 10**).

As Tables 5.1 and 5.2 show, external finance of gross investment is constrained by the flow demand for bank deposits. There is no risk of bank runs because bank deposits represent workers' wages that are kept with banks, used by workers to carry out daily transactions. With the aid of this extended and modified model, I analyze the role of finance in the cyclical and in the steady state behavior of economic growth in a non-stochastic environment. To analyze the short-run dynamics of the model, I start from an initial, pre-crisis steady state *GDP* growth rate of the model economy. An exogenous crisis (an event outside the model) severely reduces the economy's financial flows, i.e., workers' income and bank deposits, disrupting investments. Two main analytical results are (1) in the transitional adjustment to the next steady state growth path, the model clearly shows contractionary overshooting of the post-crisis steady state growth rate; and (2) absent adequate policy responses, the post-crisis steady state growth path is unambiguously below the pre-crisis one. I show that the recessionary overshooting is followed by a protracted, slow growth recovery, and ultimately to a return to a lower, post-crisis steady state growth rate.

As simple as this neoclassical growth model is, it can nonetheless account for the broad contours and dynamics of growth developments in the U.S. economy since the financial crisis of 2007–08. That the growth slowdown has been deep (contractionary overshooting) and the recovery slow are predicted by the model. The model also suggests that countercyclical policies undertaken in response to the crisis may have been insufficient to restore the pre-crisis steady state output growth rate.[3]

Section 5.2 presents and discusses the model, followed by the analytics of the reduced model in Section 5.3. Section 5.4 analyzes the short-run (transitional) and long-run (steady state) growth impacts of an exogenous collapse in financial flows. Section 5.5 discusses the growth dynamics of changes in the other structural parameters of the

[3]Fiscal policies (income taxes net of benefits, τ_i as fractions of gross income) can easily be incorporated in the model by adopting *disposable* group incomes $(1-\tau_i)Y_i$, $i = c, w$. Benefits include subsidies and tax credits.

model. Section 5.6 summarizes and draws implications for growth policies.

5.2 The Growth Model

$$Y = K^{\alpha} L^{(1-\alpha)} \tag{5.1}$$

$$r = \frac{\partial Y}{\partial K} \tag{5.2}$$

$$w = \frac{\partial Y}{\partial L} \tag{5.3}$$

$$Y_c = rK \tag{5.4}$$

$$Y_w = wL \tag{5.5}$$

$$\dot{K} = I - \delta K \tag{5.6}$$

$$I = s_c Y_c + \dot{B} \tag{5.7}$$

$$\dot{B} = \dot{D} \tag{5.8}$$

$$\dot{D} = s_w Y_w \tag{5.9}$$

$$L = AN \tag{5.10}$$

$$\frac{\dot{A}}{A} = \emptyset \frac{K}{L} + \lambda \tag{5.11}$$

$$\frac{\dot{N}}{N} = n \tag{5.12}$$

$$k = \frac{K}{L} \tag{5.13}$$

$$d = \frac{D}{L} \tag{5.14}$$

Y = GDP, K = capital stock, L = effective labor, r = rentals rate, w = real wage rate, Y_c = capitalist income, Y_w = worker income, I = gross investment, B = bank credit, D = bank deposits, A = technology/productivity multiplier, N = exogenous working population, k = ratio of K to L, d = ratio of D to L, and α, s_c, s_w,

$\varnothing$, δ, λ, n = structural parameters. A dot over a variable denotes a time derivative.

Equation (5.1) is the aggregate production function, subject to the Inada (1963) conditions.[4] Equations (5.2) and (5.3) are profit-maximizing conditions, setting the rentals rate and real wage rate equal to their respective marginal products. Equations (5.4) and (5.5) define group incomes. Equation (5.6) states that the addition to the capital stock equals gross investment less depreciation. Equation (5.7) says that gross investment is financed by capitalists' own internal saving, which is a proportion s_c of their income, and by bank credit. Equations (5.8) and (5.9) state that the flow of bank credit is financed by bank deposits, representing a proportion s_w of workers' income after paying for consumption and other current expenditures. Equation (5.10) defines effective[5] labor L as the product of labor-augmenting technology or productivity multiplier A and working population N.[6]

Equation (5.11) postulates that the increment in labor-augmenting productivity has endogenous and exogenous components. The endogenous element is a modified version of Arrow's (1962) learning by doing. Arrow (1962) hypothesizes that investment ($\dot{K}$) induces more learning-by-doing, $\frac{\dot{A}}{A} = \varnothing\left(\frac{\dot{K}}{K}\right) + \lambda$, i.e., learning-by-doing is a proportion $\varnothing$ of capital growth plus an exogenous component λ.[7] In equilibrium, Arrow's output growth is exogenously fixed at $\left(\frac{\dot{K}}{K}\right)^* = \left(\frac{\dot{L}}{L}\right)^* = \left(\frac{\dot{A}}{A}\right)^* + n = \left(\frac{\dot{Y}}{Y}\right)^* = g^{Y*} = \frac{(\lambda+n)}{(1-\varnothing)}$, which is a multiple of the S-S equilibrium output growth since $0 < \varnothing < 1$ by

---

[4]With reference to any production function, $Y = F(K, L) = Lf(k)$, where K is capital, L is labor, and k is the ratio of K to L, these conditions can be summarized as follows: $\lim \frac{\partial F}{\partial K} = \infty$ as $K \to 0$; $\lim \frac{\partial F}{\partial K} = 0$ as $K \to \infty$; $f(0) \geq 0$; $f'(k) > 0$, and $f''(k) < 0$ for all $k > 0$. Equation (5.1) satisfies these conditions.

[5]In efficiency units (for definition, see top of Table 5.1).

[6]Generally, the definition of L should be $L = APN$, where P is the labor participation rate ($0 < P \leq 1$). The working population is PN. When $P = 1$, $L = AN$. Whatever P is, it is usually assumed in growth literature as an exogenous constant, whose rate of change is zero. For an endogenous and variable P, see Villanueva (2020, **Chapter 3**).

[7]$\varnothing$ is a learning coefficient.

assumption. If Arrow's learning by doing is interpreted as driven by cumulative investments (integral of I = stock of K) per unit of L, Equation (5.11) adopts, not modifies, Arrow's learning by doing.[8] The larger the capital stock per capita, the more intense is the workers' learning-by-doing experience and hence, the higher is their productivity.[9] The exogenous component is the standard S-S (and Arrow's) constant term λ. Equation (5.12) assumes a constant rate n of exogenous population growth. The remaining Equations (5.15)–(5.16) are definitions for capital intensity k, and deposit ratio d, respectively.

There are 14 equations in 14 variables and time t (suppressed): Y, K, L, r, w, Y_c, Y_w, D, B, I, A, N, k, and d.[10] The growth model reduces to two differential equations in the state variables k and d. There are two special cases of the model: (a) If $s_w = 0$ and $\emptyset = 0$ (no financial sector and all technical change is exogenous), Equations (5.8) and (5.9) drop out and Equation (5.11) becomes $\frac{\dot{A}}{A} = \lambda$. Equation (5.7) is $I = sY$ (s = aggregate saving rate) and the growth model reduces to the S-S model; and (b) If $s_w = 0$ and $\emptyset > 0$ (no financial sector and technical change is partly endogenous via learning by doing), the model reduces to the Villanueva (1994, **Chapter 6**) model.

5.3 Reduced Model

Using Equations (5.4), (5.5), (5.8) and (5.9), Equation (5.7) becomes:

$$I = s_c rK + s_w wL. \tag{5.15}$$

Equation (5.15) into Equation (5.6), using Equations (5.1)–(5.5), (5.8) and (5.9), and dividing the result by K,

$$\frac{\dot{K}}{K} = [s_c\alpha + s_w(1-\alpha)]k^{(\alpha-1)} - \delta. \tag{5.16}$$

Equation (5.16) is the warranted rate equation.

[8]The only difference is the absence of a financial sector in the Arrow model.

[9]Using $L = AN$ and $k = K/L$, re-write Equation (5.11) as $\dot{A} = \emptyset\frac{K}{N} + \lambda \text{A}$.

[10]Time is not explicit in the model. Partly for this reason, phase diagramming is used to analyze the existence, uniqueness, and stability of the growth model.

Equations (5.10)–(5.12) need elaboration. The differential of Equation (5.10) is given by:

$$\dot{L} = \dot{A}N + A\dot{N}.$$

The increment in L is the sum of the increment in labor-augmenting technical change, specified in Equation (5.11), and the increment in the working population, specified in Equation (5.12). Equation (5.11) can be re-written as $\dot{A} = \emptyset\left(\frac{K}{N}\right) + \lambda A$ (see footnote 9). It is the size of the capital stock *per capita* that matters for learning by doing, not the growth rate of the capital stock. When laborers work with a larger capital stock possessing the latest advanced technology, they learn more as time passes, with consequent increase in productivity. Equation (5.11) is identical to the specification in Villanueva (1994, **Chapter 6**, Equation 6.4, where $\emptyset = \alpha$ and $A = T$). The model allows for a constant rate λ of exogenous labor-augmenting technical change as in the S-S (**Chapter 1**, Equation 1.5) model.

Time differentiating Equation (5.10) and substituting Equations (5.11)–(5.12),

$$\frac{\dot{L}}{L} = \emptyset k + \lambda + n. \tag{5.17}$$

Equation (5.17) is the natural rate equation.

Time differentiating Equation (5.15) and substituting into the result Equations (5.16)–(5.17) yield the proportionate rate of change in the capital intensity,

$$\frac{\dot{k}}{k} = [s_c\alpha + s_w(1-\alpha)]k^{(\alpha-1)} - \emptyset k - (\lambda + n + \delta). \tag{5.18}$$

Equations (5.1) and (5.15) imply $Y = Lk^{\alpha}$, whose time derivative is

$$\frac{\dot{Y}}{Y} = \frac{\dot{L}}{L} + \alpha\frac{\dot{k}}{k}. \tag{5.19}$$

Equation (5.19) is the growth rate of output at any moment of time. Using Equation (5.17) evaluated at the steady state $k = k^*$,[11]

[11] A constant k^* implies $\frac{\dot{K}}{K}* = \frac{\dot{L}}{L}* = \frac{\dot{Y}}{Y}* = \emptyset k^* + \lambda + n$. This balanced growth path is a consequence of the unit-homogeneous production function.

Equation (5.19) can be rewritten as

$$\frac{\dot{Y}}{Y} - n = \O k^* + \lambda + \alpha\frac{\dot{k}}{k} \tag{5.20}$$

where $\frac{\dot{k}}{k}$ is given by Equation (5.18). Equation (5.20) states that the growth rate of per capita output $\frac{\dot{Y}}{Y} - n$ will be above (below) the steady state level $= \O k^* + \lambda$ for a rising (falling) k, or whenever k is smaller (larger) than k^*.[12]

Finally, time differentiating Equation (5.16) and substituting Equations (5.1), (5.3), (5.5), (5.9) and (5.17) yield

$$\frac{\dot{d}}{d} = \frac{\{s_w(1-\alpha)\}\, k^{\alpha}}{d} - (\O k + n + \lambda). \tag{5.21}$$

Equations (5.18) and (5.21) form the reduced model in k, d, and time. The equilibrium values of k and d, denoted by k^* and d^*, are obtained by equating Equations (5.18) and (5.21) to zero, i.e.,

$$[s_c\alpha + s_w\,(1-\alpha)]\, k^{*(\alpha-1)} - \O k^* - (\lambda + n + \delta) = 0$$

$$= H\,(k^*, d^*), \tag{5.22}$$

$$\frac{\{s_w(1-\alpha)\}\, k{*}^{\alpha}}{d*} - (\O k^* + n + \lambda) = 0 = J\,(k^*, d^*), \tag{5.23}$$

whose partial derivatives are:

$$a_{11} = \frac{\partial\frac{\dot{k}}{k}}{\partial k} = H_1 = [s_c\alpha + s_w\,(1-\alpha)]\,(\alpha-1)\, k^{*(\alpha-2)} - \O < 0 \tag{5.24}$$

$$a_{12} = \frac{\partial\frac{\dot{k}}{k}}{\partial d} = H_2 = 0 \tag{5.25}$$

$$a_{21} = \frac{\partial\frac{\dot{d}}{d}}{\partial k} = J_1 = s_w\,(1-\alpha)\,\alpha k^{*(\alpha-1)} - \O = ? \tag{5.26}$$

$$a_{22} = \frac{\partial\frac{\dot{d}}{d}}{\partial d} = J_2 = -d^{*-2} s_w\,(1-\alpha)\, k^{*\alpha} < 0 \tag{5.27}$$

[12]It can also be seen from Equation (5.20) that the equilibrium growth rate of per capita output $\frac{\dot{Y}}{Y} * -n = \O k^* + \lambda$, since the third term on the right-hand side disappears when the economy reaches equilibrium at $\frac{\dot{k}}{k} = 0$.

Denoting the Jacobian matrix as A, whose elements are the a_{ij} above, the stability conditions

$$\mathrm{tr}(A) < 0$$

and

$$|\mathrm{A}| > 0$$

are met, given Equations (5.24)–(5.27). Thus, the model is stable.

The phase diagram of the reduced model is shown in Figure 5.1, depicting long-run equilibrium.[13] In both upper and lower parts, the horizontal axis measures the capital intensity k. In the upper part, the vertical axis measures bank deposits per effective worker d, while in the lower part, it measures the proportional rates of change in per capita *GDP* and capital intensity.

The upper part of Figure 5.1 plots the $\frac{\dot{k}}{k} = 0$ and $\frac{\dot{d}}{d} = 0$ lines in the k, d space. In Equation (5.18), the $\frac{\dot{k}}{k}$ relationship does not involve d so the $\frac{\dot{k}}{k} = 0$ curve is a straight line from the steady state value of k at $k^{*\prime}$. In Equation (5.21), the $\frac{\dot{d}}{d} = 0$ line is upward sloping because as k goes up, the real wage rises, stimulating higher demand for bank deposits. The long-run equilibrium values of $k = k^{*\prime}$ and $d = d^{*\prime}$ are obtained when $\frac{\dot{k}}{k} = 0$ and $\frac{\dot{d}}{d} = 0$ lines intersect at point H, which is locally stable. Starting from any point other than point H in the upper part of Figure 5.1, k and d will go back to $k^{*\prime}$ and $k^{*\prime}$, respectively. For example, any point to the right of the $\frac{\dot{k}}{k} = 0$ line indicates $k > k^{*\prime}$ $\left(\frac{\dot{k}}{k} < 0\right)$, meaning that the natural rate exceeds the warranted rate. For balanced growth to be restored, the warranted rate must rise and the natural rate must fall. The marginal returns to capital rise as k declines toward $k^{*\prime}$, encouraging investment and accelerating the warranted rate. As k falls toward $k^{*\prime}$, learning by doing slows, decelerating the natural rate. Consequently, $\frac{\dot{k}}{k}$ will be less and less negative, until it is zero at equilibrium point H, when the

[13] A phase diagram is a graphical tool to analyze the existence and stability of equilibrium for a system of two first-order differential equations not explicitly involving time.

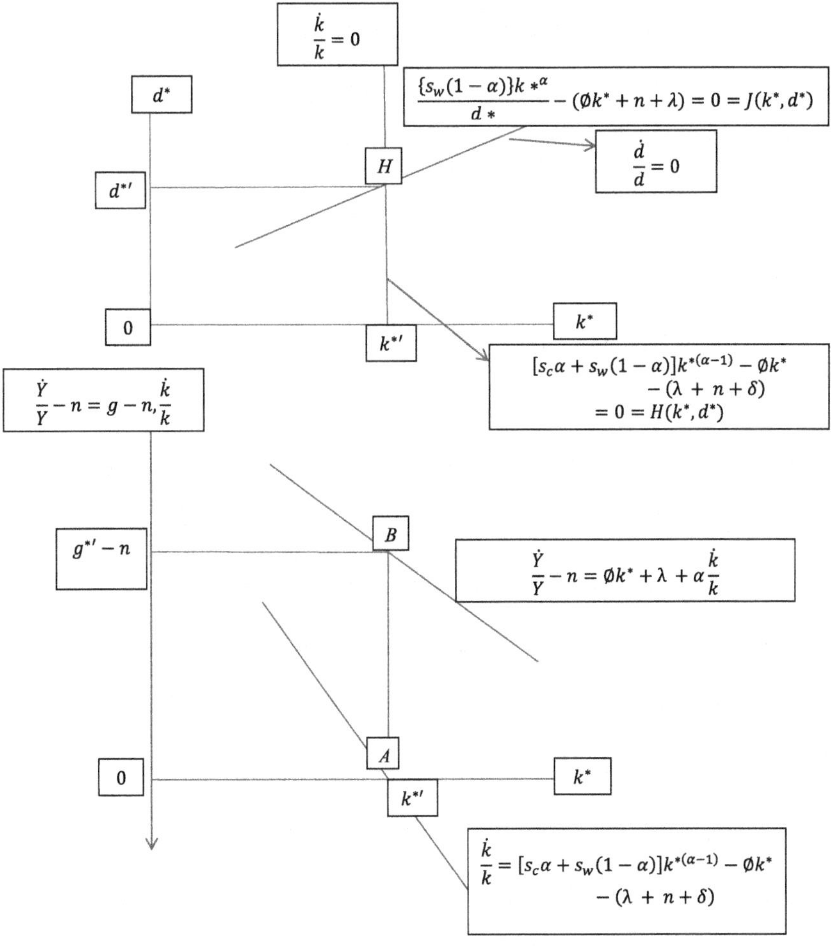

Figure 5.1. Long-run equilibrium.

warranted rate has risen to the lower natural rate restoring balanced growth at $k^{*\prime}\left(\frac{\dot{k}}{k} = 0\right)$. The opposite sequence of economic events holds at any point to the left of the $\frac{\dot{k}}{k} = 0$ line when $k < k^{*\prime}\left(\frac{\dot{k}}{k} > 0\right)$.

The $\frac{\dot{d}}{d} = 0$ line is upward sloping because inequality (5.26) says that the positive income effect of a higher k on $\frac{\dot{D}}{D}$ is greater than the positive learning-by-doing effect of a higher k^* on $\frac{\dot{L}}{L}$. Take any point below the $\frac{\dot{d}}{d} = 0$ line. To the right of $k^{*\prime}$ $(k^* > k^{*\prime})$, the higher income effect on $\frac{\dot{D}}{D}$ is larger than the higher learning-by-doing effect; d goes up. To the left of $k^{*\prime}$ ($k^* < k^{*\prime}$), as k^* goes up toward $k^{*\prime}$ the higher income effect on $\frac{\dot{D}}{D}$ is larger than the higher learning-by-doing effect; d goes up. Now, take any point above the $\frac{\dot{d}}{d} = 0$ line. To the left of $k^{*\prime}$ ($k^* < k^{*\prime}$), the lower income effect on $\frac{\dot{D}}{D}$ is larger than the lower learning-by-doing effect; d goes down. To the right of $k^{*\prime}$ ($k^* > k^{*\prime}$), as k^* goes down toward $k^{*\prime}$ the lower income effect on $\frac{\dot{D}}{D}$ is larger than the lower learning-by-doing effect; d goes down.

The lower panel of Figure 5.1 shows the instantaneous and steady state per capita *GDP* growth rate. Taking the derivatives of the $\frac{\dot{Y}}{Y} - n$ and $\frac{\dot{k}}{k}$ lines with respect to k, the $\frac{\dot{Y}}{Y} - n$ line is drawn flatter than the $\frac{\dot{k}}{k}$ line.[14] At $k^{*\prime}$, the instantaneous and steady state per capita *GDP* growth rate coincide at $g^{*\prime} - n$. At any $k < k^{*\prime}$, $\frac{\dot{k}}{k} > 0$, and the instantaneous per capita *GDP* growth rate exceeds the steady state rate ($\frac{\dot{Y}}{Y} - n > g^{*\prime} - n$). At any $k > k^{*\prime}$, $\frac{\dot{k}}{k} < 0$, and the instantaneous per capita *GDP* growth rate is below the steady state rate ($\frac{\dot{Y}}{Y} - n < g^{*\prime} - n$). Through adjustments in the capital intensity and its rate of change, the warranted and natural rates adjust towards equality to restore a balanced growth path of per capita output at the rate $\emptyset k^{*\prime} + \lambda$ (at $\frac{\dot{k}}{k} = 0$).

5.4 Short-Run and Long-Run Growth Effects of a Decline in Financial Flows

Figure 5.2 reproduces Figure 5.1. It traces the dynamic effects of a decline in the proportion s_w of workers' income so that there is a decrease in net financial flows (from s_{w0} to s_{w1}) to the capitalist/financial intermediary sector (as happened in the financial crisis of 2007–08). The initial steady state equilibrium points are $A(k^{*\prime}, 0)$ and $C(k^{*\prime}, g^{*\prime} - n)$, where $g^{*\prime} - n$ and $k^{*\prime}$, respectively, denote equilibrium growth rate of per capita output and equilibrium level of capital intensity. Given $k^{*\prime}$, the initial equilibrium deposit ratio is

---

[14] $\frac{\partial\left(\frac{\dot{Y}}{Y} - n\right)}{\partial k} = \frac{\alpha\partial\left(\frac{\dot{k}}{k}\right)}{\partial k} < \frac{\partial\left(\frac{\dot{k}}{k}\right)}{\partial k}$ in absolute value, since α is a positive fraction.

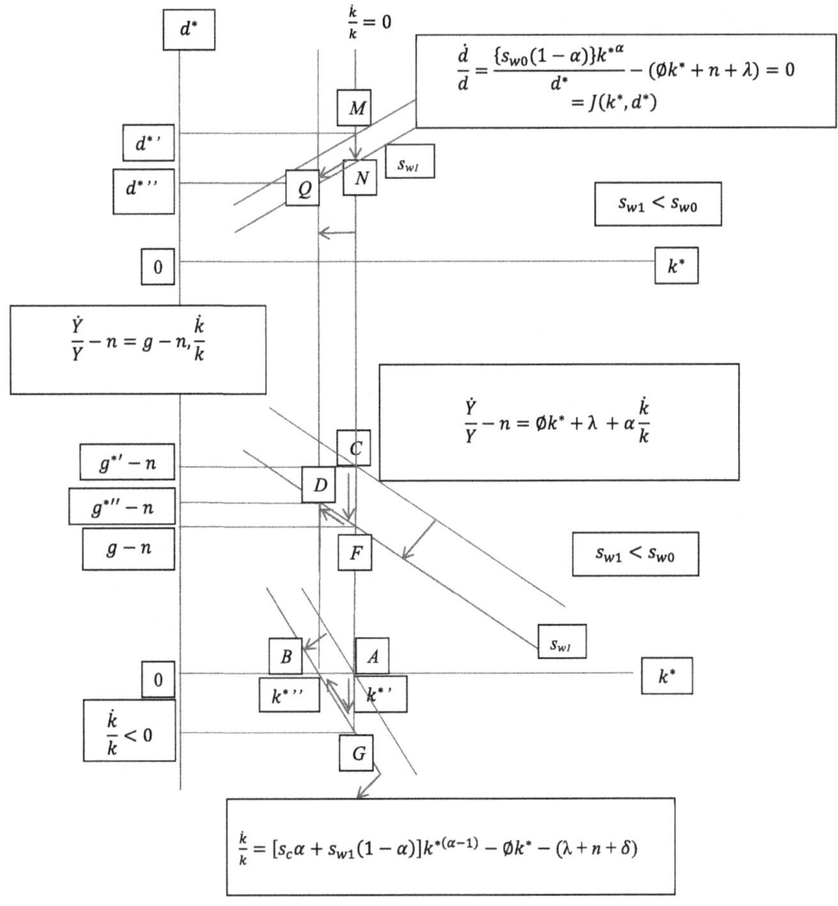

Figure 5.2. Short-run and long-run effects of a decline in net financial flows (lower s_w) on the growth rate of per capita output/income.

$d^{*\prime}$ in the upper panel. A lower s_w (s_{w1}) shifts downward both the $\frac{\dot{d}}{d}$ line in the upper panel and the $\frac{\dot{Y}}{Y} - n$ line in the lower panel of Figure 5.2. Both steady state deposit-labor ratio and capital intensity are lower at $d^{*\prime\prime}$ and $k^{*\prime\prime}$.[15] In the lower panel, the $\frac{\dot{k}}{k}$ line shifts

[15]Recall that in the Pasinetti (1962) growth model, the equilibrium rate of return to capital r^* (capital's marginal product) is inversely related to the capitalists' saving rate, but is unaffected by the workers' saving rate. This result carries over in the modified Pasinetti model with endogenous growth discussed in this chapter

downward to the left and intersects the k-axis at point $B(k^{*\prime}, 0)$. The $\frac{\dot{Y}}{Y} - n$ line also shifts downward to the left, and its new steady state equilibrium point is $D(k^{*\prime\prime},\ g^{*\prime\prime} - n)$. The short-run growth dynamics is as follows. Following the downward shift of the $\frac{\dot{k}}{k}$ line under the impact of a lower s_{w1}, and before the initial steady-state $k = k^*$ adjusts, $\frac{\dot{k}}{k} < 0$ at point G. Thus, the per capita output growth rate drops precipitously from $g^{*\prime} - n$ at point C to $g - n$ at point F. As $k^* = k^{*\prime}$ contracts toward $k^{*\prime\prime}$, the warranted rate accelerates on the strength of improvements in the marginal and average returns to capital, exceeding the decelerating natural rate, the latter reflecting lower learning-by-doing (the negative value of $\frac{\dot{k}}{k}$ becomes less and less negative) until the two rates are equal at the new steady state equilibrium point $B(k^{*\prime\prime}, 0)$.[16] Correspondingly, the per capita output growth rate recovers from $g - n$ at F and increases to $g^{*\prime\prime} - n$ at D on the strength of a rising last term $\frac{\dot{k}}{k}$ of the $\frac{\dot{Y}}{Y} - n$ line until this term is zero at D.[17] As for the dynamics of the adjustment of deposits per effective worker, d^* initially declines from point M to point N in the upper panel, and further falls from point N to the new equilibrium point Q because of lower real wages as capital intensity shrinks.

The 2007–08 global financial crisis precipitated by the U.S. financial crisis can be analyzed with the help of Figure 5.2. Following the financial shock (represented by the downward shift in s_w), credit flows to the corporate sector dried up, investments slumped, leading to a short-run precipitous drop in the growth rate of per capita output. As time went on, the recovery was excruciatingly slow and after adjustments finished, the equilibrium per capita output growth remained lower than the pre-crisis rate. The pre-crisis output growth rate at $g^{*\prime} - n$ could have been achieved with quantitatively sufficient, calibrated expansionary fiscal and monetary policies promoting investments.

(see Table 5.3). The additional new result is that r^* is also inversely related to the workers' saving rate. As workers decrease their financial savings, deposit flows into the financial system fall, capitalists' physical investment goes down and capital intensity declines, raising the equilibrium rate of return to capital r^*.

[16] Adjustment is traced by segment $G - B$.

[17] Adjustment is traced by segment $F - D$.

5.5 Other Comparative Dynamics

Table 5.3 shows the all-else-equal effects of the model's other structural parameters on equilibrium capital intensity and equilibrium per capita output growth.

$$\frac{\dot{k}}{k} = [s_c\alpha + s_w(1-\alpha)]k^{(\alpha-1)} - \emptyset k - (\lambda + n + \delta). \tag{5.28}$$

$$\frac{\dot{Y}}{Y} - n = \emptyset k^* + \lambda + n + \alpha\frac{\dot{k}}{k}. \tag{5.29}$$

The signs in Table 5.3 are obtained by equating Equation (5.28) to zero and partially differentiating with respect to each structural parameter, noting that $k^* = k^*(s_c, s_w, \emptyset,\ n, \lambda, \delta)$. For example, to find the sign of $\frac{\partial k^*}{\partial s_w}$, which is the effect of a fall in the saving rate of the working class:

$$(1-\alpha)k^{*(\alpha-1)} + \{[s_c\alpha + s_w(1-\alpha)](\alpha-1)k^{*(\alpha-2)} - \emptyset\}\frac{\partial k^*}{\partial s_w} = 0$$

or

$$\frac{\partial k^*}{\partial s_w} = \frac{-(1-\alpha)k^{*(1-\alpha)}}{\{[s_c\alpha + s_w(1-\alpha)](\alpha-1)k^{*(\alpha-2)} - \emptyset\}} > 0,$$

since $0 < \alpha < 1$.

A decline in the saving rate of the working class leads to a fall in equilibrium capital intensity, inducing lower learning by doing, and hence lower equilibrium per capita output growth, $\frac{\dot{Y}}{Y}^* - n = \emptyset k^* + \lambda$ [Equation (5.20)].

Figure 5.3 illustrates the growth effects of changes in the learning coefficient $\emptyset$. The initial equilibrium occurs at points $A(k^{*\prime}, 0)$, $B(k^{*\prime}, g^{*\prime} - n)$, and the subsequent equilibrium is at points $C(k^{*\prime\prime}, 0)$, $D(k^{*\prime}, g^{*\prime\prime} - n)$. Following the downward shift of the $\frac{\dot{k}}{k}$ line under the impact of a higher $\emptyset$, and before the initial steady-state $k = k^{*\prime}$ adjusts, $\frac{\dot{k}}{k} < 0$ at point G. Thus, per capita output growth rises only to $g - n$ at point E, less than $g^{*\prime\prime} - n$ at point D. As $k = k^{*\prime}$ contracts toward $k^{*\prime\prime}$, the warranted rate accelerates on the strength of improvements in the marginal and average returns to capital, exceeding the decelerating natural rate, the latter reflecting lower

Table 5.3. Sensitivity of k^*, r^*, and g^*-n to parameter changes.

Description	s_c	s_w	Ø	n	λ	δ
Change in k^*	+	+	−	−	−	−
Change in r^*	−	−	+	+	+	+
Change in $g^* - n$	+	+	+	−	+	−

k^* = capital intensity, r^* = rate of return to capital (marginal product of capital), $g^* - n$ = per capita output growth, s_c = capitalist saving rate, s_w = worker saving rate, Ø = learning coefficient, n = rate of exogenous population growth, λ = rate of exogenous labor-augmenting technical change, and δ = rate of capital depreciation. * indicates steady-state (equilibrium) values.

Notes: The $\frac{\dot{k}}{k} = 0$ [Equation (5.22)] is the steady-state condition with an implicit solution for k^*. The reader can easily check the signs of Table 5.3 by implicit differentiation of k^* in the equation $\frac{\dot{k}}{k} = 0$ with respect to the parameters. Substituting such changes in k^* into the partial derivatives of $r^* = \alpha k*^{(\alpha-1)}$ and of $\frac{\dot{K}}{K} = 0 = \frac{\dot{L}}{L} = 0 = \frac{\dot{Y}}{Y} = 0$ [Equations (5.16)–(5.19), evaluated at k^*] with respect to each of the six structural parameters determines the signs of the partial derivatives shown in Table 5.3.

learning by doing (the negative value of $\frac{\dot{k}}{k}$ at point G becomes less and less negative) until the two rates are equal at the new steady state equilibrium point $C(k^{*\prime\prime}, 0)$.[18] Correspondingly, the per capita output growth rate rises further from $g - n$ at E to $g^{*\prime\prime} - n$ at D on the strength of a rising last term $\frac{\dot{k}}{k}$ of the $\frac{\dot{Y}}{Y} - n$ line until this term is zero at D.[19]

Figure 5.4 shows the growth effects of an increase in population growth n. The initial equilibrium occurs at points $A(k^{*\prime}, 0)$, $B(k^{*\prime}, g^{*\prime} - n)$, and the subsequent equilibrium is at points $C(k^{*\prime\prime}, 0)$, $D(k^{*\prime\prime}, g^{*\prime\prime} - n)$, characterized by lower capital intensity and lower per capita output growth.[20] Following the downward shift of the $\frac{\dot{k}}{k}$ line

[18] Adjustment is traced by segment $G - C$.
[19] Adjustment is traced by segment $E - D$.
[20] As mentioned earlier, the Arrow (1962) model's steady state growth equation is $\frac{\dot{K}}{K}* = \frac{\dot{L}}{L}* = \frac{\dot{A}}{A} * + n = \frac{\dot{Y}}{Y}* = g^Y* = (\mu + \text{n})/(1 - Ø)$, which has the property that $\frac{d(g^{Y*} - n)}{dn} = \left[\frac{Ø}{(1-Ø)}\right] > 0$, i.e., an *increase* in the population growth rate n

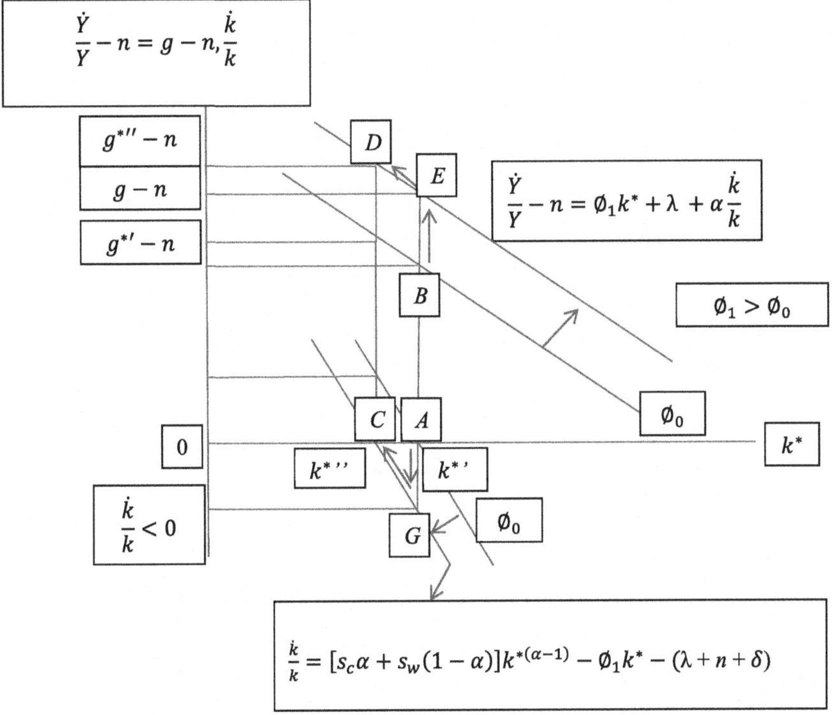

Figure 5.3. Short-run and long-run effects of an increase in the learning coefficient (higher Ø) on the growth rate of per capita output/income.

under the impact of a higher n, and before the initial steady-state $k = k^*$ adjusts, $\frac{\dot{k}}{k} < 0$ at point F. Thus, per capita output growth drops precipitously to $g - n$ at point E, less than $g^{*''} - n$ at point D. As $k = k^{*'}$ contracts toward $k^{*''}$, the warranted rate accelerates on the strength of improvements in the marginal and average returns to capital, exceeding the decelerating natural rate, the latter reflecting

---

raises the long-run growth rate of per capita output, $g^{Y*} - n$. This prediction is counterintuitive and rejected by empirical evidence. See, among others, Conlisk (1967), Otani and Villanueva (1990), Knight *et al.* (1993, **Chapter 2**), and Villanueva (1994, **Chapter 6**). However, if Arrow (1962) is interpreted as relating enhanced learning to the stock of capital per worker, the Arrow model is consistent with empirical findings. The only difference is the absence of finance in the Arrow model.

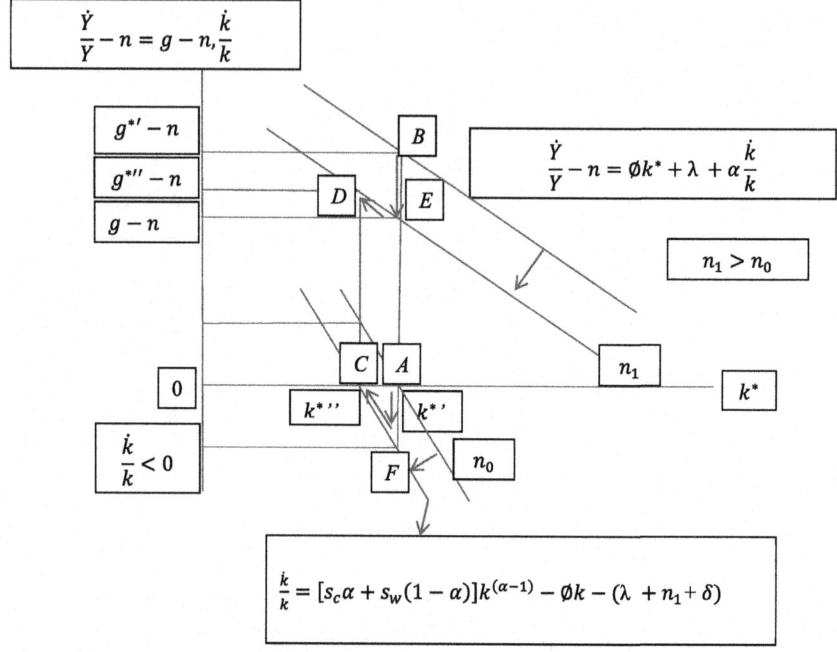

Figure 5.4. Short-run and long-run effects of an increase in population growth (higher n) on the growth rate of per capita output/income.

lower learning by doing (the negative value of $\frac{\dot{k}}{k}$ at point F becomes less and less negative) until the two rates are equal at the new steady state equilibrium point $C(k^{*\prime\prime}, 0)$.[21] Correspondingly, the per capita output growth rate rises further from $g - n$ at E to $g^{*\prime\prime} - n$ at D on the strength of a rising last term $\frac{\dot{k}}{k}$ of the $\frac{\dot{Y}}{Y} - n$ line until this term is zero at D.[22] Comparing the two equilibrium points B and D, a higher population growth n lowers the growth rate of per capita income, from $g^{*\prime} - n$ to $g^{*\prime\prime} - n$.

Finally, Figure 5.5 illustrates the growth effects of an increase in exogenous labor-augmenting technical change λ. The initial equilibrium occurs at points $A(k^{*\prime}, 0)$, $B(k^{*\prime}, g^{*\prime} - n)$, followed by the next equilibrium at points $C(k^{*\prime\prime}, 0)$, $D(k^{*\prime\prime}, g^{*\prime\prime} - n)$, characterized

[21] Adjustment is traced by segment $F - C$.
[22] Adjustment is traced by segment $E - D$.

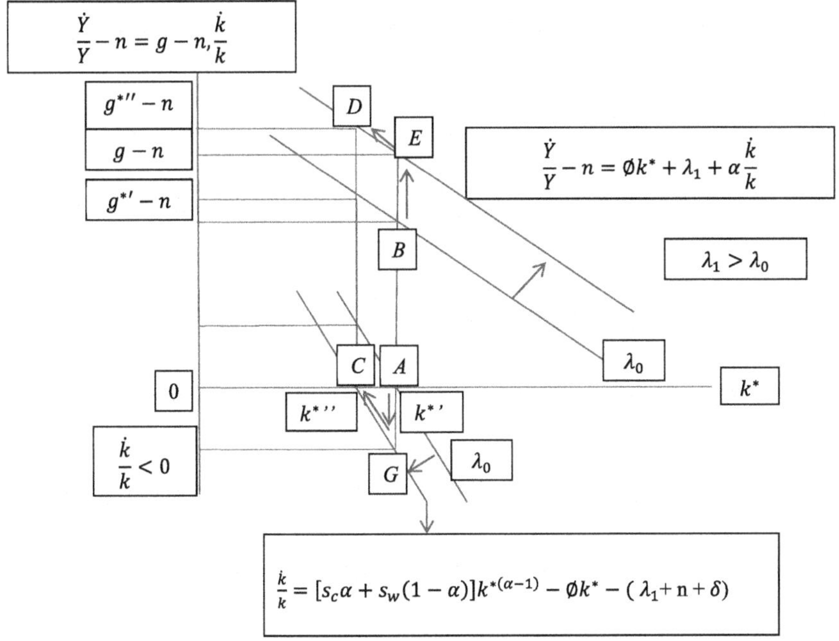

Figure 5.5. Short-run and long-run effects of an increase in exogenous labor-augmenting technical change (higher λ) on the growth rate of per capita output/income.

by lower capital intensity and higher per capita output growth. Following the downward shift of the $\frac{\dot{k}}{k}$ line under the impact of a higher λ, and before the initial steady-state $k = k^{*\prime}$ adjusts, $\frac{\dot{k}}{k} < 0$ at point G. Thus, per capita output growth rises only to $g - n$ at point E, less than $g^{*\prime\prime} - n$ at point D. As $k = k^{*\prime}$ contracts toward $k^{*\prime\prime}$, the warranted rate accelerates on the strength of improvements in the marginal and average returns to capital, exceeding the decelerating natural rate, the latter reflecting lower learning by doing (the negative value of $\frac{\dot{k}}{k}$ at point G becomes less and less negative) until the two rates are equal at the new steady state equilibrium point $C(k^{*\prime\prime}, 0)$.[23] Correspondingly, the per capita output growth rate rises further from $g - n$ at E to $g^{*\prime} - n$ at D on

[23]The adjustment is traced by segment $G - C$.

the strength of a rising last term $\frac{\dot{k}}{k}$ of the $\frac{\dot{Y}}{Y} - n$ line until this term is zero at D.[24]

Table 5.3 suggests a regression format to test the long-run growth implications of the model's structural parameters using cross-country data. The saving rates of the capitalist and working classes, population growth, and depreciation rates (all observables) can be regressors. The rate of exogenous labor-augmenting technical change can be impounded in the constant term of the regression, and the learning coefficient can be replaced by its determinants as was done by Villanueva (1994, **Chapter 6**), i.e., expenditures on education, health, public infrastructure, and foreign trade (exports plus imports) to GDP.

5.6 Conclusion

In this chapter's modified Pasinetti framework with endogenous growth, the equilibrium rate of return to capital is shown to be a function of all structural parameters, including both saving rates of the capitalist and working classes. Additionally, this chapter shows the simple analytics of the short-run and long-run growth effects of an exogenous collapse in financial flows, as happened in the global financial crisis of 2008–09. In the short run, there is an overshooting of recessionary growth. In the long run, there is an eventual return to a lower output growth path. Policies to restore the pre-crisis growth path involve appropriately calibrated expansionary monetary and fiscal policies, as well as supportive financial regulation to ensure the health of the financial sector. The objective is to ensure adequate financing of the economy's investment and capital accumulation through higher capitalists' re-invested profits and workers' financial savings.

References

Arrow, K. (1962). The economic implications of learning by doing. *Review of Economic Studies*, 29, 155–173.

[24] The adjustment is traced by segment $E - D$.

Atje, R. and B. Jovanovic (1993). Stock markets and development. *European Economic Review*, 37, 632–640.

Conlisk, J. (1967). A modified neoclassical growth model with endogenous technical change. *Southern Economic Journal*, 34, 199–208.

Conlisk, J. (1989). An aggregate model of technical change. *Quarterly Journal of Economics*, 104, 787–821.

Conlisk, J. (1996). Why bounded rationality. *Journal of Economic Literature*, 34, 669–700.

Inada, K.-I. (1963). On a two-sector model of economic growth: comments and generalization. *Review of Economic Studies*, 30, 119–127.

Knight, M., N. Loayza, and D. Villanueva (1993, **Chapter 2**). Testing the neoclassical theory of economic growth. *IMF Staff Papers*, 40, 512–541.

Mankiw, N., D. Romer, and D. Weil (1992). A contribution to the empirics of economic growth. *Quarterly Journal of Economics*, 107, 407–437.

Otani, I. and D. Villanueva (1989). Theoretical aspects of growth in developing countries: external debt dynamics and the role of human capital. *IMF Staff Papers*, 36, 307–342.

Otani, I. and D. Villanueva (1990). Long-term growth in developing countries and its determinants: an empirical analysis. *World Development*, 18, 769–783.

Pasinetti, L. (1962). Rate of profit and income distribution in relation to the rate of economic growth. *Review of Economic Studies*, 29, 267–279.

Ramsey, F. (1928). A mathematical theory of saving. *The Economic Journal*, 38, 543–559.

Samuelson, P. and F. Modigliani (1966). The Pasinetti paradox in neoclassical and more general models. *Review of Economic Studies*, 33, 269–301.

Solow, R. (1956). A contribution to the theory of economic growth. *Quarterly Journal of Economics*, 70, 65–94.

Swan, T. (1956). Economic growth and capital accumulation. *Economic Record*, 32, 334–362.

Villanueva, D. (1994, **Chapter 6**). Openness, human development, and fiscal policies: effects on economic growth and speed of adjustment. *IMF Staff Papers*, 41, 1–29.

Villanueva, D. and R. Mariano (2007, **Chapter 9**). External debt, adjustment, and growth. In T Ito and A Rose (eds.), *Fiscal Policy Management in East Asia*, NBER, Chicago, Illinois: University of Chicago Press.

Villanueva, D. (2008). *Macroeconomic Policies for Stable Growth*. Singapore: World Scientific Publishing Company.

Villanueva, D. (2020, **Chapter 3**). A modified neoclassical growth model with endogenous labor participation. *Bulletin of Monetary Economics and Banking*, 23, 83–100.

Villanueva, D. and R. Mariano (2021, **Chapter 10**). Optimal saving and sustainable foreign debt. *The Philippine Review of Economics*, 57, 170–199.

Chapter 6

Openness, Human Development, and Fiscal Policies*

The basic neoclassical growth model developed by Solow (1956) and Swan (1956) has been the workhorse of growth theory for nearly four decades.[1] Its simple structure consisting of a well-behaved neoclassical production function, investment-saving relation, and a labor growth function, is an elegant solution to the *knife-edge* problem posed by Harrod (1939) and Domar (1946). By allowing smooth factor substitution and wage-price flexibility, the capital/output ratio is made a monotonic function of the capital/labor ratio. The growth rate of the capital stock (the warranted rate) adjusts to the exogenously given growth rate of the labor force (the natural rate) to maintain full employment real output.

The Solow–Swan model, however, has certain equilibrium properties that bother many growth theorists: an increase in the saving rate, while raising the level of per capita real income, has no effect on the growth rate of output. This surprising result on growth neutrality has a simple explanation: although a higher saving rate raises the growth rate of output by increasing the investment rate, the increase in economic growth occurs only during the transition toward the next equilibrium; sooner or later, the labor input becomes a bottleneck,

*Written by Delano S. Villanueva and adapted from *International Monetary Fund Staff Papers* 41, 1–29, by the permission of the International Monetary Fund. Copyright 1994 by the International Monetary Fund.

[1] 1956–1994.

restricting further output expansion. The growth rate of output would eventually fall back to the constant natural rate of growth.

The time it takes the economy to reach this balanced growth path is of considerable interest — particularly to policy makers. In the context of the Solow–Swan model, if the objective of the macroeconomic policy were to raise the equilibrium level of per capita real income (for example, by raising the government saving rate), a fast adjustment would be desirable.

Using a Cobb–Douglas production function with constant returns to scale and Harrod-neutral technical progress, Sato (1963) has shown that the time required for the Solow–Swan model to reach equilibrium is about a hundred years![2] Moreover, the lower the rate of depreciation or the higher the share of capital in total output, the slower the adjustment. An intuitive explanation for these results is that a slower rate of depreciation or a larger share of capital would enable firms to substitute capital for labor and thus postpone for a longer period the bottleneck posed by a fixed rate of labor growth.

The Solow–Swan model's prediction that the rates of saving, depreciation, population growth, and government policies cannot affect the equilibrium growth rate of per capita real income, which is fixed by an exogenously determined rate of labor-augmenting technological progress, appears counterfactual. It seems reasonable to conjecture that, over the long haul, countries that promote saving and investment, reduce the depreciation of the capital stock, and create more open trading systems tend to grow faster and that those with rapid population growth, sluggish expansion in expenditures on human development and basic needs, and high ratios of fiscal deficits to GDP tend to grow slower.

The relatively slow adjustment of the Solow–Swan model toward its steady-state is partly due to the (assumed) inability of the natural rate to adjust to changes in capital intensity as the economy moves from one equilibrium to another in response to an exogenous shock. It seems plausible to consider that a partly endogenous natural rate,

[2]Such a slow adjustment would render somewhat irrelevant the equilibrium behavior of the model because of the likelihood that the other parameters of the system would have changed in the interim.

via learning through experience, would contribute to a faster speed of adjustment. If so, the steady-state behavior of the Solow–Swan model would assume much more relevance to policy makers.

This chapter is both theoretical and empirical and belongs to the class of new *endogenous growth* models.[3] It is a variant of Conlisk's (1967) endogenous-technical-change model and of Arrow's (1962) *learning by doing* model, wherein experience (measured in terms of either cumulative past investment or output) plays a critical role in raising labor productivity over time. The presence of learning through experience has three major theoretical consequences. First, equilibrium growth becomes endogenous and is influenced by government policies.[4] Second, the speed of adjustment to growth equilibrium is faster, and enhanced learning further reduces adjustment time. Third, both equilibrium economic growth and the optimal net rate of return to capital are higher than the sum of the exogenous rates of technical change and population growth.

The endogenous growth model's equilibrium behavior is found to be consistent with the substantial diversity in per capita growth patterns actually observed across countries. Such diverse growth experiences, which are predicted by the model, can be explained by differences in saving rates, ratios of government deficits to GDP, population growth rates, and certain parameters that influence the learning coefficient, such as changes in openness to world trade and growth in government outlays on education and health.

6.1 Endogenous Growth

The model is summarized by the following relationships:

$$Y = F(K, N) = Nf(k), \tag{6.1}$$

$$dK/\mathrm{d}t = s(\theta, .)Y - \delta(\mu)K, \tag{6.2}$$

[3]See, among others, Romer (1986), Lucas (1988), Becker *et al.* (1990), Grossman and Helpman (1990), and Rivera-Batiz and Romer (1991).

[4]Equilibrium growth in Arrow's (1962) learning by doing model, although a function of the *learning coefficient*, nevertheless remains independent of the saving rate and the depreciation rate.

$$dL/\mathrm{dt} = nL, \tag{6.3}$$

$$dT/\mathrm{dt} = \alpha(\chi, \xi, \omega, .)K/L + \lambda T, \tag{6.4}$$

$$N = TL, \tag{6.5}$$

$$k = K/N, \tag{6.6}$$

where the variables are defined as

Y = real GDP,
K = capital stock,
N = labor, man-hours in efficiency units,
L = population, man-hours,
T = labor productivity or technical-change multiplier, index number,
k = ratio of K to N,

and the parameters are defined as

s = ratio of real saving-investment to Y,
δ = depreciation of capital,
α = learning coefficient,
n = population growth rate,
χ = change in ratio to GDP of foreign trade (sum of exports and imports),
ξ = growth rate of real government expenditures on education and health,
ω = growth rate of real government expenditures for social security and housing,
μ = growth rate of real government expenditures on operations and maintenance,
θ = ratio of government deficits to GDP,
λ = rate of exogenous labor-augmenting technical change,
$\mathrm{d}(.)/\mathrm{d}t$ = time derivative.

Equation (6.1) is a standard neoclassical production function satisfying the Inada (1963) conditions.[5] Equation (6.2) is the expression

[5] $\lim \partial F/\partial K = \infty$ as $K \to 0$; $\lim \partial F/\partial K = 0$ as $K \to \infty$; $f(0) \geq 0$; $f'(k) > 0$; and $f''(k) < 0$, for all $k > 0$.

for capital accumulation: the increment in the capital stock is equal to gross domestic saving less depreciation. The proportion s of GDP saved and invested is assumed to be sensitive to government policies, in particular to the ratio of the fiscal deficit to GDP θ. High values of θ directly lower s, as the public sector dissaves. There are indirect effects as well. High levels of θ indicate large government borrowings from financial markets. Either through high interest rates or lower credit availability, private sector capital accumulation is adversely affected. Thus, it is assumed that $s'(\theta) < 0$. There are other (unspecified) factors affecting s. For example, interest rate liberalization may increase the private saving rate, which would tend to pull aggregate s up, but may also entail increases in the rate of government dissaving in the presence of a large stock of public debt, which would drag total s both directly and indirectly (via negative effects on the private saving-investment rate, as mentioned above). It is also assumed that $\delta'(\mu) < 0$ — the rate of depreciation δ is a negative function of the real growth of expenditures on operations and maintenance μ, that is, a higher μ lowers the rate of depreciation of existing capital stock K. The population grows at an exogenously constant rate n in Equation (6.3).

The key relationship in the model is given by Equation (6.4). It postulates that technical change $\mathrm{d}T/\mathrm{d}t$ improves with the aggregate capital stock per capita K/L. Output per capita Y/L can be used instead. For example, man-hours in the production of an airframe during the 1930s tended to decline with the number of airframes produced. A more current example is the introduction of both high-speed and personal computers that have improved the productivity of engineers and scientists (including economists). Since $(\mathrm{d}T/\mathrm{d}t)/T$ is a function of $Y/TL = Y/N = f(k)$, using K/L is equivalent to using Y/L as the forcing variable behind improvements in labor productivity. The parameter α is the learning coefficient. If $\alpha = 0$, T grows exogenously at a constant rate λ and the endogenous growth model collapses into the Solow–Swan model. The restrictions $\alpha \geq 0$ are assumed and empirically tested in Section 6.3. Since the assumption that $\alpha > 0$ is crucial to the arguments and propositions in this chapter, an extended discussion of its rationale is useful.

The Solow–Swan model's characterizing assumption $\alpha = 0$ may be true in a world devoid of technical change, as labor supply may be measured by the size of population. In this case, it may be plausible to assume that labor has no endogenous growth component, since population in many countries appears to grow independently of the economic system. But the real world is one of continuous technical change. While a portion of this may be exogenous, some technical change is clearly endogenous and partly labor-augmenting. Workers learn through experience, and their productivity is likely to be enhanced by the arrival of new and advanced capital goods. That is, the endogenous growth model's assumption that $\alpha > 0$ seems more plausible than the Solow–Swan model's assumption that $\alpha = 0$.[6]

In the restriction $\alpha > 0$, the learning coefficient α is allowed to vary positively with changes in the ratio of foreign trade to GDP χ, real growth of outlays on education and health ξ, social security, housing, and recreation ω, and other unspecified factors. The role of a rapid growth of foreign trade in stimulating a higher learning coefficient is twofold.[7] First, the import–export sector serves as a vehicle for technology transfer through the importation of advanced capital goods, as elucidated by Bardhan and Lewis (1970), Chen (1979), and Khang (1987), and as a channel for positive intersector externalities through the development of efficient and internationally competitive management, training of skilled workers, and the spillover consequences of scale expansion (Keesing, 1967;

---

[6]Arrow's (1962) learning by doing model has a steady-state solution for the growth rate of output equal to $(\lambda + n)/(1 - \alpha)$, wherein the technical change function is $(\mathrm{d}T/\mathrm{d}t)/T = \alpha(\mathrm{d}K/\mathrm{d}t)/K + \lambda$, $0 < \alpha < 1$. Although steady-state growth is thus a multiple of $\lambda + n$, growth remains independent of s and δ; besides, this model has the property that $\partial(g^* - n)/\partial n = \alpha/(1-\alpha) > 0$, that is, an increase in population growth *raises* equilibrium rate of *per capita* growth! This proposition is rejected by the empirical finding reported in Section 6.3.3 that an increase in the rate of population growth *depresses* the average growth rate of per capita output.

[7]See the discussion on the production linkage summarized in Khan and Villanueva (1991). Edwards (1992) and Knight *et al.* (1993, **Chapter 2**) present evidence on the relationship between trade openness and economic growth.

Feder, 1983). Second, rising exports relieve the foreign-exchange constraint. The importation of technologically superior capital goods is enlarged by growing export receipts and higher flows of foreign credits and direct investment, which take into account the country's ability to repay out of export earnings.[8]

It is also reasonable to posit that an acceleration in the growth of real outlays on education and health would be associated with a higher value of the labor's learning potential, as would growth in real expenditures on social security, housing, and recreation. Finally, Equations (6.5) and (6.6) are standard definitional relations involving N and k.

6.1.1 *Reduced Model*

The growth rate of the capital stock is derived by dividing Equation (6.2) by K, using Equations (6.1) and (6.6):

$$(\mathrm{d}K/\mathrm{d}t)/K = s(\theta,.)f(k)/k - \delta(\mu). \tag{6.7}$$

The growth rate of efficient labor is derived by differentiating Equation (6.5) with respect to time, using Equations (6.1) and (6.3)–(6.6):

$$(\mathrm{d}N/\mathrm{d}t)/N = \alpha(\chi,\xi,\omega,.)k + n + \lambda. \tag{6.8}$$

Differentiating Equation (6.6) with respect to time and substituting Equations (6.7) and (6.8), the growth rate of the capital–labor ratio k is thus equal to:

$$\begin{aligned}(\mathrm{d}k/\mathrm{d}t)/k &= (\mathrm{d}K/\mathrm{d}t)/K - (\mathrm{d}N/\mathrm{d}t)/N \\ &= s(\theta,.)f(k)/k - \alpha(\chi,\xi,\omega,.)k - [n + \lambda + \delta(\mu)]. \end{aligned} \tag{6.9}$$

[8]The transfer of efficient technologies and the availability of foreign exchange have featured prominently in recent experiences of rapid economic growth (Thirlwall, 1979).

The reduced model, Equation (6.9), is a single differential equation involving the variables $(\mathrm{d}k/\mathrm{d}t)/k$ and k alone.

Per capita income, Y/L, grows according to:

$$(\mathrm{d}Y/\mathrm{d}t)/Y - n = \alpha(\chi, \xi, \omega, .)k + \pi(k)(\mathrm{d}k/\mathrm{d}t)/k + \lambda, \qquad (6.10)$$

which is also a single-valued function of k. Here, π is the share of income going to capital; this share is in general a function of k.[9]

The equilibrium capital intensity, k^*, is the root of Equation (6.9) equated to zero,

$$s(\theta, .)f(k^*)/k^* - \alpha(\chi, \xi, \omega, .)k^* - [n + \lambda + \delta(\mu)] = 0. \qquad (6.11)$$

And the equilibrium growth rate of per capita income is given by:

$$[(\mathrm{d}Y/\mathrm{d}t)/Y]^* - n$$

$$= [(\mathrm{d}K/\mathrm{d}t)/K]^* - n = s(\theta, .)f(k^*)/k^* - [n + \delta(\mu)] \qquad (6.12a)$$

$$= [(\mathrm{d}N/\mathrm{d}t)/N]^* - n = \alpha(\chi, \xi, \omega, .)k^* + \lambda. \qquad (6.12b)$$

6.1.2 *Stability*

Given the Inada conditions on the production function, Equations (6.7)–(6.9) graph according to Figure 6.1. The upper panel graphs Equation (6.9), while the lower panel graphs Equations (6.7) and (6.8). The downward slopes of the curves representing Equations (6.7) and (6.9) and the upward slope of the curve representing Equation (6.8) follow from the assumption of a positive but diminishing marginal product of capital. The reasons why the $(\mathrm{d}k/\mathrm{d}t)/k$ curve lies partly in the first quadrant and partly in the fourth quadrant in Figure 6.1 are given by the other Inada conditions, that is, for some initial values of the capital–labor ratio, it is possible for the capital to labor ratio to grow either faster or slower than labor. It is obvious by inspection that, at any point on the $(\mathrm{d}k/\mathrm{d}t)/k_e$ curve, the economy

---

[9] For a degree β homogeneous production function $Y = F(K, N)$, $\pi(k) = kf'(k)/\beta f(k)$. The sign of $\pi'(k)$ follows the sign of $\varepsilon(k) - 1$, where $\varepsilon(k) = f'(k)[\beta f(k) - kf'(k)]/k[(\beta-1)f'(k)^2 - \beta f(k)f''(k)]$ is the elasticity of substitution. If F is Cobb–Douglas, $\pi(k) = \alpha$, where α is the constant exponent of K, and $\varepsilon(k) = 1$. If F is CES, $\pi(k) = 1/[1 + (1-\alpha)(1/\alpha)k^{-\sigma}]$ and $\varepsilon(k) = 1/(1-\sigma)$. Notice that if $\sigma = 0$, CES reduces to Cobb–Douglas.

would move in the direction indicated by the arrows. Thus, k tends to settle at an equilibrium value k_e^*, which is globally stable. Points off k_e^* along the curve imply nonzero rates of change in k, and k will change toward k_e^*. For example, in Figure 6.1, points to the left of k_e^* imply positive values of $(\mathrm{d}k/\mathrm{d}t)/k$. This means that K is growing faster than N, and the ratio K/N will rise. The increase in k reduces the returns to capital and lowers the income/capital ratio and, hence, the saving/capital and investment/capital ratios. The growth of K slows. Meanwhile, a higher k induces an increase in labor-augmenting technical change through enhanced learning and experience. The growth of N is stimulated. This process would continue until the growth rates of K and N converge at the stationary value k_e^*.[10] At this equilibrium point, K and N would grow at the same rate g_e^* and, by the constant returns assumption, output Y also would grow at this rate, given by Equations (6.12a) and (6.12b).

6.1.3 *Equilibrium Capital Intensity and Growth*

The Solow–Swan and endogenous growth models are graphically portrayed in Figure 6.1. In the lower panel, the natural rate schedule N_e is upward sloping in the endogenous growth model, owing to the presence of learning by doing and the assumption of a positive marginal product of capital. The natural rate schedule in the Solow–Swan model is shown as the horizontal line N_s with vertical height equal to a constant $g_s^*(= \lambda + n)$. The warranted rate schedule K is assumed to be identical in the two models.

In the upper panel, reflecting the different natural rate schedules, the capital accumulation schedules assume the shape and intersection (with the k-axis) indicated by the two curves, with $(\mathrm{d}k/\mathrm{d}t)/k_s$ flatter and to the right of $(\mathrm{d}k/\mathrm{d}t)/k_e$. The equilibrium positions of the two types of models are indicated by the points A and B, respectively, in the lower panel. The growth rate of output is higher in the endogenous growth model, by the magnitude $\alpha(.)f(k^*)$, that is, $g_e^* > g_s^*$. The capital/labor ratio, however, is lower in the endogenous

[10]The opposite sequence of events is true for points to the right of k_e^*, implying negative values of $(\mathrm{d}k/\mathrm{d}t)/k$.

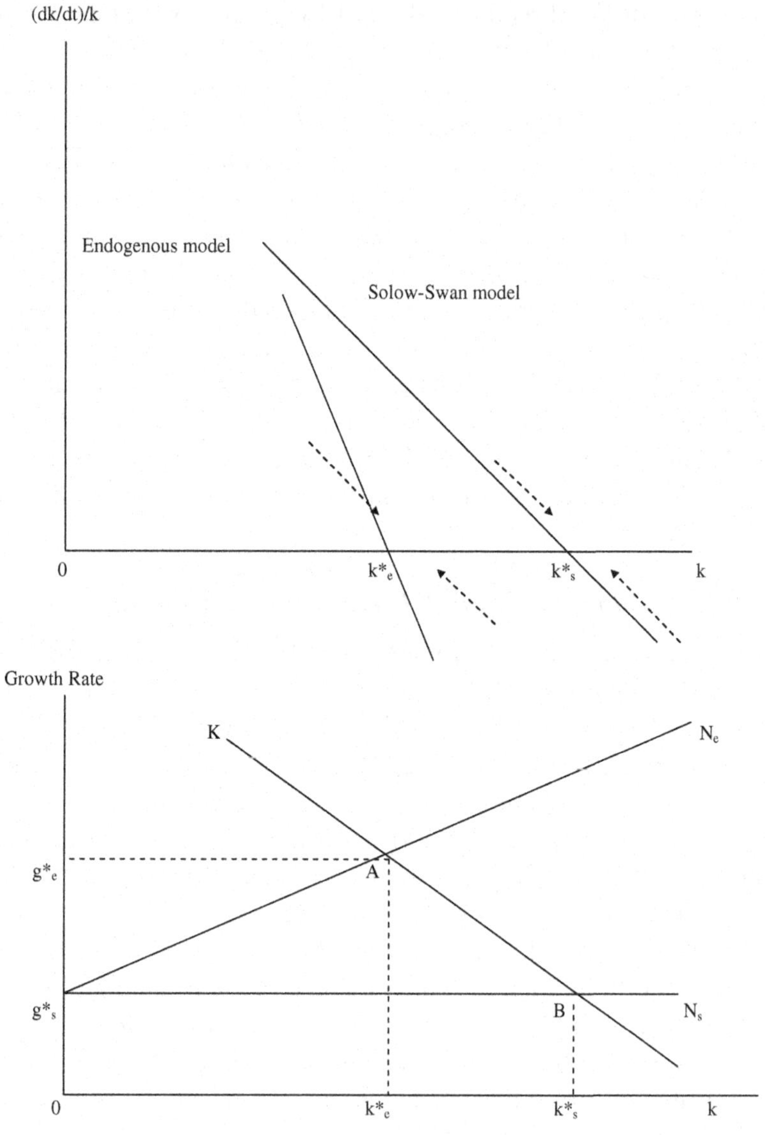

Figure 6.1. Endogenous and Solow–Swan growth models.

growth model ($k_e^* < k_s^*$). The growth rate is higher because of induced learning by doing. The model's capital intensity level is lower because of a higher level of the effective labor input.

Table 6.1. Comparative effects of structural parameters on equilibrium values of capital intensity (k^*) and per capita growth rate ($g^* - n$).

	Endogenous growth		Solow–Swan	
An increase in	k^*	$g^* - n$	k^*	$g^* - n$
Saving rate (s)	+	+	+	0
Ratio of foreign trade to GDP (χ)	+	+	na	na
Growth in real spending on education & health (ξ)	−	+	na	na
Growth in real spending on social security, etc. (ω)	−	+	na	na
Growth in real spending on operations & maintenance (μ)	+	+	na	na
Ratio of fiscal deficits to GDP (θ)	−	−	na	na
Population growth (n)	−	−	−	0
Exogenous technical change (λ)	−	+	−	+

Notes: + = increase; − = decrease; 0 = no change; na = not applicable.
Source: For the endogenous growth model, Equations (6.11), (6.12a) and (6.12b). For the Solow–Swan model, same set of equations with α set equal to zero.

6.1.4 *Comparative Dynamics*

Table 6.1 summarizes the qualitative effects of changes in the structural parameters on the equilibrium capital intensity k^* and on the equilibrium per capita growth rate of income, $g^* - n$. Algebraically, the partial derivatives of k^* and $g^* - n$ with respect to any structural parameter may be obtained by differentiation of Equations (6.11), (6.12a) and (6.12b).

6.1.4.1 *Effects of a Higher Saving Rate*[11]

The effects of an increase in the saving rate s on the transitional and equilibrium growth rate of output in the endogenous and Solow–Swan models can be analyzed in detail with the aid of Figure 6.2, in which the initial equilibrium positions in the two models are indicated by

[11]The effects of a reduction in the rate of depreciation — exogenously in the Solow–Swan model and endogenously in the endogenous growth model via a higher growth rate of real expenditures on operations and maintenance — are similar.

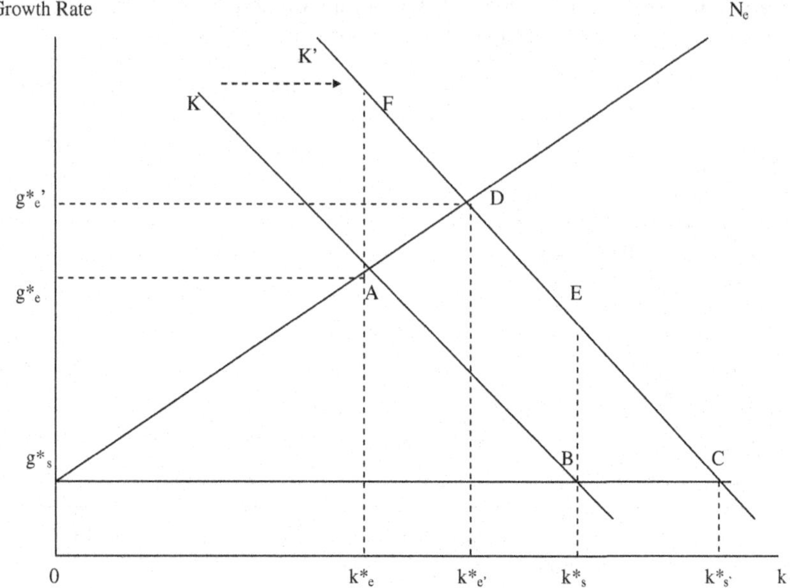

Figure 6.2. Effects of an increase in the saving rate.

points A and B, respectively. An increase in the saving rate shifts the warranted rate curve to K' in either model. The new equilibrium positions are indicated by points D in the endogenous growth model and C in the Solow–Swan model. In both endogenous and Solow–Swan models, the capital/labor ratio goes up, albeit the new ratio remains lower in the endogenous growth model (in relation to the new ratio in the Solow–Swan model), owing to positive learning by doing. However, the new equilibrium growth rate increases in the endogenous growth model, but remains unchanged in the Solow–Swan model. The discussion below traces the adjustment dynamics to the new growth equilibrium in the two models, as a result of an increase in the saving rate. The transitional dynamics of the Solow-Swan model is taken up first, followed by that of the endogenous growth model. During the transition between equilibrium points B and C, the rate of growth of output in the Solow–Swan model is momentarily higher, by EB, than the natural rate g_s^* because of a higher warranted rate occasioned by a higher ratio of saving to income.[12] The capital/labor ratio begins to rise, which slows the warranted rate. Since the natural rate is completely independent of the capital/labor ratio, only the warranted rate adjusts (downward) along the segment EC. Over time, labor becomes a bottleneck, and the growth rate slows (converges) to the constant natural rate $g_s^*(= n + \lambda)$ at C. At this point, the capital–labor ratio stops rising and settles at a new and higher level $k_s^{*\prime}$. The effect of an increase in the saving rate is thus to raise the equilibrium capital–labor ratio (from k_s^* to $k_s^{*\prime}$),[13] owing to a permanent upward shift of the warranted rate curve associated with an increase in the saving rate.

In the endogenous growth model, following an increase in the saving rate, equilibrium shifts from A to D. At the starting position A, capital would grow faster than labor (by FA), and the capital/labor ratio would rise (from k_e^* toward $k_e^{*\prime}$). As this happens, the marginal and average product of capital would fall, thus lowering the level of saving per unit of capital and slowing the warranted rate (downward along FD). On the other hand, the natural rate, instead of remaining constant as in the Solow–Swan model, would accelerate (from A to D, along the N_e curve) because of a higher rate of labor-augmenting technical change associated with a rising capital/labor ratio. This process would continue until the warranted and natural rates are equalized — through a continuous increase in the capital/labor ratio — at the new equilibrium value $k_e^{*\prime}$ at D, at which point the warranted rate would have fallen to the new and

[12]The transitional growth rate of output, $(\mathrm{d}Y/\mathrm{d}t)/Y$, is equal to $\lambda + n + \pi(k)(\mathrm{d}k/\mathrm{d}t)/k$, where $\pi(k) = kf'(k)/f(k)$. Now, both $\pi(k)$ and $(\mathrm{d}k/\mathrm{d}t)/k$ are positive anywhere between k_s^* and $k_s^{*\prime}$. It follows that $(\mathrm{d}Y/\mathrm{d}t)/Y > \lambda + n$ during the transition from B to C. At either B or C, $\pi > 0$ and $(\mathrm{d}k/\mathrm{d}t)/k = 0$, so that $(\mathrm{d}Y/\mathrm{d}t)/Y = \lambda + n$ at either equilibrium point. The convergence property of neoclassical growth models, including the Solow–Swan and endogenous growth models, can be demonstrated with the aid of Figure 6.2. As the initial capital intensity (or initial income per worker) moves farther to the left of $k_s^{*\prime}$ (or $k_e^{*\prime}$), that is, gets smaller, the average growth rate of per capita income rises, that is, the length of the line increases between C (or D) and any point on the K' curve corresponding to the initial level of capital intensity.

[13]And thus, the equilibrium level of real income per effective worker.

higher value of the natural rate, equal to the new and higher growth rate of output $g_e^{*\prime}(> g_e^*)$.

6.1.4.2 *Effects of Openness, Human Development Spending, and Technical Change*

The effects of these factors can be analyzed with the help of Figure 6.3. Since many of these parameters are absent from the Solow–Swan model,[14] the illustrations refer only to the endogenous growth model. Changes in the ratio to GDP of foreign trade (sum of exports and imports) and growth in real outlays on education, health, and social security, housing, and recreation are reflected in changes in the learning coefficient α, while changes in the exogenous rate of technical change λ enter the natural rate schedule directly. An increase in any of these parameters shifts the capital accumulation schedule in the southwest direction (upper panel) and the natural rate schedule in the northwest direction (lower panel). With reference to Figure 6.3, the adjustment dynamics are the following. After the parametric increase, the rate of change in k is negative at the old equilibrium value k_0^*. This means that the natural rate is above the warranted rate, as shown in the lower panel. Thus, the level of capital intensity begins to fall toward k_1^*. As k falls, income per unit of capital rises, stimulating saving and investment, and the warranted rate goes up. At the same time, a lower stock of capital reduces the rate at which technological progress is taking place, depressing the natural rate. This process continues until the two rates meet at k_1^*, where the rate of change in k is, again, zero. A lower level of capital intensity and a higher growth rate of per capita output and income characterize the new equilibrium position.

6.1.4.3 *Effects of Fiscal Deficits and Population Growth*

Finally, Figure 6.4 illustrates the effects of increases in the fiscal deficit ratio and in the rate of population growth on equilibrium capital intensity and on the growth rate of per capita output in the

---

[14]Except for the exogenous rate of technical change λ, whose effects on capital intensity and per capita growth are similar in the two models.

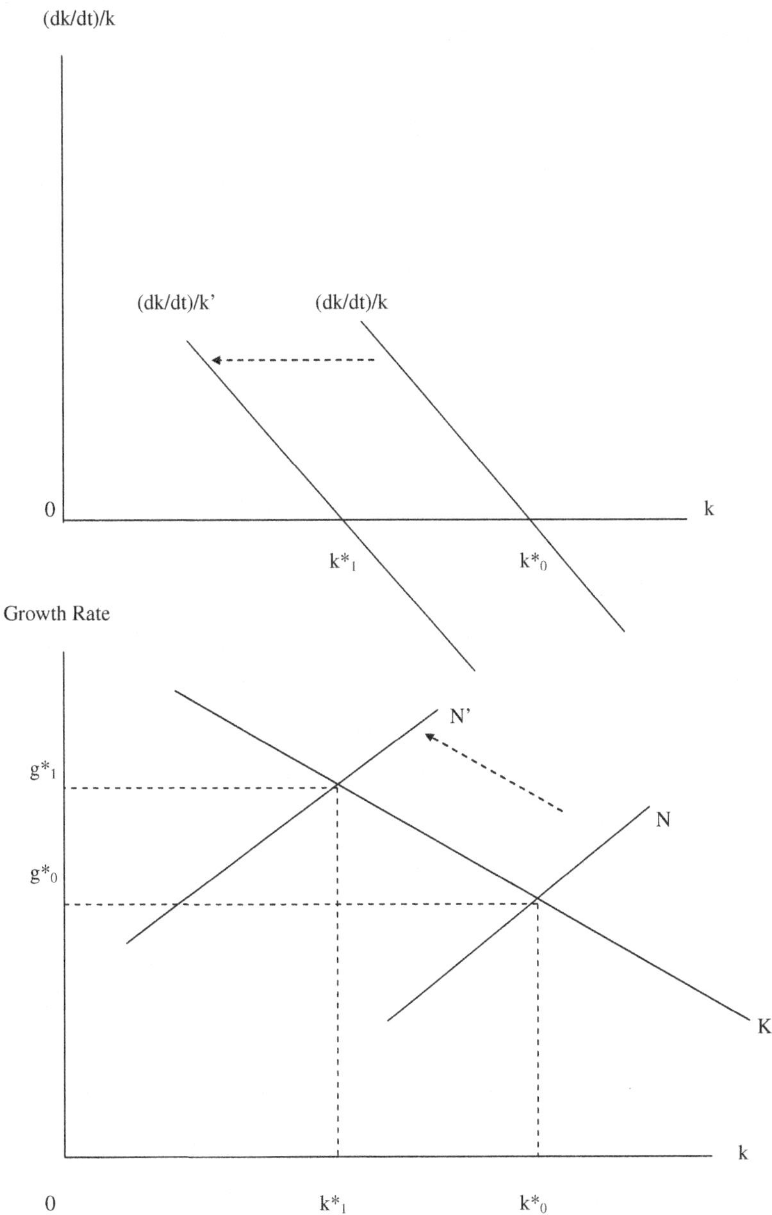

Figure 6.3. Growth effects of increased openness and expenditures on human development in the endogenous growth model.

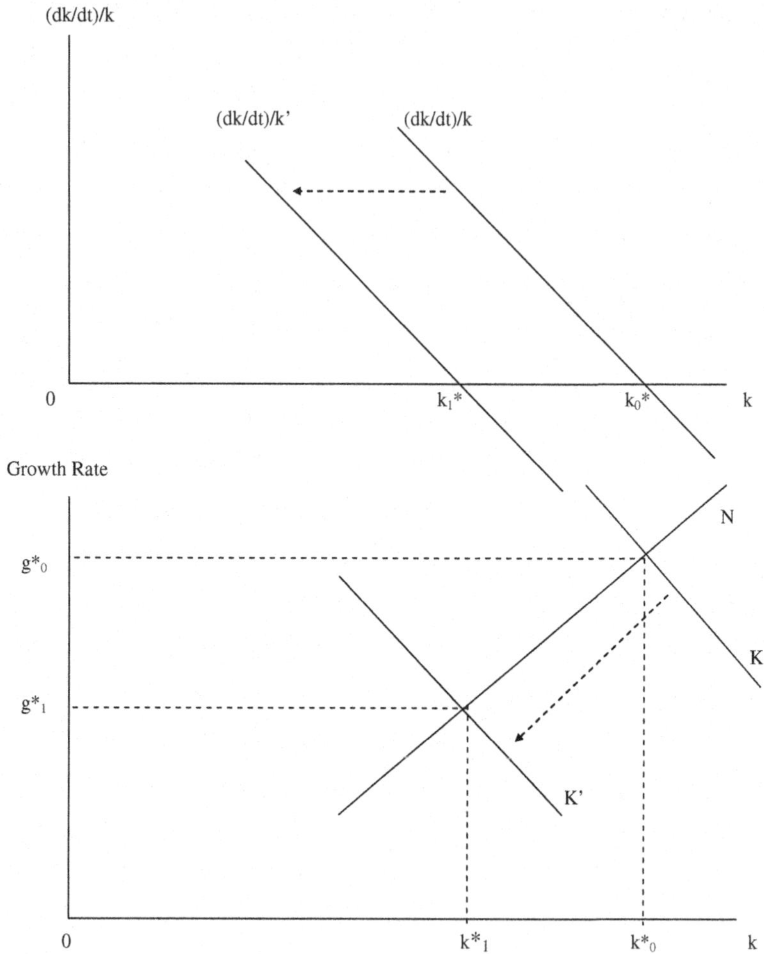

Figure 6.4. Growth effects of increases in ratio of fiscal deficits to GDP and in population growth.

endogenous growth model. An increase in population growth or in the rate of government dissaving[15] (by lowering the investment rate) shifts the capital accumulation schedule in the southwest direction

[15]As noted earlier, as the public sector dissaves less resources will be available to accumulate capital. Moreover, the ensuing large government borrowings from financial markets would tend to raise interest rates or lower available credit, adversely affecting private capital accumulation.

in both panels. At the old equilibrium capital intensity, the rate of change in k turns negative (upper panel), implying that the warranted rate falls short of the natural rate (lower panel). As k falls, income per unit of capital increases, raising saving and investment and, hence, the warranted rate. At the same time, the natural rate decreases, because a lower k induces a lower rate of learning. This process would continue until the economy settles at a new equilibrium position, characterized by a convergence of the warranted and natural rates, a lower level of capital intensity, and a slower growth rate of per capita output.

6.2 Optimal Long-Run Growth

Output per unit of effective labor in the long run is $y^* = f(k^*)$. If the level of y^* is considered a measure of the standard of living, and since $f'(k^*) > 0$, it is possible to raise living standards by increasing k^*. This can be done by adjusting the saving rate s, via, for example, lowering the fiscal deficit parameter θ. If consumption per unit of effective labor (or any monotonically increasing function of it) is taken as a measure of the social welfare of the society, the saving rate that will maximize social welfare by maximizing long-run consumption can be determined. Phelps (1966) refers to this path as the *Golden Rule of Accumulation.*

Consumption per unit of effective labor is $c = C/N = Y/N - S/N$. Y/N is $f(k)$ and $S = I = \mathrm{d}K/\mathrm{d}t + \delta(\mu)K$. Thus, $c = f(k) - [(\mathrm{d}K/\mathrm{d}t + \delta(\mu)K)]/N = f(k) - k[(\mathrm{d}K/\mathrm{d}t)/K] - \delta(\mu)k$. On the balanced growth path, $(\mathrm{d}K/\mathrm{d}t)/K = \alpha(.)k^* + \lambda + n$, where $\alpha(.) = \alpha(\chi, \xi, \omega, .)$. Thus:

$$c^* = f(k^*) - [\alpha(.)k^* + \lambda + n + \delta(\mu)]k^*. \tag{6.13}$$

Maximizing c^* with respect to s,

$$\partial c^*/\partial s = [f'(k^*) - 2\alpha(.)k^* - (\lambda + n + \delta(\mu))]\partial k^*/\partial s = 0. \tag{6.14}$$

Since $\partial k^*/\partial s > 0$, the *Golden Rule* condition is

$$f'(k^*) - \delta(\mu) = g^*(k^*) + \alpha(.)k^*, \tag{6.15}$$

where $g^*(k^*) = \alpha(.)k^* + \lambda + n$ is the equilibrium growth rate of output. The second-order condition for a maximum is satisfied, since

$$\partial^2 c^*/\partial s^2 = [f''(k^*) - 2\alpha(.)]\partial k^*/\partial s < 0. \tag{6.16}$$

Equation (6.15) says that, for social welfare to be maximized, the saving/investment ratio should be raised up to a point where the net rate of return to capital (which is equal to capital's marginal product less depreciation) equals the long-run growth rate of output plus the product of the learning coefficient and the equilibrium capital intensity. The second term is nothing more than the endogenous component of labor-augmenting technical change — the component of $(\mathrm{d}T/\mathrm{d}t)/T$ induced by learning and experience associated with a higher level of capital intensity, which, in turn, is caused by a higher saving rate. If there is no learning ($\alpha = 0$), Equation (6.15) reduces to $f'(k^*) - \delta = \lambda + n$, which is the familiar *Golden Rule* result from standard neoclassical growth theory. It is evident that the optimal net rate of return to capital should be higher than $\lambda + n$ when $\alpha > 0$ — when there is learning by doing — because of two factors. First, when the saving rate s is raised, the equilibrium growth g^* will be higher than $\lambda + n$, by the amount $\alpha(.)\partial k^*/\partial s$. Second, capital should be compensated for the effect on equilibrium output growth through the induced learning term $\alpha(.)k^*$.

An alternative interpretation of the above *Golden Rule* can be given. A standard neoclassical result is that the optimal saving rate s should be set equal to the income share of capital π. With endogenous learning by doing, the optimal saving rate should be set at a fraction of π, the fraction being equal to $(g^* + \delta)/[g^* + \delta + \alpha(.)k^*]$.[16] Here,

[16] Equations (6.11), (6.15) and the definition $\pi = k^* f'(k^*)/f(k^*)$ are used to derive this result. When $\alpha = 0$, the proportionality factor assumes a value of unity, and the standard neoclassical result holds. In terms of the parametric values assumed in the simulations reported in Table 6.2, when the learning coefficient α is greater than zero, the optimal saving rate should be set at about three quarters of the assumed income share of capital π, or at 0.3 when $\pi = 0.4$. The simulations also show that the higher the learning coefficient, the lower the optimal saving rate as a proportion of capital's income share. According to the standard model, the optimal saving rate should always be set equal to π, which is at 0.4 in the numerical examples. The higher saving rate implied by the standard model owes

$g^* + \delta + \alpha(.)k^* = f'(k^*)$, given by Equation (6.15), is the (gross) social marginal product of capital, inclusive of the positive externalities via learning experience associated with capital accumulation in the endogenous growth model. Equivalently put, income going to capital as a share of total output should be a multiple of the amount saved and invested to compensate capital for the additional output generated by endogenous growth and induced learning. A value of π equal to s, implicit in the standard model, would undercompensate capital and thus would be suboptimal from society's point of view.

6.3 The Speed of Adjustment Toward Equilibrium

The equilibrium results derived in the preceding section would not be relevant to the real world if the time period for the model to reach its equilibrium were unduly long. There are three approaches to the analysis of adjustment dynamics in the speed-of-approach literature:

1. Analytical approach, with less explicit results but without resorting to a full-scale numerical simulation;
2. Simulation, such as the work of Sato (1963), where a specific functional form for the production function and representative values of the structural parameters are used, and adjustment paths from hypothetical disequilibria are calculated to obtain estimates of the time (in years) needed to reach equilibrium; and
3. Empirical approach, where the model's equilibrium predictions are examined whether they accord with observed growth patterns of real economies over reasonably long periods.

6.3.1 *Analytical Approach*

The (negative) slope of the $(\mathrm{d}k/\mathrm{d}t)/k_e$ curve (see Figure 6.1) at the equilibrium capital intensity k_e^* is a measure of the local adjustment speed. The steeper the slope, the faster the steady-state k_e^* is reached.

---

to its neglect of endogenous growth and positive externalities through learning by doing associated with saving and capital accumulation. By contrast, in the endogenous growth model the economy benefits from such endogenous growth and positive externalities, so that a smaller saving/investment rate is all that is required (relative to the rate required by the standard model).

The absolute value (or a.v.) of the slope of the above curve at k_e^* may be obtained by differentiating Equation (6.9) with respect to k and evaluating at k_e^*:

$$\begin{aligned} V &= \text{a.v.}[(\mathrm{d}/\mathrm{d}k)\{(\mathrm{d}k/\mathrm{d}t)/k\}]^* \\ &= (n+\lambda+\delta+\alpha k_e^*)[(1-\pi(k_e^*)]/k_e^* + \alpha. \end{aligned} \tag{6.17}$$

The key feature of the endogenous growth model that distinguishes it from the Solow–Swan model is the assumed presence of learning by doing, represented by a positive learning coefficient α. In the absence of learning through experience ($\alpha = 0$), (6.17) reduces to the Solow–Swan expression. It is obvious by inspection of (6.17) that, with $\alpha > 0$, the $(\mathrm{d}k/\mathrm{d}t)/k_e$ curve is steeper than the $(\mathrm{d}k/\mathrm{d}t)/k_s$ curve (when $\alpha = 0$); see Figure 6.1. Thus, the endogenous growth model takes lesser time to reach equilibrium, compared with the Solow–Swan model. Moreover, it can be shown that enhanced learning, represented by an increase in α, would further reduce the adjustment time, provided that the elasticity of substitution is not less than one, such as when the production function is CES. This can be seen by differentiating Equation (6.17) with respect to α, which yields:

$$\begin{aligned} \partial V/\partial\alpha = \{&[(1-k_e^*)\alpha - (n+\lambda+\delta)](1-\pi(k_e^*)) \\ &- \pi'(k_e^*)(n+\lambda+\delta+\alpha k_e^*)\}(1/k_e^*)(\partial k_e^*/\partial\alpha), \end{aligned}$$

which is positive, if the production function is CES (in which case, $\pi'(k_e^*) \geq 0$), and if $k_e^* \geq 1$ (the equilibrium capital per effective worker is not less than a unit of the currency). It has been shown earlier that $\partial k_e^*/\partial\alpha < 0$. The simulations using a Cobb-Douglas production function (a special case of CES) reported in Table 6.2 show the same results.

The above results can be given an intuitive interpretation. It has been shown that the equilibrium growth rate of output is $((\mathrm{d}N/\mathrm{d}t)/N)^* = ((\mathrm{d}K/\mathrm{d}t)/K)^*$. *Both* the natural and warranted rates adjust endogenously to changes in capital intensity. With the brunt of adjustment toward equilibrium being shared by changes in the natural rate, the time needed to reach equilibrium is much less in the endogenous growth model. In sharp contrast, the time required to

Table 6.2. Estimated period of adjustment in years as y_t approaches a limit of $y_\infty(\alpha = 0)$.[a]

	$y_0 - y_\infty > 0$		$y_0 - y_\infty < 0$	
p_t	$y_0 = 0.045$	$y_0 = 0.035$	$y_0 = 0.015$	$y_0 = 0.025$
0.25	33.8	9.3	3.9	5.4
0.50	55.7	21.1	10.1	13.6
0.75	80.3	39.6	22.6	28.5
0.90	105.9	62.6	41.7	49.3
		$(\alpha = 0.01)$[b]		
	$y_0 - y_\infty > 0$		$y_0 - y_\infty < 0$	
p_t	$y_0 = 0.08$	$y_0 = 0.07$	$y_0 = 0.01$	$y_0 = 0.05$
0.25	6.4	4.3	1.5	2.6
0.50	13.5	9.8	3.9	6.5
0.75	23.3	18.6	9.1	13.6
0.90	34.7	29.4	17.5	23.5
		$(\alpha = 0.02)$[c]		
	$y_0 - y_\infty > 0$		$y_0 - y_\infty < 0$	
p_t	$y_0 = 0.08$	$y_0 = 0.07$	$y_0 = 0.01$	$y_0 = 0.05$
0.25	3.8	3.0	1.3	2.1
0.50	8.4	6.9	3.3	5.1
0.75	15.3	13.2	7.6	10.5
0.90	23.6	21.2	14.2	18.0

[a]With $a = 0.4$, $\delta = 0.04$, $\lambda = 0.005$, $n = 0.025$, $s = 0.2$. With these parametric values, $k^* = 5.75$ and $y_\infty = 0.03$.
[b]With $a = 0.4$, $\delta = 0.04$, $\lambda = 0.005$, $n = 0.025$, $s = 0.2$. With these parametric values, $k^* = 3.00$ and $y_\infty = 0.06$.
[c]With $a = 0.4$, $\delta = 0.04$, $\lambda = 0.005$, $n = 0.025$, $s = 0.2$. With these parametric values, $k^* = 2.40$ and $y_\infty = 0.08$.

reach equilibrium is much longer in the Solow–Swan model because the adjustment burden is borne *entirely* by changes in the warranted rate.

6.3.2 *Simulation*

The reduced model, Equation (6.9), is

$$(\mathrm{d}k/\mathrm{d}t)/k = sf(k)/k - \alpha k - (n + \lambda + \delta).$$

Assuming a Cobb–Douglas form for $f(k) = k^a$, where $0 < a < 1$ is the exponent of the capital stock (in this particular case, also equal to capital's share in income π, which is constant and independent of k), the reduced model becomes:

$$\mathrm{d}k/\mathrm{d}t = sk^a - \alpha k^2 - (n + \lambda + \delta)k = g(k). \tag{6.18}$$

The solution to this differential equation is complicated because it is a nonlinear function. However, a linear approximation is possible in the neighborhood of the steady-state constant value k^*[17]:

$$\begin{aligned}\mathrm{d}k/\mathrm{d}t &= g(k^*) + g'(k^*)(k - k^*)\\ &= [ask^{*a-1} - 2\alpha k^* - (n + \lambda + \delta)](k - k^*),\end{aligned}$$

since $g(k^*) = 0$.

Or,

$$\mathrm{d}k/\mathrm{d}t = A(k - k^*), \tag{6.19}$$

where $A = ask^{*a-1} - 2\alpha k^* - (n + \lambda + \delta) < 0$.[18]

Equation (6.19) is of a "variables separable" form, which can be separated as:

$$[1/(k - k^*)]\mathrm{d}x = A\mathrm{d}t. \tag{6.20}$$

Integrating both sides,

$$\begin{aligned}&\int [1/(k - k^*)]\mathrm{d}x = At + \text{constant},\\ &\log(k - k^*) = At + \text{constant},\\ &k - k^* = \text{constant } e^{At},\\ &k = k^* + Ce^{At},\end{aligned} \tag{6.21}$$

[17]The constant k^* is the unique root of (6.18) equated to zero: $sk^{*a} - \alpha k^{*2} - (n + \lambda + \delta)\, k^* = 0$. Given $s = 0.2$, $a = 0.4$, $\alpha = 0.01$, $n = 0.025$, $\lambda = 0.005$, and $\delta = 0.04$, k^* assumes the value of 3.00, and the balanced growth path is equal to an annual rate of 0.06. If $\alpha = 0$, as in the Solow–Swan model, and assuming the other parameters unchanged, k^* solves to a higher level at 5.75, and balanced growth to a lower rate of 0.03 per annum.

[18]As mentioned in the preceding footnote, for values of the parameters and of k^* assumed therein, a particular value for A equal to -0.0886 is obtained for $\alpha = 0.01$.

where C is a constant of integration.[19]

Substituting (6.21) into (6.19)

$$(\mathrm{d}k/\mathrm{d}t)/k = A[1 - (k^*/\{k^* + Ce^{At}\})]. \tag{6.22}$$

Now, from (6.10), the growth rate of output is given by:

$$(\mathrm{d}Y/\mathrm{d}t)/Y = y_t = a(\mathrm{d}k/\mathrm{d}t)/k + y_\infty, \tag{6.23}$$

where:

$$y_\infty = \alpha k^* + \lambda + n. \tag{6.24}$$

Substituting (6.22) and (6.24) into (6.23),

$$y_t = aA[1 - (k^*/\{k^* + Ce^{At}\})] + y_\infty, \tag{6.25}$$

Setting $y_t = y_0$ and $t = 0$ in (6.25),

$$y_0 = aA[1 - (k^*/\{k^* + C\})] + y_\infty, \tag{6.26}$$

which can be solved for the constant C,

$$C = (y_0 - y_\infty)k^*/(y_\infty - y_0 + aA). \tag{6.27}$$

Substituting (6.27) into (6.25),

$$y_t = aA[1 - (k^*/\{k^* + ((y_0 - y_\infty)k^*/(y_\infty - y_0 + aA))e^{At}\})] + y_\infty. \tag{6.28}$$

Next, define the adjustment ratio p_t as:

$$p_t = (y_t - y_0)/(y_\infty - y_0). \tag{6.29}$$

Substituting (6.28) into (6.29) solves for the time t (in years) required to get a fraction p_t of the way from y_0 to y_∞, from which Table 6.2 is computed:

$$t = (1/A)LN[(1 - p_t)(y_\infty - y_0 + aA)/((1 - p_t)(y_\infty - y_0) + aA)], \tag{6.30}$$

where LN is the natural logarithm operator.

[19]Note that as t goes to infinity, the second term on the right-hand side of (6.21) goes to zero (since $A < 0$), and k approaches k^*.

Table 6.2 reveals that the adjustment times in an endogenous growth model are generally only about a quarter or a third of those in an exogenous growth model, depending on the value of the learning coefficient α. For example, whereas an exogenous growth model ($\alpha = 0$) takes from 42 to 106 years for equilibrium growth to be nearly reached, an endogenous growth model ($\alpha > 0$) takes anywhere from 14 to 35 years to achieve 90 percent adjustment to the steady-state growth path, depending on the learning coefficient α (Table 6.2 alternately uses values of 0, 0.01, and 0.02 for α).

Table 6.2 also illustrates the effects of an increase in the learning coefficient from 0.01 to 0.02: the equilibrium capital intensity falls from 3.00 to 2.40 and equilibrium growth rises from 6 to 7.8 percent annually; moreover, adjustment times are reduced by 30–50 percent.[20]

6.3.3 *Empirical Approach*

The model's predictions about the per capita output growth and capital stock trends, which have been summarized in Table 6.1, are reproduced below, where the directional impact is given by the sign above each argument inside the two functions.

$$g^* - n = \psi(\overset{+}{s}, \overset{-}{\theta}, \overset{+}{\chi}, \overset{+}{\xi}, \overset{+}{\omega}, \overset{+}{\mu}, \overset{-}{n}, \overset{+}{\lambda}) \tag{6.31}$$

$$k^* = \phi(\overset{+}{s}, \overset{-}{\theta}, \overset{-}{\chi}, \overset{-}{\xi}, \overset{-}{\omega}, \overset{+}{\mu}, \overset{-}{n}, \overset{-}{\lambda}) \tag{6.32}$$

Equations (6.31) and (6.32) are in general nonlinear functions. Without the fiscal deficit variable θ, a linear approximation to (6.31) and (6.32) can produce coefficient estimates of arbitrary magnitude and significance. For example, suppose that growth rates initially rise and then fall as the growth of government expenditures continuously increases, with attendant heavy financing burdens, measured by rising values of θ. In this case, positive coefficients of government expenditures will be obtained for linear regressions using data with

[20]These simulation results are confirmed by the qualitative analysis of the endogenous growth model summarized in Table 6.1.

low θ, negative coefficients for those that rely on high θ, and coefficients biased toward zero for linear regressions using both low and high θ. The endogenous growth model and the linear regression results reported below thus include the ratio θ of government deficits to GDP.

No data for k^* exist in developing countries, so that Equation (6.32) cannot be estimated. However, since there are data on $g^* - n$, Equation (6.31) can be tested. In general, the average per capita growth rate $g^* - n$ is inversely related to the starting value of per capita real income y_0, the familiar convergence property of neoclassical growth models (including the present one). Thus, for empirical testing, the following linear specification can be considered:

$$g^* - n = a0 + a1s + a2\chi + a3\xi + a4\omega + a5\theta + a6n + a7y_0 + a8\lambda + a9\mu. \tag{6.33}$$

Of the nine explanatory variables in Equation (6.33), data on only the last two are unavailable. Recall that μ is the real growth of expenditures on operations and maintenance of capital assets, while λ is the exogenous rate of labor-augmenting technological progress. The parameter λ can be interpreted as capturing all the unobserved country-specific factors that raise labor productivity (cultural, social, ethnic, political, and religious). Regional dummy variables will be included to reflect such factors. The unobserved series μ is assumed to enter the error term in a well-behaved manner. For present purposes, the following multiple regression can be estimated:

$$g^* - n = a0 + a1s + a2\chi + a3\xi + a4\omega + a5\theta + a6n + a7y_0 + a8 \text{ dummy}. \tag{6.34}$$

The endogenous growth model's equilibrium predictions (where the learning coefficient $\alpha > 0$) are that $a1$, $a2$, $a3$, $a4 > 0$, and $a5$, $a6$, $a7 < 0$. The Solow–Swan model (where $\alpha = 0$) predicts that $a1 = a2 = a3 = a4 = a5 = a6 = 0$, and $a7 < 0$. The data set consists of annual averages of observations over the period 1975–1986 for 36 developing countries from five geographic regions.[21]

The regression results are reported below, where the insignificant coefficients of the regional dummy variables are suppressed (t-values are in parentheses):

$$\begin{aligned} g^* - n = {} & \underset{(0.50)}{0.01} + \underset{(3.06)}{0.183s} + \underset{(2.43)}{0.038\chi} + \underset{(1.91)}{0.093\xi} + \underset{(1.54)}{0.063\omega} - \underset{(2.39)}{0.189\theta} \\ & - \underset{(1.90)}{0.665n} - \underset{(2.59)}{0.000015y_0} \qquad (6.35) \\ R^2 = {} & 0.7952; \quad SEE = 0.0144. \end{aligned}$$

An R^2 of close to 0.8 is relatively high for a cross-country regression.[22] All the regression coefficients have the expected signs. The coefficients for the saving rate, ratio of foreign trade to GDP, the ratio of fiscal deficits to GDP, and the initial level of per capita income are statistically significant at the 5 percent level or better. The coefficients for the growth of real expenditures on education and health and for the rate of population growth are statistically significant at the 10 percent level or better. The coefficient for the growth of real expenditures on social security, housing, and recreation is marginally significant.

Since θ (government dissaving) is a part of total s, a discussion of the coefficients of s and θ in the above regression would be useful. The endogenous growth model divides the total long-run impact of changes in s on $g^* - n$ into two components: (1) an element arising from changes in the private saving rate induced by changes in its determinants other than changes in θ; and (2) a composite factor stemming from changes in s directly as a result of changes in θ and indirectly via induced changes in the private saving rate. Component (1) is measured by the coefficient of s in the above regression equation, while component (2) is captured by the

[21] See Appendix 6.A for the data, sources, and definitions, and list of countries in the sample.

[22] Ramanathan (1982) notes that typical values of R^2 for equations estimating the growth performance in developing countries using cross-country data fall in the range $0.3 \approx 0.4$.

coefficient of θ in the same regression. Since the estimates of these two coefficients are nearly identical (with opposite signs), the results suggest a symmetric response of $g^* - n$, in opposite direction, either to a change in the private saving rate or to a change in the rate of government dissaving.

The empirical results clearly show that the following factors promote per capita economic growth: steady increases in saving/ investment rates, in the ratio of foreign trade (exports plus imports) to GDP, and in the growth of real expenditures on education and health. On the other hand, rapid population growth rates and high ratios of fiscal deficits to GDP are followed by slow average growth rates of per capita output. There is also empirical support for the convergence property of the endogenous growth and Solow–Swan models — the significant negative relationship between the initial level of per capita real income and subsequent average growth.

6.4 Summary and Conclusions

This chapter has presented a simple neoclassical growth model with endogenous technical change and contrasted its equilibrium properties with those of the standard Solow–Swan model. It is found that, contrary to the predictions of the latter model, the equilibrium growth rate of per capita output is influenced in a systematic way by changes in the private rates of saving and depreciation, population growth, and in public policies with regard to opening up of the economy (trade liberalization), fiscal deficits, spending for human resource development (the growth of real expenditures on education and health), and net investment (public capital formation and real expenditures on operations and maintenance of existing capital assets).

In the absence of learning by doing, the model's optimal net rate of return to capital is equal to the sum of the population growth n and the exogenous rate of labor-augmenting technical change λ, or that the optimal saving rate should be set equal to the share of capital in aggregate output — these are familiar *Golden Rule* theorems from standard optimal growth theory. With learning by doing, these standard *Golden Rule* results are revised: The optimal net rate of return to capital is higher than $n + \lambda$, or alternatively, the optimal saving rate should be set at only a fraction of capital's income share, because of endogenous growth and the induced learning associated with increases in the capital stock.

The analytic and simulation results appear to favor the endogenous growth over the Solow–Swan model. Simulations show that the speed of adjustment toward equilibrium is substantially faster in a model of endogenous growth. Moreover, an increase in learning by doing further reduces the adjustment time. The empirical results also validate the endogenous growth model, particularly those relating to the positive per capita growth effects of public policies for greater openness of the trading system, high saving rates, and rapid growth in expenditures on human development, and those relating to the negative per capita growth effects of rapid population growth and high ratios of fiscal deficits to GDP. Finally, the convergence property of the endogenous growth model has been confirmed (as has the convergence of the Solow–Swan model). However, the result on the saving rate-growth relationship is tenuous, in view of the short time interval (12 years) of the sample. Since the realized growth dynamics in the Solow–Swan model over this relatively short period would also show a positive relationship, the empirical results would hardly invalidate the Solow–Swan approach, pending additional research. Efforts are currently underway to use the very long time series (from 1950 to 1985) from Summers and Heston (1988) in testing the equilibrium relationships among the growth rates of per capita real income, saving rates, population growth rates, and the growth and size of government. The 36 years spanned by this data set would meet the adjustment time estimates of 14–35 years for equilibrium growth to be reached (but not the adjustment time estimates of 42–106 years in a model without endogenous learning).

The policy implications are straightforward. Public policies that raise the capital/labor ratio have magnified effects on the growth rate of per capita income, owing to induced learning by doing associated with a rising capital stock. Policies that enhance the learning process also accelerate the speed of adjustment toward the balanced growth path. Examples of such policies include measures to raise saving and investment, permit the steady expansion of the tradable sector, and accelerate the growth of real expenditures on education and health. On the other hand, there are clear limits to the size of government in relation to GDP, because of the increasingly heavy costs of burgeoning deficits.

Appendix 6.A: Data Used in the Study

The data, except for foreign trade flows, are drawn from Orsmond (1990), which are based on the IMF Government Financial Statistics and International Financial Statistics. Foreign trade flows are taken from the World Economic Outlook database. The sample consists of observations averaged over the period 1975 through 1986 for 36 developing countries.

PYG: Real per capita GDP growth rate, annual average;
KY: Gross investment divided by nominal GDP, annual average;
XC: Change in ratio of sum of nominal exports and imports to nominal GDP between 1975 and 1986;
EG: Growth rate of government expenditures on education and health, annual average, deflated by GDP deflator for budget year;
SG: Growth rate of government expenditures on social security, housing, and recreation, annual average, deflated by GDP deflator for budget year;
DY: Nominal fiscal deficits divided by nominal GDP, annual average;
PG: Population growth rate, annual average;
GDP75: Per capita income level in 1975 US dollars;
DUM(i): Dummy variable that assumes the value of 1 for region i, zero otherwise, i = AFRICA, ASIA, MIDDLE EAST, WESTERN HEMISPHERE.

List of Countries

The countries in the sample are:

Botswana	Mexico
Burkina Faso	Morocco
Cameroon	Myanmar
Chile	Nepal
Costa Rica	Pakistan
Dominican Republic	Panama
Egypt	Singapore
El Salvador	Sri Lanka
Ethiopia	Tanzania
Fiji	Thailand
Guatemala	Togo
Indonesia	Tunisia
Iran	Turkey
Kenya	Uruguay
Korea	Yemen Arab Republic
Liberia	Zambia
Mauritius	Zimbabwe

The Data

	PYG	KY	XC	EG	SG	DY	PG	GDP75
Botswana	7.4	29.8	3.5	17.5	38.7	−4.2	4.7	350.0
Korea	7.1	28.8	10.6	10.2	12.9	1.7	1.4	580.0
Singapore	5.7	40.3	35.6	12.8	12.8	−1.7	1.2	2540.0
Yemen Arab Rep.	3.7	27.9	−9.4	32.1	2.0	10.8	2.8	140.0
Pakistan	3.4	17.0	1.1	10.1	32.2	7.5	3.1	140.0
Cameroon	3.1	22.4	−7.6	0.0	13.3	0.5	3.0	310.0
Mali	3.9	24.1	11.1	9.0	6.1	4.1	2.1	360.0
Indonesia	4.0	24.4	−4.0	9.3	2.0	2.2	2.0	210.0

(*Continued*)

(*Continued*)

	PYG	KY	XC	EG	SG	DY	PG	GDP75
Paraguay	2.6	23.7	11.6	1.2	9.2	0.3	3.2	550.0
Myanmar	3.2	15.9	−0.3	7.0	10.0	−0.1	2.4	150.0
Sri Lanka	3.6	23.3	13.8	6.7	0.8	10.5	1.6	220.0
Tunisia	2.5	29.4	2.5	5.0	9.5	4.7	2.6	710.0
Kenya	0.8	20.9	−15.8	5.8	5.1	5.7	4.2	230.0
Panama	1.9	23.4	−26.7	4.1	9.1	7.6	2.6	1,030.0
Mauritius	3.1	24.4	−3.1	7.7	−0.5	8.5	1.3	300.0
Burkina Faso	2.7	22.9	4.6	6.7	18.7	0.3	1.6	100.0
Egypt	1.8	25.8	25.2	9.4	0.3	13.1	2.5	310.0
Turkey	2.1	20.2	15.4	0.7	2.7	4.3	2.0	830.0
Chile	2.2	14.7	8.0	3.4	7.3	−0.3	1.7	860.0
Morocco	1.3	25.2	−4.3	5.3	6.5	10.8	2.5	500.0
Nepal	0.9	17.7	10.7	11.3	14.3	4.6	2.8	110.0
Mexico	0.9	21.1	5.2	4.0	0.0	6.6	2.6	1,360.0
Ethiopia	−1.2	10.3	8.0	6.3	10.8	6.0	4.6	90.0
Dominican Republic	0.4	21.2	−8.9	2.0	1.6	2.1	2.8	670.0
Costa Rica	0.0	21.8	−38.9	1.5	9.5	3.3	3.1	950.0
Zimbabwe	−0.5	17.8	−29.8	10.9	5.0	7.9	2.9	570.0
Fiji	0.2	20.6	−14.3	4.8	13.0	3.8	2.0	1030.0
Guatemala	−0.4	15.3	−16.5	13.9	−1.2	2.7	2.5	570.0
Togo	−0.9	29.1	0.4	5.9	6.6	11.3	2.9	260.0
Tanzania	−1.8	18.5	−16.0	−5.6	3.8	8.8	3.6	160.0
Venezuela	−1.4	26.4	−17.4	2.7	2.6	0.7	3.1	2,380.0
Uruguay	0.8	13.3	5.8	−1.8	3.8	2.6	0.6	1,370.0
Iran	−2.6	22.7	−58.9	3.5	10.1	5.8	3.8	1,449.7
Zambia	−3.2	18.6	9.0	−3.4	−0.5	13.7	3.5	550.0
Liberia	−3.3	22.4	−29.2	6.1	13.7	7.8	3.3	410.0
El Salvador	−2.1	15.9	−21.1	−3.4	0.3	2.8	1.9	440.0

Appendix 6.B[23]: The Endogenous Growth Model in a Ramsey Framework

6.B.1 *The Model*

Assume the following institutional arrangements of a closed, perfectly competitive economy with rational agents and a unit-homogeneous aggregate production function. One good is produced that can be consumed or invested. Enterprises rent capital K from households and hire workers L to produce output in each period. Households own the physical capital stock and receive income from working, renting capital, and managing the enterprises. Profits Π from managing enterprises are:

$$\Pi = F(K, L) - rK - wL$$

in which r is the rental rate and w is the real wage rate. The budget constraint of a representative household is

$$C + \dot{K} + \delta K = rK + wL + \Pi,$$

where C is consumption and δ is depreciation. Dividing both sides by L,

$$c + \dot{k} + (\delta + g^L)k = rk + w + \pi, \tag{6.B.1}$$

where, as before, lower case letters are expressed as ratios to effective labor L, and g^L is given by

$$\dot{L}/L = g^L = (\dot{A}/A) + n, \tag{6.B.2}$$

where A is labor-augmenting technology and n is the exogenous growth rate of the working population.

The representative household maximizes a discounted stream of lifetime consumption C, subject to the budget constraint (6.B.1) in

[23]This appendix is previously unpublished. It is added to this chapter to extend the analysis to the Ramsey (1928)–Cass (1965)–Koopmans (1965) optimal control framework.

which instantaneous utility is of the CRRA form[24]:

$$N(0)^{1-\theta}\int_0^{\infty}\frac{(C/L)}{1-\theta}^{1-\theta}A^{1-\theta}e^{-\rho*t}dt. \tag{6.B.3}$$

For the integral to converge, I adopt the standard assumption that $\rho^* = \rho - (1-\theta)n > 0$.

In maximizing (6.B.3) subject to (6.B.1), each household takes as parametrically given the time paths of r, w, π, and A. When making decisions about consumption and capital accumulation, each household is small enough to affect r, w, π, and A.

The household's Hamiltonian is

$$H = e^{-\rho*t}[(c^{(1-\theta)}/(1-\theta]A^{(1-\theta)} + \varphi[rk + w + \pi - c - (\delta + g^L)k]. \tag{6.B.4}$$

After substituting Equation (6.B.2) and $\rho^* = \rho - (1-\theta)n$, the first-order conditions yield:

$$\dot{c}/c = (1/\theta)[(r - \delta - \rho - \theta n - \theta(\dot{A}/A)] \tag{6.B.5}$$

$$\dot{k} = rk + w + \pi - c - [\delta + n + (\dot{A}/A)]k. \tag{6.B.6}$$

Now, the economy-wide resource constraint is

$$C + \dot{K} + \delta K = F(K, L).$$

Dividing both sides by L,

$$c + \dot{k} + (\delta + g^L)k = f(k). \tag{6.B.7}$$

In competitive equilibrium, $r = f'(k)$ and $w = f(k) - kf'(k)$, implying $\pi = 0$. Substituting these expressions for r, w, and π, and

[24]For brevity, the time t is suppressed for all variables.

for

$$\dot{A} = \phi(K/N) + \mu A \tag{6.B.8}$$

into Equations (6.B.5) and (6.B.6), the optimal time paths for c and k are as follows:

$$\dot{c}/c = (1/\theta)[(f'(k) - \delta - \rho - \theta(n + \mu) - \theta\phi k], \tag{6.B.9}$$

$$\dot{k} = f(k) - c - (\delta + n + \mu)k - \phi k^2. \tag{6.B.10}$$

The transversality condition is:[25]

$$\lim_{t\to\infty} \mathrm{e}^{-\rho * t}\varphi k = 0\,. \tag{6.B.11}$$

If there is no learning by doing ($\phi = 0$), the model (6.B.9) and (6.B.10) reduces to the extended Ramsey (1928)–Cass (1965)–Koopmans (1965) model that allows for population growth n and exogenous technical progress μ, with the key property that the equilibrium growth rate of per capita output is fixed entirely by μ and thus is independent of preferences and policy.

6.B.2 *The Reduced Model*

The system (6.B.9) and (6.B.10) represents the reduced model in c, k, and time t. The equilibrium (asymptotic) values c^* and k^* are the roots of (6.B.9) and (6.B.10) equated to zero.

$$f'(k^*) - \delta - \rho - \theta\mu - \theta n - \theta\phi k^* = 0 \tag{6.B.12}$$

$$f(k*) - c^* - (\delta + n + \mu)k^* - \phi k^{*2} = 0. \tag{6.B.13}$$

Let J be the Jacobian associated with the system (6.B.12) and (6.B.13).

$$J = \begin{bmatrix} 0 & (c/\theta)(f''(k) - \theta\phi) \\ -1 & (f'(k) - \delta - \mu - n - 2\phi k) \end{bmatrix}.$$

[25] As a standard condition, the no-Ponzi game is also imposed.

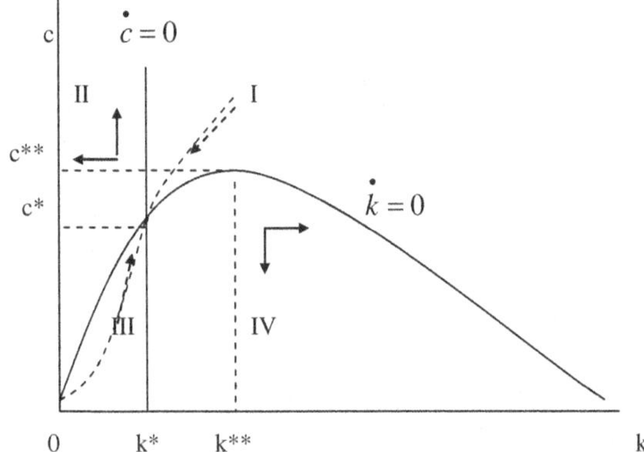

Figure 6.B.1. Long-run equilibrium.

Evaluated in the neighborhood of the steady-state k^*, c^*,[26]

$$J = \begin{bmatrix} 0 & -0.0249 \\ -1 & 0.0400 \end{bmatrix}.$$

The associated eigenvalues are $\lambda_1 = -0.13904$ and $\lambda_2 = 0.17907$.[27]

Figure 6.B.1 shows the phase diagram in c, k space with equilibrium values k^*, c^*. The pair (k^*, c^*) is saddle path stable and is the *Golden Utility* solution, while the pair (k^{**}, c^{**}) is the *Golden Rule* solution.[28] While the latter maximizes c at c^{**}, the former maximizes intertemporal utility. The equilibrium capital intensity k^* is a function of all the parameters of the model, including the parameters of the preference or utility function, namely the discount rate ρ and the coefficient of relative risk aversion θ or its reciprocal, the elasticity of intertemporal substitution $(1/\theta)$, and other parameters, notably the learning coefficient ϕ and the

[26]Parameter values used are: $\alpha = 0.3$, $\delta = 0.04$, $\mu = 0.01$, $\theta = 1.5$, $\phi = 0.003$, $\rho = 0.04$, and $n = 0.02$. The parameter α is the exponent in the Cobb–Douglass production $f(k) = k^{\alpha}$. The solutions for k and c are $k^* = 3.31$, $c^* = 1.17$. The optimal saving rate is 0.1846 and the steady-state growth rate of per capita output is 0.02, of which the endogenous component is half at 0.01 and the other half is μ.

[27]The median lag is 5 years $(\ln 2/|\lambda_1|)$. For more details, see Section 6.8.4.

[28]The transversality condition (6.B.11) rules out quadrants II and IV in Figure 6.B.1. On the *Golden Rule* solution, see Phelps (1966).

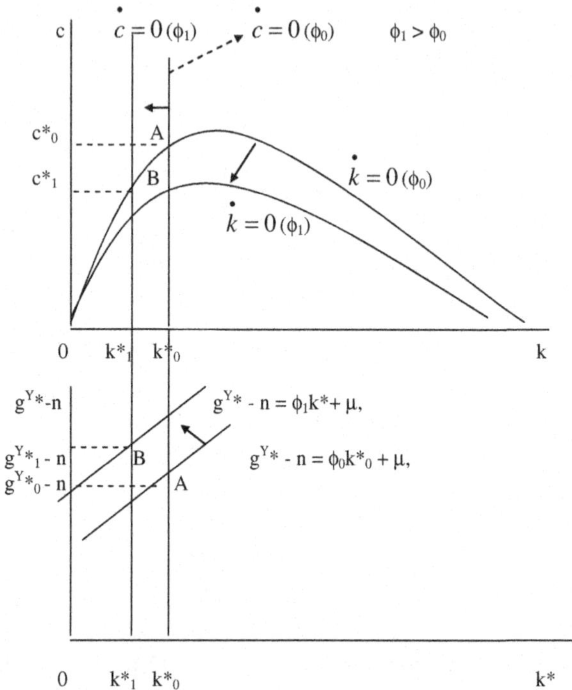

Figure 6.B.2. Growth effects of an increase in learning by doing.

parameters and form of the production function $f(k^*)$. Since the equilibrium growth rate of per capita output $g^{Y*} - n$ equals $\phi k^* + \mu$, any public policy that enhances the equilibrium capital intensity k^* and the learning coefficient ϕ raises long-run per capita output growth.

6.B.2.1 *Comparative Dynamics*

Figure 6.B.2 illustrates the growth effects of an increase in learning by doing.

In the upper panel, the intersection at point $A(k_0^*, c_0^*)$ shows the initial equilibrium corresponding to a given level of the learning coefficient ϕ_0. In the lower panel, the vertical axis measures the equilibrium growth rate of per capita output, and the horizontal axis measures equilibrium capital intensity. The $g^{Y*} - n$ curve, $\phi k^* + \mu$, has a positive slope equal to ϕ. Assume that public policy

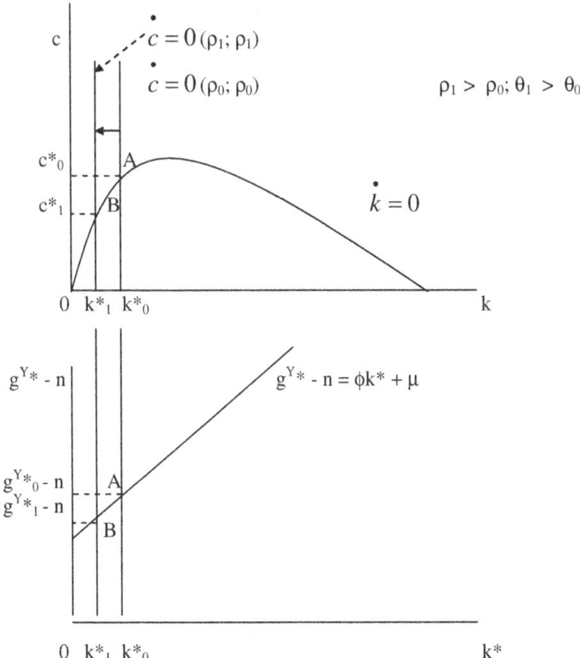

Figure 6.B.3. Growth effects of higher discounting and lower inter-temporal elasticity of substitution.

subsidizes on-the-job-training at enterprises, resulting in an increase in the learning coefficient from ϕ_0 to ϕ_1. In the upper panel, the new equilibrium shifts to point $B(k_1^*, c_1^*)$, with both equilibrium consumption per effective worker and equilibrium capital intensity lower than at point A. In the lower panel, the $g^{Y*} - n$ curve shifts upward to $g^{Y*} - n = \phi_1 k_1^* + \mu$, with the equilibrium growth rate of per capita output higher.

Figure 6.B.3 illustrates the effects of a higher discounting of future consumption or a higher degree of relative risk aversion (lower intertemporal elasticity of substitution). The initial equilibrium is at point $A(k_0^*, c_0^*)$, shown in the upper panel. The increase in ρ shifts the $\dot{c} = 0$ curve to the left, intersecting the stationary $\dot{k} = 0$ curve at point $B(k_1^*, c_1^*)$. Both equilibrium consumption per effective worker and equilibrium capital intensity are lower than before. In the lower panel, as k^* falls from k_0^* to k_1^*, learning by doing drops

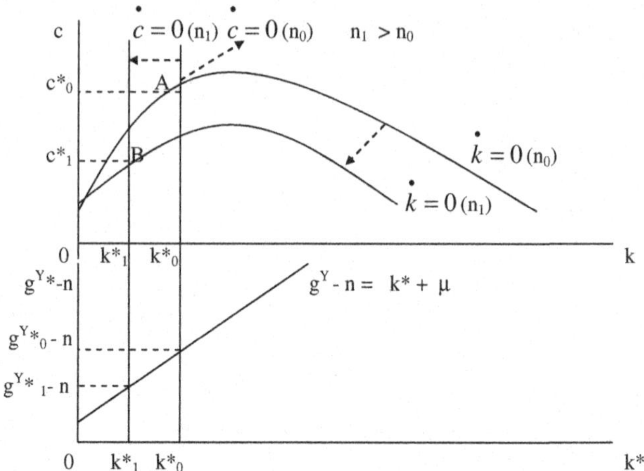

Figure 6.B.4. Growth effects of an increase in population growth.

and so does the equilibrium growth rate of per capita output, from $g_0^{Y*} - n$ to $g_1^{Y*} - n$ (downward movement along the $g^{Y*} - n$ curve). For similar reasons, a higher degree of relative risk aversion θ or a lower intertemporal elasticity of substitution, $1/\theta$, would have similar negative effects on the steady-state growth rate of per capita output.

Finally, the model yields a more empirically plausible prediction about the effect of population growth n on the steady-state growth rate of per capita output, as illustrated in Figure 6.B.4, a result that is particularly relevant to developing countries. In the upper panel, an increase in n from n_0 to n_1 shifts the $\dot{c} = 0$ curve to the left and the $\dot{k} = 0$ curve downward.

The steady-state equilibrium moves from point A to point B, with lower equilibrium consumption per efficient labor and lower equilibrium level of capital intensity. In the lower panel, the decline in the equilibrium stock of capital per efficient worker cuts learning by doing and leads to lower steady-state growth rates of productivity and per capita output.[29]

[29]The effects of an increase in the depreciation rate of physical capital are similar. An increase in δ shifts the consumption growth curve to the left and the capital intensity growth downward, with the two curves intersecting at a lower equilibrium c^* and k^*. A lower k^* means lower degree of learning by doing

6.B.3 *Optimal Saving Rate*

From Equations (6.B.12) and (6.B.13), the endogenously derived optimal saving rate is given by:

$$s = \{(n + \mu + \phi k^* + \delta)/[\theta(n + \mu + \phi k^*) + \delta + \rho]\}\alpha. \tag{6.B.14}$$

If $\rho = 0$, $\phi = 0$, and $\theta = 1$, then the optimal saving rate is

$$s = \alpha, \tag*{(6.B.14)$'$}$$

which is the standard Solow–Swan result in a world of exogenous technical change. That is, the saving rate must be set equal to the income share of capital.[30] If $\rho = 0$, $\theta = 1$, and $\phi > 0$, then the saving rate must be set equal to $[(n+\mu+\phi k^* + \delta)/(n+\mu+\phi k^* + \delta)]\alpha = \alpha$. However, if $\rho > 0$, $\theta > 1$, and $\phi > 0$, then the optimal saving rate is not only a function of the deep parameters ρ, θ, ϕ, μ, δ, and n, as well as k^*, but must also be set equal to a fraction of capital's income share, with the fraction equal to the term $\{(n + \mu + \phi k^* + \delta)/[\theta(n + \mu + \phi k^*) + \delta + \rho]\}$.[31]

6.B.4 *The Speed of Adjustment to Equilibrium*

This section addresses the question whether the presence of learning by doing increases the speed of adjustment of the model to its steady-state. The nonlinear system is described by Equations (6.B.9) and (6.B.10). Linearize this system around the steady-state values c^*, k^*.

$$\begin{pmatrix} \dot{c} \\ \dot{k} \end{pmatrix} = J \begin{pmatrix} c - c^* \\ k - k^* \end{pmatrix} \tag{6.B.15}$$

in which J is the Jacobian matrix. Denote by v_1 and v_2 the two given eigenvectors and $\lambda_1 < 0$ and $\lambda_2 > 0$ the two eigenvalues associated

---

and thus lower productivity and, consequently, lower equilibrium growth rate of per capita output.

[30]In Figure 6.B.1, this condition is associated with maximum consumption per L at $c^{**} > c^*$.

[31]In Figure 6.B.1, this condition is associated with maximum utility at $c^* < c^{**}$.

with J. Then,

$$\begin{pmatrix} c - c^* \\ k - k^* \end{pmatrix} = C_1 v_1 \mathrm{e}^{\lambda 1t} + C_2 v_2 \mathrm{e}^{\lambda 2t}. \tag{6.B.16}$$

$C_2 = 0$ must hold for $k \to k^*$. $C_2 > 0$ violates the transversality condition; if $C_2 < 0$, then $k \to 0$ in quadrant II, Figure 6.B.1, which is also a violation of the transversality condition. Therefore,

$$c_t = c^* + e_1^{\lambda t}(c_0 - c^*) \tag{6.B.17}$$

$$k_t = k^* + e_1^{\lambda t}(k_0 - k^*). \tag{6.B.18}$$

Next, define the adjustment ratio,

$$p_t = (g_t - g_0)/(g^* - g_0), \tag{6.B.19}$$

in which $g_t = g * + \alpha(\dot{k}/k_t)$, g^* is the steady-state growth rate of output, and $(\dot{k}/kt)$ is given by (6.B.15) and (6.B.18). The denominator is the distance the output growth rate at time t has to adjust to reach its steady-state value from an initial value. The numerator is the distance the growth rate has adjusted by t. Substituting (6.B.15) and (6.B.18) into (6.B.19) solves for t (in years) required for a fraction p_t of the way from g_0 to g^*, from which Tables 6.B.1–6.B.3 are computed.

Table 6.B.1. Estimated adjustment in years to the steady-state from initial high growth rate ($g_0 = 0.09$) and low intertemporal elasticity of substitution ($1/\theta = 0.53$).

	p_t	$\phi = 0$ $g^{Y*} = 0.0300$	$\phi = 0.004$ $g^{Y*} = 0.0417$	$\phi = 0.008$ $g^{Y*} = 0.0501$
	0.25	1.6	1.4	1.3
	0.50	4.2	3.6	3.3
	0.75	9.6	7.9	7.0
	0.90	17.8	14.0	12.3
Memorandum item:				
Endogenous growth component (ϕk^*)		0.0000	0.0117	0.0201
Saving rate (s^*)		0.1765	0.1735	0.1719

Table 6.B.2. Estimated adjustment in years to the steady-state from initial high growth rate ($g_0 = 0.09$) and medium intertemporal elasticity of substitution ($1/\theta = 0.67$).

	p_t	$\phi = 0$ $g^{Y*} = 0.0300$	$\phi = 0.004$ $g^{Y*} = 0.0427$	$\phi = 0.008$ $g^{Y*} = 0.05196$
	0.25	1.4	1.3	1.2
	0.50	3.7	3.2	3.0
	0.75	8.5	7.1	6.4
	0.90	15.7	12.8	11.3
Memorandum item:				
Endogenous growth component (ϕk^*)		0.0000	0.0127	0.0219
Saving rate (s^*)		0.1826	0.1851	0.1865

Table 6.B.3. Estimated adjustment in years to the steady-state from initial high growth rate ($g_0 = 0.09$) and high intertemporal elasticity of substitution ($1/\theta = 0.91$).

	p_t	$\phi = 0$ $g^{Y*} = 0.0300$	$\phi = 0.004$ $g^{Y*} = 0.0437$	$\phi = 0.008$ $g^{Y*} = 0.0543$
	0.25	1.2	1.1	1.1
	0.50	3.1	2.8	2.7
	0.75	7.2	6.3	5.8
	0.90	13.4	11.3	10.3
Memorandum item:				
Endogenous growth component (ϕk^*)		0.0000	0.0138	0.0243
Saving rate (s^*)		0.1891	0.1992	0.2054

Tables 6.B.1–6.B.3 assume an initial growth rate of 9 percent per annum.[32] The steady-state annual growth rate ranges from 3 percent to 5.4 percent, depending on the elasticity of intertemporal substitution and the learning coefficient. Szpiro (1986) tested the CRRA utility function used in this appendix on the basis of data for 15 industrial countries using property/liability insurance data, and found that the CRRA cannot be rejected. His estimate of θ

[32]This is a realistic initial position in developing countries with relatively small stocks of capital per efficient worker.

is between 1 and 2.[33] Therefore, each table assumes a particular value for the intertemporal substitution elasticity, from low (0.53) to medium (0.67) to high (0.91), corresponding to $\theta = 1.9$, 1.5, and 1.1. The first columns of the tables show the fraction p_t of adjustment. Subsequent columns show estimates of adjustment speed in years corresponding to various values of the learning coefficient ranging from a zero value (standard model, $\phi = 0$ or no learning by doing) to $\phi = 0.004$ and $\phi = 0.008$. The memorandum items show (1) the values for the endogenous growth component (equal to the product of the learning coefficient and the equilibrium capital intensity), ranging from zero when $\phi = 0, 1.4$ percentage points when $\phi = 0.004$ and 2.4 two percentage points when $\phi = 0.008$; and (2) the optimal saving rate, ranging from 0.1765 when $(1/\theta) = 0.53$ and $\phi = 0$, to 0.2054 when $(1/\theta) = 0.91$ and $\phi = 0.008$. In all numerical simulations, the Cobb–Douglas production function used is $f(k) = k^{\alpha}$, with the following parameter values: $\alpha = 0.3$, $\rho = 0.04$, $\mu = 0.01$, $\delta = 0.04$, and $n = 0.02$.[34]

Tables 6.B.1–6.B.3 clearly show that, for each given degree of the elasticity of intertemporal substitution, the presence of learning by doing ($\phi > 0$, as opposed to $\phi = 0$) not only leads to higher long-run growth rate of per capita output, but also to a faster speed of adjustment to the steady-state. Moreover, an increase in the degree of learning by doing (increase in ϕ) contributes to an even faster adjustment speed. The intuitive reason for the latter result is that the learning by doing component of the effective labor growth equation (natural rate) adjusts to any discrepancy between the capital growth equation (warranted rate) and the natural rate. The Solow–Swan model focuses *exclusively* on the adjustment of the warranted rate. The extended model of this paper relies on *both* the adjustments of the warranted and natural rates of growth, so that the speed of adjustment to the steady-state (defined by equality between the two rates) is a lot faster.

[33]Szpiro's estimate of θ for the United States is 1.19, which implies an estimate of 0.84 for the elasticity of intertemporal substitution.

[34]The computations reported in Tables 6.B.1–6.B.3 use Microsoft EXCEL's *Goal Seek* and *Solver* tools.

The tables also show that, holding the learning coefficient constant, adjustment to the steady-state is faster as the elasticity of intertemporal substitution increases. Looking at the last columns of each table, in which the endogenous component of technical change adds at least 2 percentage points to the steady-state growth rate of output, whereas it takes between 13 and 18 years for the standard model with no learning by doing to reach 90 percent of the time required to reach its steady-state GDP growth path, depending on the elasticity of intertemporal substitution, it would take only between 10 and 12 years for the model with learning by doing to converge to the steady-state growth path.[35]

Figure 6.B.5 graphs the adjustment of the annual growth rate of output to its steady-state level when the learning coefficient $\phi = 0.008$ (the endogenous growth component adds 2.4 percentage points to the steady-state growth rate of output) and $(1/\theta) = 0.91$ (high elasticity of intertemporal substitution). The initial and steady-state annual growth rates of output are 9 percent and 5.4 percent, respectively. The initial conditions, shown in Figure 6.B.1 somewhere in quadrant III, are more relevant to the developing world that is initially understocked with capital, and therefore, its assumed initial growth rate (0.090) is above the steady-state level (0.054).[36]

At time $t = 0$, the growth rate is 9 percent per annum. After the first year, the growth rate is 8.1 percent; after nearly 3 years, it is 7.2 percent; after 6 years, it is 6.3 percent; and after 10 years, it is 5.8 percent, just 0.4 percentage point off the steady-state growth rate. This is a plausible adjustment speed, since many developing countries (notably in East Asia) have been growing at over 5 percent annually for at least a decade.

I ran a numerical simulation for the United States, using the following parameter values and initial conditions: $\alpha = 0.3$, $\delta = 0.04$,

[35]That is, 10 years for the high substitution elasticity of 0.91, 11 years for the medium elasticity of 0.67, and 12 years for the low elasticity of 0.53.

[36]The initial growth rate is based on initial $k_0 = 1.54$ and initial $c_0 = 0.8283$, both levels below the steady-state values $k^* = 3.04$ and $c^* = 1.1091$.

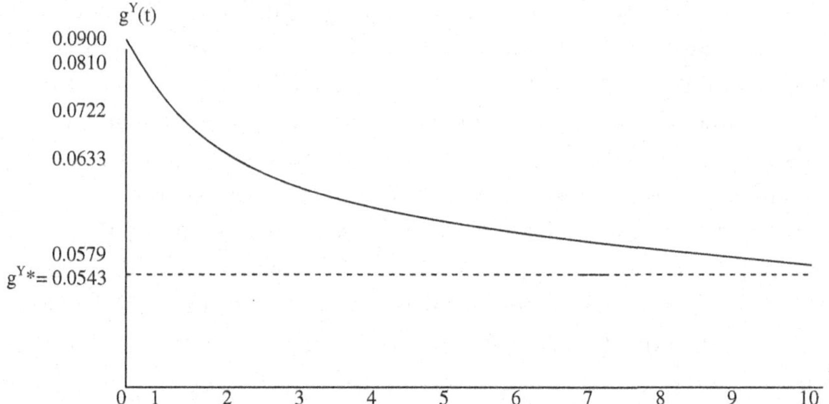

Figure 6.B.5. The developing world: Adjustment to the optimal steady-state growth path.

$\phi = 0.003$,[37] $\mu = 0.01$, $\theta = 1.19$, $\rho = 0.04$, $n = 0.02$; and $g_0^Y = 0.01$, based on $k_0 = 4.51$ and $c_0 = 1.654$. The estimate for $\theta = 1.19$ owes to Szpiro (1986). The steady-state optimal values are: $g^{Y*} = 0.04$, $k^* = 3.51$, and $c^* = 1.175$. These initial conditions, shown in Figure 6.B.1 somewhere in quadrant I, are more relevant to the United States; owing to its advanced state, it is initially overstocked with capital, and therefore, its assumed initial growth rate (0.01) is below the steady-state level (0.04). Figure 6.B.6 graphs the adjustment of the growth rate of output toward the steady-state level plotted against time (in years). With its high degree of intertemporal substitution, from an initial growth rate of one percent, it would take 16 years for the US economy to reach a 3.7 percent annual GDP growth rate, equivalent to 90 percent of the time required to reach its steady-state GDP growth path of 4 percent per annum. This is indeed a reasonable adjustment speed, since the United States (and many other advanced economies) has been growing at this rate for at least this long.

[37]This value adds a percentage point to the steady-state growth rate of output $[\phi k^* = 0.003(3.51)]$. This lower contribution of endogenous growth (compared to its larger contribution in developing countries) partly reflects the existence of a large R&D sector in the United States, not explained endogenously by the model. That is to say, learning by doing via on-the-job training is much larger in developing countries.

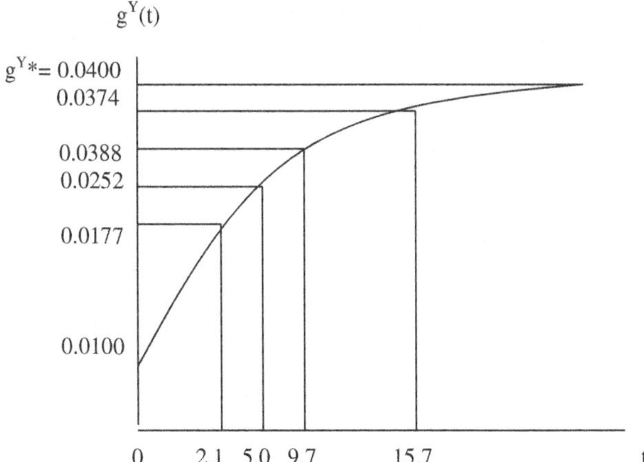

Figure 6.B.6. The United States: Adjustment to the optimal steady-state growth path.

6.B.5 *Conclusion*

This appendix has adopted a more realistic specification of learning by doing and embedded it in a Ramsey optimal growth framework without invoking increasing returns to aggregate capital and without an R&D sector. A simple extension of the Solow–Swan growth model in an optimizing framework produces empirically plausible and testable predictions about the per capita output growth effects of changes in preferences, in population growth, and in public policies that affect the equilibrium capital intensity and, directly or indirectly, any or all the model's parameters, particularly the degree of learning by doing associated with the economy's stock of capital per efficient worker. Numerical simulations also indicate the extended model's faster adjustment to the steady-state from an initial disequilibrium position.

References

Arrow, K (1962). The economic implications of learning by doing. *Review of Economic Studies*, 29, 155–173.

Bardhan, P and S Lewis (1970). Models of growth with imported inputs. *Economica*, 37, 373–385.

Becker, G, K Murphy and R Tamura (1990). Human capital, fertility, and economic growth. *Journal of Political Economy*, 98, S12–S37.

Cass, D (1965). Optimum growth in an aggregative model of capital accumulation. *Review of Economic Studies*, 32, 233–240.

Chen, E (1979). *Hyper-Growth in Asian Economies: A Comparative Study of Hong Kong, Japan, Korea, Singapore, and Taiwan.* NY: Holmes and Meier.

Conlisk, J (1967). A modified neo-classical growth model with endogenous technical change. *Southern Economic Journal*, 34, 199–208.

Domar, E (1946). Capital expansion, rate of growth, and employment. *Econometrica*, 14, 137–147.

Edwards, S (1992). Trade orientation, distortions and growth in developing countries. *Journal of Development Economics*, 39, 31–57.

Feder, G (1983). On exports and economic growth. *Journal of Development Economics*, 12, 59–73.

Grossman, G and E Helpman (1990). Comparative advantage and long-run growth. *American Economic Review*, 80, 796–815.

Harrod, R (1939). An essay in dynamic theory. *Economic Journal*, 49, 14–33.

Inada, K-I (1963). On a two-sector model of economic growth: Comments and generalization. *Review of Economic Studies*, 30, 119–127.

Keesing, D (1967). Outward-looking policies and economic development. *Economic Journal*, 77, 303–320.

Khan, M and D Villanueva (1991). Macroeconomic policies and long-term growth: A conceptual and empirical review. *International Monetary Fund Working Paper 91/28.*

Khang, C (1987). Export-led economic growth: The case of technology transfer. *Economic Studies Quarterly*, 38, 131–147.

Knight, M, N Loayza, and D Villanueva (1993). Testing the neoclassical theory of economic growth: A panel data approach. *IMF Staff Papers*, 40, 512–541.

Koopmans, T (1965). On the concept of optimal economic growth. In Ch. 4, *The Economic Approach to Development Planning.* Amsterdam: North-Holland Publishing.

Lucas, R (1988). On the mechanics of economic development. *Journal of Monetary Economics*, 22, 3–42.

Phelps, E (1966). *Golden Rules of Economic Growth.* NY: W.W. Norton & Company.

Orsmond, D (1990). The size of government and economic growth a methodological review. Unpublished manuscript. Washington, DC: International Monetary Fund.

Ramanathan, R (1982). *Introduction to the Theory of Economic Growth.* Berlin: Springer-Verlag.

Ramsey, F (1928). A mathematical theory of saving. *Economic Journal*, 38, 543–559.

Rivera-Batiz, L and P Romer (1991). International trade and endogenous technical change. *NBER Working Paper 3594.*

Romer, P (1986). Increasing returns and long-run growth. *Journal of Political Economy*, 94, 1002–1037.

Sato, R (1963). Fiscal policy in a neo-classical growth model — an analysis of the time required for equilibrium adjustment. *Review of Economic Studies*, 30, 16–23.

Solow, R (1956). A contribution to the theory of economic growth. *Quarterly Journal of Economics*, 70, 65–94.

Summers, R and A Heston (1988). A new set of international comparisons of real product and price levels estimates for 130 countries, 1950–85. *Review of Income and Wealth*, 34, 1–25.

Swan, T (1956). Economic growth and capital accumulation. *Economic Record*, 32, 334–362.

Szpiro, G (1986). Relative risk aversion around the world. *Economic Letters*, 20, 19–21.

Thirlwall, A (1979). The balance of payments constraint as an explanation of international growth rate differences. *Banca Nazionale del Lavoro Quarterly Review*, 32, 45–53.

Chapter 7

Does Monetary Policy Matter for Long-Run Growth?*

...the most urgent current analytical need was for a way of fitting together short-run macroeconomics, when the main action consists of variations in aggregate demand, with the long run factors represented by the neoclassical growth model, when the main action is on the supply side.

— Robert M. Solow, Nobel Prize Lecture,
Nobel Prize Outreach AB 2022

7.1 Introduction

Does monetary policy matter for long-run growth? No is the answer from modern macroeconomics. Monetary policy affects only inflation in the long-run. The level and growth rate of potential output are functions of productive inputs (capital, labor, and technology) and their rates of change. Therein lies the puzzle. If inflation is influenced by monetary policy in the long-run, and investment is affected by expected inflation, among other variables, why would potential output not change when investment changes as a result of changes in expected inflation induced by monetary policy?[1] Certainly

---

*Written by Delano S. Villanueva and adapted from *Macroeconomic Policies for Stable Growth*, 211–236, by the permission of World Scientific Publishing Company. Copyright 2008 by World Scientific Publishing Company.

[1]See Section 7.2 on the theoretical and empirical relevance of rational vs adaptive expectations in determining expected inflation, noting that bounded rationality favors adaptive expectations and that the adaptive model fits the data better.

capital accumulation would be encouraged (discouraged) by lower (higher) inflation in the long-run. This chapter argues that, not only the levels, but also the growth rates of potential output and real GDP change in economically sensible ways when monetary policy changes. To demonstrate these results, I modify and extend the modern macroeconomic model of economic fluctuations as explained, for example, by Hall and Taylor (1997), and link it formally to the Solow (1956)–Swan (1956) growth model.

Section 7.2 presents the modified model and discusses the submodels of economic fluctuations and economic growth. Section 7.3 analyzes the short- and long-run effects of disinflation. Section 7.4 solves for the optimal inflation target and the optimal monetary policy that maximize a social welfare function. Section 7.5 estimates the model's speed of adjustment (in years) to its steady-state (long-run equilibrium). Section 7.6 summarizes and concludes. Appendix 7.A contains a formal analysis of the reduced model, existence and stability of equilibrium, and a summary of the regression work on US data on which the solution of the optimal program is partly based.

7.2 The Modified Model

$$R - R^{\text{eq}} = -b\hat{Y} \quad \text{(IS curve)} \tag{7.1}$$

$$R = \pi + \beta\hat{Y} + \phi(\pi - \pi^t) + R^f \quad \text{(Monetary policy rule)} \tag{7.2}$$

$$\pi = \varphi\hat{Y} + \pi^e + Z \quad \text{(Price-adjustment)} \tag{7.3}$$

$$Y^p = K^\alpha L^{1-\alpha} \quad \text{(Potential output)} \tag{7.4}$$

$$I/L = i_0 - i_1 R^b - i_2\pi^e \quad \text{(Investment function)} \tag{7.5}$$

$$R^b = r_0 + r_1 R \quad \text{(Corporate bond rate)} \tag{7.6}$$

$$\dot{K} = I - \delta K \quad \text{(Capital growth)} \tag{7.7}$$

$$\dot{L} = \theta K + (n + \lambda)L \quad \text{(Labor growth)} \tag{7.8}$$

$$\dot{\pi}^e = \gamma(\pi - \pi^e) \quad \text{(Expectation-generating function)} \tag{7.9}$$

$$k = K/L \quad \text{(Capital–labor ratio)} \tag{7.10}$$

Notation:

Y : real GDP,
Y^p : potential output,
$\hat{Y}$: output gap $= Y/Y^p - 1$,
I : real investment,
R^b : Corporate bond interest rate (Moody's Aaa seasoned rate),
R : Federal funds interest rate,
R^{eq} : equilibrium Federal funds interest rate (consistent with full employment),
R^f : coefficient,
π : inflation rate,
π^e : expected inflation,
π^t : target inflation,
Z : price shock,
K : capital stock,
L : labor in efficiency units,
k : capital/effective labor ratio,
b : $s_1 k^\alpha$,
$\beta, \phi, \gamma, \alpha, \theta, \lambda, \delta, \varphi, n, r_0, r_1, i_0, i_{1,}, i_2, s_1$ are parameters.[1]

Equation (7.1) embeds an IS relationship that includes an investment function like

$$I/L = i_0 - i_1(R^b - \pi^e) - i_2'\pi^e, \tag{7.5$'$}$$

in which (a) $-i_1(R^b - \pi^e)$ measures the negative effect on investment of the user cost of capital; and (b) $-i_2'\pi^e$ measures the negative effect on investment of the distortions and instabilities associated with expected inflation. Specifically, effects (b) include:

(b.1) increased riskiness of long-term investment projects;
(b.2) decreased average maturity of commercial lending;
(b.3) distorted information content of relative prices; and
(b.4) pronounced macroeconomic instability and a country's inability to control macroeconomic policy.

[1]The parameter s_1 is defined below.

Investment Equation (7.5)$'$ can be re-written as

$$I/L = i_0 - i_1 R^b - i_2 \pi^e, \tag{7.5}$$

in which $i_2 = (i_2' - i_1)$. Equation (7.5) can be fitted on the data on investment, the interest rate, and expected inflation. If the investment effect of expected inflation is only via the user cost of capital [effect (a)] and effects (b) are absent, i.e., $i_2' = 0$, then the coefficient of π^e in Equation (7.5) would be $+i_1$. However, when effects (b) are present, negative and significant, then the coefficient of π^e in Equation (7.5) would be $|i_2' - i_1| > 0$, implying that $|i_2'| > |i_1|$, that is, effects (b) outweigh effect (a). Empirical work on US and UK data confirms these coefficient restrictions — there is a large and significant negative effect of expected inflation on investment; the coefficients of both the nominal interest rate and expected inflation are negative and significant, and the negative coefficient of expected inflation is often larger in absolute value than the coefficient of the interest rate. See, among others, Fair (2004) and Turner (2007).[2]

Thus, the IS curve embedded in Equation (7.1) and the investment Equation (7.5) show different coefficients of the nominal interest rate and expected inflation, with both having a negative impact on investment. Equation (7.1) posits a negative relation between the

---

[2]My own OLS regressions using alternative measures of the interest rate in the investment function (Federal funds rate, Moody's Aaa seasoned corporate bond rate, and US prime rate) from 1970 to 2006 also confirm these empirical regularities. See Appendix 7.A. In earlier papers, Tobin (1965), Stein (1966), and Sidrauski (1967) hypothesize that long-run growth is affected by monetary policy, but in an empirically implausible manner. They argue that an expansionary monetary policy, by inducing higher expected inflation, would encourage investment because of substitution from money to capital. Additionally, by lowering the nominal interest rate, an expansionary monetary policy would lower the user (opportunity) cost of capital [effect (a) above]. Since the distortions and instabilities associated with high expected inflation [effects (b) above] are assumed absent or nil, investment and thus, long-run growth would be enhanced by an expansionary monetary policy. A contractionary monetary policy would lower investment and growth by raising the user cost of capital through a higher nominal interest rate and lower expected inflation. As noted, available empirical evidence confirms the existence of large effects (b) that overturn the long-run growth implications of monetary policy that Tobin and others hypothesize.

gap of actual and equilibrium interest rate and the gap of actual and potential output. If actual output is lower (higher) than its potential level — if $\hat{Y}$ is negative (positive) — the actual interest rate is higher (lower) than its equilibrium level. The equilibrium interest R^{eq} is the interest rate level along the IS curve that corresponds to potential output (corresponding to full employment of capital and labor).

The derivation of Equation (7.1) is as follows. Assume the following basic macroeconomic model:

$$Y/L = C/L + I/L + G/L + \text{CAB}/L \quad \text{(Income identity)} \tag{7.11}$$

$$C/L = c_0 + c_1 Y/L \quad \text{(Consumption)} \tag{7.12}$$

$$I/L = i_0 - i_1 R^b - i_2 \pi^e \quad \text{(Investment)} \tag{7.5}$$

$$G/L = g_0 + g_1 Y/L \quad \text{(Government expenditures)}^3 \tag{7.13}$$

$$\text{CAB}/L = m_0 - m_1 Y/L \quad \text{(Net export demand)}^4 \tag{7.14}$$

$$R^b = r_0 + r_1 R \quad \text{(Corporate bond rate)} \tag{7.6}$$

in which Y is GDP, C is private consumption, I is gross private investment, G is government spending, and CAB is net exports of goods and services (current account balance), all in constant prices, L is effective labor, R^b is the corporate bond rate, R is the Federal funds rate, and π^e is expected inflation. Equations (7.11)–(7.14), (7.5) and (7.6) collapse into an equation for the interest rate R:

$$R = s_0 - s_1(Y/L) - s_2\pi^e \quad \text{(IS curve)} \tag{7.15}$$

in which $s_0 = (c_0+g_0+m_0+i_0-i_1r_0)/i_1r_1$, $s_1 = (1-c_1-g_1+m_1)/i_1r_1$, and $s_2 = i_2/i_1r_1$. The equilibrium interest rate R^{eq} is the rate at the full employment point, Y^p:

$$R^{\text{eq}} = s_0 - s_1(Y^p/L) - s_2\pi^e \quad \text{(IS curve at full employment)} \tag{7.16}$$

[3]The intercept g_0 includes exogenous shifts in fiscal policy.
[4]The intercept m_0 includes exogenous shifts in net exports.

Subtract (7.16) from (7.15):

$$R - R^{\text{eq}} = -b\hat{Y} \tag{7.1}$$

in which $b = s_1(Y^p/L) = s_1k^\alpha$ and $\hat{Y} = Y/Y^p - 1$ is the output gap.[5] Equation (7.16) states that an increase in either potential GDP or expected inflation reduces the equilibrium interest rate, and from Equation (7.1) implies a negative output gap.[6]

Equation (7.2) is a Taylor-type monetary policy rule — the Fed sets the short-term interest rate (Federal funds rate) in response to the output gap and the deviation of inflation from its target level, with the coefficient of inflation exceeding unity.[7] R^f is a monetary policy coefficient. The positive coefficient of the output gap means that as actual output gets smaller in relation to potential output ($\hat{Y} < 0$) the Federal Reserve would lower the interest rate to lift actual GDP as close as possible to the potential level, and vice-versa.

Equation (7.3) is an expectations-augmented Phillips curve — inflation is the sum of the expected rate, a proportion of the output gap, and a shock term (e.g., a change in oil price). The positive coefficient of the output gap means that there would be upward pressure on inflation when actual GDP gets larger in relation to potential output ($\hat{Y} > 0$). Equations (7.1)–(7.3) represent a system of three equations in three unknowns (π, $\hat{Y}$ and R) as functions of given values of k, π^e, π^t, R^f, and Z.[8]

The remaining Equations (7.4)–(7.10) comprise the long-run growth component of the extended model. A Cobb–Douglass production function is specified in Equation (7.4). Equation (7.5)

[5]Equations (7.4) and (7.10) are used in defining the variable b.

[6]An increase in full employment income raises saving, and an increase in expected inflation lowers investment. In either case, the result is excess saving over investment. The equilibrium interest rate must fall to increase investment and clear the market for goods and services. The above derivation of Equation (7.1) follows the procedure used by Hall and Taylor (1997).

[7]When setting the interest rate, the Fed aims at raising the interest rate by $1+\phi$. For example, if $\phi = 0.5$, then the interest rate is raised by 1.5 percentage points in response to a one percentage point rise in inflation.

[8]R^{eq}, which appears in Equation (7.1), is a function of k and π^e, as noted in Equation (7.16), recalling from Equations (7.4) and (7.10) that $Y^p/L = k^\alpha$.

states that investment per effective worker is a negative function of the corporate bond interest rate and the expected inflation rate. Equation (7.6) links the corporate bond rate to the Federal funds rate. Equations (7.7) and (7.8) specify the growth of the capital stock and effective labor, respectively.[9] Endogenous capital-augmenting technical change is embodied in new capital goods, I. Exogenous capital-augmenting technical change, if any, lowers the depreciation rate δ. Endogenous labor-augmenting technical change positively depends on the size of the capital stock K. Exogenous labor-augmenting technical change, if any, is captured by λ. The working population grows at a constant rate n.

Several researchers have found that inflationary expectations are more appropriately described by the backward-looking adaptive variety. Kiefer (2008) finds that the implications of rational expectations as inflation forecasts by economic agents "do not conform well to observed outcomes when applied to endogenous stabilization; an adaptive model fits the data better. The adaptive rule, often labeled naive, could be the rational strategy in an uncertain world." Lovell (1986) rejects the unbiasedness and efficiency predictions of rational expectations on the basis of survey data on expectations of inflation and other variables. In an empirical study using firm-level data, Schenkerman and Nadiri (1984) conclude that their econometric results strongly reject the rational and static expectations hypotheses in favor of adaptive expectations. Chow (1989), Fair (2004), and Curto Millet (2007) reach similar conclusions.[10] Equation (7.9) is a process of adaptive expectation — inflationary expectations change in proportion, measured by γ, to the deviation of actual inflation from its expected level.[11] Finally, Equation (7.10) defines the capital

[9]See Villanueva (1994, **Chapter 6**) for a detailed explanation of the effective labor growth Equation (7.8).

[10]The Curto Millet (2007) study used inflation expectations data in consumer surveys in eight European countries.

[11]Conlisk (1988) has shown that rational expectations need not be the solution to a properly specified optimization problem if the cost of optimization is substantial. An adaptive expectation hypothesis may well be the right (least cost) solution as suggested by bounded rationality.

stock in intensive form, that is, its level per unit of the effective labor force. As explained below, Equations (7.4)–(7.10) can be reduced to two differential equations in two variables, k and π^e.

Substituting Equation (7.2) into Equation (7.1) and repeating Equation (7.3),

$$\hat{Y} = -[(1+\phi)/(\beta+b)]\pi + \phi\pi^t/(\beta+b) - (R^f - R^{\text{eq}})/(\beta+b) \text{(Inflation-output gap curve)} \quad (7.17)$$

$$\pi = \varphi\hat{Y} + \pi^e + Z \quad \text{(Expectations-augmented Phillips curve).} \quad (7.18)$$

Equations (7.17) and (7.18) involve two variables, output gap $\hat{Y}$ and inflation π, as functions of state variables capital intensity k and expected inflation π^e, and of exogenous inflation target π^t, monetary policy coefficient R^f, price shock Z, and exogenous shifts in fiscal policy, and net exports included in the equation for the equilibrium interest rate, R^{eq}.[12] The solutions for inflation and the output gap are

$$\pi = (B+\varphi A)/[1+\varphi(1+\phi)/(\beta+b)] = \pi(k,\pi^e) \quad (7.19)$$

$$\hat{Y} = [A - B(1+\phi)/(\beta+b)]/[1+\varphi(1+\phi)/(\beta+b)] = \hat{Y}(k,\pi^e) \quad (7.20)$$

in which $A = \phi\pi^t/(\beta+b) - (1/(\beta+b)(R^f - R^{\text{eq}})$, $B = \pi^e + Z$, $R^{\text{eq}} = s_0 - b - s_2\pi^e$, and $b = s_1 k^\alpha$.

The solution for the Federal funds interest rate is

$$R = (1+\phi)\pi(k,\pi^e) + \beta\hat{Y}(k,\pi^e) - \phi\pi^t + R^f = R(k,\pi^e). \quad (7.21)$$

Equations (7.17) and (7.18) represent the submodel of economic fluctuations, which is discussed more fully in the next section on disinflation. For the submodel of growth, time differentiate Equation (7.10), substitute Equations (7.4)–(7.8), (7.10), and repeat

[12] In addition, text Equation (7.16) for the equilibrium interest rate includes in s_0 exogenous shocks to consumption, investment, and the corporate bond interest rate.

Equation (7.9) to obtain,

$$\dot{k}/k = [i_0 - i_1 r_0 - i_1 r_1 R(k, \pi^e) - i_2 \pi^e]/k - \theta k - (n + \lambda + \delta), \tag{7.22}$$

$$\dot{\pi}^e = \gamma[\pi(k, \pi^e) - \pi^e], \tag{7.23}$$

which are two differential equations in k and π^e.

The equilibrium values k^* and π^{e*} are the roots of the reduced model (7.24) and (7.25):

$$\dot{k}/k = [i_0 - i_1 r_0 - i_1 r_1 R(k^*, \pi^{e*}) - i_2 \pi^{e*}]/k^* - \theta k^* - (n + \lambda + \delta) = 0, \tag{7.24}$$

$$\dot{\pi}^e = \gamma[\pi(k^*, \pi^{e*}) - \pi^{e*}] = 0. \tag{7.25}$$

Figure 7.1 is a phase diagram of the reduced model. The right panel plots Equations (7.24) and (7.25) and the left panel plots the growth rates of the capital stock, effective labor, and potential GDP for a given steady-state rate of expected inflation π^{e*}. The $\dot{k}/k = 0$ curve shows pairs of π^e and k that produce no change in capital intensity. It slopes downward because as expected inflation decreases, investment, and hence capital growth (warranted rate) increases to a rate above the growth of effective labor (natural rate), i.e., $\dot{k}/k > 0$.

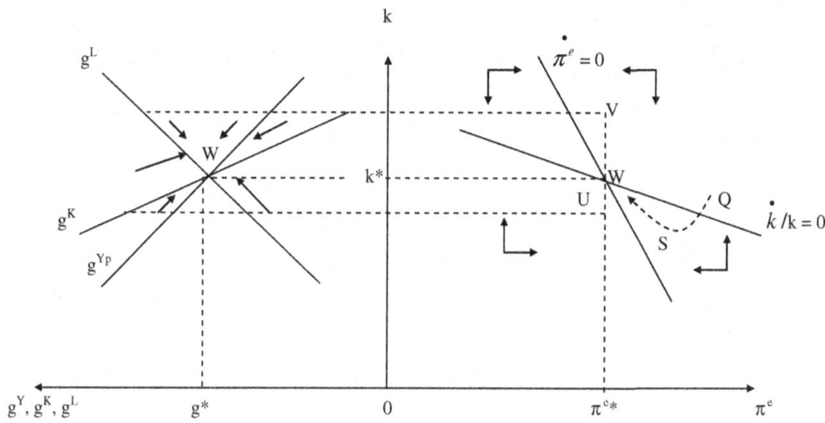

Figure 7.1. Phase diagram of the growth model. *Notes:* $g^{Yp} = \lambda + n + \theta k + \alpha[\dot{k}/k(\pi^{e*})]$; $g^L = \theta k + n + \lambda$; $g^K = I[R(k, \pi^{e*}), \pi^{e*}]/k - \delta$; "$g$" is the growth rate operator $(dx/dt)/x$ for $x = Y, L, K$.

For the latter to be zero, capital intensity k must increase to pull the warranted rate down and the natural rate up.[13] The $\dot{\pi}^e = 0$ curve shows pairs of π^e and k that produce no change in expected inflation. It also slopes downward because an increase in capital intensity reduces the output gap[14] and, hence, inflation, implying $\dot{\pi}^e < 0$. For the latter to be zero, expected inflation must also decrease.[15]

The steady-state equilibrium values π^{e*} and k^* are determined at point W, associated with a given initial inflation target π_0^t and initial values of the other exogenous variables.[16] The steady-state equilibrium is locally stable (see Appendix 7.A for proof). The arrows indicate the tendency of the system to return to equilibrium from any point other than W. For instance, consider point Q, at which the initial capital intensity is below the steady-state level, and the initial expected inflation is above the steady-state rate. These initial conditions typify a capital-scarce economy with high inflationary expectations. At point Q, the initial high rate of expected inflation discourages investment and lowers capital intensity. Also, high expected inflation drives the equilibrium interest rate below

[13]The increase in k has two opposing effects on the warranted rate: the interest rate effect and the base effect. The positive interest rate effect $= I_R R_k/k$, in which $I_R < 0$ and $R_k < 0$. An increase in k, by reducing the output gap and inflation, lowers the interest rate and stimulates investment. The negative base effect $= -I(R)/k^2 < 0$. For a given $I(R)$, a higher k reduces capital growth. The latter effect usually swamps the former effect, resulting in a decline in capital growth (warranted rate). At the same time, a higher k, by increasing learning by doing, raises labor growth (natural rate).

[14]The output gap turns negative on two counts. First and directly, a rise in capital intensity pulls up potential output (per L) [from Equations (7.4) and (7.10)]. Second and indirectly, a higher potential GDP reduces the required interest rate below the actual interest rate, decreasing real GDP below potential [from Equations (7.1) and (7.17)].

[15]The right panal of Figure 7.1 shows that the $\dot{\pi}^e = 0$ curve is steeper than the $\dot{k}/k = 0$ curve. The reason is empirical, based on the evaluation of the partial derivatives of the reduced model in the neighborhood of the steady-state. See Appendix 7.A for the derivation of the slopes of these two curves and for stability analysis.

[16]An asterisk on any variable denotes its long-run, steady-state value. Lower case variables, unless otherwise stated, are expressed in terms of L (e.g., $y = Y/L$, $y^p = Y^p/L$, and so forth).

the actual interest rate; the resulting negative output gap exerts downward pressure on inflation and on expected inflation.[17] Thus, both capital intensity and expected inflation decline. At some point such as S, when expected inflation has declined far enough, capital accumulation turns positive and capital intensity begins to rise. Meanwhile, expected inflation continues to fall pari passu actual inflation, owing to a sustained negative output gap (the latter reinforced directly by a rising level of potential output, y^p induced by a rising ratio of capital to effective labor, k). This process continues until capital intensity has risen to k^* and expected inflation has fallen to π^{e*} at W.

In the left panel, the natural rate schedule $g^L = (\dot{L}/L)$ is drawn with a positive slope [Equations (7.8) and (7.10)]. As capital intensity rises, endogenous labor-augmenting technical change goes up, and effective labor grows faster. The warranted rate schedule $g^K = (\dot{K}/K)$ has a negative slope [Equations (7.5), (7.6), (7.7), and (7.10)]. The capital stock grows slower with increases in capital intensity.[18] The g^K $(\dot{K}/K)$ curve is drawn for a given equilibrium expected inflation π^{e*}. The instantaneous growth rate of potential output is derived by time differentiating Equation (7.4), using (7.7), (7.8), and (7.10),

$$g^Y = \dot{Y}^p/Y^p = \lambda + n + \theta k + \alpha\dot{k}/k,$$

shown in the left panel as downward-sloping and intersecting the warranted and natural rate schedules at the equilibrium point W.[19] The growth rate of potential GDP can be restated as $\dot{Y}^p/Y^p =$

[17]From Equations (7.16), (7.1), and (7.3).

[18]As mentioned in an earlier footnote, as k increases, the negative base effect is typically larger in absolute value than the positive interest rate effect.

[19]The $\dot{Y}^p/Y^p$ curve is drawn for a given steady-state rate of expected inflation π^{e*}, whose slope is: $\partial(\dot{Y}^p/Y^p)/\partial k = \theta + \alpha(\partial\dot{k}/k)/\partial k = 0.003 + 0.3(-0.02461) = -0.004382$. The slope of the capital growth curve is: $\partial(\dot{K}/K)/\partial k = -(1/k)(i_1\partial R/\partial k) - (1/k^2)(i_0 - i_1R - i_2\pi^e) = (1/3.08)(-0.624)(-0.024) - (1/3.08^2)[0.287 - 0.624(0.0427) - 0.840(0.0130)] = -0.01944$. These partial derivatives are evaluated in the neighborhood of equilibrium (see Appendix 7.A). Given these partial derivatives, the $(\dot{K}/K)$ curve is steeper than the $(\dot{Y}^p/Y^p)$ curve, as shown in the left panel of Figure 7.1.

$g^*+\alpha\dot{k}/k$, in which $g^* = \lambda+n+\theta k^*$ is the steady-state natural growth rate of the economy, at which balanced growth takes place (warranted rate equals natural rate). Consider the short-run adjustment when the initial position is at point U in the right panel of Figure 7.1. At point U, where the initial capital intensity is below k^* and expected inflation is at its steady-state level, the warranted rate exceeds the natural rate (left panel) and thus, $\dot{k}/k > 0$, implying that $\dot{Y}^p/Y^p > g^*$. As k rises, the gap between the warranted and natural rates narrows and disappears at $k = k^*$ (indicated by the arrows in the left panel), at which point $\alpha\dot{k}/k = 0$. Thus, $\dot{Y}^p/Y^p$ declines toward the limiting value g^*.[20] The opposite sequence of events is true when the initial position is at point V where the initial capital intensity is above k^* (the natural rate exceeds the warranted rate).

7.3 The Effects of Disinflation[21]

Figure 7.2 (consisting of three quadrants) provides a graphic summary of the short- and long-run effects of disinflation. Quadrants II and III repeat Figure 7.1.[22] The new quadrant I graphs the sub model of economic fluctuations [Equations (7.17) and (7.18)], and illustrates the short- and long-run adjustments of the *levels* of real and potential GDP. The line D is the aggregate demand-inflation curve

[20]A simple explanation is the following: in an initially capital-scarce economy with stable expected inflation, capital's net marginal product is relatively high (in relation to its steady-state value), encouraging larger investments and thus a higher warranted rate. At the same time, a low level of capital intensity is associated with a low rate of endogenous labor-augmenting technology and thus with a low natural rate. The positive gap between the warranted and natural rates means that the capital/effective labor ratio rises. The resulting higher capital intensity level lowers capital's marginal product owing to diminishing returns, and enhances the endogenous component of labor-augmenting technology. The warranted rate falls and the natural rate rises, and the gap between the two narrows. The process continues until capital intensity has risen to k^*, at the point of equality between the warranted and natural rates.

[21]The effects of an expansionary monetary policy (an increase in π^t), an expansionary fiscal policy (an increase in g_0), or an exogenous increase in net exports (an increase in m_0) are in the opposite direction from the sequence detailed in this section.

[22]The g^Y curve is suppressed to avoid further cluttering quadrant III.

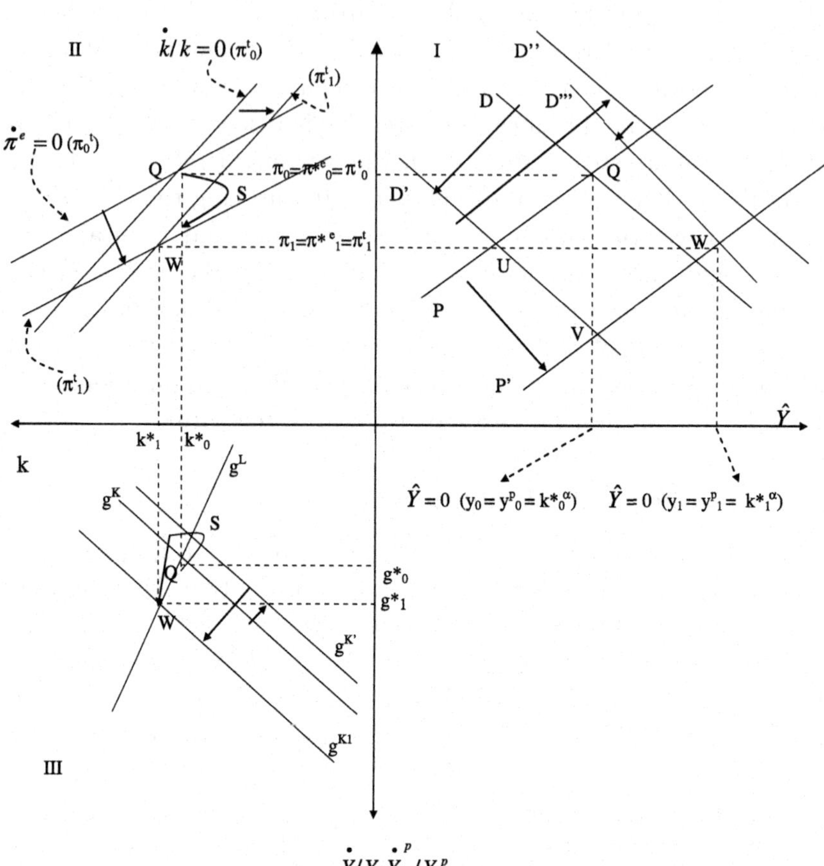

Figure 7.2. Short- and long-run effects of disinflation. *Notes:* $y = Y/L$; $y^p = Y^p/L$; $D = D(\pi_0^t, k_0^*, \pi_0^{*e})$; $D' = D'(\pi_1^t, k_0^*, \pi_0^{*e})$; $D'' = D''(\pi_1^t, k_0^*, \pi_1^{*e})$; $D''' = D'''(\pi_1^t, k_1^*, \pi_1^{*e})$; $P = P(\pi_0^{*e})$; $P' = P'(\pi_1^{*e})$; $g^L = n + \lambda + \theta k$; $g^K = I[R^0(k, \pi_0^{e*})]/k - \delta$; $g^{K'} = I[R'(k, \pi_0^{e*})]/k - \delta$; $g^{K1} = I[R^1(k, \pi_1^{e*})]/k - \delta$; $R' > R^0 > R^1$; $\pi_1^t < \pi_0^t$.

[Equation (7.17)], with a negative slope equal to $-(\beta + b)/(1 + \phi)$. P is the price-adjustment line [Equation (7.18)], with a positive slope equal to φ. The demand-inflation curve D is drawn for given levels of capital intensity and expected inflation, and also of target inflation, monetary policy coefficient, fiscal policy and exogenous shifts in net exports (and other exogenous shocks). Changes in those variables shift this curve. The price-adjustment line P is drawn for given expected inflation and price shocks, changes in which shift this curve. At the initial target inflation π_0^t, equilibrium occurs at point Q, with capital intensity k_0^* and expected inflation π_0^{e*}. The actual inflation rate is equal to its expected and target levels ($\pi_0 = \pi_0^{*e} = \pi_0^t$) and real GDP is equal to its potential level ($y_0 = y_0^p = k_0^{*\alpha}$).[23]

Now, suppose the Fed lowers the target inflation rate from π_0^t to π_1^t (say, from 4 percent to 2 percent).[24] When the target inflation is lowered from π_0^t to π_1^t, the Fed raises the interest rate, shifting the D curve downward to D'. Real GDP falls below potential and inflation declines (the line Q–U traces this short-run adjustment). In response to these developments, the Fed cuts the interest rate. At the same time, the price-adjustment line P shifts downward to P', anchored by a lower expected inflation π_1^{e*} consistent with the lower inflation target π_1^t. The line U–V traces the increase in real GDP and the continued decrease in inflation. At point V, real GDP returns to its previous potential level it had at point Q. The only effect of monetary policy *at this point* is to reduce the inflation rate. However, the story does not end here. As shown in quadrant II and discussed in detail immediately below, the continued decrease in inflation lowers expected inflation, boosting investment and shifting the D' curve upward to D''. Equilibrium capital intensity rises from k_0^* to k_1^*. Because of the higher capital intensity, potential GDP rises; the required equilibrium interest rate falls below the actual interest rate, which reduces real GDP further below potential GDP. The higher capital intensity shifts the demand-inflation curve downward from D'' to D''', intersecting the P' line at point W, at which a higher level of real GDP per L equals its higher potential level at $y_1 = y_1^p = k_1^{*\alpha}$, while actual and expected inflation matches the lower target level at

[23]In equilibrium (at point Q, for instance), $R^{\text{eq}} = R$; thus, $R^f - R^{\text{eq}} = R^f - R = -\pi$, and from Equation (7.17), $\hat{Y} = [(-1 - \phi + \phi)\pi + \pi = -\pi + \pi]/(\beta + b) = 0$. $\hat{Y} = 0$ implies $\pi = \pi^e = \pi^t$ for any π^t. The price shock term Z is assumed to be zero in equilibrium.

[24]See Appendix 7.A for proof of the extent of the shifts in the D and P curves shown in quadrant I in response to changes in the target inflation, expected inflation, and capital intensity.

$\pi_1 = \pi_1^{*e} = \pi_1^t$.[25] The path Q–U–V–W traces the adjustment of the *levels* of real and potential GDP to the lower target inflation.

Quadrant II shows the comparative dynamics and adjustments of expected inflation and capital intensity. The Fed's lowering of the target inflation rate *shifts* the $\dot{k}/k = 0$ curve to the (π_1^t) position because of higher interest rates and the $\dot{\pi}^e = 0$ to the π_1^t position as actual and expected inflation declines.[26] The two curves intersect at point W, at which the new equilibrium capital intensity is higher at k_1^*, and the actual and expected inflation is lower at target rate π_1^{*e}.

The curved line Q–S–W traces the adjustment path of expected and actual inflation and capital intensity. Following the Fed's interest rate increase, capital intensity declines to a level below k_0^* on impact. As inflation falls toward the lower target level, the Fed cuts the interest rate. After some point, such as S, when expected inflation has fallen enough, capital intensity recovers and begins to rise. Expected inflation keeps on its downward trajectory, further raising investment. This process continues until capital intensity passes its previous equilibrium level at k_0^*, and ultimately reaches a higher equilibrium level k_1^* at W, at which point expected and actual inflation matches the lower targeted level $\pi_1 = \pi_1^{*e} = \pi_1^t$.

Quadrant III shows the short- and long-run *growth* dynamics. Given the initial target inflation $\pi_0^t (= \pi_0^{*e} = \pi_0)$, equilibrium is at point Q where balanced growth is equal to $g_0^* = g_0^{K*} = g_0^{L*}$. On impact, a lowering of the target inflation prompts the Fed to raise the interest rate that depresses capital accumulation, reflected by the northeast shift of the g^K curve to $g^{K'} = [R'(k, \pi_0^{*e})]/k - \delta$,

[25]The D''' is also steeper, reflecting a larger slope (in absolute value) as k^* increases, i.e., $|\partial^2\pi/\partial\hat{Y}^2| = (\partial b/\partial k^*)/(1+\phi) = s_1\alpha k^{*(\alpha-1)}/(1+\phi)$. The net change in the intercept of the D curve $= -0.333 + 0.505 - 0.0343 = 0.1377$ (shift from D to D'''). The first decimal measures the decrease in the intercept resulting from a lower inflation target (shift from D to D'); the second measures the increase in the intercept resulting from lower expected inflation (shift from D' to D''); and the third measures the decrease in the intercept resulting from a higher capital intensity (shift from D'' to D'''). These magnitudes are based on values of parameters discussed later in the next section and Appendix 7.A.

[26]Appendix 7.A shows that the downward shift of the $\dot{\pi}^e = 0$ curve is larger than the downward shift of the $\dot{k}/k = 0$ curve, as reflected in quadrant II.

intersecting the g^L curve at point S. The growth rate of potential GDP falls below g_0^*. The lower expected inflation, matching the lower target and realized level, and subsequent lowering of the interest rate by the Fed stimulate capital accumulation, reflected by the southwest shift of the g^K curve to $g^{K1} = I[R^1(k, \pi_1^{e*})]/k - \delta$, intersecting the stationary labor growth curve at a higher equilibrium growth rate of potential output $g_1^* = g_1^{K*} = g_1^{L*}$ at point W.[27] Recovery begins from point S and economic growth steadily increases toward the new higher steady-state rate g_1^*. The movement along the natural rate curve, Q–S–W, traces the adjustment path of economic growth.

From Figure 7.2, the key result of the modified model is that the disinflation program, while creating unemployment in the short run, raises the levels *and* growth rates of real and potential GDP in the long-run. As noted in the preceding section, the equilibrium growth rate g^* of potential GDP is given by:

$$g^{Yp*} = (\dot{Y}^p/Y^p)^* = n + \lambda + \theta k^*.$$

Since k^* goes up from k_0^* to k_1^*, the equilibrium growth rate of potential GDP is higher, and so is the equilibrium growth rate of real GDP.[28]

7.4 Optimal Monetary Policy and Optimal Long-Run Growth

There is indeterminacy about the analytical results so far. There is no unique value for the target inflation rate. Different inflation targets are associated with different capital intensities and levels and growth rates of real GDP. Moreover, given the preferred weights β and ϕ placed on the output gap and deviation of inflation from target, different values for the monetary policy coefficient R^f would

[27]Owing to lower inflation, the equilibrium interest rate is lower at point W than at point $Q(R^1 < R^0)$. In between Q and W, the interest rate rises at first from its level at $Q(R' > R^0)$ and then falls to its lower level at $W(R^1 < R^0 < R')$.
[28]In the long-run, $\hat{Y}^* = Y^*/Y^{p*} - 1 = 0$, or $Y^*/Y^{p*} = 1$, implying that $Y^* = Y^{p*}$ and $(\dot{Y}/Y)^* = (\dot{Y}^p/Y^p)^*$.

produce different economic outcomes for the interest rate R. But when the output gap is zero in equilibrium, $R = R^{\text{eq}}$. And the latter is determined by capital intensity and expected inflation, which vary depending on the value of R^f. Thus, there is no unique value for the monetary policy coefficient. Also in long-run equilibrium, expected, actual, and target rates of inflation are equal to each other. Thus, the interest rate must equal the target rate of inflation plus the monetary policy coefficient in equilibrium. Since neither π^t nor R^f is unique, there is no unique equilibrium interest rate even when the output gap is zero and actual inflation is on target. Additionally, for optimal investment, the net marginal product of capital (net of depreciation) must equal the real corporate bond interest rate adjusted for financial markups and various risk factors. Such a premium depends on capital intensity, among others. To pin down a unique set of values for the inflation target, the monetary policy coefficient, and the interest rate premium, a social welfare function is needed.

In the long-run, potential output per unit of effective labor is $y^{p*} = k^{*\alpha}$. In the steady-state, because the output gap is zero, $y^{p*} = y^*$. If y^* is considered a measure of the standard of living, and since $(dy^*/dk^*) = \alpha k^{*(\alpha-1)} > 0$, it is possible to raise living standards by increasing k^*. Monetary policy has a role in increasing k^* by focusing on reducing inflation and inflationary expectations and thereby encouraging long-run investment. For monetary policymakers, the practical questions are: Are there optimal values for the inflation target and the monetary policy coefficient? That is to say, what are the values for π^t and R^f that maximize living standards? If consumption per unit of effective labor (or any monotonically increasing function of it) is taken as a measure of the social welfare of society, the monetary policy coefficient and target inflation that maximize social welfare by maximizing long-run consumption per unit of effective labor can be determined.[29]

[29]The k^* that maximizes $(C/L)^*$ is also the k^* that maximizes the long-run level $(Y/L)^*$ and growth (g^*) of real GDP, since all are functions of k^*.

Long-run consumption per unit of effective labor is

$$\begin{aligned} c^* &= (C/L)^* = (Y/L)^* - (I/L)^* - (G/L)^* - (\mathrm{CAB}/L)^*, \\ &= (i_1 r_0 - i_0 - g_0 - m_0) + (1 - g_1 + m_1)k^{\alpha *} + i_1 r_1 \pi^* \\ &\quad + i_1 r_1 R^f + i_2 \pi^{e*}, \end{aligned} \tag{7.26}$$

in which $(Y/L)^* = (Y^p/L)^* = k^{*\alpha}$, $\pi^* = (B + A\varphi)/E, A = \phi\pi^t/(\beta + b) - (R^f - R^{\mathrm{eq}})/(\beta + b)$, $B = \pi^{e*} + Z, E = 1 + \varphi(1 + \phi)/(\beta + b)$, $R^{\mathrm{eq}} = s_0 - s_1 k^* - s_2\pi^{e*}$, and $b = s_1 k^{*\alpha}$.[30]

The constrained optimization is

Max (7.26) with respect to k^*, π^{e*}, π^t, R^f, and ρ, subject to the following constraints:

$$\begin{aligned} &\dot{k}/k = 0; \quad \dot{\pi}^e = 0; \quad \pi^* - \pi^t = 0; \quad \text{and} \\ &\alpha k^{*(\alpha-1)} - \delta - R^b + \pi^{e*} - \rho/k^* = 0. \end{aligned} \tag{7.27}$$

The first two constraints are the equations of the reduced model. The third constraint is the achievement of the inflation target. The fourth constraint is the optimal condition for investment, which is undertaken up to the point at which the marginal product of capital, net of depreciation, equals the expected real interest rate on high-grade corporate bonds plus a variable term ρ/k^*, which includes financial mark-ups and risk factors. This variable term is assumed to be inversely related to the steady-state capital intensity because the earnings of the productive sector are directly linked to the level of capital intensity it has. The higher k^* is, the more productive are workers, and the less is the additional premium the

[30] $(I/L)^* = (i_0 - i_1 r_0) - i_1 r_1 \pi^* - i_1 r_1 R^f - i_2 \pi^{e*}$, $(G/L)^* = g_0 + g_1 (Y/L)^*$, and $(\mathrm{CAB}/L)^* = m_0 - m_1 (Y/L)^*$. Z is assumed to be zero in long-run equilibrium. The following parameter values are used in the constrained optimization: $s_0 = 0.4038$, $s_1 = 0.2506$, $s_2 = 0.7579$, and $n = 0.0178$. The first three are based on the regression estimates of the consumption, investment, government spending, net export demand, and corporate bond equations reported in Appendix 7.A. The estimate for n is obtained from the BLS, US Department of Labor. In line with standard practice, I assume $\alpha = 0.3$. The other parameters are assigned plausible values: $\phi = 0.5$, $\beta = 0.5$, $\varphi = 0.25$, $\gamma = 0.7$, $\delta = 0.04$, $\lambda = 0.008$, and $\theta = 0.003$.

corporate sector has to pay to borrow from the global corporate bond market. Using Microsoft's Excel's *Solver*, optimal values of the monetary policy coefficient and the optimal inflation target are obtained and summarized in Table 7.1.[31] For maximum consumer welfare, the optimal inflation target should be set at 1.30 percent and the monetary policy coefficient at 2.97 percent. The long-run equilibrium Federal funds rate is 4.27 percent and the long-run equilibrium corporate bond interest rate is 7.22 percent.[32] The difference between the net marginal product of capital and the expected real corporate bond interest rate is estimated to be 3.73 percent.[33] Among the real variables, the long-run equilibrium ratio of capital to effective labor is 3.08, implying a long-run capital–output ratio of 2.19. The long-run equilibrium marginal product of capital, net of depreciation, is 9.65 percent. The long-run growth rates of real GDP and per capita real GDP are 3.5 and 1.7 percent, respectively. The implied equilibrium levels of government expenditures, investment,

---

[31]In Excel, click *Tools*, then *Solver*. Microsoft's *Solver* uses the Generalized Reduced Gradient (GRG2) nonlinear optimization code developed by Leon Lasdon, University of Texas at Austin, and Allan Waren, Cleveland State University. For more information on the internal solution process used by Solver, contact: Frontline Systems, Inc. at http://www.frontsys.com. Appendix 7.A shows details of the OLS regressions involving consumption, investment, government expenditures, current account balance, and the corporate bond yield, using US annual data from 1970 to 2006. The estimated regression parameters are used in the constrained maximization process.

[32]The differential between the Federal funds rate and the corporate bond interest rate is nearly 3 percentage points, consistent with the finding of Goodfriend and McCallum (2007) that the difference between the interbank policy rate and the short rates can be as much as 4 percentage points. The expected real corporate bond yield is 5.92 percent. Since the corporate bond used is the high grade, seasoned Aaa Moody's rate, the 3.73 percent difference between the net marginal product of capital, which is 9.65 percent, and the expected real corporate bond interest rate, reflects financial markups and various risk factors summarized by the variable ρ/k^*.

[33]Goodfriend and McCallum (2007) find that the difference between the T-bill rate and the net marginal product of capital is over 3 percent.

consumption, and external current account balances[34] as ratios to GDP are broadly in line with historical averages.[35]

7.5 The Speed of Adjustment to Long-Run Equilibrium

The equilibrium optimal results derived in the preceding section would not be relevant to the real world if the time period for the modified model to reach its equilibrium were unduly long. This section uses a numerical simulation procedure used by Sato (1963, 1964) to calculate adjustment paths from a hypothetical disequilibrium to obtain estimates of the time (in years) needed to reach long-run equilibrium.

The reduced growth model (7.22) and (7.23) is repeated here:

$$\dot{k}/k = [i_0 - i_1 r_0 - i_1 r_1 R(k, \pi^e) - i_2 \pi^e]/k - \theta k - (n + \lambda + \delta), \tag{7.22}$$

$$\dot{\pi}^e = \gamma[\pi(k, \pi^e) - \pi^e]. \tag{7.23}$$

Linearize (7.22) and (7.23) around the steady-state:

$$\begin{bmatrix} \dot{k} \\ \dot{\pi}^e \end{bmatrix} = \begin{bmatrix} a_{11} & a_{12} \\ a_{21} & a_{22} \end{bmatrix} \begin{bmatrix} (k - k^*) \\ (\pi^e - \pi^{e*}) \end{bmatrix} \tag{7.28}$$

$$\begin{aligned} a_{11} &= -i_1 r_1 (\partial R/\partial k) - 2k\theta - (\lambda + n + \partial) \\ a_{12} &= -i_1 r_1 (\partial R/\partial \pi^e) - i_2; \\ a_{21} &= \gamma(\partial \pi/\partial k); \\ a_{22} &= \gamma[(\partial \pi/\partial \pi^e) - 1]. \end{aligned}$$

[34]In an optimal two-country intertemporal framework, a steady-state current account deficit to GDP ratio for the United States may be explained by a lower degree of relative risk aversion relative to that of surplus trading partners, such as Japan, that has a higher degree of relative risk aversion. See Harashima (2005).

[35]The price adjustment coefficient φ is a key parameter, measuring the proportion of the output gap that translates into inflation. Table 7.1 uses $\varphi = 0.25$. The optimal results reported in Table 7.1 are robust to alternative values $\varphi = 0.20$ or $\varphi = 0.29$, with no changes in the results.

Table 7.1. Optimal monetary policy and inflation target (percent, except for $Y^* = Y^{p*}$).

R^{f*}	2.97
$\pi^t = \pi^{e*} = \pi^*$	1.30
$R^* = R^{\text{eq}*}$	4.27
$R^* - \pi^{e*}$	2.97
R^{b*}	7.22
$R^{b*} - \pi^{e*}$	5.92
$(\rho/k)^{*\text{a}}$	3.73
$\text{NMPK}^{*\text{b}}$	9.65
$k^{*\text{c}}$	3.08
$Y^* = Y^{p*\text{d}}$	9,206.592
$(C/N)^{*\text{e}}$	44,350
$\dot{Y}/Y = \dot{Y}^p/Y^{p*}$	3.5
$\dot{Y}/Y - n = \dot{Y}^p/Y^p - n^*$	1.7
Memorandum items:	
$(G/Y)^*$	20.21
$(I/Y)^*$	16.51
$(C/Y)^*$	65.60
$(\text{CAB}/Y)^*$	−2.36

*Denotes steady-state values.
[a]The optimal $\rho = 0.1147$.
[b]Net Marginal Product of Capital (net of depreciation) = $\alpha k^{*(\alpha-1)} - \delta$, in which $\alpha = 0.3$ and $\delta = 0.04$.
[c]The implied long-run capital output ratio is 2.914. The formula for the long-run capital output ratio is $k^{*(1-\alpha)}$.
[d]In billions of constant chained dollars, based on the 2006 working population.
[e]Optimal consumption per worker in constant chained dollars, based on the 2006 working population.
Source: Output from Microsoft Excel *Solver* maximization of text Equation (7.26) subject to the text constraints (7.27).

The general solutions to the system (7.28) are[36]:

$$k_t = [C_1 a_{12}/(\mu_1 - a_{11})]e^{\mu_1 t} + [C_2 a_{12}/(\mu_2 - a_{11})]e^{\mu_2 t} + k^*, \quad (7.29)$$

$$\pi_t^e = C_1 e^{\mu_1 t} + C_2 e^{\mu_2 t} + \pi^{e*}, \quad (7.30)$$

[36]See Klein (1998, p. 469).

in which C_1 and C_2 are constants. The characteristic roots (μ_1, μ_2) are real and distinct, with values $\mu_1 = -0.0608$ and $\mu_2 = -0.3372$.[37] The specific solutions are obtained by setting $t = 0$ in (7.29) and (7.30), specifying initial values k_0 and π_0^e, and solving for C_1 and C_2 in terms of those initial values, the characteristic roots, the elements of the first row of the a_{ij} matrix in (7.28), and the asymptotic values k^* and π^{e*}.[38] The constants are: $C_1 = 0.05314$ and $C_2 = 0.05387$.

The specific solution for $\dot{k}$ is

$$\dot{k}/k = [a_{11}(k_t - k^*) + a_{12}(\pi_t^e - \pi^{e*})]/k_t, \tag{7.31}$$

in which $k(t)$ and $\pi^e(t)$ are given by (7.29) and (7.30).

Now, from (7.4), (7.8), and (7.10), the instantaneous growth rate of potential output is

$$g_t = \alpha(\dot{k}/k) + g^*, \tag{7.32}$$

in which $g^* = \theta k^* + \lambda + n$.

Next, define the adjustment ratio,

$$p_t = (g_t - g_0)/(g^* - g_0). \tag{7.33}$$

The denominator is the distance the output growth rate at time t has to adjust to reach its steady-state value from an initial value. The numerator is the distance the output growth rate has adjusted by time t. Substituting (7.32) into (7.33) solves for the time t (in years) required for a fraction p_t of the way from g_0 to g^*, from which Table 7.2 is computed.[39]

---

[37]The partial derivatives in the system (7.28) are evaluated at the steady-state values $k^* = 3.08$ and $\pi^{e*} = 0.013$ and using the parameter values cited in Section 7.3.

[38]For reasons discussed below, the initial values chosen are: $k_0 = 0.4$ and $\pi_0^e = 0.12$. The equilibrium values of k and π are $k^* = 3.08$, $\pi^* = 0.013$; and $a_{11} = -0.0757$, $a_{12} = -0.8009$.

[39]The initial values $k_0 = 0.4$ and $\pi_0^e = 0.12$ imply the initial value $g_0 = 0.10$ ($> g^* = 0.035$). Microsoft Excel *Solver* was used to solve text Equation (7.33) for the time t, given alternative values of p_t.

Table 7.2. Estimated period of adjustment in years as g_t approaches its limit g^* ($g^* = 0.035; \theta = 0.003$).

Percentage adjustment p_t	Positive initial disequilibrium ($g_0 = 0.10$)[a] t (years)
0.25	3.5
0.50	6.1
0.75	12.1
0.90	23.5

[a]Corresponding to $k_0 = 0.4$ and $\pi_0^e = 0.12$.
Source: Output from Microsoft Excel *Solver* in solving Equation (7.33) for alternative values of p_t.

A negative initial disequilibrium ($g_0 - g^* < 0$) implies that the model economy is initially overstocked with capital.[40] In the real world, the typical adjustment is from a capital-scarce situation to an advanced state. Thus, a positive initial disequilibrium ($g_0 - g^* > 0$) is more relevant. The second column of Table 7.2 involves a large positive initial disequilibrium (the initial growth rate is 10 percent per annum).[41] It takes about 24 years for the model economy to adjust 90 percent of the time required to reach its steady-state growth path.[42] This is indeed a reasonable adjustment speed, since many

[40]A negative initial disequilibrium implies a positive initial disequilibrium for the capital–output ratio, since the latter is equal to $k^{1-\alpha}$, and $k_0 > k^*$, where k_0 is the initial capital–labor ratio.

[41]The assumed initial expected inflation rate is also large, at 12 percent per annum. In terms of Figure 7.1, with reference to point W as the equilibrium point, the assumed initial position is at point Q, in which the initial capital intensity is lower than k^* and the initial expected inflation is higher than π^{e*}, and the adjustment path to Q is traced by the curved line Q–S–W.

[42]A modest value for θ of 0.003 adds about 0.9 percent to the equilibrium annual growth rate of 3.5 percent. Another 0.8 percent is contributed by exogenous technical change, i.e., independent of capital intensity. The growth rate of the working population accounts for the remaining 1.8 percent. A higher value for θ would further reduce adjustment times. The intuitive reason is this: In the modified model in which labor-augmenting technical change is completely exogenous ($\theta = 0$), the adjustment burden to reach long-run equilibrium is borne entirely by changes in the warranted rate. In sharp contrast, in the modified model in which labor-augmenting technical change is partly endogenous ($\theta > 0$), the brunt of adjustment toward equilibrium is shared with changes in the natural

advanced economies have been growing from a capital-scarce state at least this long.

7.6 Summary and Conclusions

This chapter has modified and extended the modern macroeconomic model of economic fluctuations and linked it formally to the Solow–Swan model of economic growth. The key result is that changes in monetary policy have transitory and permanent effects on the levels and growth rates of real and potential GDP. A disinflation program, while creating temporary unemployment, produces in the long-run a permanent increase in the levels and growth rates of real GDP and potential output. Conversely, although an expansionary monetary policy may temporarily keep the economy at full employment, such a policy would lead to higher expected inflation and eventually to a permanent reduction in the levels and growth rates of real and potential GDP. For maximum long-run consumption per effective worker, the inflation target should be set at 1.3 percent and the monetary policy coefficient at 2.97 percent. The estimated adjustment time for the modified model to reach its steady-state growth of 3.5 percent per annum from an initial growth rate of 10 percent per annum is about 24 years. In the real world where technical change is partly endogenous (it absorbs some of society's resources), the adjustment time would be further reduced by a higher value of the labor-augmenting technical change parameter θ because of the natural rate's enhanced adjustment to changes in capital intensity pari passu the warranted rate during the approach to the steady-state.

Appendix 7.A: The Reduced Model and Stability Analysis

Equations (7.22) and (7.23) comprise a system of two differential equations in two unknowns, k and π^e.

$$\dot{k}/k = (i_0 - i_1 r_0 - i_1 r_1 R - i_2 \pi^e)/k - \theta k - (n + \lambda + \delta), \quad (7.A.1)$$

$$\dot{\pi}^e = \gamma(\pi - \pi^e), \quad (7.A.2)$$

rate. The modified model's adjustment speed would be faster because both the warranted and natural rates adjust endogenously to changes in capital intensity.

in which

$$\pi = (B + \varphi A)/[1 + \varphi(1 + \phi)/(\beta + b)], \tag{7.A.3}$$

$$\hat{Y} = [A - B(1 + \phi)/(\beta + b)]/[1 + \varphi(1 + \phi)/(\beta + b)], \tag{7.A.4}$$

$$R = (1 + \phi)\pi + \beta\hat{Y} - \phi\pi^t + R^f, \tag{7.A.5}$$

$$A = \phi\pi^t/(\beta + b) - (1/(\beta + b)(R^f - R^{\text{eq}}), \quad B = \pi^e + Z,$$
$$R^{\text{eq}} = s_0 - s_1 k^\alpha - s_2\pi^e, \quad \text{and} \quad b = s_1 k^\alpha.$$

Differentiating (7.A.1) and (7.A.2) with respect to k and π^e,[43]

$$\begin{aligned}
\partial(\dot{k}/k)/\partial k &= a_{11} \\
&= (1/k)[-i_1 r_1 \partial R/\partial k - (1/k^2)(i_0 - i_1 r_0 - i_1 r_1 R - i_2\pi^e) \\
&\quad - \theta \\
&= -0.02461 < 0; \\
\partial(\dot{k}/k)/\partial\pi^e &= a_{12} = (1/k)[-i_1 r_1(\partial R/\partial\pi^e) - i_2] = -0.26011 < 0; \\
\partial\dot{\pi}^e/\partial k &= a_{21} = \gamma\partial\pi/\partial k = -0.00488 < 0; \quad \text{and} \\
\partial\dot{\pi}^e/\pi^e &= a_{22} = \gamma[(\partial\pi/\partial\pi^e) - 1] = -0.32223 < 0.
\end{aligned}$$

A necessary and sufficient condition for stability is that the eigenvalues of the a_{ij} matrix have negative real parts, and necessary and sufficient conditions for this are that $a_{11} + a_{22} < 0$ and $a_{11}a_{22} - a_{12}a_{21} > 0$. Both these conditions are satisfied, since $a_{11} + a_{22} = -0.34683$ and $a_{11}a_{22} - a_{12}a_{21} = 0.006658$.

The determinant condition that $a_{11}a_{22} - a_{12}a_{21} > 0$ is equivalent to the condition $|a_{22}/a_{21}| = 65.973 > |a_{12}/a_{11}| = 10.571$, i.e., the $\dot{\pi}^e = 0$ curve be steeper than the $\dot{k}/k = 0$ curve. Thus, in the neighborhood of equilibrium, the $\dot{\pi}^e = 0$ and $\dot{k}/k = 0$ curves assume their slopes and positions in Figures 7.1 and 7.2. There is at least one intersection between the two curves, and the point of intersection is locally stable.

[43]The signs of these partial derivatives are determined by evaluating them in the neighborhood of the steady-state, using the parameter values discussed in this appendix.

The long-run equilibrium values k^* and π^{*e} are obtained by equating (7.A.1) and (7.A.2) to zero:

$$\dot{k}/k = [i_0 - i_1 r_0 - i_1 r_1 R(k^*, \pi^{e*}) - i_2 \pi^{e*}]/k^* - \theta k^* - (n + \lambda + \delta)$$
$$= 0, \tag{7.A.6}$$
$$\dot{\pi}^e = \gamma[\pi(k^*, \pi^{e*}) - \pi^{e*}] = 0, \tag{7.A.7}$$

in which the $R(.)$ and $\pi(.)$ functions are defined by Equations (7.A.3)–(7.A.5) above. Given the values of the parameters, the long-run equilibrium values are $k^* = 3.0793$ and $\pi^{e*} = 0.01298$.[44]

To show the extent of the relative shifts of the D and P curves in Figure 7.2, take the partial derivatives of the aggregate demand-inflation relationship (7.17) with respect to π^t, π^e, and k:

(a) Shift in the D curve resulting from change in π^t: $\phi/(1+\phi) = 0.5/1.5 = 0.333$;
(b) Shift in the D curve resulting from change in π^e: $-s_2/(1+\phi) = -0.757/1.5 = -0.505$;
(c) Shift in the D curve resulting from change in k: $-s_1\alpha k^{\alpha-1}/(1+\phi) = -0.251(0.3)(3.08)^{-0.7} = -0.0343$;
(d) Shift in the D curve from D to D''': $-0.333 + 0.505 - 0.0343 = 0.1377$;
(e) Shift in the P curve from P to P' resulting from change in π^e: 1.0.

To show that the downward shift in the $\dot{\pi}^e = 0$ in Figures 7.1 and 7.2 is larger than the downward shift of the $\dot{k}/k = 0$ curve, take the partial derivatives of Equations (7.A.6) and (7.A.7) with respect to π^t:

(a) Shift in the $\dot{k}/k = 0$ curve: $(i_1 r_1 b/k^*)\phi/[\beta + b + \varphi(1+\phi)] > 0$;
(b) Shift in the $\dot{\pi}^e = 0$ curve: $\gamma\varphi\phi/[\beta + b + \varphi(1+\phi)] > 0$.

Since $\phi/[\beta + b + \varphi(1+\phi)]$ is a common multiplier in (a) and (b), it suffices to show that $\gamma\varphi > i_1 r_1 b/k^*$. Evaluating at $k^* = 3.079$, $b^* = s_1 k^{*\alpha} = 0.351$, $\gamma\varphi = 0.175 > i_1 r_1 b/k^* = 0.040$. ■

[44]Microsoft Excel's *Solver* tool was used to maximize Equation (7.26) subject to the set of constraints (7.27). One constraint is the reduced model (7.A.6)–(7.A.7).

Regressions

The following OLS regressions were run on a sample of 37 annual observations of US data from 1970 to 2006 involving these variables:

C : Private consumption,
I : Gross private investment,
G : Government expenditures,
CAB : Exports of goods and service less imports of goods and services,
Y : Gross domestic product,
CPI : Consumer price index,
N : Total employment,
R^b : Corporate bond yield, Moody's Aaa Seasoned series,
R : Federal funds rate.

The data on C, I, G, CAB, and Y were obtained from the Bureau of Economic Analysis, US Department of Commerce. The data on CPI and N were from the Bureau of Labor Statistics, Department of Labor. Finally, the data on R and R^b were from the Board of Governors, Federal Reserve System. The national income accounts data are in Year 2000-chained dollars. The CPI index is based on 1982–1984 = 100. The expected inflation variable π^e is constructed as the sum of the preceding two years' actual inflation rates, with weights of 0.7 for $t-1$ and 0.3 for $t-2$, respectively. The coefficient of inflationary expectations is consistent with $\gamma = 0.7$ used in the constrained optimization program. The regressions use discrete observations on inflation, and the adaptive expectations process is specified as $\Delta\pi_t^e = 0.7(\pi_{t-1} - \pi_{t-1}^e)$. The Koyck lag infinite series was truncated at $t-2$. The per worker data on C/N, I/N, CAB$/N$, and G/N are expressed in thousands of constant price dollars. The data on interest rates were first averaged daily, then monthly, and finally annually, and are expressed as decimals (t-statistics in parentheses). I tried the Federal funds rate, prime rate, and corporate bond interest rate in the investment function, and I decided to use the corporate bond interest rate.

Consumption function

$$C/N = -8.48361 + 0.805755Y/N$$
$$(13.1) \qquad (81.9)$$
$$\overline{R}^2 = 0.99; \quad \text{SE} = 0.5128$$

Investment function[45]

$$I/N = 13.7240 - 29.8162R^b - 40.1278\pi^e$$
$$(10.8) \qquad (1.6) \qquad (2.7)$$
$$\overline{R}^2 = 0.44; \quad \text{SE} = 1.8005$$

Government spending

$$G/N = 10.30096 + 0.04827Y/N$$
$$(13.5) \qquad (4.1)$$
$$\overline{R}^2 = 0.31; \quad \text{SE} = 0.6058$$

---

[45]The prime rate and the Federal funds rate were tried as alternative interest rate variables. The coefficient of the prime rate had the wrong sign and was insignificant,

$$I/N = 11.5 + 7.99\text{PRIME} - 61.92\pi^e$$
$$(12.4) \qquad (0.6) \qquad (4.3)$$
$$\overline{R}^2 = 0.40; \quad \text{SE} = 1.8555,$$

while the coefficient of the Federal funds rate had the correct sign and was insignificant,

$$I/N = 12.3 - 11.05R - 47.50\pi^e$$
$$(17.5) \quad (0.9) \quad (3.23)$$
$$\overline{R}^2 = 0.41; \quad \text{SE} = 1.8440.$$

However, since the Federal funds rate affects the corporate bond interest rate, which in turn affects investments, the Fed rate influences the latter indirectly.

Net export demand

$$\mathrm{CAB}/N = \underset{(7.4)}{7.27405} - \underset{(8.9)}{0.13186}Y/N$$
$$\overline{R}^2 = 0.6844; \quad \mathrm{SE} = 0.7733$$

Corporate bond interest rate

$$R^b = \underset{(11.3)}{0.048226} + \underset{(9.7)}{0.563173}R$$
$$\overline{R}^2 = 0.72; \quad \mathrm{SE} = 0.0115$$

The theoretical macroeconomic model is cast in terms of the effective labor force, L, which is defined as TN, where T is a labor-augmenting technological multiplier (or skills-augmented index), and N is the number of employed workers. The regressions, however, are expressed in terms of N, because T is unobservable. To translate the estimated intercepts and coefficients of the interest rate and expected inflation in terms of units of L, the identity (a) $T = (Y/N)^{\mathrm{ave}}/k^{\alpha}$ is used, in which $(Y/N)^{\mathrm{ave}}$ is the average GDP per worker during the sample (1970–2006).[46] The variable k is now in terms of the effective labor force ($k = K/L$). The intercepts and the coefficients of the interest rate and expected inflation variables in the regression equations for $C/N, I/N, G/N$, and CAB/N were adjusted by dividing them by the index T given by definition (a), so that in effect these variables are now expressed as ratios to L in conformity with the theoretical model. The optimal program is solved, in which the identity (a) is embedded into the regression estimates of the intercepts and relevant coefficients.

References

Chow, G. (1989). Rational versus adaptive expectations in present value models. *The Review of Economics and Statistics*, 71, 376–384.

[46] $(Y/N)^{\mathrm{ave}} = 66{,}940$ constant chained dollars.

Conlisk, J. (1988). Optimization cost. *Journal of Economic Behavior and Organization*, 9, 213–228.

Curto Millet, F. (2007). Inflation expectations, the Phillips curve and monetary policy. *Kiel Working Paper 1339*. Kiel Institute for World Economics.

Fair, R. (2004). *Estimating How the Macro Economy Works*. Boston, MA: Harvard University Press.

Goodfriend, M. and B. McCallum (2007). Banking and interest rates in monetary policy analysis: Quantitative exploration. *NBER Working Paper 13207*.

Hall, R. and J. Taylor (1997). *Macroeconomics*. NY: W.W. Norton & Company.

Harashima, T. (2005). *Endogenous Growth Models in Open Economies: A Possibility of Permanent Current Account Deficits*. Tsukuba, Japan: Graduate School of Systems and Information Engineering, University of Tsukuba.

Kiefer, D. (2008). Inflation targeting, the natural rate and expectations. *Department of Economics Working Paper No. 2008-03*. Salt Lake City, UT: University of Utah.

Klein, M. (1998). *Mathematical Methods for Economics*. New York, NY: Addison-Wesley.

Lovell, M. (1986). Tests of the rational expectations hypothesis. *American Economic Review*, 76, 110–124.

Sato, R. (1963). Fiscal policy in a neo-classical growth model: An analysis of the time required for equilibrium adjustment. *Review of Economic Studies*, 30, 16–23.

Sato, R. (1964). The Harrod-Domar model versus the neoclassical growth model. *Economic Journal*, 74, 380–387.

Schenkerman, M. and M. Nadiri (1984). Investment in R&D, cost of adjustment and expectations, In Z. Griliches (ed.), *R&D, Patents and Productivity*. Chicago, IL: University of Chicago Press.

Sidrauski, M. (1967). Inflation and economic growth. *Journal of Political Economy*, 75, 796–810.

Solow, R. (1956). A contribution to the theory of economic growth. *Quarterly Journal of Economics*, 70, 65–94.

Stein, J. (1966). Money and capacity growth. *Journal of Political Economy*, 74, 451–465.

Swan, T. (1956). Economic growth and capital accumulation. *Economic Record*, 32, 334–362.

Tobin, J. (1965). Money and economic growth. *Econometrica*, 33, 671–684.

Turner, P. (2007). Some UK evidence on the forward-looking IS equation. *WP 2007–16*. Loughborough University.

Villanueva, D. (1994, **Chapter 6**). Openness, human development, and fiscal policies: Effects on economic growth and speed of adjustment. *International Monetary Fund Staff Papers*, 41, 1–29.

Chapter 8

Outward-Oriented Trade Policies and Economic Growth*

8.1 Introduction

One of the robust empirical determinants of long-term output growth in many countries, particularly the developing ones, has been the whole gamut of outward-looking exchange and trade policies designed to promote the expansion and diversification of the export sector.[1] The explanation why such strategies improve growth performance has, however, proven elusive, despite several formal theoretical models, notably that of Feder (1983).[2] While the conclusion that strong export performance promotes long-run economic growth seems intuitively reasonable, it is a clear implication of the standard neoclassical model that exports cannot exert a *sustained* long-run effect on the economy's *growth rate.* As Lucas (1988, pp. 12–15) puts it, "The empirical connections between trade policies and economic growth that Krueger (1983) and Harberger (1984) document are of evident importance, but they seem to me to pose a real paradox

*Written by Delano S. Villanueva and adapted from Staff Papers No. 58, *Exports and Economic Development*, by the permission of the South East Asian Central Banks (SEACEN) Research and Training Centre. Copyright for the year 1997 was obtained by the SEACEN Centre.

[1]For a partial survey of the literature, see Khan and Villanueva (1991), and the references cited therein.

[2]Feder's two-sector (exports and nonexports) model has the standard long-run (steady-state) property that the growth rate of aggregate output is equal to the exogenously determined growth rate of the labor force, adjusted for an exogenous rate of labor-augmenting technical change. See Section 8.2.

to the neoclassical theory we have, not a confirmation of it." There is thus a gap between the empirical work on the nexus of export expansion and the economic growth on the one hand, and standard neoclassical growth theory (Solow, 1956; Swan, 1956) on the other.

Many economists have long recognized the importance of the export sector to the development process. The literature on this subject identifies two channels through which sustained *growth* effects of export activity are expected to be transmitted. First, Keesing (1967) emphasized *learning* effects, the improvement of *human capital*, and the value of competition and close communication with advanced countries. This important channel is reiterated recently by Feder (1983, p. 61) with the observation that exports positively enhance labor productivity via the training of skilled workers, "who find themselves subjected to greater pressures to perform and to train others." Second, Goldstein and Khan (1982) cite production and demand linkages, including the opening up of *investment* opportunities in areas far removed from the actual export activity as the need to supply inputs rises, and as productive facilities are created utilizing inputs and outputs that were nonexistent prior to the expansion of exports. The increase in income that comes directly from exports leads in time to a rise in demand for a wide range of products, including nontradables. These demand pressures are reflected in a higher rate of capacity utilization and ultimately involve investment in facilities providing such products.[3]

Export expansion tends to mobilize domestic and foreign resources in several ways. First, domestic saving may rise because of the general increase in incomes associated with the initial rise in exports. As argued by Maizels (1968), the marginal propensity to save in the export sector could be higher than in other sectors, in which case the rise in saving would be magnified. The rise in saving translates into a rise in investment in physical and human capital,

[3]There are several other growth effects, which are just as important. Balassa (1978) cites the improvement in overall factor productivity arising from the transfer of factors from the rest of the economy to the export sector, which is typically the most productive. This, however, represents a one-time shift in the aggregate production function.

and thus in the rate of economic growth. Second, foreign direct investment and foreign loans may be encouraged by the expansion of the export sector, since investment and lending decisions take into account a country's ability to repay out of export earnings. By enhancing profitability and the capacity to service the external debt (thereby improving creditworthiness), the expansion of the export sector induces higher flows of direct foreign investment and foreign loans that permit an even higher rate of investment (and thus a higher rate of growth). Third, exports provide the necessary foreign exchange to import advanced capital goods and raw materials for which there are no convenient domestic substitutes (Khang, 1968; Bardhan and Lewis, 1970). The transfer of efficient technologies and the availability of foreign exchange have featured prominently in recent experiences of rapid economic growth (Khang, 1987; Thirlwall, 1979). Of course, the superior foreign technology embodied in foreign produced capital goods is widely recognized as a powerful factor in transmitting technological innovations directly to developing economies. Export earnings and export-induced foreign direct investment and loans serve to facilitate the importation of these advanced capital goods. To the extent that these capital imports are stimulated by brisk export activity, the production and demand linkages identified by Goldstein and Khan (1982) are reinforced.

This chapter formally incorporates one important channel in the linkage between exports and growth, namely the learning effect that leads to the improvement of human capital identified by Keesing (1967) and Feder (1983). It does so by incorporating this effect into a modified neoclassical model with endogenous growth.[4] A key result is that the long-run equilibrium growth rate of output is a positive function of, among other variables, the domestic saving rate and the

[4]See, among others, Conlisk (1967), Villanueva (1971, 1994, 2007), Romer (1986), Lucas (1988), Otani and Villanueva (1989), Grossman and Helpman (1990), and Becker *et al.* (1990). These approaches fall into the category of what has been termed *endogenous growth* models. A common feature of these models is the endogeneity of technological progress, particularly the rate of labor-augmenting or Harrod-neutral technical change.

rates of utilization of capital and labor in the export sector. The empirical growth literature (Khan and Villanueva, 1991) confirms these hypotheses. Following a critical review of the literature on the exports-growth relationship, Section 8.2 presents and contrasts the standard growth-cum-exports model and the modified model proposed in this chapter, discusses more fully a two-sector version of the modified model, and extends it in several directions. Section 8.3 derives new Golden Rule results relating to the optimal saving rate, taking into account the positive externalities of export activities operating through an endogenous rate of labor augmenting technological progress. Section 8.4 summarizes and concludes with several policy implications.

8.2 The Growth Model

In the theoretical literature on the relationship between exports and economic growth, a typical approach has been to adopt the standard neoclassical assumption of an exogenously determined rate of labor-augmenting technical change, and to include the export variable as a third factor (in addition to capital and labor) in the aggregate production function, on the premise that exports engender scale effects and externalities.[5] A model developed by Feder (1983) typifies this approach, and has been invoked in empirical studies of the exports-growth nexus.[6]

Feder (1983) presents a two-sector model consisting of exports and nonexports. The two-sector production functions employ capital and labor, with the marginal factor productivities in the export sector assumed to be higher than those in the nonexport sector. Intersector externalities are incorporated by introducing the output of the export sector as a third input in the production function of the nonexport sector. Feder shows that the off-steady state (or transitional) growth

[5]See, among others, Balassa (1978), Tyler (1981), Feder (1983), and Ram (1985). Balassa (1978, p. 185) argues that since "exports tend to raise total factor productivity..., the inclusion of exports in a production function-type relationship is warranted..."

[6]See, among others, Ram (1985) and references cited therein.

rate of total output (exports plus nonexports) is a function of the aggregate investment/output ratio, the growth rate of the total labor force, and the ratio of the change in exports to the level of output. Feder then estimates the parameters of such a growth rate function using cross-country data *averaged over long periods.*[7] However, such long run observations correspond more to the steady-state, than to the year-to-year transitional growth rate of output. Long-run cross-section regressions are more appropriate in testing the steady-state behavior of growth models. As will be shown below, in the long run, the growth rates of the capital stock and of the export input in a Feder-type model would be constrained by the constant rate of growth of the labor force, adjusted for exogenous labor-augmenting technical change. Feder (1983) argues that, given identical marginal factor productivities in both export and nonexport sectors and in the absence of inter-sector externalities, the empirical growth equation reduces to the familiar neoclassical formulation without the export variable. Or does it?

8.2.1 *The Standard vs. Modified Models: An Overview*

The Feder (1983) model may be simplified without sacrificing its main features. It can then be compared with the basic modified model proposed in this chapter. Table 8.1 provides a summary of the two models, with the Feder-type model labeled as the standard one. Both standard and modified models have a two-sector structure, involving two neoclassical production functions for exports and nonexports. For simplicity, it is assumed that the export sector employs a constant uniform rate ε of the total amounts of K and L, with $1-\varepsilon$ being the employment rate prevailing in the nonexport sector.[8] Both models also assume significant intersector externalities involving exports and that the marginal productivities in the export sector are higher than

[7]Many others follow a similar approach. See, for example, Balassa (1978), Tyler (1981), and Ram (1985).

[8]The strict two-sector version of the modified model, characterized by different utilization rates of K and L, is discussed in detail below.

Table 8.1. The standard and modified growth models.

Standard model	Modified model	
$Z = (1-\varepsilon)Lf(k,x)$	$Z = (1-s)Lf(k,x)$	(8.1)
$X = \varepsilon Lg(k)$	$X = \varepsilon Lg(k)$	(8.2)
$L = EN$	$L = EN$	(8.3)
$k = K/L$	$k = K/L$	(8.4)
$x = X/L$	$x = X/L$	(8.5)
$\mathrm{d}K/\mathrm{d}t = sQ - \delta K$	$\mathrm{d}K/\mathrm{d}t = sQ - \delta K$	(8.6)
$(\mathrm{d}E/\mathrm{d}t)/E = \lambda$	$(\mathrm{d}E/\mathrm{d}t)N = h(X) + \lambda L; h' > 0$	(8.7)
$(\mathrm{d}N/\mathrm{d}t) = nN$	$\mathrm{d}N/\mathrm{d}t = nN$	(8.8)
$Q = Z + X$	$Q = Z + X$	(8.9)
Reduced model		
$(\mathrm{d}k/\mathrm{d}t)/k = sk^{-1}\{1-\varepsilon)f[k,\varepsilon g(k)] + \varepsilon g(k)\{sk^{-1}\{1-\varepsilon)f[k,\varepsilon g(k)] + \varepsilon g(k)\}h[\varepsilon g(k)] - (\lambda+\delta+n) - (\lambda+\delta+n)$		(8.10)
Equilibrium capital–labor ratio (k^*)		
Root of the equation:		
$sk^{*-1}\{1-\varepsilon)f[k^*,\varepsilon g(k^*)] + \varepsilon g(k^*)\} -(\lambda+\delta+n) = 0$	$sk^{*-1}\{1-\varepsilon)f[k^*,\varepsilon g(k^*)] + \varepsilon g(k^*)\} -h[\varepsilon g(k^*)] - (\lambda+\delta+n) = 0$	(8.11)
Equilibrium growth rate of output $(Q/Q)^*$		
$[(\mathrm{d}Q/\mathrm{d}t)/Q]^* = [(\mathrm{d}K/\mathrm{d}t)/K]^*$	$[(\mathrm{d}Q/\mathrm{d}t)/Q]^* = [(\mathrm{d}K/\mathrm{d}t)/K]^* = sk^{*-1}\{1-\varepsilon)f[k^*,\varepsilon g(k^*)] + \varepsilon g(k^*)\} - \delta$	(8.12a)
$= [(\mathrm{d}L/\mathrm{d}t)/L]^* = \lambda + n$	$[(\mathrm{d}L/\mathrm{d}t)/L]^* = h[\varepsilon g(k^*)] + \lambda + n$	(8.12b)
or,		
$[(\mathrm{d}Q/\mathrm{d}t)/Q]^* = J(s,\varepsilon,\delta,\lambda,n)$, 0 0 0 1 1	$(Q/Q)^* = J(s,\varepsilon,\delta,\lambda,n)$ + + − + +	(8.12c)

Notation

- Q: total output (GDP), constant dollars
- X: output of the export sector, constant dollars
- Z: output of the non-export sector, constant dollars
- L: labor, in efficiency units, man-hours
- K: capital stock, constant dollars
- E: technical change or productivity multiplier, index number
- N: working population
- $f(\cdot)$: production function for non-exports, intensive form
- $g(\cdot)$: production function for exports, intensive form
- $h(\cdot)$: a unit-homogeneous learning function
- $J(\cdot)$: asymptotic (equilibrium) growth function
- ε : rate of employment of capital and labor in the export sector
- s: saving rate
- δ: depreciation rate
- λ: exogenous rate of labor-augmenting technical change
- n: exogenous rate of working population growth

those in the nonexport sector. Reflecting these assumptions, the production functions for nonexports in both the standard and the modified models include exports as a separate input (Equation (8.1) in Table 8.1). Both models measure the labor input in efficiency units (Equation (8.3)),[9] and employ the neoclassical capital accumulation function (Equation (8.6)), where the net increase in the capital stock is equal to gross saving minus depreciation.

It turns out that the standard assumption of a direct effect of exports on the output of the non-export sector is not essential to the different equilibrium growth implications of the two models (compare equilibrium growth expressions in (8.12c) of Table 8.1). Rather, the critical differences between the standard and modified models lie in their alternative assumptions about the nature of labor-augmenting technical change in relation to the size of the export sector (compare equilibrium growth equations in (8.12b)).[10] In particular, the standard model assumes that the rate of labor-augmenting technical change is independent of export activity. In contrast, the modified model formalizes the observation made by Keesing (1967) and Feder (1983) that the export sector tends to improve the quality (productivity) of the labor input by providing a valuable learning experience (compare the technical change functions in (8.7)). In other words, even if the modified model adopts the standard model's production function for nonexports, in which the export variable appears as another factor input, important differences between the two models would remain. The assumption about the rate of labor-augmenting technical change turns out to be crucial. The standard model's hypothesis that $h' = 0$ means that labor-augmenting technical change is not affected by export activity, and is taking place at an exogenous constant rate λ. In the real world, while a portion of technical change may indeed be

---

[9]If a 1990 man-hour is equivalent as an input in the production function to two man-hours in the base period, say 1960, then the ratio K/L is the amount of capital per half-hour 1990 or per man-hour 1960.

[10]Notice that the two models are identical except for the technical change function.

exogenous, some technical change is clearly endogenous, partly labor-augmenting, and positively enhanced by the expansion of exports, as argued by Keesing (1967) and Feder (1983) and empirically verified by Romer (1990).[11] That is, the hypothesis of this chapter that $h' > 0$, as against the standard assumption that $h' = 0$, appears plausible and merits serious consideration.

Suppose that $h' = 0$, as assumed in the standard model. Where does this assumption lead? It is relatively straightforward to show that the equilibrium growth path would be one on which $([\mathrm{d}Q/\mathrm{d}t)/Q])^* = n + \lambda$ (see the standard model's Equation (8.12b)). Per capita output grows at the exogenous labor-augmenting technical change λ. The saving, export, employment, and depreciation rates do not affect the long-run growth rate of per capita output. This is inconsistent with the robust empirical result that saving behavior and exports raise the long-term growth rate of output. Again, the alternative hypothesis $h' > 0$ deserves to be considered. This hypothesis says that labor-augmenting technological innovations are transmitted to the domestic economy partly through the export sector. In the modified model, the export variable has two effects on output. First, through its role as a factor input in the production of nonexportables, and second, through its influence on the rate of labor-augmenting technical progress. The first channel is a transitory *level* effect (a one-time shift in the production function for nonexports). The second channel is a permanent *growth* effect. Of these two mechanisms, the second one on technical change is pivotal. Reflecting this difference in assumptions about the presence or absence of any link between exports and technological progress, the conclusions regarding the long-run growth rate of output are strikingly dissimilar. In the standard model, as in the neoclassical model without exports, the steady-state growth rate of output is fixed by the constant growth rate of the working population n plus the

---

[11]Romer (1990) finds that a high ratio of exports to GDP is associated with a higher rate of technological change in a cross-section of 90 industrial and developing countries over the period 1960–1985. Thus, by implication, he would probably reject the hypothesis $h' = 0$ in favor of the alternative hypothesis $h' > 0$.

exogenous rate of labor-augmenting technical change λ. By contrast, in the modified model, in addition to being affected by λ and n, the steady-state growth rate of output can be raised by increasing the employment rate ε in the export sector and the aggregate saving rate s, and by lowering the rate of depreciation of capital δ (compare the signs of the partial derivatives of the growth functions in (8.12c) of Table 8.1).

Figure 8.1 illustrates the workings of two models. The vertical and horizontal axes measure, respectively, the growth rates of capital and labor (in efficiency units) and the capital/labor ratio. Panels A and B, respectively, depict the standard and modified models. In either model, the relationship between the rate of capital accumulation and the capital/labor ratio (the KK curve) is downward sloping because of the diminishing marginal productivity of capital. In the standard model, the labor growth schedule (L_sL_s curve) is horizontal with vertical height equal to $\lambda + n$ for all levels of the capital/labor ratio because, by assumption, labor-augmenting technical change is independent of the export/labor ratio and thus of the capital/labor ratio (that is, $h' = 0$). In the modified model, the labor growth curve is now upward-sloping because the rate of labor-augmenting technological progress is a positive function of output per unit of labor in the export sector and, hence, of the capital/labor ratio.[12]

Now, suppose that the rate of utilization of capital and labor in the export sector ε rises for some reason (for example, vigorous implementation of export promotion policies, including competitive exchange rate policy, trade liberalization, and tariff reform). In the standard model (panel A of Figure 8.1), the higher value of ε shifts the KK curve to the right, to $K'K'$, and the new equilibrium is established at point $C(k^*_{s1}, \lambda + n)$, which is characterized by a higher

[12]The export employment rate ε itself may be made an increasing function of the capital–labor ratio k. Given reasonable assumptions that labor productivity in the export sector is higher than in the rest of the economy and that, as labor's productivity increases with a brisk pace of export activity (and a rise in capital intensity), the economy will devote a larger share of resources to expand the export sector and hire more workers.

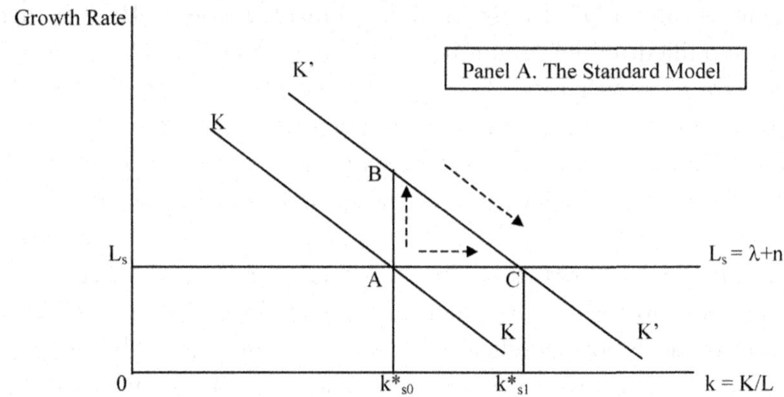

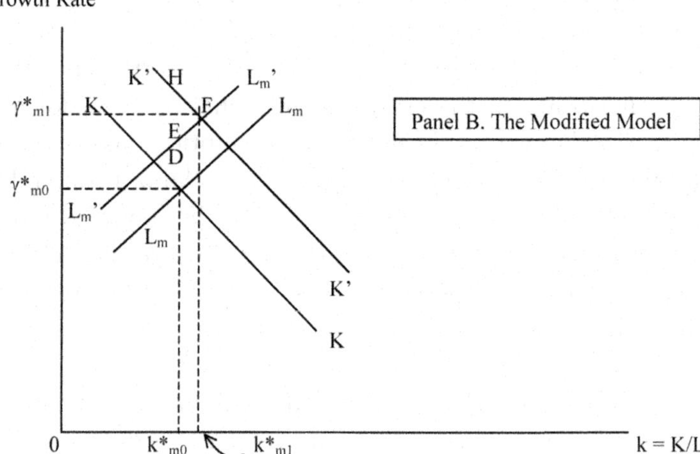

Figure 8.1. Long-run growth equilibrium.

capital/labor ratio but an unchanged growth rate of output.[13] The path *A–B–C* traces the transitional dynamics. The growth rate

[13]In general the effects of a rise in ε on the KK curve work in opposite directions. On the one hand, an increase in ε means less resources are available for production in the nonexport sector. On the other hand, this is offset by higher output in this sector induced by positive externalities generated by rising exports. Additional to this effect is a direct increase in the output of the export sector. Assuming with Feder (1983) that the export sector's marginal factor productivities are higher than those of the nonexport sector, the net effect is to raise the economy-wide

of the capital stock initially jumps to point B, exceeding that of the growth rate of labor by an amount equal to AB. This rise in the growth rate of the capital stock and, hence, of output, is only temporary and cannot be sustained over time, since the labor input ultimately becomes a bottleneck in the production process.[14] As the capital/labor ratio rises from $k*_{s0}$ toward $k*_{s1}$, the marginal productivity of capital declines, and firms will slow the rate of investment until the growth rate of the capital stock is brought down to the constant rate of growth of the labor force at point C. Labor growth, being independent of the capital/labor ratio, slides horizontally from A to C. Thus, in the long run, the rise in the export employment rate ε raises capital intensity and the levels of exports and output, but leaves the growth rate of per capita output unaffected this being fixed by the exogenous rate of labor-augmenting technical change λ.[15]

Turning to the workings of the modified model, the rise in the export employment rate ε shifts the KK curve to the right, to $K'K'$. However, the L_mL_m curve also shifts upward to the left, to $L'_mL'_m$, intersecting the $K'K'$ at point F. Like in the standard model, the growth rate of the capital stock initially jumps to point H, exceeding labor growth by EH. But, unlike the standard model, the modified model's new equilibrium is now characterized by a higher growth rate of output (with the growth rate increasing from γ_{m0} to γ_{m1}).[16]

aggregate output and thus the savings needed for investment. The net effect is an upward shift of the KK curve in the northeast direction.

[14]This temporary growth effect of the export parameter ε is basically the exports-growth relationship emphasized in standard theoretical models, such as Feder's (1983). Standard empirical growth models, such as Knight *et al.* (1993, **Chapter 2**), also find that opening up the domestic economy through reductions in import-weighted average tariffs on intermediate and capital goods tends to raise the transitional growth rate of per capita output.

[15]The levels of exports and output per labor are higher because of the higher capital intensity. The result on higher output per labor is Solow's (1956) conclusion that changes in saving rates, and for that matter changes in the parameter ε in the context of standard neoclassical growth models with exports, are level, *not* growth effects.

[16]The new equilibrium capital/labor ratio may be higher or lower, depending on the magnitudes of the relative shifts in the KK and LL curves. Panel B,

The main difference between two models lies in the behavior of the growth rate of labor. Referring to panel B, Figure 8.1, the initial rise in the capital/labor ratio resulting from the increase in the export employment rate ε leads to an increase in the growth rate of the labor input, instead of remaining constant as in the standard model, for two reasons. First, an increase in ε directly raises exports per labor and thus the rate of labor-augmenting technical change (this is represented by the shift from $L_m L_m$ to $L'_m L'_m$), an increase shown by the distance DE. Second, as the capital/labor rises, a proportion of the increase is used to raise the output of the export sector further, providing additional boost to the rate of labor-augmenting technological improvements (this is represented by the *movement* along the new $L'_m L'_m$ curve), an increase traced by $E-F$.[17] While the growth of the capital stock is falling after an increase in capital/labor ratio (from H to F, owing to diminishing marginal productivity of capital), the growth rate of the labor input rises from D to E to F. After adjustments are completed, the growth rates of capital and labor converge at F. Therefore, in the modified model with endogenous technical change, the long-run growth rate of per capita output increases when the export employment rate is raised.

The available long-run cross-section empirical studies reviewed in Khan and Villanueva (1991) find that the saving rate (or investment rate) and some measure of export activity influence positively and significantly the growth rate of potential output. These findings are consistent with the steady-state behavior of the modified model. They do not support the hypotheses of the standard model that ε and s have no long-run effects on output growth.

To sum up, the restrictive assumption behind most export-cum-growth models is that technical change is given exogenously, typically

Figure 8.1 assumes that the shift in the KK curve is larger, resulting in a higher equilibrium capital–labor ratio. If the shift in the KK curve is smaller than the shift in the LL curve, the new equilibrium capital–labor ratio would be lower, but the new equilibrium output growth rate would remain higher.

[17]There is a third reason. An improvement in labor productivity induced by an increased size of the export sector provides an incentive to raise the share ε of capital and labor utilized in this important sector. This would mean another round of increases in the rate of growth of output.

as a constant rate of labor-augmenting, or Harrod-neutral technical change λ. The modified model allows for an export-induced component of technical change,[18] in addition to an exogenous component. While the inclusion of exports in the standard neoclassical model enriches the transitional growth dynamics, the (asymptotic) long-run growth rate of per capita output remains fixed by the constant rate λ.[19] Thus, the robust empirical result that exports and the growth rate of output are positively correlated in the long run appears to be consistent with the modified model, whereas it is not consistent with those of the standard theoretical models formulated to underpin existing empirical work.

8.2.2 *A Two-Sector Modified Model*

The foregoing discussion suggests the irrelevance of exports as a third factor of production to the steady-state behavior of the growth rate of output, and the crucial importance of exports as a determinant of the rate of Harrod-neutral technological progress. This subsection develops a two-sector modified neoclassical growth model wherein exports enhance the rate of labor-augmenting technical change. This is essentially a formalization of the mechanism identified by earlier authors, notably Keesing (1967). Consider the following model, summarized in Table 8.2. The sector production functions for nonexports and exports, respectively, are given in Equations (8.13) and (8.14). These functions are assumed to satisfy the Inada (1963) conditions.[20] The labor inputs are measured in efficiency units, as before. The sector resource allocation coefficients, μ and θ, are assumed to be given in (8.15) and (8.16), subject to changes by

[18]This is supported by empirical work done by Romer (1990).

[19]As mentioned earlier, the inclusion of exports directly in the production function for nonexports represents a static, one-time upward shift in the production possibilities curve. A ten percent increase in the level of output induced by export expansion, though seemingly large, translates into a small annual growth of only half of a percentage point over 20 years.

[20]That is, with reference to a production function $F(K, L) = Lf(k)$, where K is capital, L is labor, and k is the ratio of K to L, the Inada conditions can be summarized as follows; $\lim \partial F/\partial K = \infty$ as $K \to 0$; $\lim \partial F/\partial K = 0$ as $K \to \infty$; $f(0) \geq 0$; $f'(k) > 0$, and $f''(k) < 0$, for all $k > 0$.

Table 8.2. The modified two-sector model.

$$Z = F(K_{z'}, E_z N_z) \tag{8.13}$$
$$X = G(K_{x'}, E_x N_x) \tag{8.14}$$
$$K_x/K_z = \mu \tag{8.15}$$
$$N_x/N_z = \theta \tag{8.16}$$
$$K = K_x + K_z \tag{8.17}$$
$$N = N_x + N_z \tag{8.18}$$
$$\mathrm{d}K_x/\mathrm{dt} = \chi X - \delta K_x \tag{8.19}$$
$$\mathrm{d}K_z/\mathrm{dt} = \eta Z - \delta K_z \tag{8.20}$$
$$E_x/E_z = 1 + \alpha; \quad \alpha \geq 0 \tag{8.21}$$
$$(\mathrm{d}E_z/\mathrm{dt})/N_z = h(X) + \lambda E_z N_z; \quad h' > 0 \tag{8.22}$$
$$\mathrm{d}N/\mathrm{dt} = nN \tag{8.23}$$
$$k' = K/E_z N \tag{8.24}$$
$$Q = X + Z \tag{8.25}$$

Reduced Model

$$(\mathrm{d}k'/\mathrm{dt})/k' = \chi G[(\mu/(1+\mu)), (1+\alpha)/(1+\theta^{-1})k'] + \eta F[(1/(1+\mu)), 1/(1+\theta)k'] - h(G[(\mu/(1+\mu)(1+\theta)k', (1+\alpha)\theta] - (\lambda + n + \delta) \tag{8.26}$$

Equilibrium capital–labor ratio (k'^{*})
Root of the equation:

$$\chi G[(\mu/(1+\mu)), (1+\alpha)/(1+\theta^{-1})k'^{*}] + \eta F[(1/(1+\mu)), 1/(1+\theta)k'^{*}] - hG[\mu/(1+\mu))(1+\theta)k'^{*}, (1+\alpha)\theta] - (\lambda + n + \delta) = 0 \tag{8.27}$$

Equilibrium growth rate of output $[(\mathrm{d}Q/\mathrm{dt})/Q]^{*}$

$$[(\mathrm{d}Q/\mathrm{dt})/Q]^{*} = [(\mathrm{d}K/\mathrm{dt})/K]^{*} = \chi G[(\mu/(1+\mu)), (1+\alpha)/(1+\theta^{-1})k'^{*}] + \eta F[(1/(1+\mu)), 1/(1+\theta)k'^{*}] - \delta \tag{8.28a}$$

$$[(\mathrm{d}Q/\mathrm{dt})/Q]^{*} = [(\mathrm{d}E_z/\mathrm{dt})/E_z]^{*} + [(\mathrm{d}N/\mathrm{dt})/N]^{*} = hG[\mu/(1+\mu))(1+\theta)k'^{*}, (1+\alpha)\theta] + \lambda + n \tag{8.28b}$$

Notation
The notation is identical for the same variables appearing in Table 8.1. The subscripts x and z refer to exports and nonexports, respectively. The new variables and parameters are

k': ratio of K to $E_z N$
χ : saving rate of the export sector
η : saving rate of the nonexport sector
μ : ratio of sectoral capital stocks
θ : ratio of sectoral labor services
α : a proportional factor by which E_x exceeds E_z

policy and, possibly, by relative profitability in the two sectors. The sector stocks of capital and quantities of labor services add up to the economy-wide totals in (8.17) and (8.18). Constant proportions of sector outputs are saved and invested in (8.19) and (8.20), where the net increases in the sector capital stocks are equal to sector gross saving less depreciation (the same depreciation rate is assumed to apply to the capital stock in each sector).[21]

Equation (8.21) says that the export sector is at least as technologically advanced as the nonexport sector, such that the labor-augmenting technical change multiplier E_x is at least as large as E_z. This is a very plausible assumption. Equation (8.22) is the most important relationship in the modified model. It hypothesizes that, as a form of intersector externality, the productivity of labor employed in the nonexport is influenced positively by export activity ($h' > 0$), and partly by exogenous factors. The modified model collapses to the standard Feder-type model if it is assumed that $h' = 0$, that is, labor productivity in the nonexport sector is independent of export activity. As demonstrated earlier, intersector externalities that assign exports the role of an additional input in the production function of the nonexport sector (à la Feder) make no difference to the asymptotic behavior of the growth model. Finally, Equation (8.24) defines a new variable k' as the ratio of K to $E_z N$. Equation (8.25) is the same as in Table 8.1.

8.2.2.1 *Equilibrium Behavior*

The growth rate of the effective capital stock, denoted $\omega(k')$, may be derived by differentiating Equation (8.17) with respect to time and substituting (8.13)–(8.16), (8.19)–(8.21), and Equation (8.24):

$$\begin{aligned}\omega(k') = \chi G[(\mu/(1+\mu)), (1+\alpha)/(1+\theta^{-1})k'] \\ + \eta F[(1/(1+\mu)), 1/(1+\theta)k'] - \delta. \qquad (8.29)\end{aligned}$$

Similarly, the growth rate of the effective labor input, denoted $\Psi(k')$, may be derived by differentiating Equation (8.18) with respect to time and substituting (8.13), (8.15)–(8.16), and (8.21)–(8.24):

$$\Psi(k') = hG[(\mu/(1+\mu))(1+\theta)k', (1+\alpha)\theta] + \lambda + n. \qquad (8.30)$$

[21]The assumption of a uniform depreciation rate simplifies the mathematics and does not change the main thrust of the analysis.

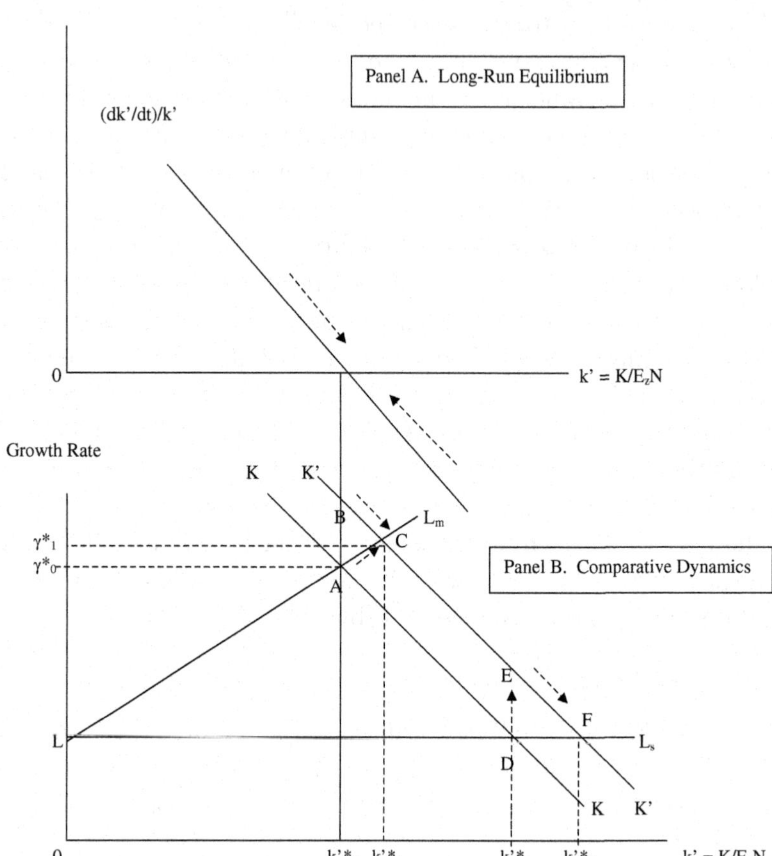

Figure 8.2. The two-sector model.

The growth rate of the capital–labor ratio, k', is thus equal to (see Equation (8.26), Table 8.2):

$$(\mathrm{d}k'/dt)/k' = \omega(k') - \Psi(k'). \tag{8.31}$$

The reduced model, Equation (8.31), is a single equation involving the variables $(\mathrm{d}k'/\mathrm{d}t)/k'$ and k' alone. Given the assumed properties of the neoclassical production function (the Inada 1963 conditions), Equation (8.31) graphs according to Figure 8.2, panel A. The downward slope of the $(\mathrm{d}k'/\mathrm{d}t)/k'$ equation follows from the assumption of positive but diminishing marginal products of capital in the two sectors. The reasons why the curve representing Equation (8.31) lies partly in the first quadrant and partly in the fourth quadrant are given by the other Inada (1963) conditions, namely, for some initial values of the capital/labor ratio, it is possible for capital to grow either faster or slower than labor.

It is obvious by inspection that, at any point on the $(\mathrm{d}k'/\mathrm{d}t)/k'$ curve, the economic system would move in the direction indicated by the arrows. Thus, k' tends to settle at an equilibrium value k'^*. At this point, K and E_zN would grow at the same rate and, by the constant returns assumption, output Q also would grow at this rate. Indicating this equilibrium growth rate γ:

$$\gamma(k'^*) = \chi G[(\mu/(1+\mu)), (1+\alpha)/(1+\theta^{-1})k'^*] + \eta F[(1/(1+\mu)), 1/(1+\theta)k'^*] - \delta \quad (8.32a)$$

$$\gamma(k'^*) = hG[(\mu/(1+\mu))(1+\theta)k'^*, (1+\alpha)\theta] + \lambda + n. \quad (8.32b)$$

Given the production functions F, G, and the learning function h, and since k'^* is a function of the structural parameters of the model, γ is in general a function of χ, η, μ, θ, α, δ, n, and λ. Note that this function $\gamma = \gamma(\chi, \eta, \mu, \theta, \alpha, \delta, n, \lambda|G, F, h)$ has partial derivatives with signs $+, +, +, +, +, -, +, +$. The exact form of the growth rate γ-function is implied by the production functions G, F and the learning function h. However, even for a simple Cobb–Douglas production function and a linear learning function, an explicit solution for the γ-function is generally difficult, if at all possible.

8.2.2.2 *The Dynamic Effects of Exports on Economic Growth*

With the aid of Figure 8.2, panel B the effects of an increase in the rate of investment in the export sector on the equilibrium growth path can be analyzed in greater detail. In Figure 8.2, panel B the initial equilibrium position is indicated by point A, characterized by equilibrium values of capital intensity, $k_0'^*$ and growth rate of output, γ_0^*. An increase in χ from χ_0 to χ_1 shifts the KK curve upward to $K'K'$. The next equilibrium position is indicated by point

C, characterized by a higher growth rate of output, γ_1^*, and a higher capital–labor ratio, $k_1'^*$. How does the system move from A to C?

An increase in χ has direct and indirect effects on the growth rate of the capital stock. An increase in χ directly raises the rate of investment in the export sector, by the amount AB (reflected in the upward shift of the $\omega(k')$ schedule from KK to $K'K'$). The indirect effect is transmitted via a change in investment behavior induced by changes in the marginal product of capital as the level of capital intensity adjusts to the new value of χ (a movement along the $K'K'$ curve), a point elaborated below.

Following an increase in χ, the economy finds itself momentarily at point B, where capital grows faster than labor. Consequently, the ratio of capital to labor begins to rise from $k_0'^*$ to $k_1'^*$. As this happens, the marginal product of capital falls, slowing investment per unit of capital. The dynamic adjustment of the growth rate of capital is traced by the path A–B–C. Similarly, there is an indirect effect on the growth rate of the labor force. As the capital–labor ratio rises, the output–labor ratio increases and with it exports per unit of labor. A higher value of exports per unit of labor, given that $h' > 0$ means an increase in the rate of labor-augmenting technical change along the stationary LL_m schedule, thereby raising the labor growth rate. The path A–C traces the dynamic adjustment. This process continues until the growth rates of capital and labor are equalized by a continuous increase in the capital–labor ratio to the new equilibrium level $k_1'^*$ at point C. At this point, capital growth has decelerated to the new and higher growth rate of labor, and the equilibrium growth rate of output has gone up to γ_1^*.

For comparison, the standard model may be described by the horizontal line LL_s, whose vertical height is equal to $(n + \lambda)$. The initial equilibrium is at point $D(k_2'^*, \lambda + n)$. An increase in χ shifts the capital growth rate schedule upward as before, and the new equilibrium is established at F, characterized by a higher equilibrium capital–labor ratio, but an *unchanged* equilibrium growth rate of output. However, in the short and medium run — between E and F — the rate of growth of output is momentarily higher than $n + \lambda$, because of a higher rate of capital accumulation (by the amount DE)

induced by the expansion of the export sector.[22] As capital intensity rises from $k_2'^*$ to $k_3'^*$, the marginal product of capital falls, slowing the rate of investment. Capital growth decelerates, traced by the path E–F. In the long run, the labor input becomes a bottleneck, and the equilibrium growth rate of output converges to a constant rate $n+\lambda$; the effect of an increase in χ is to raise the equilibrium capital–labor ratio owing to a higher investment rate in the export sector and thus the equilibrium *level* of output per labor.

8.2.2.3 *Some Extensions*

The basic growth model (see the modified model, Table 8.1) can be extended in several directions. Maizels (1968) has argued that the marginal propensity to save in the export sector could be larger than elsewhere, in which case the overall saving-income ratio, s, would increase with an expanding export sector. This hypothesis can be incorporated in the model by assuming that $s = s(\chi)$, with $s' > 0$. The growth effects of export expansion would be magnified by this extension, because of an additional channel (via a higher overall saving–income ratio) through which increased export activity raises the growth rate of the capital stock.

The model can also be extended to incorporate fiscal variables by defining domestic saving into private and government saving: $S = S^p + \tau Q - C^g$, where S^p is private saving, τ is the average income tax rate, and C^g is government real current expenditure on goods and services. Allowing for a degree of debt neutrality or incomplete Ricardian equivalence, private saving can be assumed to be a constant fraction of disposable income: $S^p = \sigma(1-\beta\tau)Q - (1-\beta)(\tau Q - C^g)$, where σ is the private saving ratio, $l-\beta$ is the proportion of a change in government saving offset by an opposite change in private saving ($\beta = 0$ means full debt neutrality or complete Ricardian equivalence).[23] Assuming that $C^g = \Gamma Q$, where

[22]This is the growth effect alluded to by Feder (1983) and others resulting from increased export activity, and by Knight *et al.* (1993) as a consequence of lower tariffs on imported intermediate and capital goods.

[23]For a review of the general literature on debt neutrality or Ricardian equivalence, see Leiderman and Blejer (1987). For empirical evidence on incomplete

Γ is a policy parameter, the aggregate saving ratio now becomes: $s = [\sigma(\chi)(1 - \beta\tau) + (\tau - \Gamma)\beta]$, with $\sigma'(\chi) > 0$. As explained in the preceding paragraph, an increase in χ would have a magnified growth effect through an increase in the private saving rate $\sigma(\chi)$. The growth effects of changes in the average income tax rate τ and the current expenditure ratio Γ can also be analyzed in this extended model. As long as Ricardian equivalence is incomplete, that is, β is nonzero, an increase in the tax/income ratio would raise the overall domestic saving ratio and thus the equilibrium growth rate of output. The opposite effects would be brought about by an increase in the current government expenditure rate Γ.[24]

8.3 Optimal Saving

Long-run output per unit of effective labor in the basic modified growth model (Table 8.1) is $q^* = (Q/L)^* = (1 - \varepsilon)f[k^*, \varepsilon\gamma(k^*)] + \varepsilon\gamma(k^*) = j(k^*)$. If we take the level of q^* as a measure of the standard of living, and since $j'(k^*) > 0$,[25] it is possible to raise living standards by increasing $k*$. This can be done by adjusting the saving rate s, either directly by raising the government saving rate or by providing incentives to increase the private saving rate. If we take consumption per unit of effective labor (or any monotonically increasing function of it) as a measure of the social welfare of the society, we can determine the domestic saving rate that will maximize social welfare by maximizing the level of long-run consumption per effective labor.[26]

Consumption per unit of effective labor is $c = C/L = Q/L - (\mathrm{d}K/\mathrm{d}t + \delta K)/L$, where the last term is gross investment per unit of effective labor. Q/L is $j(k)$ and $(\mathrm{d}K/\mathrm{d}t + \delta K)/L$ is equal to

---

Ricardian equivalence in developing countries, see Haque and Montiel (1989). Also, see IMF (1989, Chapter IV, Appendix).

[24]Strictly speaking, the growth effects of an increase in the tax rate can go either way, depending on the distortionary cost of taxation, the relative productivities of private and public capital, whether the tax revenues are applied to government consumption or investment, etc.

[25]This follows from the assumption that $f_{k*}, g_{k*} > 0$.

[26]Phelps (1966) refers to this path as the *Golden Rule of Accumulation*.

$k(\mathrm{d}K/\mathrm{d}t + \delta)$. In long-run equilibrium, $(\mathrm{d}K/\mathrm{d}t)/K = h[\varepsilon\gamma(k^*)] + n + \lambda$. Thus, we have the equilibrium level of consumption per unit of effective labor:

$$c^* = (C/L)^* = j(k^*) - \{h[\varepsilon\gamma(k^*)] + n + \lambda + \delta\}k^*. \tag{8.33}$$

Maximizing c^* with respect to s:

$$\partial c^*/\partial s = [j'(k^*) - \gamma^* - \delta - k^*h'\varepsilon\gamma'(k^*)]\partial k^*/\partial s = 0, \tag{8.34}$$

where $\gamma^* = h[\varepsilon\gamma(k^*)]+n+\lambda$ is the equilibrium growth rate of output. Since $\partial k^*/\partial s > 0$, the *Golden Rule* condition is[27]

$$j'(k^*) = \gamma^* + \delta + k^*h'\varepsilon\gamma'(k^*). \tag{8.35}$$

Note that in the standard model, since the parameter $h' = 0$ (that is, export expansion has no effects on human resource development), the *Golden Rule* condition reduces to the familiar one: The gross marginal product of capital $j'(k^*)$ should be equal to the steady-state growth rate of output $\gamma^* = n + \lambda$ plus the depreciation rate δ.

The revised condition (8.34) says that, when an expanding export sector continuously improves human skills and productivity, the optimal gross rate of return to capital should be set at a rate higher than the standard magnitude $n + \lambda + \delta$ for two basic reasons. First, when the saving rate is raised, the steady-state growth rate of output will be higher than $n + \lambda$ (the rate obtained from the standard models). Second, capital should be compensated for its additional effect on the equilibrium growth rate of output through what Keesing (1967, p. 305) has termed "the learning effects and improvement of human resources" (that is, the h-function) involved in the mutually reinforcing stages of export expansion and capital accumulation. In view of the positive externalities of export activities and their interaction with capital accumulation, the social marginal of capital exceeds the private marginal product of capital. If capital is paid only the standard rate $n + \lambda + \delta$, its indirect effect on output through the human resource development associated with export

[27]The second-order condition for a maximum is satisfied as long as $h'' < 0$, which implies diminishing returns to the learning function.

expansion, which is in turn dependent on capital accumulation, is not compensated. One way to deal with this problem is to pay capital and labor a proportion ζ of the corresponding marginal product, where ζ is determined so as to exhaust total output:

$$\zeta = j(k^*)/[j(k^*) + h'\varepsilon\gamma'(k^*)\{j(k^*) - k^*j'(k^*)\}]. \tag{8.36}$$

Since ζ is a function of k^* only, it is stationary in the steady-state, and so is the share of capital in output. Rents will remain constant and wages per worker N will grow at the rate $h[\varepsilon\gamma(k^*)] + \lambda$.

8.4 Summary and Conclusions

This chapter has explored several mechanisms through which exports affect, and are affected by, long-term economic growth, namely, production and demand linkages, learning effects and improvement of human resources, adoption of superior technology embodied in foreign produced capital goods, and the general easing of the foreign exchange constraint associated with the expansion of the export sector. Of these various elements, the learning effects that lead to human capital improvements were introduced into a formal growth model via the dependence of technological progress on exports and vice-versa. A key analytical result is that, both in the short run and in the long run, an increase in resources devoted to expanding the export sector will raise the growth rate of output. The long-run result is at variance with the standard theoretical result that the long-run growth rate of output is independent of export activity. Another important analytical result is that, for long-run consumption per effective labor to be maximized, the optimal rate of return to capital should be established at a rate higher than the standard population growth rate adjusted for any exogenous labor-augmenting technical change in order to compensate capital for its additional effect on the long-run growth rate of output through the learning effects and improvement of human resources associated with export activities and their interaction with the saving-investment process. The empirical literature on the growth-exports nexus favors the modified over the standard model.

Because of the central role of exports in the absorption of the latest technology, and the interdependence of investment, technical change, and the size of the export sector, there are several important policy implications that can be drawn from the analysis.

A key policy objective should be to adopt an outward-looking strategy to export manufactures early in the process of industrial development. High protective tariffs tend to create an inefficient industrial sector, prevent the introduction of modern techniques, and stunt factor productivity. This chapter has provided a theoretical rationale for such an outward-looking strategy in the light of recent developments in the *new growth theory* characterized by the improvement of human resources and advances in technology.

A crucial policy instrument is a competitive, market-determined or at least, market-related, level of the real exchange rate, complemented by low, nondiscriminatory tariffs and the elimination of nontariff import barriers. A competitive exchange rate, combined with the protection afforded by transport cost, should reduce the need for tariff protection of domestic consumer goods industries, but more importantly will eliminate anti-export bias.

Strong anti-inflationary financial policies are essential to keep local input prices and wages low, so as to maintain external competitiveness. These policies would necessitate strict limits on fiscal subsidies, tax exemptions, and credit expansion.

References

Balassa, B. (1978). Exports and economic growth: Further evidence. *Journal of Development Economics*, 5, 181–189.

Bardhan, P. and S. Lewis (1970). Models of growth with imported inputs. *Economica*, 57, 575–585.

Becker, G., K. Murphy, and R. Tamura (1990). Human capital, fertility, and economic growth. *Journal of Political Economy*, 98, S12–S37.

Conlisk, J. (1967). A modified neo-classical growth model with endogenous technical change. *Southern Economic Journal*, 54, 199–208.

Feder, G. (1983). On exports and economic growth. *Journal of Development Economics*, 12, 59–73.

Goldstein, M. and M. Khan (1982). The effects of slowdown in industrial countries on growth in non-oil developing countries. *Occasional Paper 12*. Washington, DC: International Monetary Fund.

Grossman, G. and E. Helpman (1990). Comparative advantage and long-run growth. *American Economic Review*, 80, 796–815.

Harberger, A. (ed.) (1984). *World Economic Growth.* San Francisco, CA: ICS Press.

Haque, N. and P. Montiel (1989). Consumption in developing countries: Tests for liquidity constraints and finite horizons. *Review of Economics and Statistics*, 71, 408–415.

Inada, K. (1963). On a two-sector model of economic growth: Comments and generalization. *Review of Economic Studies*, 30, 119–127.

International Monetary Fund (1989). *Staff Studies for the World Economic Outlook.* Washington, DC: International Monetary Fund.

Keesing, D. (1967). Outward-looking policies and economic development. *Economic Journal*, 77, 303–320.

Khan, M. and D. Villanueva (1991). Macroeconomic policies and long-term growth: A conceptual and empirical review. *Working Paper 91/28.* Washington, DC: International Monetary Fund.

Khang, C. (1968). A neoclassical growth model of a resource-poor open economy. *International Economic Review*, 9, 329–338.

Khang, C. (1987). Export-led economic growth: The case of technology transfer. *Economic Studies Quarterly*, 38, 31–47.

Knight, M., N. Loayza, and D. Villanueva (1993). Testing the neoclassical theory of economic growth: A panel data approach. *IMF Staff Papers*, 40, 512–541.

Krueger, A. (1983). *The Developing Countries' Role in the World Economy.* Lecture given at the University of Chicago. Chicago, Illinois.

Leiderman, L. and M. Blejer (1987). Modeling and testing Ricardian equivalence: A survey. *International Monetary Fund Working Paper 87/35.*

Lucas, R. (1988). On the mechanics of economic development. *Journal of Monetary Economics*, 22, 3–42.

Maizels, A. (1968). *Exports and Economic Growth of Developing Countries.* Cambridge: Cambridge University Press.

Otani, I. and D. Villanueva (1989). Theoretical aspects of growth in developing countries: External debt dynamics and the role of human capital. *IMF Staff Papers*, 36, 307–342.

Phelps, E. (1966). *Golden Rules of Economic Growth.* NY: W.W. Norton & Company.

Ram, R. (1985). Exports and economic growth: Some additional evidence. *Economic Development and Cultural Change*, 33, 415–425.

Romer, P. (1986). Increasing returns and long-run growth. *Journal of Political Economy*, 94, 1002–1037.

Romer, P. (1990). Capital, labor, and productivity. *Brookings Papers on Economic Activity*. Washington: The Brookings Institution, 337–367.

Solow, R. (1956). A contribution to the theory of economic growth. *The Quarterly Journal of Economics*, 70, 65–94.

Swan, T. (1956). Economic growth and capital accumulation. *Economic Record*, 32, 334–362.

Thirlwall, A. (1979). The balance of payments constraint as an explanation of international growth rate differences. *Banca Nazionale del Lavoro Quarterly Review*, 32, 45–53.

Tyler, W. (1981) Growth and export expansion in developing countries: Some empirical evidence. *Journal of Development Economics*, 9, 121–130.

Villanueva, D. (1971). A note on Professor Fei's 'Per Capita Consumption and Growth'. *The Quarterly Journal of Economics*, 75, 704–709.

Villanueva, D. (1994, **Chapter 6**). Openness, human development, and fiscal policies. *IMF Staff Papers*, 41, 1–29.

Villanueva, D. and R. Mariano (2007, **Chapter 9**). External debt, adjustment, and growth. In T Ito and A Rose (eds.), *Fiscal Policy and Management in East Asia*, pp. 199–221. National Bureau of Economic Research: The University of Chicago Press.

Chapter 9

External Debt, Adjustment, and Growth*

9.1 Introduction

High ratios of external debt to GDP in selected Asian countries have contributed to the initiation, propagation, and severity of the financial and economic crises in recent years, reflecting runaway fiscal deficits and excessive foreign borrowing by the private sector. More importantly, the servicing of large debt stocks has diverted scarce resources from investment and long-term growth. Applying and calibrating the formal framework proposed by Villanueva (2003) to Philippine data, we explore the joint dynamics of external debt, capital accumulation, and growth. The relative simplicity of the model makes it convenient to analyze the links between domestic adjustment policies, foreign borrowing, and growth. We estimate the optimal domestic saving rate that is consistent with maximum *steady-state* real consumption per unit of effective labor. As a by-product, we estimate the steady-state ratio of net external debt to GDP that is associated with this optimal outcome.

The framework is an extension of the standard neoclassical growth model that incorporates endogenous technical change and global capital markets. The steady-state ratio of the stock of net

*Written by Delano S. Villanueva and Roberto S. Mariano and adapted from *Fiscal Policy and Management in East Asia*, edited by Takatoshi Ito and Andrew Rose, 199–221, by the permission of the University of Chicago Press. Copyright for the year 2007 was obtained by the National Bureau of Economic Research.

external debt to GDP is derived as a function of the real world interest rate, the spread and its responsiveness to the external debt burden and market perception of country risk, the propensity to save out of gross national disposable income, rates of technical change, and parameters of the production function.

Being concerned primarily with the long-run interaction between external debt, growth, and adjustment, our nonstochastic paper is not about solvency or liquidity per se. However, a continuous increase in the foreign debt to GDP ratio will, sooner or later, lead to liquidity and, ultimately, solvency problems. Steady-state ratios of external debt to GDP belong to the set of indicators proposed by Roubini (2001, p. 6): "... *a non-increasing foreign debt to GDP ratio* is seen as a practical sufficient condition for sustainability: a country is likely to remain solvent as long as the ratio is not growing." Cash-flow problems, inherent in liquidity crises, also emerge from an inordinately large debt ratio that results from an unabated increase over time. In our proposed analytical framework, we allow debt accumulation beyond the economy's steady-state growth rate as long as the expected net marginal product of capital exceeds the effective real interest rate in global capital markets. When the return-cost differential disappears, net external debt grows at the steady-state growth of GDP, and the debt ratio stabilizes at a constant level, a function of structural parameters specific to a particular country. Among all such steady-state debt ratios, we estimate an optimal debt ratio that is associated with the value of the domestic saving rate that maximizes *steady-state* real consumption per unit of effective labor.

The main results of the extended model:

1. The optimal domestic saving rate is a fraction of the income share of capital (the standard result is that the optimal saving rate is equal to capital's income share).
2. Associated with the optimal saving rate and maximum welfare is a unique steady-state net foreign debt to GDP ratio.
3. The major policy implications are that fiscal consolidation and the promotion of private saving are critical, while overreliance on foreign saving (net external borrowing) should be avoided,

particularly in an environment of high cost of external borrowing that is positively correlated with rising external debt.

4. For debtor countries facing credit rationing in view of prohibitive risk spreads even at high expected marginal product of capital and low risk-free interest rates, increased donor aid targeted at expenditures on education, health, and other labor productivity enhancing expenditures would relax the external debt and financing constraints while boosting per capita GDP growth.

The plan of this chapter is as follows: Section 9.2 describes the structure of our open-economy growth model with endogenous technical change. We begin with a brief review of the relevant literature, and incorporate some refinements to the closed economy model. First, Gross National Disposable Income (GNDI) instead of GDP is used, since net interest payments on the net external debt use part of GDP, while positive net transfers add to GDP, leaving GNDI as a more relevant variable in determining domestic saving.[1] Second, the marginal real cost of external borrowing is the sum of the risk-free interest rate and a risk premium, which is an increasing function of the ratio of the stock of net external debt to the capital stock. That is to say, inter alia, as the proportion of external debt rises, the risk premium goes up, and so does the effective cost of external borrowing, even with an unchanged risk-free interest rate. Third, via enhanced learning by doing, technical change is made partly endogenous.[2] On the balanced growth path, we then derive the optimal value of the domestic saving rate that maximizes the steady-state level of real consumption per unit of effective labor. Section 9.3 applies the optimal growth framework to the Philippines. Section 9.4 draws some implications for fiscal policy and external debt management. Section 9.5 concludes. Appendices 9.A and 9.B, respectively, analyze the model's stability and describe the data used in the calibrations to the Philippine experience.

[1]In the Philippines, workers' remittances included in private transfers average \$7–\$8 billion per year or some 12 percent of GDP.

[2]See Villanueva (1994, **Chapter 6**).

9.2 The Formal Framework

9.2.1 *Brief Survey of the Literature*

The Solow (1956)–Swan (1956), or S–S, model has been the workhorse of standard neoclassical growth theory. It is a closed-economy growth model where exclusively domestic saving finances aggregate investment. In addition, the standard model assumes that labor-augmenting technical change is exogenous, which determines the equilibrium growth of per capita output.

There have been two developments in aggregate growth theory since the S–S model appeared. First, technical change was made partly endogenous and partly exogenous. Conlisk (1967) was the first to introduce endogenous technical change into a closed-economy neoclassical growth model, in which the saving rate was assumed fixed. This was followed by the recent endogenous growth literature using endogenously and optimally derived saving rate-models (Romer, 1986, 1990; Lucas, 1988; Becker *et al.*, 1990; Grossman and Helpman, 1990, 1991; Rivera-Batiz and Romer, 1991; Barro and Sala-i-Martin, 1995; Villanueva, 2007, **Chapter 9**, among others). Among all classes of closed-economy growth models, the steady-state properties of fixed (Villanueva, 1994, **Chapter 6**) and optimally derived saving rate models are the same.[3]

The second development was to open up the Conlisk (1967) model to the global capital markets. An early attempt was made by Otani and Villanueva (1989), followed by Agénor (2000), and Villanueva (2003). The fixed saving rate models of Otani and Villanueva (1989) and Villanueva (2003) are variants of Conlisk's (1967) endogenous technical change model and Arrow's (1962) *learning by doing* model, wherein experience (measured in terms of either output or cumulative past investment) plays a critical role in raising productivity over time.

[3]Lucas (1988) specifies the effective labor $L = uhN$, where h is the skill level, u is the fraction of non-leisure time devoted to current production, and $1 - u$ to human capital accumulation. His uh variable is our variable A in $L = AN$ (the variable is T in Otani and Villanueva (1989) and Villanueva (1994, **Chapter 6**, Equation (6.12))), interpreted as a labor-augmenting technology or labor productivity multiplier.

In Villanueva (2003), the aggregate capital stock is the accumulated sum of domestic saving and net external borrowing (the current account deficit). At any moment of time, the difference between the expected marginal product of capital, net of depreciation, and the marginal cost of funds[4] in the international capital market determines the proportionate rate of change in the external debt-capital ratio. When the expected net marginal product of capital matches the marginal cost of funds at the equilibrium capital–labor ratio, the proportionate increase in net external debt (net external borrowing) is fixed by the economy's steady-state output growth, and the external debt/output ratio stabilizes at a constant level. Although constant in long-run equilibrium, the steady-state external debt ratio shifts with changes in the economy's propensity to save out of national disposable income, the marginal cost of funds in world capital markets, the depreciation rate, the growth rates of the working population and any exogenous technical change, and the parameters of the risk-premium, production, and technical change functions.

The major shortcoming of the Villanueva (2003) model is its inability to pin down the steady-state external debt ratio that is consistent with maximum consumer welfare. We correct this shortcoming in the present paper. On the balanced growth path, if consumption per unit of effective labor (or any monotonically increasing function of it) is taken as a measure of the social welfare of society, we choose the domestic saving rate that maximizes social welfare by maximizing long-run consumption per unit of effective labor. Consistent with this optimal outcome is a steady-state ratio of net external debt to total output. Using parameters for the Philippines to calibrate the extended model, we show that it is locally stable, with a steady-state solution characterized by a constant capital/effective labor ratio, an optimal domestic saving rate, and

[4]Risk-free interest rate plus a risk premium. The LIBOR, US Prime Rate, US Federal Funds Rate, or US Treasury, deflated by changes in an appropriate price index in the United Kingdom or United States of America, typically represents the risk-free interest rate. The risk premium is country specific and a positive function of a country's external debt burden and other exogenous factors capturing market perceptions of country risk.

a unique external debt/capital ratio.[5] The latter interacts with long-run growth and domestic adjustment and is determined jointly with other macroeconomic variables, including a country's set of structural parameters.

9.2.2 *The Extended Model*

Our model can be summarized as follows[6]:

$$Y = Lk^{\alpha} \quad \text{(Gross Domestic Product)} \tag{9.1}$$

$$\text{GNDI} = Y - \text{NFP} + \text{NTR} \quad \text{(Gross National Disposable Income)} \tag{9.2}$$

$$\text{CAD} = S^f = C + I - \text{GNDI} \quad \text{(Current Account Deficit)} \tag{9.3}$$

$$C = \text{cGNDI} \quad \text{(Consumption function)} \tag{9.4}$$

$$\text{NFP} = rD \quad \text{(Net factor payments)} \tag{9.5}$$

$$\text{NTR} = \tau Y \quad \text{(Net transfers)} \tag{9.6}$$

$$\dot{D} = \text{CAD} \quad \text{(Net debt issue)} \tag{9.7}$$

$$d = \frac{D}{K} \quad \text{(Debt/capital ratio)} \tag{9.8}$$

$$\dot{d}/d = \alpha k^{\alpha-1} - \delta - r \quad \text{(External Borrowing Function)} \tag{9.9}$$

---

[5]For empirical external debt research using various statistical techniques, see Manasse *et al.* (2003); Reinhart *et al.* (2003); Kraay and Nehru (2004); Patillo *et al.* (2004); and Manasse and Roubini (2005). For a survey, see Kraay and Nehru (2004).

[6]The numéraire is the foreign price of the investment good. Thus, P^d/eP^f is multiplied by residents' saving (in constant dollars), where P^d is the price of domestic output, e is the exchange rate in quantity of local currency units per unit of foreign currency, and P^f is the price of the investment good in foreign currency. Foreign saving denominated in foreign currency is deflated by P^f to get the real value. Similarly, the marginal real cost of external borrowing is the sum of the world interest rate and risk premium in foreign currency less the rate of change in P^f. Since model simplicity is our primary concern, we abstract from the effects of movements of these variables by arbitrarily assigning unitary values to these price and exchange rate indices without loss of generality. Incorporation of these variables in the extended model is straightforward and is done in Otani and Villanueva (1989).

$$r^e = r^f + \phi d \quad \text{(Effective Interest Rate)} \tag{9.10}$$

$$\dot{K} = I - \delta K \quad \text{(Capital growth)} \tag{9.11}$$

$$L = AN \quad \text{(Effective labor)} \tag{9.12}$$

$$N = nN \quad \text{(Working population growth)} \tag{9.13}$$

$$\dot{A} = \theta \frac{K}{N} + \lambda A \quad \text{(Technical change function)} \tag{9.14}$$

$$k = \frac{K}{L} \quad \text{(Capital/effective labor ratio)} \tag{9.15}$$

Here, Y is aggregate output produced according to a standard neoclassical production function,[7] K is physical capital stock, L is effective labor (in efficiency units, man-hours or man-days), A is labor-augmenting technology (index number), N is working population, k is the capital/effective labor ratio, GNDI is gross national disposable income, NFP is net factor payments, NTR is net transfers, CAD is external current account deficit, S^f is saving by nonresidents, C is aggregate consumption, I is gross domestic investment, D is net external debt,[8] d is the net external debt/capital ratio, r is the marginal real cost of net external borrowing, r^e is the effective world interest rate, r^f is the risk-free interest rate; τ, δ, ϕ, n, λ, and α are positive constants, and θ is the learning coefficient, as in Villanueva (1994, **Chapter 6**). In a closed economy (when $D = 0, S^f = 0$) with technical change partly endogenous ($\theta > 0$), the model reduces to the Villanueva (1994, **Chapter 6**) model; additionally, if technical change is completely exogenous ($\theta = 0$), the model reduces to the S–S model.

Consumption in the extended model reflects the openness of the economy — consumption is gross national disposable income plus foreign saving less aggregate investment.[9] Here, $s = 1 - c$ is the

[7] Any production function will do, as long as it is subject to constant returns to scale and satisfies the Inada (1963) conditions.

[8] D is defined as external liabilities minus external assets; as such, it is positive, zero, or negative as external liabilities exceed, equal, or fall short of, external assets.

[9] From the national income identity (Equation (9.3)).

propensity to save out of gross national disposable income. After we solve for the balanced growth path, we choose a particular value of s that maximizes social welfare (long-run consumption per unit of L).[10]

The transfers/grants parameter τ may be allowed to vary positively with the domestic savings effort s. Donors are likely to step up their aid to countries with strong adjustment efforts. Finally, donor aid τ earmarked for education, health, and other labor-productivity enhancing expenditures is expected to boost the learning coefficient θ.

Foreign saving is equivalent to the external current account deficit, which is equal to the excess of domestic absorption over national income or, equivalently, to net external borrowing (capital plus overall balance in the balance of payments) — noted in Equations (9.3) and (9.7).

The derivation of the effective cost, r, of net external debt, $D(= D^{\text{gross}} - A^f)$ is as follows: Assume a linear function for the effective interest rate $r^e = r^f + \phi d$, where $0 < \phi < 1$ (Equation (9.10)); the second term is the spread that is increasing in d.[11] Net interest payments on net external debt

$$
\begin{aligned}
&= r^e D^{\text{gross}} - r^f A^f, \\
&= (r^f + \phi d) D^{\text{gross}} - r^f A^f \\
&= r^f (D^{\text{gross}} - A^f) + \phi d D^{\text{gross}} \\
&= r^f (D^{\text{gross}} - A^f) + \phi \frac{D}{K} D^{\text{gross}} \\
&= r^f D + \phi \frac{D}{K} D^{\text{gross}}.
\end{aligned}
$$

---

[10] Thus, the saving ratio $s = 1 - c$ will be chosen endogenously.

[11] An increase in d raises the credit risk and thus the spread. The parameter ϕ is likely to be negatively correlated with the domestic saving effort. Countries with high domestic saving rates appear to enjoy low spreads (for given debt ratios) because of the quality of their adjustment policies — sound fiscal policy, conservative monetary policy, and the like.

Dividing both sides by D,

$$r = r^f + \frac{\phi D^{\text{gross}}}{K} = r^f + \frac{\phi(D + A^f)}{K} = r^f + \phi d + \frac{\phi A^f}{Y} k^{(\alpha-1)}$$

$$r = r^f + \phi[d + \varepsilon k^{(\alpha-1)}], \tag{9.16}$$

where D^{gross} is gross external liabilities, A^f is gross external assets, $D = D^{\text{gross}} - A^f$, and $A^f/Y = \varepsilon$. Assume that the gross external assets, A^f, are a constant (minimum) fraction of GDP: $A^f = \varepsilon Y$.[12] In the case of the Philippines, $\varepsilon = 0.214$ at present.

The optimal decision rule for net external borrowing is specified in Equation (9.9); at any moment of time, net external borrowing as percent of the total outstanding net stock of debt is undertaken at a rate equal to the growth rate of the capital stock plus the difference between the expected marginal product, net of depreciation, and the marginal real cost of funds, r.[13] A more general law of motion for external capital is

$$\frac{\dot{d}}{d} = \beta[\alpha k^{(\alpha-1)} - \delta - r], \tag{9}'$$

where $\beta > 0$ measures the speed of adjustment of external capital to the discrepancy between capital's expected net marginal product and the world real interest rate. In his discussion of the Villanueva (1994, **Chapter 6**) model in the context of open global capital markets, Agénor (2000, p. 594) obtains the key result that the steady-state values of capital intensity and the debt-to-capital ratio are locally stable if and only if the *adjustment speed of external capital is sufficiently large* (Appendix 9.A demonstrates local stability of long-run equilibrium), i.e., $\beta > \{[\eta + s(1 - \eta)]/(1 - \alpha)\}d_0$, where η is the ratio of tax revenue to national income, s is the ratio of domestic

[12] A rule of thumb is that the variable A^f represents 3–4 months of imports.

[13] Equations (9.7) and (9.9) equate net foreign saving with net foreign borrowing, not strictly true. Net foreign saving (sum of capital, financial, and overall accounts in the balance of payments) includes debt (bonds and loans) and nondebt-creating flows (equities and foreign direct investment); both flows use up a portion of GDP, with the latter as dividends and profit remittances abroad. Our variables D and r, respectively, should be interpreted broadly to include equities and foreign direct investment, as well as dividends and profit remittances.

saving to national income, α is the elasticity of output with respect to the capital stock, and d_0 is the initial debt-to-capital ratio.[14]

When the expected yield-cost differential is zero and k is at its steady-state value k^*,[15] the net external debt as ratio to output stabilizes at a constant level.[16] However, this constant debt level may not necessarily be optimal in the sense of being associated with maximum consumer welfare. For it to be so, it has to be associated with a particular value of the domestic saving rate that maximizes long-run consumption per effective labor.

9.2.3 *The Reduced Model*

By successive substitutions, the extended model reduces to a system of two differential equations in k and d.[17]

$$\frac{\dot{k}}{k} = \left\{ \frac{s[(1+\tau)k^{(\alpha-1)} - rd]}{1-d} \right\} + \left[\frac{(\alpha k^{(\alpha-1)} - \delta - r)d}{1-d} \right] - \left[\frac{\delta}{1-d} \right] - \theta k - n - \lambda = H(k,d) \tag{9.17}$$

$$\frac{\dot{d}}{d} = \alpha k^{(\alpha-1)} - \delta - r = J(k,d), \tag{9.18}$$

where r is a function of k and d — given by Equation (9.16).

---

[14]In the application of our framework to the Philippines, fully described in Section 9.3, using $s = 0.188$, $\eta = 0.186$, $d_0 = 0.13$ (historical averages from 1993–1998), and $\alpha = 0.4$, the adjustment speed β should be at least 0.073. Our assumed unitary value is much larger than this minimum.

[15]An asterisk denotes steady-state value of any variable.

[16]The steady-state current account balance may be positive (deficit), zero (in balance), or negative (surplus). This follows from the steady-state solution $(\frac{\dot{D}}{Y})^* = \frac{g^* d^*}{k^{*(\alpha-1)}}$, where g^* is the steady-state growth rate of output, d^* is the steady-state debt/capital ratio, and k^* is the steady-state capital/effective labor ratio. As defined by Equation (9.8), the variable d^* is the ratio of net external debt (external liabilities minus external assets) to the capital stock and can be positive, zero, or negative. More precisely, $-1 < d^* < 1$, depending on whether the accumulated sum of domestic savings is less than, equal to, or greater than the aggregate capital stock (accumulated sum of aggregate investments).

[17]It can be seen that in a closed economy, $d = \tau = 0$, Equation (9.18) drops out and, thus, Equation (9.17) is identical to the Villanueva (1994, **Chapter 6**) model (Equation (6.9)). Further, with $\theta = 0$, Equation (9.17) reduces to the Solow–Swan model.

Long-run equilibrium is obtained by setting the reduced system (9.17) and (9.18) to zero, such that k is constant at k^* and d is constant at d^*. It is characterized by balanced growth: K, L, and D grow at the same rate $\theta k^* + n + \lambda$. It also implies the condition $\alpha k^{*\alpha-1} - \delta - r(d^*, k^*; r^f) = 0$, which is the optimal rule for external net borrowing to cease at the margin.[18]

The steady-state solutions for k^*, d^*, and r^* are

$$\left\{\frac{s[(1+\tau)k^{*(\alpha-1)} - r^* d^*]}{1-d^*}\right\} - \frac{\delta}{1-d^*} - \theta k^* - n - \lambda = 0 \quad (9.19)$$

$$d^* = \frac{[(\alpha - \phi\varepsilon)k^{*(\alpha-1)} - \delta - r^f]}{\phi} \quad (9.20)$$

$$r^* = r^f + \phi d^* + \phi\varepsilon k^{*(\alpha-1)}. \quad (9.16)'$$

Long-run equilibrium is defined by point $Q(d^*, k^*)$ in Figure 9.1.[19] In regions N and W, the dynamics force d to increase, and in regions S and E, the dynamics force d to decrease. In regions N and E, the dynamics force k to decrease, and, in regions S and W, the dynamics force k to increase. Any initial point, like point A, leads to a movement toward the equilibrium point Q, with a possible time path indicated by point A.

9.2.4 *Restrictions on External Financing*

Using the definition of d (Equation (9.8)), the law of motion for external capital as specified in Equation (9.9) can be restated as:

$$\frac{\dot{D}}{D} = \frac{\dot{K}}{K} + \alpha k^{(\alpha-1)} - \delta - r. \quad (9.9)'$$

Using the definition of k (Equation (9.15)) and substituting Equations (9.12)–(9.14) into Equation (9.17), we obtain $\dot{K}/K =$

---

[18]When the yield-cost differential is zero, net external borrowing as percent of the outstanding net stock of debt proceeds at the steady-state growth rate of output.
[19]For the derivation of the slopes of the curves shown in Figure 9.1, see Appendix 9.A.

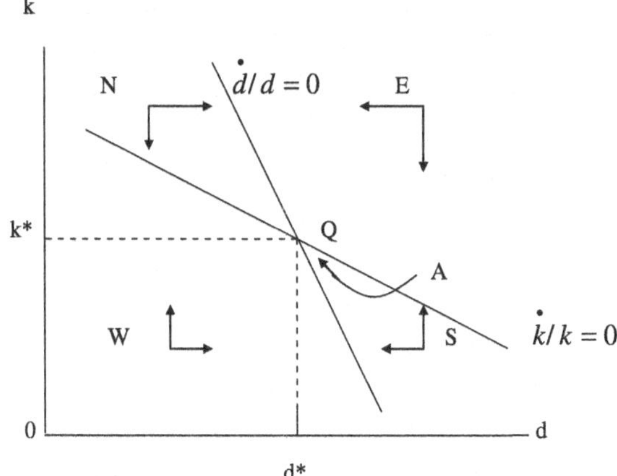

Figure 9.1. Phase diagram of the extended model.

$\theta k + n + \lambda + H(k, d)$. Substituting this into Equation (9.9)′,

$$\frac{\dot{D}}{D} = \theta k + n + \lambda + H(k, d) + \alpha k^{(\alpha-1)} - \delta - r, \quad \text{where } r = r(d, k; r^f). \tag{9.9}''$$

Equation (9.9)″ says that at any moment of time, the amounts of external financing vary with levels of k and d. In long-run equilibrium (i.e., in the steady-state), external financing as percent of the debt stock is equal to the GDP growth g^* (noting that $H[k, d)] = 0$ and $\alpha k^{(\alpha-1)} - \delta - r = 0$, and that, by the assumption of constant returns, GDP grows at the same rate as capital and effective labor),

$$(\dot{D}/D)^* = (\dot{K}/K)^* = (\dot{Y}/Y)^* = g^*(k^*, d^*). \tag{9.9}'''$$

In other words, in the short run, there are no limits on the absolute level of the debt stock or on its increment. External financing is ruled in the short run by Equation (9.9)″ (a function of k and d, given r^f). In the long run, external debt grows at the same rate as GDP, given by Equation (9.9)‴ (a function of k^* and d^*).

In Figure 9.1, the speed of adjustment to long-run equilibrium (characterized by, among other conditions, a zero return-cost differential in global capital markets) varies with the initial values of k and d. In growth modeling, the speed of adjustment of state variables like d and k usually refers to the number of periods (e.g., years) it takes for the variables to adjust to their long-run equilibrium values.

In Figure 9.1, an adjustment trajectory may be that, if initially, $d < d^*$, but $k > k^*$, d increases at first slowly, then accelerates toward d^*, aided by k falling to k^* and thus raising capital's net marginal product, which in turn induces higher capital inflows. Or, if initially both $d < d^*$ and $k < k^*$, d monotonically increases toward d^* (as does k toward k^*), with more or less than the same speed each period. There are other trajectory paths with different adjustment speeds in the north, east, and south quadrants of Figure 9.1. Adjustment speeds of our model have been numerically solved by Chen (2006), confirming different adjustment speeds depending on the initial values of output growth (a function of initial values of k and d), and on whether the adjustment starts from above or below g^*. A finite albeit slow adjustment of external capital is what is observed empirically, both domestically and especially for foreign capital.

9.2.5 *Optimal Growth*

In the steady-state, output per unit of effective labor is $y^* = k^{*\alpha}$. If y^* is considered a measure of the standard of living, and since $dy^*/dk^* > 0$, it is possible to raise living standards by increasing k^*. This can be done by adjusting the domestic saving rate s, for example, by raising the public sector saving rate and assuming imperfect Ricardian equivalence.[20] If consumption per unit of effective labor is taken as a measure of the social welfare of the society, the saving rate s that maximizes social welfare by maximizing long-run consumption can be determined. Phelps (1966) refers to this path as the *Golden Rule of Accumulation.*

From Equation (9.3), steady-state consumption per unit of effective labor is

$$\begin{aligned}(C/L)^* &= (\text{GNDI}/L)^* + (S^f/L)^* - (I/L)^* \\ &= (1+\tau)k^{*\alpha} - r^*d^*k^* + \{[(dK/dt)/K]^* \\ &\quad + \alpha k^{*(\alpha-1)} - \delta - r^*\}d^*k^* - \{[(dK/dt)/K]^* + \delta\}k^*,\end{aligned}$$

[20] There is ample empirical evidence (Haque and Montiel, 1989) that, at least for developing countries, the private sector saving rate does not offset one-to-one the increase in the public sector saving rate.

and since $\alpha k^{*(\alpha-1)} - \delta - r^* = 0$,

$$= (1+\tau)k^{*\alpha} - r^*d^*k^* - (1-d^*)k^*[(dK/dt)/K]^* - \delta k^*,$$

where $r^* = r^f + \phi[d^* + \varepsilon k^{*(\alpha-1)}]$.

Also in the steady-state,

$$[(dK/dt)/K]^* = \theta k^* + n + \lambda.$$

Thus,

$$(C/L)^* = (1+\tau)k^{*\alpha} - r^*d^*k^* - (1-d^*)(\theta k^* + n + \lambda)k^* - \delta k^*. \tag{9.21}$$

Maximizing $(C/L)^*$ with respect to s, and noting that

$$d^* = [(\alpha - \phi\varepsilon)k^{*(\alpha-1)} - \delta - r^f]/\phi \quad \text{and} \quad r^* = r^f + \phi[d^* + \varepsilon k^{*(\alpha-1)}],$$

$$\begin{aligned}
&\partial(C/L)^*/\partial s \\
&\quad = \{(1+\tau)\alpha k^{*(\alpha-1)} - r^*d^* - \delta - (1/\phi)[(r^* + \phi d^*)(\alpha - \varepsilon\phi)] \\
&\qquad \times (\alpha-1)k^{*(\alpha-1)} - (1-d)\theta k^* - [2(\alpha - \varepsilon\phi) + \varepsilon](\alpha-1)d^*k^{*(\alpha-1)} \\
&\qquad - [1 - d^* - (\alpha - \varepsilon\phi)(\alpha-1)(1/\phi)k^{*(\alpha-1)}]g^*\}\partial k^*/\partial s = 0.
\end{aligned} \tag{9.22}$$

Since $\partial k^*/\partial s > 0$, the Golden Rule condition is[21]

$$\begin{aligned}
&(1+\tau)\alpha k^{*(\alpha-1)} - r^*d^* - \delta \\
&\qquad = [1 - d^* - (\alpha - \varepsilon\phi)(\alpha-1)(1/\phi)k^{*(\alpha-1)}]g^* \\
&\qquad\quad + [2(\alpha - \varepsilon\phi) + \varepsilon](\alpha-1)d^*k^{*(\alpha-1)} \\
&\qquad\quad + (1/\phi)[(r^* + \phi d^*)(\alpha - \varepsilon\phi)](\alpha-1)k^{*(\alpha-1)} + (1-d)\theta k^*
\end{aligned}$$

or

$$M = sUZ + V + W + X - U\delta/(1-d^*),$$

[21]The second-order condition for a maximum, $\partial^2(C/L)^*/\partial s^2 < 0$, is a tediously long algebraic expression that, when evaluated at the steady-state values solved for the Philippines, yields a value of -0.01847. See last page of Appendix 9.A.

or

$$s = [M - V - W - X + U\delta/(1 - d^*)]/UZ,^{22} \tag{9.23}$$

where

$$M = (1 + \tau)\alpha k^{*(\alpha-1)} - r^* d^* - \delta;$$

$$U = [1 - d^* - (\alpha - \varepsilon\phi)(\alpha - 1)(1/\phi)k^{*(\alpha-1)}];$$

$$V = [2(\alpha - \varepsilon\phi) + \varepsilon](\alpha - 1)d^* k^{*(\alpha-1)};$$

$$W = (1/\phi)[(r^* + \phi d^*)(\alpha - \varepsilon\phi)](\alpha - 1)k^{*(\alpha-1)};$$

$$X = (1 - d^*)\theta k^*; \quad \text{and}$$

$$Z = [(1 + \tau)k^{*(\alpha-1)} - r^* d^*]/(1 - d^*).$$

M is capital's net (of depreciation) marginal product less interest payments on the stock of net external debt. The first-order condition (9.22) says that for social welfare to be maximized the domestic saving rate should be raised to a point where the net return to capital is a multiple of the long-run growth rate of output. X is nothing more than the open-economy[23] version of the endogenous component of labor-augmenting technical change — the component of $(dA/dt)/A$ induced by learning that occurs at a higher level of capital intensity, which, in turn, is caused by a higher domestic saving rate. If there are no learning ($\theta = 0$), no net external debt ($d^* = 0$) and no net transfers ($\tau = 0$), Equation (9.22) reduces to $\alpha k^{*(\alpha-1)} - \delta = \lambda + n$, which is the familiar Golden Rule result from standard neoclassical growth theory, i.e., the optimal net rate of return to capital equals the natural growth rate. If there is learning ($\theta > 0$) and there are no net external debt ($d^* = 0$) and no net transfers ($\tau = 0$), Equation (9.22) reduces to the Villanueva (1994, **Chapter 6**) *Golden Rule* result, $\alpha k^{*(\alpha-1)} - \delta = g^* + \theta k^*$, where $g^* = \theta k^* + \lambda + n$. The effect of opening up the economy to global capital and labor markets is to

[22]This expression for the optimal s uses the relation $g^* = \theta k^* + n + \lambda = \{s[(1 + \tau)k^{(\alpha-1)} - r^* d^*] - \delta\}/(1 - d^*)$, substituting it for g^* in Equation (9.22).

[23]Reduced by a factor $(1 - d^*)$. When $d = 0$, this term becomes θk^* in Villanueva (1994, **Chapter 6**).

raise the optimal net rate of return to capital beyond $\lambda + n$ or even beyond $g^* + \theta k^*$ when $\theta > 0$ — when there is learning by doing — because of four factors.

First, when the domestic saving rate s is raised, the equilibrium growth rate g^* will be higher than $\lambda + n$, by the amount of $\theta \partial k^*/\partial s$. Second, capital should be compensated for the effect on equilibrium output growth through the induced learning term θk^*. Third, when the domestic saving rate is raised, the equilibrium debt stock d^* will be lower, releasing resources toward more capital growth; the effective interest rate r^* also will be lower pari passu with a lower spread, further increasing domestic resources for investment and growth. Fourth, the availability of foreign saving to finance capital accumulation enhances long-run growth, up to a point.

An alternative interpretation of the above *Golden Rule* can be given. A standard neoclassical result is that the optimal saving rate s should be set equal to the income share of capital, α. To see this, set $d^* = \tau = \theta = 0$, and since $\partial k^*/\partial s > 0$, the *Golden Rule* condition is the standard relation

$$\alpha k^{*(\alpha-1)} - \delta = n + \lambda,$$

i.e., the net (of depreciation) return to capital equals the steady-state natural growth rate.

Since $sk^{*(\alpha-1)} - \delta = n + \lambda$,

$$sk^{*(\alpha-1)} - \delta = \alpha k^{*(\alpha-1)} - \delta,$$

or

$$s = \alpha.$$

If $d^* = \tau = 0$ and technical change is partly endogenous ($\theta > 0$), the modified *Golden Rule* is

$$\alpha k^{*(\alpha-1)} - \delta = g^* + \theta k^*,$$

which is Villanueva's result (1994, **Chapter 6**).

Since $sk^{*(\alpha-1)} - \delta = g^*$,

$$\alpha k^{*(\alpha-1)} = sk^{*(\alpha-1)} + \theta k^*,$$

or

$$s = \alpha - \theta k^{*(2-\alpha)}.$$

In general, Villanueva (1994, **Chapter 6**) shows that for any income share of capital $\pi = k^* f'(k^*)/f(k^*)$, where $f(.)$ is the intensive form of the production function, $s = \sigma\pi$, where the fraction $\sigma = (g^* + \delta)/(g^* + \delta + \theta k^*)$.[24] Here, $g^* + \delta + \theta k^* = f'(k^*)$ is the gross social marginal product of capital, inclusive of the positive externalities arising from the learning associated with capital accumulation in an endogenous growth model. Equivalently put, income going to capital as a share of total output should be a multiple of the amount saved and invested in order to compensate capital for the additional output generated by endogenous growth and induced learning. A value of π equal to s, implicit in the standard model, would under compensate capital and thus be suboptimal from a societal point of view.

The open economy's optimal domestic saving rate, given by Equation (9.23), is higher than $\alpha - \theta k^{*(2-\alpha)}$ given by Villanueva (1994, **Chapter 6**), reflecting the inherent risks involved in foreign borrowing.[25]

In general, the existence, uniqueness, and stability of the steady-state equilibrium are not guaranteed. However, Appendix 9.A shows that for a Cobb–Douglas production function, linear *learning by doing* and risk-premium functions, and values of the parameters for the Philippines, the extended model's equilibrium is locally stable in the neighborhood of the steady-state.[26]

[24]For derivation, see Villanueva (1994, **Chapter 6**).

[25]In the calibration of the model to Philippine data in the next subsection, the optimal s estimated for the open-economy and closed-economy versions are 0.34 and 0.30, respectively. Both values are less than the share of income going to capital, equal to 0.40, consistent with the result first shown by Villanueva (1994, **Chapter 6**) in an endogenous growth model.

[26]Outside the neighborhood of the steady-state, multiple equilibria, jumps, and the like are theoretically possible.

9.3 Application to the Philippines

Developments in fiscal policies and in access to external sources of capital in East Asia (as elsewhere) often raise important external debt issues. This section presents an illustrative numerical example[27] using representative parameters for the Philippines: $\alpha = 0.4$, $\delta = 0.04, \tau = 0.07$, $n = 0.025, \lambda = 0.02$, $r^f = 0.03$, $\phi = 0.41$, and $\theta = 0.005$.[28] Using Microsoft Excel's *Goal Seek* tool, the solution values are $d^* = 0.07$ and $k^* = 6.8$. Note that d^* and k^* are functions of s in the reduced model (Equations (9.16), (9.17), and (9.18)), while the (optimal) s is a function of d^* and k^* (Equation (9.23)). Therefore, iterations were performed to obtain a unique value for s that satisfies Equations (9.16), (9.17), (9.18), and (9.23). The resulting optimal value of the domestic saving rate $s = 0.3429$.

Steady-state per capita GDP growth is 5.4 percent per year, of which the endogenous component is 3.4 percent per year.[29] The steady-state risk premium is 288 basis points, steady-state gross external debt is 43.5 percent of GDP, and steady-state net external debt/GDP ratio is 22.1 percent of GDP.[30] Steady-state interest payments are 2.6 percent of GDP. Using the relation,

$$\left(\frac{\dot{D}}{D}\right)^* = \left(\frac{\dot{K}}{K}\right)^* = \left(\frac{\dot{L}}{L}\right)^* = g^* = \left(\frac{\dot{Y}}{Y}\right)^* \quad \text{(in the steady-state)},$$

or

$$\left(\frac{\dot{D}}{Y}\right)^* = \left(\frac{\dot{Y}}{Y}\right)^* \left(\frac{D}{Y}\right)^* = g^* d^* / [k^{*(\alpha-1)}]$$

$$= (0.079)(0.07)/[(6.8)^{-0.6}] = 0.017; \qquad (9.24)$$

---

[27] The next section discusses the linkages between fiscal policy and the management of external debt in the Philippines. The discussion in this section is specific to the Philippine case and, in particular, does not cover a situation where the state is part of a federal currency union.

[28] $\phi = \phi^* k^{*(1-\alpha)}$, where $\phi^* = 0.13$ was estimated using averages of the ratio of changes in the risk spread to changes in the ratio of external debt to GDP. See Appendix 9.B.

[29] It would take about 13 years for per capita GDP to double.

[30] $(D/Y)^* = d^*/k^{*(\alpha-1)}$.

Table 9.1. Sensitivity calculations.

$\phi^* = \Delta$ spread/Δ debt/GDP	0.10	0.13	0.15
Optimal domestic saving rate	0.3519	0.3429	0.3372
Gross external debt/GDP	0.5274	0.4353	0.3883
Net external debt/GDP	0.3134	0.2213	0.1743
Per capita GDP growth	0.0558	0.0540	0.0532
Years to double per capita income	12.54	12.96	13.13

the steady-state external current account deficit is 1.7 percent of GDP.[31]

The above calculations are based on a 0.13 average ratio of changes in spread to changes in the external debt/GDP ratio estimated over the period 2000–2003. Table 9.1 shows the sensitivity of the results to alternative values of this ratio.

The estimated optimal domestic saving rate, steady-state per capita GDP growth rate, and the number of years it would take for per capita GDP to double are robust to alternative values of the ratio of changes in spread to changes in the external debt/GDP ratio of 0.10 to 0.15. However, as expected, the steady-state gross external debt/GDP ratio declines from 53 percent to 39 percent, and the steady-state net external debt/GDP ratio from 31 percent to 17 percent, as the sensitivity of the spread to the debt ratio rises from 0.10 to 0.15.[32]

In the Philippines, optimal long-run growth requires raising the domestic saving rate from the historical average of 18.8 percent of GNP (IMF, 1999, Table 5) during 1993–1998 to a steady-state 34 percent over the long term.This is necessary to achieve external viability while maximizing long-run (steady-state) consumption per effective labor. The savings effort should center on fiscal consolidation and adoption of incentives to encourage private saving,

[31]Recall that $-1 < d^* < 1$. When $-1 < d^* < 0$, Equation (9.24) solves for the external current account surplus (e.g., Singapore). When $d^* = 0$, the long-run current account is in balance.

[32]If the sensitivity parameter is 0.15, it means that a one percent increase in the net external debt/GDP ratio is associated with an increase of 15 basis points in the spread.

including market-determined real interest rates. From the national income identity (9.3), the external current account deficit CAD is equal to the excess of aggregate investment I over domestic saving $S(= \text{GNDI} - C)$, or CAD $= I - S$. Decomposing I and S into their government and private components CAD $= (I_g - S_g) + (I_p - S_p)$, where the subscripts g and p denote government and private, respectively. The first term is the fiscal balance, and the second term is the private sector balance. Fiscal adjustment is measured in terms of policy changes in S_g (government revenue less consumption) and in I_g (government investment). Given estimates of the private sector saving-investment balance and its components, the optimal government saving-investment balance may be derived as a residual; from this, the required government saving ratio can be calculated because the optimal growth model implies a government-investment ratio.

Assume, however, the following *hypothetical* worst case-scenario for the Philippines. For whatever reason (political, social, etc.), owing to the initial high level of the external debt, market perceptions reach a very high adverse level. Despite a high expected marginal product of capital, the risk premium is prohibitively high at any level of the debt ratio and the risk-free interest rate, such that the Philippine public sector faces credit rationing.[33] In such circumstances, as Agénor (2000, pp. 595–596) suggests, increased foreign aid targeted at investment broadly defined to include physical and human capital may benefit the Philippines, provided that economic policies are sound.

9.4 Implications for Fiscal Policy and External Debt Management

The implications for fiscal policy and external debt management are clear for the Philippines. The first step is to launch an effective external debt management strategy that will articulate the

[33]The credit risk is included in the risk premium. The higher is the credit risk assigned by international creditors/investors, the higher is the risk premium and consequently, the higher is the effective real interest rate.

short- and long-run objectives of fiscal policy and debt management and ensure effective centralized approval and monitoring of primary debt issues to global financial markets, aided by (a) detailed electronic data on external debt, both outstanding and new debt, by borrowing institution, maturity, terms, etc., and by (b) an interagency desk exclusively responsible for top quantitative and analytic work on external debt for the benefit of policy makers.

The level of external debt can be reduced only by cutting the fiscal deficit immediately and at a sustained pace over the medium term. In this context, the privatization of the National Power Corporation (NAPOCOR) is essential, since a big chunk of sovereign debt issues is on behalf of NAPOCOR.

Interest payments on total government debt currently eat up a significant share of government revenues, leaving revenue shortfalls to cover expenditures on the physical infrastructure and on the social sectors (health, education, and the like). With a successful and steady reduction of the stock of debt and the enhancement of domestic savings led by the government sector (via increases in S_g), the sensitivity of the risk spread to the external debt would decrease, resulting in interest savings that would provide additional financing for the infrastructure and social sectors. Furthermore, there are clear implications for both revenue-raising and expenditure-cutting measures. On the revenue side, although the recently enacted and signed VAT bill is welcome, there remains low compliance on the VAT, resulting in very low collections. There is evidence of VAT sales being substantially under declared on a regular basis. Our concrete proposal would be to set up a computerized system of VAT sales wherein an electronic copy of the sales receipt is transmitted in real time by merchants, producers, and service providers to the Bureau of Internal Revenue (BIR). In this manner total sales subject to the VAT submitted cum tax time can be compared by the BIR against its own electronic receipts. It is estimated that if only 50 percent of total sales were collected from VAT, the current budget deficit (some P200+ billion) could be wiped out. This proposal easily beats current proposals to raise taxes because as they stand, marginal tax rates are already very high (resulting in tax evasion and briberies).

The imposition of *sin* taxes (on cigarettes and liquor sales) would provide little relief. Individual and corporate tax reforms are also necessary — different tax brackets should be consolidated into a few, with significant reductions in marginal income tax rates; at the same time, the number of exemptions should be drastically reduced to widen the tax base. The whole customs tariffs structure should be reviewed with the aim of reducing average tariff rates further, while eliminating many exemptions. The role of the customs assessor and collector should be severely restricted, with computerized assessment and collection being put in place, similar to our VAT proposal.

9.5 Summary and Conclusions

This chapter has explored the joint dynamics of external debt, capital accumulation, and growth. In developing countries in East Asia and elsewhere, external debt issues are often associated with public policy decisions about fiscal policy. This has been especially relevant since the Asian financial crisis in the late 1990s. The relative simplicity of our model makes it convenient to analyze the links between domestic adjustment policies, foreign borrowing, and growth. We estimate the optimal domestic saving rate for the Philippines that is consistent with maximum real consumption per unit of effective labor in the long run. As a by-product, we estimate the steady-state ratio of net external debt to GDP that is associated with this optimal outcome. The framework is an extension of the standard neoclassical growth model that incorporates endogenous technical change and global capital markets. Utilizing this framework, the linkages between fiscal policy and external debt management are discussed in the context of a calibrated model for the Philippines. The major policy implications are that in the long run, fiscal adjustment and the promotion of private saving are critical; reliance on foreign saving in a globalized financial world has limits, and when risk spreads are highly and positively correlated with rising external debt levels, unabated foreign borrowing depresses long run welfare.

The obvious policy conclusions of the extended model are:

1. Fiscal consolidation and strong incentives for private saving are essential to achieving maximum per capita GDP growth.
2. The domestic saving rate should be set below the share of capital in total output, owing to positive externalities arising from learning by doing associated with capital accumulation. Equivalently put, income going to capital as a share of total output should be a multiple of the amount saved and invested in order to compensate capital for the additional output generated by endogenous growth and induced learning.
3. Reliance on foreign savings (external borrowing) has limits, particularly in a global environment of high interest rates and risk spreads.
4. When real borrowing costs are positively correlated with rising external indebtedness, the use of foreign savings is even more circumscribed; and
5. When risk spreads are prohibitively large despite high-expected marginal product of capital, there is a role for increased foreign aid earmarked for education and health, provided that economic policies are sound.

Appendix 9.A: Stability Analysis

Partially differentiating Equations (9.16), (9.17), and (9.18) with respect to k and d and evaluating in the neighborhood of the steady state yield

$$\begin{aligned} a_{11} = H_k = {} & [s(1+\tau) - \varepsilon\phi d^*][1/(1-d^*)](\alpha-1)k^{*\alpha-2} \\ & + (\alpha - \varepsilon\phi)[(\alpha-1)d^* k^{*\alpha-2}][1/(1-d^*)] - \theta = \ ? \end{aligned} \tag{9.A.1}$$

$$\begin{aligned} a_{12} = H_d = {} & -[s(1-d^*)^{-2}][(1+\tau)(k^{*\alpha-1}) - r^* d^*] \\ & - s(r^* + \phi d^*)(1-d^*)^{-1} - \phi d^*(1-d^*)^{-1} + \delta(1-d^*)^{-2} = \ ? \end{aligned} \tag{9.A.2}$$

$$a_{21} = J_k = (\alpha - \varepsilon\phi)(\alpha-1)k^{*\alpha-2} = \ ? \tag{9.A.3}$$

$$a_{22} = J_d = -\phi < 0. \tag{9.A.4}$$

In the steady-state, Equations (9.19) and (9.20) are equated to zero:

$$H(k, d) = 0 \tag{9.A.5}$$

$$J(k, d) = 0. \tag{9.A.6}$$

Totally differentiating (9.5) and (9.6) with respect to k and d yields,

$$Hk(dk/dd) + H_d = 0 \tag{9.A.7}$$

$$Jk(dk/dd) + J_d = 0. \tag{9.A.8}$$

The slope of the $\dot{k}/k = 0$ curve is given by:

$$(dk/dd)|\dot{k}/k = 0 = -H_d/H_k = -a_{12}/a_{11} = ? \tag{9.A.9}$$

The slope of the $\dot{d}/d = 0$ curve is given by:

$$(dk/dd)|\dot{d}/d = 0 = -J_d/J_k = -a_{22}/a_{21} = ? \tag{9.A.10}$$

Let A be the matrix of partial derivatives defined by Equations (9.A.1)–(9.A.4). For stability, a necessary and sufficient condition is that the eigenvalues of A have negative real parts, and a necessary and sufficient condition for this is that:

$$\text{tr}(A) < 0, \tag{9.A.11}$$

and

$$|A| > 0. \tag{9.A.12}$$

Since the signs of Equations (9.A.1)–(9.A.3) are ambiguous, both trace (9.A.11) and determinant (9.A.12) conditions are indeterminate. The trace condition is

$$a_{11} + a_{22} < 0.$$

The determinant condition is

$$a_{11}a_{22} - a_{12}a_{21} > 0.$$

Assuming values of parameters estimated for the Philippines and evaluating the matrix of partial derivatives in the neighborhood of the steady state, $a_{11} = -0.4226$, $a_{12} = -0.2516$, $a_{21} = -0.0112$, and $a_{22} = -0.4107$. Thus, the trace condition (9.A.11) $a_{11} + a_{22} < 0$ is met. The determinant condition (9.A.12) is also met. The extended model's phase diagram shown in Figure 9.1 reflects these considerations.

The second-order condition for maximum consumption per unit of L is

$$\begin{aligned}
&\partial^2(C/L)/^*\partial s \\
&\quad = (1+\tau)\alpha(\alpha-1)k^{*(\alpha-2)} - r^*(dd^*/dk^*) \\
&\qquad - d^*[(\partial r^*/\partial k^*) + (\partial r^*/\partial d^*)(dd^*/dk^*)] \\
&\qquad - (1/\phi)[(r^* + \phi d^*)(\alpha - \phi\varepsilon)](\alpha-1)(\alpha-1)k^{*(\alpha-2)}] \\
&\qquad - (1/\phi)(r^* + \phi d^*)(\alpha - \varepsilon\phi)(\alpha-1)(\alpha-1)k^{*(\alpha-2)} \\
&\qquad - (1/\phi)(\alpha-1)k^{*(\alpha-1)}[(\alpha-\varepsilon\phi)((\partial r^*/\partial k^*) + (dd^*/dk^*))] \\
&\qquad - (1-d^*)\theta + \theta k^*(dd^*/dk^*) \\
&\qquad - [2(\alpha-\varepsilon\phi)+\varepsilon][d^*(\alpha-1)k^{*(\alpha-2)} + k^{*(\alpha-1)}(dd^*/dk^*)] \\
&\qquad - [1 - d^* - (\alpha-\varepsilon\phi)(\alpha-1)(1/\phi)k^{*(\alpha-1)}]\theta + g^*[(dd^*/dk^*) \\
&\qquad + (\alpha-\varepsilon\phi)(\alpha-1)(1/\phi)(\alpha-1)k^{*(\alpha-2)}] < 0, \qquad (9.A.13)
\end{aligned}$$

where

$$\begin{aligned}
(dd^*/dk^*) &= (\alpha-\varepsilon\phi)(\alpha-1)k^{*(\alpha-2)}(1/\phi) \\
(\partial r^*/\partial k^*) &= \phi\varepsilon(\alpha-1)k^{*(\alpha-2)} \\
(\partial r^*/\partial d^*) &= \phi(\partial d^*/\partial k^*) \\
g^* &= \theta k^* + \lambda + n.
\end{aligned}$$

When evaluated at the steady-state, $\partial^2(C/L)^*/\partial s = -0.01847 < 0$ and, thus, satisfies the second-order condition (9.A.13) for a maximum.

Appendix 9.B: Data

9.B.1 *Definitions*

1. C: Deflated Consumption Expenditures.
2. GNP: Deflated Gross National Product.
3. GNDI: Deflated Gross National Disposable Income.
4. CAB: Deflated Current Account Balance.
5. JACI: JPMorgan Asia Credit Index on Asian US dollar denominated bonds, containing more than 110 bonds, using their dirty prices and weights according to respective market capitalization. It includes sovereign bonds, quasi-sovereign bonds, and corporate bonds from those countries.

9.B.2 *Data Sources*

1. JACI Spread: JP Morgan Markets.
2. US GDP Deflator: International Financial Statistics (IFS).
3. US CPI for all urban consumers: US Bureau of Labor Statistics (USBLS).
4. Philippine External Debt: Bangko Sentral ng Pilipinas (BSP).
5. External Assets: Bangko Sentral ng Pilipinas (BSP).
6. Nominal GDP: IFS.
7. Average Exchange Rates: BSP.
8. Consumption, GNP, GNDI, CAB, Current Transfers, GDP Deflator: (IFS).

9.B.3 *Sample Period*

Philippine JACI Spreads: 2000–2003.

9.B.4 *Software Used*

Philippine Optimal Domestic Saving Rate: Microsoft Excel, "Goal Seek".

References

Agénor, P-R. (2000). *The Economics of Adjustment and Growth*, pp. 591–596. San Diego, CA: Academic Press.

Arrow, K. (1962). The economic implications of learning by doing. *Review of Economic Studies*, 29, 155–173.

Becker, G. and K. Murphy (1990). Human capital, fertility, and economic growth. *Journal of Political Economy*, 98, S1237.

Chen, S. (2006). External debt and growth dynamics. M.A. thesis, School of Economics and Social Sciences, Singapore Management University.

Conlisk, J. (1967). A modified neo-classical growth model with endogenous technical change. *The Southern Economic Journal*, 34, 199–208.

Grossman, G. and E. Helpman (1990). Comparative advantage and long-run growth. *American Economic Review*, 80, 796–815.

Grossman, G. and E. Helpman (1991). *Innovation and Growth in the Global Economy.* Cambridge, MA: MIT Press.

Haque, N. and P. Montiel (1989). Consumption in developing countries: Tests for liquidity constraints and finite horizons. *Review of Economics and Statistics*, 71, 408–415.

Inada, K-I. (1963). On a two-sector model of economic growth: Comments and generalization. *Review of Economic Studies*, 30, 119–127.

Kraay, A. and V. Nehru (2004). When is external debt sustainable? *World Bank Policy Research Working Paper 3200.*

Lucas, R. (1988). On the mechanics of economic development. *Journal of Monetary Economics*, 22, 3–42.

Manasse, P. and N. Roubini (2005). Rules of thumb for sovereign debt crises. *International Monetary Fund Working Paper 05/42.*

Manasse, P. and N. Roubini and A. Schimmelpfenning (2003). Predicting sovereign debt crises. Manuscript. University of Bologna, IMF and New York University.

Otani, I. and D. Villanueva (1989). Theoretical aspects of growth in developing countries: External debt dynamics and the role of human capital. *IMF Staff Papers*, 36, 307–342.

Patillo, C., H. Poirson and L. Ricci (2004). What are the channels through which external debt affects growth? *International Monetary Fund Working Paper 04/15.*

Phelps, E. (1966). *Golden Rules of Economic Growth.* NY: W.W. Norton & Company.

Reinhart, C., K. Rogoff and M. Savastano (2003). Debt Intolerance. *Brookings Papers on Economic Activity.*

Rivera-Batiz, L. and P. Romer (1991). International trade with endogenous technical change. *Working Paper 3594.* Washington: National Bureau of Economic Research.

Romer, P. (1986). Increasing returns and long-run growth. *Journal of Political Economy*, 94, 1002–1037.

Romer, P. (1990). Endogenous technological change. *Journal of Political Economy*, 98 (Part 2), S71–S102.

Roubini, N. (2001). Debt sustainability: How to assess whether a country is insolvent. Manuscript. Stern School of Business: New York University.

Solow, R. (1956). A contribution to the theory of economic growth. *The Quarterly Journal of Economics*, 70, 65–94.

Swan, T. (1956). Economic growth and capital accumulation. *Economic Record*, 32, 334–362.

Villanueva, D. (1994, **Chapter 6**). Openness, human development, and fiscal policies: Effects on economic growth and speed of adjustment. *IMF Staff Papers*, 41, 1–29.

Villanueva, D. (2003). External debt, capital accumulation, and growth. *SMU-SESS Discussion Paper Series in Economics and Statistics.*

Villanueva, D. and R. Mariano (2007, **Chapter 9**). External debt, adjustment, and growth. In T Ito and A Rose (eds.), *Fiscal Policy and Management in East Asia.* pp. 199–221. National Bureau of Economic Research: The University of Chicago Press.

Chapter 10

Optimal Saving and Sustainable Foreign Debt*

10.1 Introduction

High ratios of external debt to gross domestic product (GDP) in several Asian countries, exacerbated by the current COVID19 pandemic, have contributed to the initiation, propagation, and severity of financial and economic crises in the last two and a half decades, reflecting runaway fiscal deficits and excessive foreign borrowing by both public and private sectors.[1] The servicing of large debt stocks has diverted scarce resources from investment and economic growth.

Applying and calibrating the formal framework developed by Villanueva (2003) to Philippine data, Villanueva and Mariano (2007, **Chapter 9**) (henceforth VM1) explored the joint dynamics of external debt, capital accumulation, and growth.[2] The relative

---

*Written by Delano S. Villanueva and Roberto S. Mariano and adapted from *The Philippine Review of Economics* 57, 170–199, by the permission of the Philippine Review of Economics. Copyright 2021 by the Philippine Review of Economics.

[1] "Amid rising debt risks in low-income developing countries and emerging markets, the IMF and the WB have been implementing a multipronged approach (MPA) to address debt vulnerabilities. Amplification of debt risks owing to COVID19 has upped the urgency to implement the MPA and highlights the importance of debt sustainability and transparency for long-term financing for development. At the same time, it should be noted that countries have limited capacities which are further stretched by COVID19 and that implementation of the MPA by itself may not be sufficient to address debt vulnerabilities and risks from global economic shocks." (IMF, 2020).

[2] The VM1 model was developed and discussed in a paper, External Debt, Adjustment, and Growth, presented at the Conference on Fiscal Policy and

simplicity of the VM1 model made it convenient to analyze the links between domestic adjustment policies, foreign borrowing, and growth.[3] Using the Golden Rule criterion suggested by Phelps (1966), VM1 calculated the optimal domestic saving rate at 34 percent of GDP and the ratio of gross external debt at 44 percent of GDP, consistent with maximum steady-state real consumption per effective labor. In a comment on the VM1 paper, Lui (2007) noted that the ambitious saving rate of 34 percent may be due to the inattention to consumer preferences and attitudes toward risk. An optimal control procedure explicitly incorporating preference and risk is developed and discussed in Ramsey (1928)-Cass (1965)-Koopmans (1965), henceforth RCK. The RCK setup maximizes the discounted stream of lifetime consumption in search of optimal saving. This Golden Utility level of saving is a function of deep parameters such as, among others, the rate of time preference and the coefficient of relative risk aversion, or its reciprocal, the elasticity of intertemporal substitution.[4] How do these deep parameters affect the optimal saving rate? Is it possible that the relatively high domestic saving rate estimated by VM1 is exaggerated by the absence of explicit consideration of consumer tastes and attitudes toward risk?

To answer the above questions, this paper presents an open-economy growth (henceforth VM2) model, employing the RCK optimal control procedure and modifying the Arrow (1962) learning-by-doing framework in which workers learn through experience on

Management in East Asia, hosted jointly by the National Bureau of Economic Research and the Philippine Institute for Development Studies, and held in Manila on June 23–25, 2005. That paper was subsequently published as Ch. 6 in Ito and Rose (eds.) (2007).

[3]Ito and Rose (eds.) (2007: 4) comment: "Villanueva and Mariano use a model that focuses on external debts, while providing an explicit set of economic dynamics that links borrowing to growth, capital accumulation and productivity. They apply their model to Philippine data. Their key findings are eminently reasonable; they imply that increased saving by the public and private sectors is the only way to escape future disaster. If this seems like common sense, it is; the depressing realization is that increasing savings is still a task beyond the ability of most governments."

[4]Using a Constant Relative Risk Aversion (CRRA) utility function.

the job, thereby increasing their productivity. The VM2 model finds that the Golden Rule domestic saving rate of 34 percent of GDP estimated by the VM1 model is associated with an implicitly high value of the elasticity of intertemporal substitution or an unrealistically low degree of relative risk aversion. Using a range of elasticities of intertemporal substitution estimated by Szpiro (1986), the VM2 model implies much lower Golden Utility domestic saving rates of 18–22 percent of GDP.[5] This range of optimal saving rates is dynamically efficient and achievable in developing and emerging market economies. The associated sustainable net foreign debt to GDP ratio is in the range of 12-23 percent of GDP.[6] Given the 27 percent average ratio of gross foreign assets to GDP during 1970–2004 for the Philippines (Lane and Milesi-Ferretti 2006), the sustainable gross foreign debt is in the range of 39–50 percent of GDP.[7]

Section 10.2 is a brief survey of the relevant literature. The model is introduced and explained in Section 10.3, followed by an analysis and discussion of its transitional and steady-state dynamics in Section 10.4. Section 10.5 derives optimal saving rates and sustainable foreign borrowing. Section 10.6 concludes with implications for saving, debt, and growth policies.

10.2 A Brief Survey of the Literature

The evolution of aggregate growth theory involves three levels: (1) closed vs. open economy; (2) fixed-exogenous saving rate vs.

---

[5]Corresponding to the estimated intertemporal substitution elasticity of 0.5, 0.7, and 0.9 from Table 10.2, Section 10.5.

[6]For derivation and discussion, see text and notes to Table 10.2, Section 10.5.

[7]Net foreign debt = gross foreign debt (liabilities) minus gross foreign assets (US$). Using gross international reserves as a proximate measure of gross foreign assets, Philippine gross foreign assets at end-2019 were 23.3 percent of GDP (BSP 2019). Taking 17.5 percent of GDP as the sustainable net foreign debt to GDP ratio (corresponding to 0.7 for the intertemporal substitution elasticity in Table 10.2, Section 10.5), the associated sustainable gross foreign debt of 40.8 percent of GDP falls within the sustainable gross range of 39–50 percent of GDP. Philippine gross foreign debt at end-2019 was 22.2 percent of GDP (BSP 2019), well below the sustainable gross range, suggesting ample room for additional foreign borrowing.

optimally derived endogenous saving rate; and (3) exogenous natural rate via exogenous technical change vs. endogenous natural rate via endogenous technical change or endogenous labor participation (see Table 10.1).[8]

Ramsey (1928) began with a closed economy, optimally derived endogenous saving rate, exogenous technical change growth model, joined later by Cass (1965), and Koopmans (1965), henceforth RCK. Next were the closed-economy, fixed-exogenous saving rate, exogenous technical change models of Solow (1956) and Swan (1956), henceforth S-S, and of Arrow (1962). These were followed by the closed-economy, fixed-exogenous saving rate, endogenous technical change growth models of Conlisk (1967) and Villanueva (1994, **Chapter 6**), and by the open-economy, fixed-exogenous saving rate, endogenous technical change models of Otani and Villanueva (1989), Villanueva (2003), and Villanueva and Mariano (2007, **Chapter 9**). Villanueva (2020, **Chapter 3**) is a closed-economy and fixed-exogenous saving rate growth model that generalizes the S-S model by incorporating an endogenously determined natural rate through endogenous labor participation.[9] Villanueva (2021, **Chapter 4**) presents a closed-economy, fixed-exogenous saving rate, endogenous technical change growth model with two inputs: physical capital stock and combined stock of human and intellectual capital. In flow terms, these correspond to Solow's (1991) physical, human, and intellectual investments. The model finds that a higher saving rate raises both the steady-state and transitional growth rate through increases in physical capital, and human and intellectual capital (higher labor productivity). Finally, the present contribution is an open-economy growth model with optimally derived endogenous saving rates and sustainable foreign borrowing.

S-S is a closed-economy growth model where domestic saving finances aggregate investment. This reference model assumes a fully exogenous natural rate via exogenous labor-augmenting

---

[8]Table 10.1 contains definitions of these three levels and related terminology.

[9]All other growth models in Table 10.1 assume exogenous labor participation.

Table 10.1. Aggregate growth models: summary features.

	C	O	EXS	ENS	EXT	ENT	EXP	ENP
Ramsey (1928)	*			*	*		*	
Solow (1956)	*		*		*		*	
Swan (1956)	*		*		*		*	
Arrow (1962)	*		*		*		*	
Cass (1965)	*			*	*		*	
Koopmans (1965)	*			*	*		*	
Conlisk (1967)	*		*			*	*	
Romer (1986)	*			*		*	*	
Lucas (1988)	*			*		*	*	
Otani &Villanueva (1989)		*	*			*	*	
Grossman & Helpman (1990)	*			*		*	*	
Otani & Villanueva (1990)		*	*			*	*	
Romer (1990)	*			*		*	*	
Grossman & Helpman (1991)	*			*		*	*	
Rivera-Batiz & Romer (1991)	*			*		*	*	
Rebelo (1991)	*		*		*		*	
Aghion & Howitt (1992)	*			*		*	*	
Knight, Loayza & Villanueva (1993)	*		*		*		*	
Villanueva (1994)	*		*			*	*	
Barro & Sala-i-Martin (1995)	*			*		*	*	
Villanueva (2003)		*	*			*	*	
Villanueva & Mariano (2007)		*	*			*	*	
Villanueva (2020)	*		*		*			*
Villanueva (2021)	*		*			*	*	

C = Closed, O = Open, EXS = Exogenous Saving, ENS = Endogenous Saving,
EXT = Exogenous Natural Rate via Exogenous Technical Change,
EXP = Exogenous Natural Rate via Exogenous Labor Participation
ENT = Endogenous Natural Rate via Endogenous Technical Change,
ENP = Endogenous Natural Rate via Endogenous Labor Participation,
L (effective labor) = APN, A = technology or productivity multiplier (index number),
P = labor participation (0 < P ≤ 1), N = population, $\dot{L}/L = \dot{A}/A + \dot{P}/P + \dot{N}/N$,
$\dot{L}/L$ = natural rate.
$\dot{N}/N = n$ = exogenous population growth rate.

(Harrod-neutral) technical change, which determines the equilibrium or steady-state growth rate of per capita output.[10]

Conlisk (1967) was first to introduce endogenous technical change in a closed-economy neoclassical growth model. Employing a constant-returns, well-behaved neoclassical production function $Y = F(K, L) = Lf(k)$, where Y = GDP, K = capital, and L = effective[11] labor, the Conlisk (1967) model consists of the following relations:

$$\dot{K}/K = sY/K - \delta = sf(k)/k - \delta \quad \text{and}$$

$$\dot{L}/L = hY/L + \mu + n = hf(k) + \mu + n,$$

where $L = AN$, A = technology or productivity index, N = working population, $k = K/L$, δ = rate of depreciation, μ = rate of exogenous technical or productivity change, n = population growth rate, and a dot over a variable = time derivative, $\dot{K} = (d(K)/dt$. A fixed fraction, s, of Y is invested in K and another proportion, h, of Y is used to increase A.[12]

The equilibrium or steady-state growth rate of GDP is,

$$\dot{Y}/Y^* = \dot{K}/K^* = \dot{L}/L^* = hY/L^* + \mu + n = hf(k^*) + \mu + n,$$

which is a positive function of the equilibrium capital-labor ratio k^*. The latter is a function of all the model's structural parameters s, h, μ, n and δ, and of the form of the intensive production function $f(k^*)$.

Villanueva (1994, **Chapter 6**) developed and discussed a variant of the Conlisk (1967) model, combining it with a modified Arrow (1962) learning-by-doing model wherein experience on the job plays

---

[10]A major strength of the S-S model is its rich transitional dynamics, elegant simplicity, as well as empirical relevance. For details, see Appendix.

[11]In efficiency units. Denoting K as capital and L as effective labor, if a 2020 man-hour is equivalent as an input in the production function to two man-hours in the base period, say, 2000, then the ratio K/L is the amount of capital per half-hour 2020 or per man-hour 2000.

[12]Representing expenditures, for example, on secondary and tertiary education, on-the-job training, and health (Villanueva, 1994, **Chapter 6**). The proportion h is a composite parameter that translates expenditures in dollars into units of L in man-hours.

a critical role in raising labor productivity, that is,

$$\dot{A}/A = \varnothing k + \mu, \quad 0 < \varnothing < 1$$

where $\varnothing$ is a learning coefficient. The idea is that as the *per capita* stock of capital with embodied advanced technology gets larger, the learning experience makes workers more productive.[13] Together with $\dot{N}/N = n$, the equilibrium or steady-state growth rate of GDP is,

$$\dot{Y}/Y^* = \dot{K}/K^* = \dot{L}/L^* = \varnothing k^* + \mu + n,$$

which is similar to the Conlisk growth expression above, with $hf(k^*)$ replaced by $\varnothing k^*$. In efforts to explain the endogenous technical change in the context of an optimal choice of the consumption path, the literature on endogenous growth exploded during the eighties and nineties, beginning with contributions by Romer (1986), Lucas (1988), Romer (1990), Grossman and Helpman (1990), Rivera-Batiz and Romer (1991), Aghion and Howitt (1992), and Barro and Sala-i-Martin (1995). These endogenous growth models conclude that the economy's steady-state output can grow as fast as or faster than, the capital stock, and public policies with regard to saving and investment affect long-run economic growth. In the AK model (Rebelo, 1991), output grows at the same rate as the capital stock K, equal to sA, where s (larger than the saving rate of the S-S model by the amount of investment in human capital) is the fraction of income saved and invested, and $A$is a technological constant. There are the R&D models of Romer (1986), Grossman and Helpman (1991), Aghion and Howitt (1992), and Barro and Sala-i-Martin (1995), in which firms operating in imperfectly competitive markets undertake R&D investments that yield increasing returns, which are ultimately the source of long-run per capita output growth. Among all classes of closed-economy growth models, the equilibrium properties of fixed (Conlisk, 1967 and Villanueva, 1994, **Chapter 6**) and optimally derived saving rate-endogenous growth models are similar.[14]

[13]Using $L = AN$ and $k = K/L$, rewrite the above equation as $A = \varnothing(K/N) + \mu A$.

[14]Lucas (1988) specifies effective labor $L = uhN$, where h is the skill level, u is the fraction of non-leisure time devoted to current production, and $1 - u$ to human

The next development was to open up Conlisk's (1967) and Villanueva's (1994, **Chapter 6**) growth models to foreign trade and global lending. An early attempt was made by Villanueva (2003). The fixed-saving rate model of Villanueva (2003) is an open-economy variant of Conlisk's (1967) endogenous technical change model and Arrow's (1962) learning-by-doing model wherein on-the-job experience plays a critical role in raising labor productivity over time.

In Villanueva (2003), the aggregate capital stock is the accumulated sum of domestic saving and net external borrowing (current account deficit). At any moment, the difference between the expected marginal product of capital, net depreciation, and the marginal cost of funds in the international lending market determines the proportionate rate of change in the external debt-capital ratio.[15]

When the expected net marginal product of capital matches the marginal cost of funds at the equilibrium capital-labor ratio, the proportionate increase in net external debt (net external borrowing) is fixed by the economy's equilibrium output growth, and the external debt/output ratio stabilizes at a constant level. Although constant in long-run equilibrium, the external debt ratio shifts with changes in the economy's propensity to save out of national disposable income, the marginal cost of funds in the world lending market, depreciation rate, growth rates of the working population, and exogenous technical change, and the parameters of the risk premium, production, and technical change functions.

A major shortcoming of the Villanueva (2003) model is its inability to pin down the saving rate and equilibrium external debt to GDP ratio that is consistent with maximum consumer welfare. The Villanueva-Mariano (2007, **Chapter 9**) (VM1) model corrected this shortcoming by employing Phelp's (1966) *Golden Rule* maximization criterion. On the balanced growth path, if consumption per unit of effective labor (or any monotonically increasing function

---

capital accumulation. The $(1-u)h$ variable is VM2 model's variable A in $L = AN$ in Section 10.3. This variable is T in Villanueva (1994, **Chapter 6**), defined as technical change or labor productivity multiplier.

[15]The marginal cost of funds is the risk-free interest rate plus a risk premium. For details, see Equation (10.8), Section 10.3.

of it) is taken as a measure of the social welfare of society, the domestic saving rate that maximizes the consumption per unit of effective labor is chosen. Consistent with this, the optimal outcome is a sustainable ratio of net external debt to total output. Using parameters for the Philippines to calibrate the model, the VM1 growth model's steady-state solution is characterized by a constant capital-effective labor ratio, an optimal domestic saving rate, and a unique external debt-capital ratio.[16] The latter ratio interacts with long-run growth and domestic adjustment and is determined jointly with other macroeconomic variables, including a country's set of structural parameters.

A weakness of the VM1 growth model is its lack of micro-foundation, a criticism leveled by Lui (2007). The RCK setup is suitable to determine unique values of the optimal saving rate and foreign debt to GDP ratio. As Table 10.1 shows, all the micro-founded optimally derived saving–rate growth models are closed- economy models. The VM2 model extends a micro-founded growth model such as RCK to an open economy with access to foreign trade and global lending. Most importantly, the VM2 model incorporates a modified Arrow learning-by-doing feature. Imports of capital goods with embodied advanced technology allow learning-by-doing to raise labor productivity and, thus, long-run growth (see Figure 10.2, Section 10.4, and related discussion).

10.3 The VM2 Model

Before presenting the VM2 model, the following background is a useful summary of the closed-economy RCK model and the original Arrow learning-by-doing framework. In the RCK model with a *CRRA* utility function and fully exogenous labor-augmenting technical change and population growth, the equations for the optimal growth of consumption, c, and capital intensity, k, consistent with

[16]For research on the sustainability of external debt using various statistical procedures, see Manasse and Schimmelpfenning (2003), Reinhart *et al.* (2003), Kraay and Nehru (2004), Patillo *et al.* (2004), and Manasse and Roubini (2005). For an excellent survey, see Kraay and Nehru (2004).

maximum discounted stream of intertemporal consumption are:

$$\dot{c}/c = 1/\theta[f'(k) - \delta - \rho - \theta(n + \mu)]; \quad \dot{k} = f(k) - c - (\delta + n + \mu)k,$$

wherein c $=$ C/L, k $=$ K/L, f(k) $=$ $F(K, L)/L$, $F(\cdot)$ $=$ unit-homogeneous production function, C = is consumption, K = physical capital, L = effective labor = AN,[17] A = labor productivity or technology index, N = population, ρ = time preference or discount rate, θ = degree of relative risk aversion, δ = capital's depreciation rate, $\dot{A}/A = \mu$, and $\dot{N}/N = n$. The asymptotic (equilibrium) values c^* and k^* are the roots of the above equations equated to zero:

$$f'(k^*) - \delta - \rho - \theta(n + \mu) = 0; \quad f(k^*) - c^* - (\delta + n + \mu)k^* = 0.$$

Given a specific form of $f(k^*)$, the first equation solves for k^*. Plugging k^* in the second equation solves for c^*. Given k^* and a well-behaved, *constant-returns* neoclassical production function, the equilibrium growth rate of per capita output, $\dot{Y}/Y^* - n$ is fixed entirely by the rate of exogenous Harrod-neutral technical change, μ, and is independent of consumer preferences and technology.[18] Nearly six decades ago, Arrow (1962) proposed a learning-by-doing growth model,

$$\dot{A}/A = \varnothing(\dot{K}/K) + \mu, \quad 0 < \varnothing < 1, \tag{10.1}$$

in which $\varnothing$ is a learning coefficient. Equation (10.1) states that the proportionate growth in labor productivity is the sum of the learning coefficient $\varnothing$ multiplied by the proportionate growth in the capital stock plus a constant rate of exogenous technical or productivity change μ. The faster the growth of the capital stock, the more

[17]Generally, the L definition should be $L = APN$, where P is the labor participation rate, which measures the percentage of the population in the labor force ($0 < P \leq 1$). The working population is PN. When $P = 1$, $L = AN$. Whatever P is, it is usually assumed in current literature as an exogenous constant, whose rate of change is zero. For an endogenous and variable P, see Villanueva (2020, **Chapter 3**).

[18]$\dot{Y}/Y^* = \dot{K}/k^* = \dot{L}/L^* = \dot{A}/A + \dot{N}/N = \mu + n$.

intensive the learning experience on the job, and the higher the growth in labor productivity is.

Given Equation (10.1), definition $L = AN$, and assumptions, $\dot{N}/N = n$, $\dot{A}/A = \mu$, a constant steady-state capital intensity $k^*(= K/L)^*$ implies the following equilibrium growth rate of output:

$$\dot{K}/K^* = L/L^* = A/A^* + n = Y/Y^* = g^{Y^*} = (\mu = N)/(1 - \varnothing).^{19} \tag{10.2}$$

Although a multiple of the S-S equilibrium output growth rate $(\mu + n)$, equilibrium output growth, $Y/Y^* = g^{y^*}$ remains equal to a constant involving only three parameters μ, $\varnothing$, and n. That is, g^{y^*} is independent of the preference and risk parameters ρ and θ, and the form of the intensive production $f(k^*)$.[20] Besides, the Arrow model has the property that, $(d[g^{Y^*} - n]/dn = [\varnothing/((1 - \varnothing))] > 0$, i.e., an increase in the population growth rate n raises the long-run growth rate of per capita output, $g^{y^*} - n$.[21] This prediction is counterintuitive and rejected by empirical evidence.[22]

Turning now to the VM2 growth model, assume the following institutional arrangements of an open and perfectly competitive economy with rational agents. One good is produced that is partly consumed and the remainder exported, using an aggregate production function with inputs of labor, and imported capital goods with embodied advanced technology. Enterprises rent capital from households and hire workers to produce output in each period. Households own the physical capital stock and receive income from working, renting capital, and managing the enterprises. To finance

---

[19]The unit-homogeneous production function $Y = F(K, L)$ is subject to constant returns to K and L jointly, implying balanced growth in Y, K, and L.

[20]Refer back to the basic RCK model, second paragraph of the current section.

[21]Subtracting n from both sides of Equation (10.2) yields $(g^{y^*} - n) = [\mu((1 - \varnothing))] + [\varnothing((1 - \varnothing))]n$.

[22]See Conlisk (1967), Otani and Villanueva (1990), Knight *et al.* (1993, **Chapter 2**) and Villanueva (1994, **Chapter 6**).

imports of capital goods, households use export earnings and borrow from abroad.[23]

The VM2 model's key innovation is a modification of Arrow's learning-by-doing equation as follows:

$$A = \varnothing(K/N) + \mu A. \tag{10.3}$$

The difference between Arrow Equation (10.1) and VM2 Equation (10.3) is the endogenous component [the first term on the right-hand side (RHS)]. Both equations have an exogenous component in the second term on the RHS involving the labor-augmenting technical change or productivity parameter μ. In the first term's endogenous component, instead of assuming that learning-by-doing is proportional to the growth rate of the aggregate capital stock, $\dot{K}/K$ as in Arrow Equation (10.1), the VM2 model assumes that the endogenous component is proportional to the level of the aggregate capital stock per capita, K/N. This is particularly relevant to developing countries whose K is imported and embodies the most advanced technology produced by the advanced industrial countries. A large stock of K/N enables workers in developing countries to engage in learning-by-doing on a significant scale.[24] In these

[23]The numeraire is the foreign price of the imported capital good. Thus, if Pd is the price of the domestic consumer good, Pf is the price of the foreign good, and e is the exchange rate expressed as quantity of local currency units per unit of foreign currency, Pd/ePf is multiplied by residents' saving to obtain domestic saving (in constant dollars). Foreign borrowing denominated in foreign currency is deflated by Pf to get the real value. Similarly, the marginal real cost of foreign borrowing is the sum of the world interest rate and risk premium in foreign currency less the rate of change in Pf. Since model simplicity and long-run growth are our primary concerns, the VM2 model abstracts from the effects of movements of these variables by arbitrarily assigning unitary values to these price and exchange rate indices without loss of generality. Incorporation of these variables in the VM2 model is straightforward and is done in Otani and Villanueva (1989). Imports of capital goods are financed by the European Ex-Im Bank and American Ex-Im Bank, global commercial banks, and international and regional development banks.

[24]The empirical results from Villanueva (1994, **Chapter 6**) suggest that the learning coefficient $\varnothing$ is positively influenced by the openness of the economy (sum of exports and imports) and expenditures on education and health, and negatively by fiscal deficits, all three variables expressed in percent of GDP.

countries, starting from a low level of K/N, even a very high growth rate of the capital stock would barely make a dent on learning by doing to have significant effects on labor productivity and growth rate of aggregate per capita output. The R&D sector in developing countries is virtually nonexistent. Owing to its large real resource (including financial) costs, R&D development is left for the rich industrial countries to pursue. The resource-poor developing countries have a cheaper alternative: Import capital goods with embodied advanced technology, learn from using these goods in the production process, and thereby raise labor productivity and long-run growth. The presence of learning through experience on the job has three major consequences: First, equilibrium or steady-state growth becomes endogenous and is influenced by preferences, technology, and government policies. Second, the speed of adjustment to growth equilibrium is faster, and enhanced learning-by-doing further reduces adjustment time.[25] Third, capital's income share is higher than the optimal saving rate to compensate capital for the additional GDP growth generated by endogenous growth and learning by doing.[26]

The VM2 model's aggregate production function adopts the S-S model's assumption of constant returns to K and L jointly, and diminishing returns to K and L separately, and in the context of perfectly competitive markets with full wage-price flexibility.[27] Like the S-S, Conlisk (1967), and Villanueva (2003) models, the VM2 model employs a well-behaved unit-homogeneous neoclassical production function $Y = F(K, L) = Lf(k)$, where Y, K, L, and k have been defined earlier, subject to the Inada (1963) conditions: $\lim \partial F/\partial K = \infty$ as $K \to 0$; $\lim \partial F/\partial K = 0$ as $K \to \infty$; $f(0) \geq 0$; $f'(k) > 0$ and $f'(k) < 0$ for all $k > 0$.

[25]See Villanueva (1994, **Chapter 6**) for analytical approach and simulation that explain reduced adjustment time towards the steady state.

[26]See Section 10.5 for proof.

[27]Unlike the models of Romer (1986), Grossman and Helpman (1991), Aghion and Howitt (1992), and Barro and Sala-i-Martin (1995) that are subject to increasing returns to capital operating in imperfect markets.

The Cobb-Douglas production function, used to calibrate the VM2 model, satisfies these conditions.

From the definition $L = AN$, noting that $\dot{N} = nN$,

$$\dot{L}/L = g^L = \dot{A}/A + n. \tag{10.4}$$

Substituting Equation (10.3) into Equation (10.4),

$$\dot{L}/L = g^L = \varnothing k + \mu + n. \tag{10.5}$$

In the steady-state, k $= k^*$ (a constant), and from the *constant-returns* assumption,

$$\dot{K}/K^* = \dot{L}/L^* = \dot{Y}/Y^* = g^{Y^*} = \varnothing k^* + \mu + n, \tag{10.6}$$

i.e., the steady-state growth rate of per capita output $= g^{Y^*} - n = \varnothing k^* + \mu$.

Comparing Equations (10.2) and (10.6), the key difference is the presence of equilibrium capital intensity k^* in the expression for the equilibrium growth rate of per capita output in the VM2 model, and the absence of k^* in the growth equation of the Arrow model. The VM2 model solves for optimal values of k^*, c^*, and d^* Equations (10.24)–(10.26) in an open-economy RCK optimal control setup using a CRRA utility function, wherein k^*, c^*, d^* and $g^{Y^*} - n$ are functions of consumer tastes, technology, and policy parameters. Besides this key property, the VM2 model implies a more empirically plausible prediction (opposite to Arrow's) that an increase in the population growth rate depresses the long-run growth rate of per capita output, $d(g^{Y^*} - n)/dn = \varnothing(\partial k^*)/\partial n < 0$[28] because $\partial k^*/\partial n < 0$ as shown in Figure 10.4, Section 10.4.

The budget constraint of a representative household is:

$$C + \dot{K} + \delta K = \delta K + wL + \Pi + \dot{D} - iD, \tag{10.7}$$

C = consumption, K = physical capital, D = net foreign debt (foreign liabilities less foreign assets),[29] r = capital's rental rate,

[28]Subtract n from both sides of Equation (10.6) and take its derivative with respect to n. For empirical evidence that $d(g^{Y^*} - n)/dn < 0$, see Conlisk (1967), Otani and Villanueva (1990), Knight *et al.* (1993, **Chapter 2**) and Villanueva (1994, **Chapter 6**).

[29]If foreign assets exceed foreign liabilities, D is negative.

w = real wage rate, Π = total profit in managing and owning the enterprises, and i = real effective interest rate.

Equation (10.7) is the budget constraint that total uses of funds equal total sources of funds. Total uses are consumption and gross investment. Total sources are GDP and foreign borrowing net of interest payments. Restating Equation (10.7), $rK+wL+\Pi = C+K+\delta K - (D - iD)$, where $(D - iD) = M - X$ = balance of payments identity, M = imports (of capital goods), X = exports, $M - X$ = current account balance, and D = change in net foreign liabilities. Gross capital formation $\dot{K} + \delta K = rK + wL + \Pi - C + D - iD$, i.e., capital accumulation is financed by an unconsumed output that is exported, and by foreign borrowing net of interest payments on debt.

The real interest $i$is the global real interest rate i^f plus a risk premium equal to a proportion λ of the foreign debt stock $d = DL$.[30]

$$i = i^f + \lambda d, \quad 0 < \lambda < 1. \tag{10.8}$$

The second term on the RHS of Equation (10.8) is the risk premium representing the combined effects of risk factors and financial markups that foreign lenders take into account prior to extending loans. When i^f is held constant, a higher debt stock d, by raising the probability of default, increases the risk premium and thus i.

Dividing both sides of Equation (10.7) by L,

$$c + k + (\delta + g^L)k - \dot{d} - g^L d = rk + w + \pi - id, \tag{10.9}$$

wherein

$$d = \beta(r - \delta - i)d \quad 0 < \beta \leq \infty, \tag{10.10}$$

and, as before, lower case letters are expressed as ratios to effective labor L, and g^L is given by Equation (10.4).

[30]The risk-free interest rate is i^f. The risk premium is $i - i^f$. The LIBOR (to be ended in 2021 and replaced by new benchmark rates), US Prime Rate, US Federal Funds Rate, or US Treasury, deflated by changes in an appropriate price index in the United Kingdom or United States of America, typically represents the risk-free interest rate. The risk premium is country-specific and a positive function of a country's external debt burden and other exogenous factors capturing market perceptions of country risk.

Equation (10.10) postulates that foreign borrowing is undertaken in response to a positive differential between the expected capital's net marginal product and the effective real interest rate, with the coefficient β measuring the response speed (an aggregate lending offer function from global lenders).

Inserting Equation (10.10) into Equation (10.9):

$$c + \dot{k} + (\delta + g^L)k - \beta(r - \delta - i)d - g^L d = rk + w + \pi - id. \quad (10.11)$$

The representative household maximizes a discounted stream of lifetime consumption C, subject to constraints Equations (10.9) and (10.10), in which instantaneous utility is of the CRRA form (for brevity, time t is suppressed for all variables):

$$N(0)^{(1-\theta)} \int_0^\infty \frac{\left(\frac{C}{L}\right)^{(1-\theta)}}{(1-\theta)} A^{(1-\theta)} e^{-\rho * t} \mathrm{d}t. \quad (10.12)$$

For the integral to converge, the standard restriction $\rho^* = \rho - (1-\theta)n > 0$ is imposed. In maximizing Equation (10.12) subject to Equations (10.9) and (10.10), each household takes as parametrically given the time paths *of* r, w, π, i and A. When making decisions about consumption, capital accumulation, and net foreign borrowing, the representative household is small enough to affect r, w, π, i and A.

The household's Hamiltonian is

$$H = e^{-p*t}\left[\frac{c^{1-\theta}}{(1-\theta)}\right] A^{(1-\theta)} + \varphi_1[rk + w + \pi - c - id - (\delta + g^L)k$$
$$+ \beta(r - \delta - i)d + g^L d] - \varphi_2[\beta(r - \delta - i)d]. \quad (10.13)$$

After substituting Equations (10.3), (10.4), and conditions are $\rho^* = \rho - (1-\theta)n$, the first-order conditions are,

$$\dot{c}/c = (1/\theta)[(r - \delta - \rho - \theta n - \theta(\varnothing k + \mu))] \quad (10.14)$$

$$\dot{k} = rk + w + \pi - c - id + \beta(r - \delta - i)d + g^L d - (\delta + g^L)k \quad (10.15)$$

$$\dot{d} = \beta(r - \dot{\delta} - i)d. \quad (10.16)$$

The economy-wide resource constraint is:

$$C + \dot{K} + \delta K = F(K, L) - iD + \dot{D}. \tag{10.17}$$

Dividing both sides by L,

$$c + \dot{k} + (\delta + g^L)k = f(k) - id + \dot{d} + g^L d. \tag{10.18}$$

In competitive equilibrium, $r = f'(k)$, and $w = f(k) - kf'(k)$, implying $\pi = 0$. Substituting these expressions for r, w, and π into Equations (10.14)–(10.16) and (10.18), the optimal time paths for c, k, and d are:

$$\dot{c}/c = (1/\theta)[(f'(k) - \delta - \rho - \theta n - \theta(\varnothing k + \mu) \tag{10.19}$$

$$k = f(k) - c - id + \beta[(f'(k) - \delta - i)]d + g^L d$$
$$-(\delta + g^L)k \tag{10.20}$$

$$\dot{d} = \beta(f'(k) - \delta - i)d, \tag{10.21}$$

wherein $g^L = \varnothing k + \mu + n$ and $i = i^f + \lambda d$. The transversality conditions are:

$$\lim_{t\to\infty} e^{-\rho * t}\varphi_1 k = 0 \tag{10.22}$$

$$\lim_{t\to\infty} e^{-\rho * t}\varphi_2 d = 0^{31}. \tag{10.23}$$

In the absence of learning by doing $\varnothing = 0$ and net foreign debt ($d = 0$), the above model reduces to the closed-economy RCK model that allows for population growth n and fully exogenous technical progress μ, with the key property that the equilibrium growth rate of per capita output is fixed entirely by μ and is independent of preferences, technology,[32] and policy.[33]

---

[31]The time paths for φ_1 and φ_2 are given by $\dot{\varphi}_1 = \rho^*\varphi_1 - \partial H/\partial k$, $\dot{\phi}_2 = \rho^*\phi_2 - \partial H/\partial d$, wherein $\partial H/\partial k$ and $\partial H/\partial d$ are functions of k and d. As a standard condition, the no-Ponzi game is imposed, i.e., non-negative present values of the household holdings k and d.

[32]Form of the production function $f(k^*)$.

[33]The optimal paths for c and k are: $\dot{c}/c = 1/\theta[f'(k) - \delta - \rho - \theta(n + \mu)]$ and $\dot{k} = f(k) - c - (\delta + n + \mu)k$. These are identical expressions for the optimal

The system (19)–(21) represents the reduced model in c, k, d, and time t. The asymptotic (equilibrium) values c^*, k^*, and d^* are the roots of Equations (10.19)–(10.21) equated to zero:

$$f'(k^*) - \delta = \rho + \theta\mu + \theta n + \theta \varnothing k^* \tag{10.24}$$

$$f'(k^*) - \delta = i = i^f + \lambda d^* \tag{10.25}$$

$$f'(k^*) - c^* + (d^* - k^*)(\varnothing k^* + \mu + n)$$
$$-d^*(i^f + \lambda d^*) - \delta k^* = 0. \tag{10.26}$$

The model's phase diagrams, shown as Figures 10.1–10.4, are based on calibrated values specified in Equations (10.24)–(10.26), using the following parameters: $\alpha = 0.3$, $\delta = 0.04$, $\mu = 0.005$, $\theta = 1.4$,[34] $\varnothing = 0.01$, $\rho = 0.03$, $\beta = 1$, $\lambda = 0.25$, $i^f = 0.05$, and $n = 0.02$.

The parameter α = exponent in the Cobb-Douglas production function $f(k) = k^\alpha$. The other parameters are: δ = capital's depreciation rate, μ = rate of exogenous labor-augmenting technical change, θ = coefficient of relative risk aversion, $\varnothing$ = learning coefficient, ρ = rate of time preference, β = speed of adjustment of foreign borrowing to the gap between capital's net marginal product and the effective cost of foreign borrowing, λ = linear response of the borrowing spread to the debt stock i^f = world interest rate, and n = growth rate working population.

The solutions are $k_0^* = 2.7$ and $s^* = 0.20$.[35] For comparison, the following solutions for the VM1 model are $k^{**} = 6.8$ and $s^{*'} = 0.34$. Note that the lower steady-state value of capital intensity is consistent with the prediction that the *Golden Utility* capital intensity level is lower than the *Golden Rule* level (see Figure 10.1).

growth of consumption and capital intensity delineated at the beginning of the current section.

[34]Corresponding to the estimate of 0.7 for the intertemporal substitution elasticity (Szpiro, 1986) shown in Table 10.2, Section 10.5.

[35]Microsoft's Solver tool is used to solve the first-order conditions. The program searches the optimal k^*, c^*, and d^* such that Equations (10.24)–(10.26) are met. The Solver tool uses the Generalized Reduced Gradient nonlinear optimization code developed by Leon Lasdon and Allan Waren.

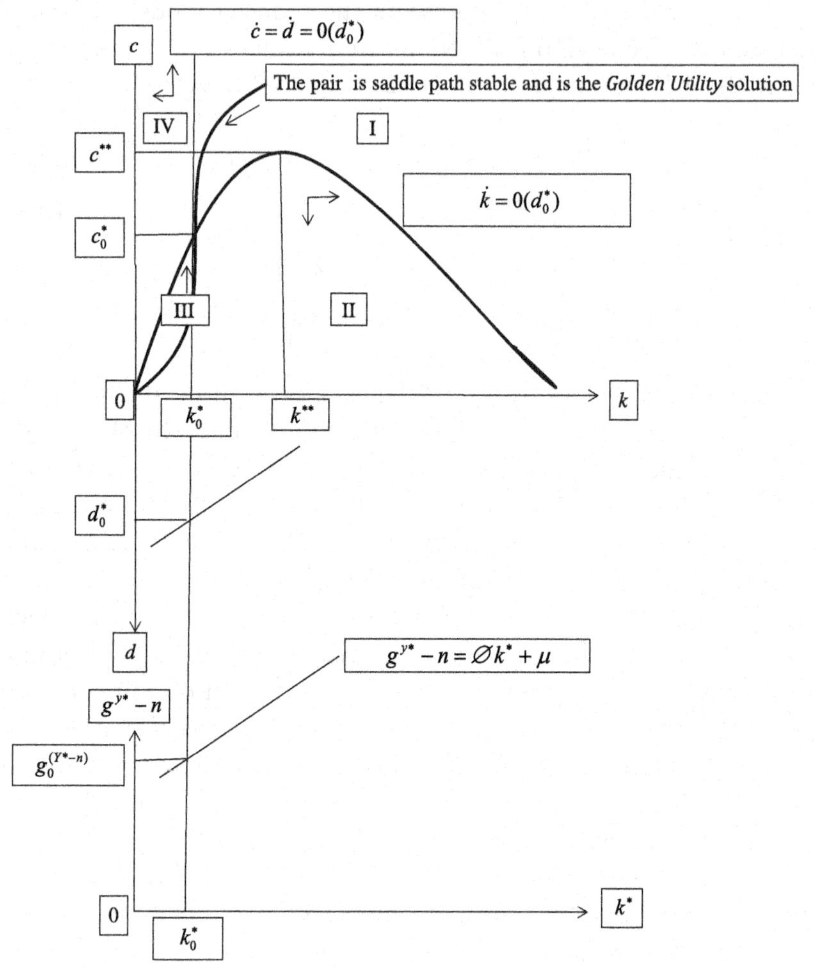

Figure 10.1. Long-run equilibrium.

While the latter maximizes consumption per effective labor at c^{**}, the former maximizes consumer utility at c^* and is dynamically efficient.

Figure 10.1 is the phase diagram of the VM2 model. The upper panel plots the $k = 0$ curve and the $d = \dot{c} = 0$ curve in k, c space. Equations (10.24)–(10.25) imply:

$$i^f + \lambda d^* = \rho + \theta\mu + \theta n + \theta\varnothing k^*. \tag{10.27}$$

This is the $\dot{d} = \dot{c} = 0$ curve. For a given d, say d_0^*, it is a vertical line in the k, c space in the upper panel of Figure 10.1. The bell-shaped curve represents the $\dot{k} = 0$ relationship, which is drawn for a given level of d, say d_0^* [Equation (10.26)]. This curve's slope has the property that $\partial c/\partial k \geq 0$ for $k \leq k^{**}$, and $\partial c/\partial k < 0$ for $k > k^{**}$. The middle panel plots the $\dot{d} = 0$ line in the k, d space with a negative slope. That is to say, when d rises above d_0^* and pushes up the real interest rate above capital's net marginal product at $k_0^*, d < 0$ and d tends to fall. For d to remain constant, capital's net marginal product must increase, requiring k *to* decrease below k_0^*. Thus, the $\dot{d} < 0$ line slopes downward. The lower panel plots the growth rate of per capita output $g^{Y^*} - n = \varnothing k^* + \mu$. This curve slopes upward.

Figure 10.1 shows the equilibrium values k_0^*, c_0^* in the upper panel, d_0^* in the middle panel, and $g_0^{(Y^*-n)}$ in the lower panel. The pair (k_0^*, c_0^*) is saddle path stable and is the *Golden Utility* solution.[36] While c_0^* is below the maximum *Golden Rule* (Phelps, 1966) level at c^{**}, c_0^* maximizes intertemporal utility and is thus dynamically efficient. The equilibrium capital intensity k_0^* is a function of all the parameters of the VM2 model, including the parameters of the utility function, namely the discount rate and the coefficient of relative risk aversion or its reciprocal, the elasticity of intertemporal substitution, and other parameters, including the learning coefficient, the global real interest rate, and the parameters and form of the production function. Since the equilibrium growth rate of per capita output $g^{Y^*} - n$ equals $\varnothing k^* + \mu$, any public policy that enhances the equilibrium capital intensity k^* and the learning coefficient $\varnothing$ raises the long-run growth rate of per capita output. This stands in sharp contrast to the open-economy RCK model with *no* learning by doing ($\varnothing = 0$), wherein $g^{Y^*} - n = \mu$.[37]

10.4 Comparative Dynamics

Figure 10.2 illustrates the growth effect of an increase in learning by doing. In the upper and middle panels, the intersection at $A(k_0^*, c_0^*)$

[36]The transversality conditions rule out quadrants II and IV in Figure 10.1.

[37]In this special case, the $g^{Y^*} - n$ line in the lower panel of Figure 10.1 turns horizontal with intercept equal to μ.

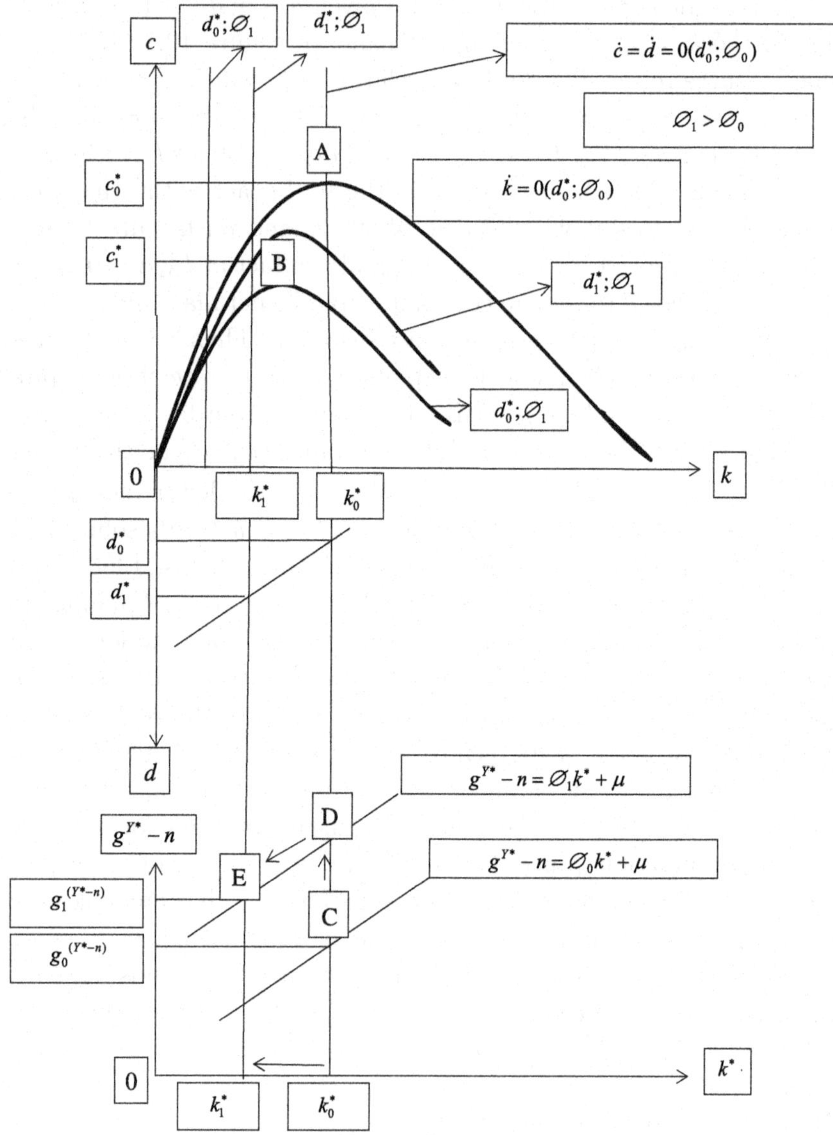

Figure 10.2. Growth effect of an increase in learning by doing.

shows the initial equilibrium point corresponding to a given level of the learning coefficient $\varnothing_0$ and equilibrium debt stock d_0^*. In the lower panel, the equilibrium growth rate of per capita output is and $g_0^{(Y^*-n)}$ given by the capital intensity level k_0^*.

Now, assume that public policy subsidizes on-the-job training at enterprises, resulting in an increase in the learning coefficient from $\varnothing_0 \to \varnothing$. From Equations (10.3), (10.5), and (10.19), labor productivity and g^L go up, slowing consumption growth, i.e., $\dot{c}/c < 0$. For $\dot{c}/c = 0$, k^* has to decrease, so that capital's marginal product rises. In the upper panel of Figure 10.2, the $\dot{c} = \dot{d} = 0(d_0^*; \varnothing_0)$ curve shifts leftward to $\dot{c} = \dot{d} = 0(d_0^*; \varnothing_1)$. In the middle panel, when k^* declines, capital's marginal product goes up, encouraging larger amounts of foreign borrowing, that is, $\dot{d} > 0$. For $\dot{d} = 0$, the real marginal cost of borrowing must increase, and so must d^*, as shown in the middle panel. Going back to the upper panel, as d^* goes up from d_0^* to d_1^*, $\dot{c} = \dot{d} = 0(d_0^*; \varnothing_1)$ the shifts rightward to $\dot{c} = \dot{d} = 0(d_1^*; \varnothing_1)$.

What happens to the $\dot{k} = 0$ curve? In the upper panel, when the learning coefficient increases, the higher effective labor growth implies $\dot{k} < 0$; for $\dot{k} = 0$, consumption has to fall; and the $\dot{k} = 0$ curve shifts downward to $\dot{k} = 0(d_0^*; \varnothing_1)$. However, increased foreign borrowing leads to higher debt stock at d_1^*, finances higher levels of consumption and capital intensity, so that the $\dot{k} = 0$ curve shifts upward to $\dot{k} = 0(d_0^*; \varnothing_1)$. The new equilibrium shifts to point B (k_1^*, c_1^*), with both equilibrium consumption per effective worker and equilibrium capital intensity lower than at point A.

In the lower panel, the increase in the learning coefficient from $\varnothing_0$ to $\varnothing_1$ shifts the per capita output growth curve upward from $g_0^{(Y^*-n)} - n = \varnothing_0 k_0^* + \mu \to g_1^{(Y^*-n)} = \varnothing_1 k^* + \mu$. Equilibrium shifts from $C(k_0^*, g_0^{(Y^*-n)})$ to $E(k_1^*, g_1^{(Y^*-n)})$, characterized by lower capital intensity and higher per-capita output growth.

At the old equilibrium capital intensity k_0^*, the transition jumps from C to D, the latter characterized by per capita output growth temporarily higher than the next equilibrium rate $g_1^{(Y^*-n)}$ at E. As capital intensity goes down from k_0^* to k_1^*, per capita output growth declines toward $g^{(Y^*-n)} > g_0^{(y^*-n)}$.[38] Thus, an increase in the learning

[38]Adjustment is traced by the segment DE.

coefficient leads to a short-run overshooting of the new and higher long-run per capita output growth rate.

Figure 10.3 illustrates the effects of higher discounting of future consumption or higher degree of relative risk aversion (lower elasticity of intertemporal substitution). The initial equilibrium is at point A (k_0^*,c_0^*), shown in the upper panel, corresponding to an initial value for ρ_0 and a given level of the debt stock d_0^*, shown in the middle panel. The equilibrium growth rate of per capita GDP at $g_0^{(Y^*-n)}$, corresponding to capital intensity k_0^*, is shown in the lower panel. The increase in ρ shifts the $\dot{c} = \dot{d} = 0$ curve to the left, lowering both c^* and k^*. A lower k^* implies a higher d^*, as shown in the middle panel. When d^* rises from d_0^* to d_1^*, the $\dot{c} = \dot{d} = 0$ curve shifts to the right, while the $\dot{k} = 0$ curve shifts downward. The new equilibrium intersection is at point B (k_1^*, c_1^*). Both the equilibrium consumption per effective worker and equilibrium capital intensity are lower. In the lower panel, as k^* falls from k_0^* to k_1^*, learning by doing drops and so does the equilibrium rate of per capita output, from $g_0^{(Y^*-n)}$ to $g_1^{(Y^*-n)}$.[39] The economic explanation is that higher discounting of future consumption means higher degree of relative risk aversion due, for instance, to increased uncertainty and macroeconomic and financial instability. The domestic saving rate falls, lowering the equilibrium capital intensity, lower imports of advanced capital goods and the associated decline in learning by doing. The equilibrium growth rate of per capita output goes down. The opposite economic adjustment follows from a reduction in uncertainty aided, for example, by a strong set of policies aimed at strengthened macroeconomic and financial stability.

Finally, the VM2 model yields a more empirically plausible prediction that an increase in population growth lowers the steady-state growth rate of per capita output, as illustrated in Figure 10.4, a result that is particularly relevant to developing countries.

In the upper panel, an increase in n from n_0 to n_1 shifts the $\dot{c} = \dot{d} = 0$ curve to the left and the $\dot{k} = 0$ curve downwards. As k falls, d rises; a higher d^* shifts the $\dot{c} = \dot{d} = 0$ curve to the right

[39]Reflecting a downward movement along the $(g^{Y^*} - n)$ curve.

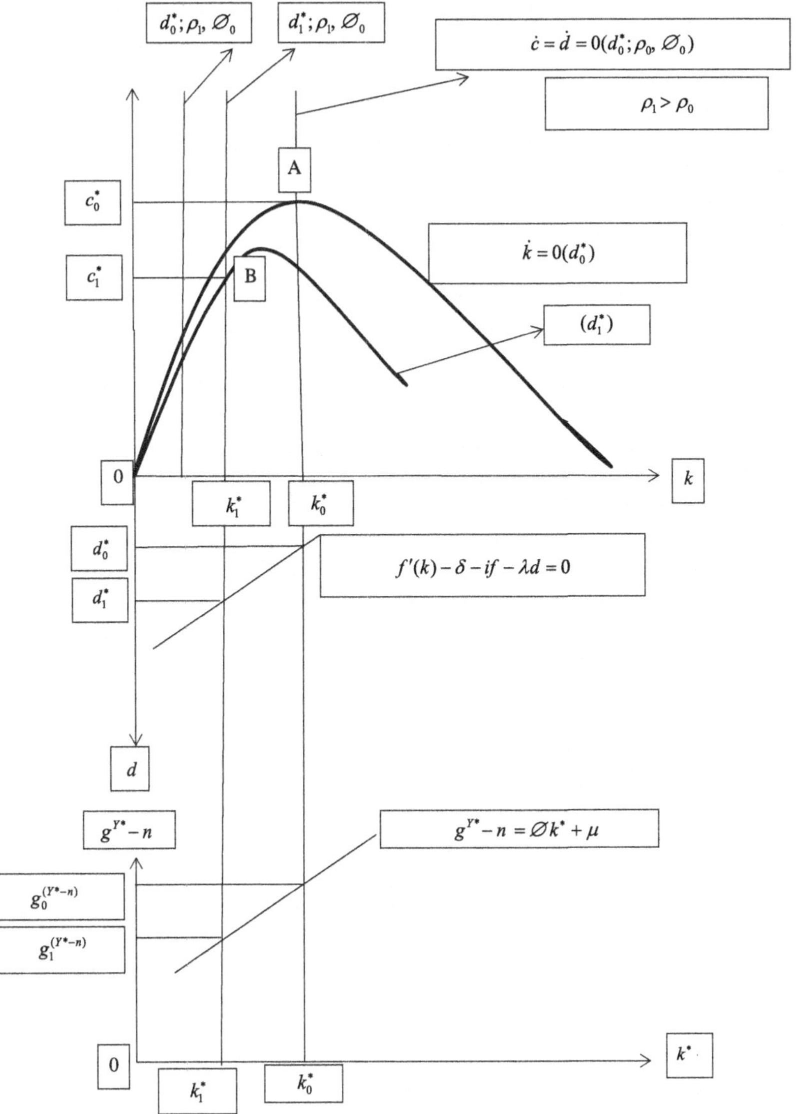

Figure 10.3. Growth effect of higher discounting or lower intertemporal substitution elasticity.

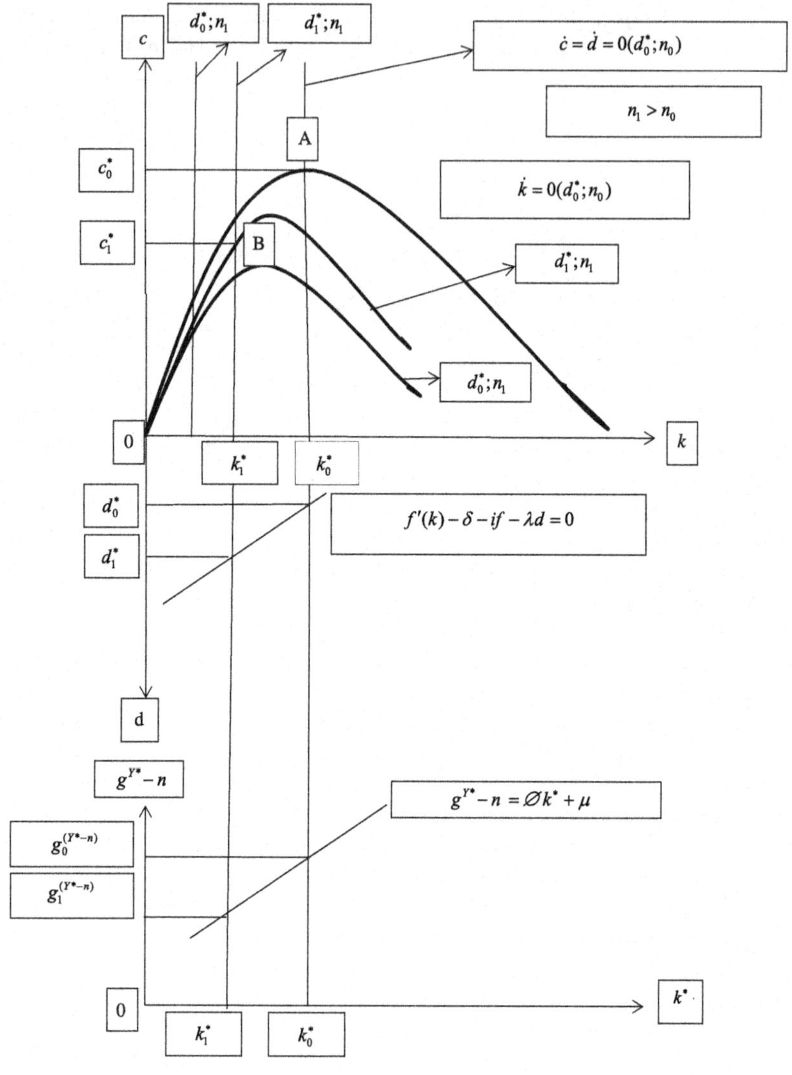

Figure 10.4. Growth effect of an increase in population growth.

and the $\dot{k} = 0$ upwards. The new equilibrium settles at point B, characterized by a lower c^* and k^* and, as shown in the middle panel, a higher d^*. In the lower panel, the decline in the equilibrium stock of capital per effective worker cuts learning by doing and leads to lower equilibrium growth rates of productivity and per capita output.[40]

10.5 Optimal Saving and Sustainable Foreign Debt

Assuming a Cobb-Douglas production function $f(k) = k^{\alpha}$ and from Equations (10.19)–(10.20), the endogenously derived optimal saving rate is given by:

$$s^* = \{[\{i^* - g^{Y^*})(d^*/k^*) + \delta + g^{Y^*}]/(\rho + \delta + \theta g^{Y^*})\}\alpha, \qquad (10.28)$$

in which $g^{Y^*} = \varnothing k^* + \mu + n$ and $i^* = i^f + \lambda d^*$. If $d^* = 0$ (closed economy), $\rho > 0$, $\theta > 1$, and $\varnothing = 0$ (all technical change is exogenous), then

$$s^{**} = \{(\mu + n + \delta)/[(\theta(\mu + n) + \delta + \rho)]\}\alpha. \qquad (10.29)$$

Evaluated in the steady state, the fraction in braces of Equation (10.28) is in range 0.60–0.74, depending on the elasticity of intertemporal substitution, and the fraction in braces of Equation (10.29) falls in range 0.55–0.67, so that s^* is in range 0.18–0.22 and s^{**} in range 0.17–0.20 (see Table 10.2). The optimal saving rate in the presence of partly endogenous learning by doing is larger than the optimal saving rate in a world of entirely exogenous learning by doing. The intuitive reason is this: learning-by-doing uses some portion (about a percentage point of GDP) of society's resources (endogenous variable), so a larger proportion of society's income must be saved for this purpose.

As noted in Section 10.1, the sustainable net foreign debt to GDP ratio is in range of 12-23 percent of GDP. Lane and Milesi-Ferretti's (2006) estimate for the Philippine average ratio of gross foreign assets to GDP during 1970–2004 is 27 percent, implying that

[40]The growth effect of a higher depreciation rate of capital is similar.

Table 10.2. Sensitivity of optimal results.[a]

	Elasticity of intertemporal substitution[b]		
	0.5	0.7	0.9
s^*	0.1805	0.1963	0.2236
s^{**}	0.1659	0.1813	0.2000
d^*/y^*	0.2277	0.1754	0.1228
d^*/k^*	0.1237	0.0868	0.0541
$(i^* - i^f)^c$	0.0729	0.0584	0.0427
$g^{Y^*} - n$	0.0289	0.0323	0.0370

s^* = optimal saving ratio in an open economy with partly endogenous technical change,
s^{**} = optimal saving ratio in an open economy with fully exogenous technical change,
d^*/y^* = debt-GDP ratio, d^*/k^* = debt/capital ratio, i^* = real interest rate, i^f = real global interest rate, $g^{Y^*} - n$ = per capita output growth rate.
[a]Based on maximization of a discounted stream of lifetime consumption Equation (10.12), subject to Equations (10.9)–(10.10), in which instantaneous utility is of the CRRA form. Microsoft's Solver tool is used to solve the frst-order conditions for a maximum.
[b]Estimates from Szpiro (1986).
[c]Risk premium Equation (10.8), reflecting combined effects of risk factors and financial markups.

the sustainable gross foreign debt is in range of 39–50 percent of GDP.[41]

If $\rho = 0$, $\theta = 1$ (utility function is ln c), and $\varnothing \geq 0$, then the optimal saving rate is:

$$s^{***} = \alpha, \tag{10.30}$$

the S-S result. In the RCK framework, if the time preference discount is close to zero (but not zero) and the utility function is ln c, the saving rate must be set equal to the income share of capital, whether

[41]Refer back to footnote 7 for the most recent Philippine gross foreign assets and debt ratios (Bangko Sentral ng Pilipinas, 2019).

or not learning by doing is partly endogenous. It is also true that $s^{***} > s^{*} > s^{**}$.

As the elasticity of intertemporal substitution increases, Table 10.1 reveals the following:

- Optimal saving ratio and the equilibrium growth rate of per capita GDP rise; and
- The debt to GDP ratio declines.[42]

When $\rho = 0$, $\theta = 1$, and $\varnothing \geq 0$, Equation (10.28) says that the optimal saving rate is not only a function of the deep parameters $\rho, \theta, \varnothing, \mu, \delta$, and n, as well as k^*, but must be set equal to a fraction of capital's income share α, with the fraction equal to $\{[\{i^* - g^{Y^*})(d^*/k^*) + \delta + g^{Y^*}]/(\rho + \delta + \theta g^{Y^*})\}$.[43] An alternative interpretation is that capital's income share should be a multiple of the optimal saving rate in order to compensate capital for the additional GDP growth generated by endogenous growth and learning by doing. Setting capital's income share equal to the saving rate, implicit in the S-S model, would be welfare-reducing because of the under-compensation of capital.

10.6 Concluding Remarks

This paper has developed and discussed the VM2 model, which is an open-economy growth model, employing the RCK optimal control setup and modifying Arrow's learning-by-doing framework in which workers learn through experience on the job to raise their productivity.

- The VM2 model produces empirically plausible and testable predictions about per capita GDP growth effects of parameters describing preferences, technology, and population growth, as well

[42] Households become less risk-averse, so they save more and borrow less, raising the growth rate of per capita GDP, and lowering the debt to GDP ratio. To be precise, a higher saving rate increases the equilibrium capital-labor ratio, lowering the marginal product of capital, foreign borrowing, and the debt to GDP ratio.

[43] In Figure 10.1, this condition is associated with maximum utility at c_0^*.

as public policies that affect equilibrium capital intensity and, directly or indirectly, the model's parameters, especially the extent of learning-by-doing associated with the economy's stock of capital per effective labor. Such predictive hypotheses can be tested empirically using panel data.[44]

- The high *Golden Rule* domestic saving rate of 34 percent of GDP reported in the VM1 model is associated with high elasticity of intertemporal substitution (a low degree of relative risk aversion). Lower empirical estimates of the elasticity of intertemporal substitution imply lower *Golden Utility* domestic saving rates of 18–22 percent of GDP that are dynamically efficient and feasible targets for most governments in Asia and emerging markets. The sustainable gross foreign debt is in the range of 39–50 percent of GDP.
- The domestic saving rate should be set below the share of capital in total output, owing to positive externalities arising from learning by doing associated with capital intensity. Equivalently put, income going to capital as a share of total output should be a multiple of the amount saved and invested in order to compensate capital for the additional output generated by endogenous growth and induced learning-by-doing.
- Fiscal consolidation and strong incentives for private saving are essential to achieving maximum per capita GDP growth. Reliance on foreign savings (foreign borrowing) has limits, particularly in a global environment of high interest rates and risk premiums.
- When real borrowing costs are positively correlated with rising external indebtedness, foreign borrowing is even more circumscribed, and efficient foreign debt management is critically important.
- When risk spreads are large despite the high expected marginal product of capital, there is a role for public policies to achieve and maintain macroeconomic and financial stability to mollify risk-averse global lenders.

[44]For the mechanics and application of a panel data procedure, see Knight *et al.* (1993, **Chapter 2**).

- The international community should increase aid including subsidized loans earmarked for imports of advanced capital goods, workers' education, on-the-job training, and health, provided that economic policies are sound.
- In view of current low global interest rates and the actual gross foreign debt remaining well below the sustainable level (as a ratio to GDP) in the Philippines, there is room for additional foreign borrowing to cover imports of advanced capital goods, subsidies to on-the-job training at enterprises, and costs of controlling the COVID19 pandemic and other public health expenditures. Such measures will increase learning-by-doing and labor productivity, leading to a short-run overshooting of a long-run, higher rate of per capita GDP growth.
- The record of the Philippines on fiscal consolidation, external accounts surplus and high and sustained growth is remarkable, earning high marks from credit-rating agencies. Thus, a temporary breach of the limits on foreign borrowing in the current environment of COVID19 is allowed. It is expected that such a breach disappears as the COVID pandemic passes.

References

Aghion, P. and P. Howitt (1992). A model of growth through creative destruction. *Econometrica*, 60, 323–352.

Arrow, K. (1962). The economic implications of learning by doing. *Review of Economic Studies*, 29, 155–173.

Bangko Sentral ng Pilipinas (2019). *Annual Report.* Manila, Philippines.

Barro, R. and X. Sala-i-Martin (1995). *Economic Growth.* NY: McGraw Hill.

Cass, D. (1965). Optimum growth in an aggregative model of capital accumulation. *Review of Economic Studies*, 32, 233–240.

Conlisk, J. (1967). A modified neo-classical growth model with endogenous technical change. *The Southern Economic Journal*, 34, 199–208.

Grossman, G. and E. Helpman (1990). Comparative advantage and long-run growth. *American Economic Review*, 80, 796–815.

Grossman, G. and E. Helpman (1991). *Innovation and Growth in the Global Economy.* Cambridge, MA: MIT Press.

International Monetary Fund (2020). Update on the joint IMF-WB multi-pronged approach to address debt vulnerabilities. *IMF Policy Paper*, December 7.

Ito, T. and A. Rose (eds.) (2007). *Fiscal Policy and Management in East Asia.* National Bureau of Economic Research: University of Chicago Press.

Knight, M., N. Loayza, and D. Villanueva (1993). Testing the neoclassical theory of economic growth: a panel data approach. *IMF Staff Papers*, 40, 512–541.

Koopmans, T. (1965). On the concept of optimal economic growth. In: *The Economic Approach to Development Planning*, Ch. 4. Amsterdam: North-Holland Publishing.

Kraay, A. and V. Nehru (2004). When is external debt sustainable? *World Bank Policy Research Working Paper 3200.*

Lane, P. and G.-M. Milesi-Ferretti (2006). The external wealth of nations: mark II: revised and extended estimates of foreign assets and liabilities, 1970–2004. *IMF Working Paper 06/69.*

Lucas, R. (1988). On the mechanics of economic development. *Journal of Monetary Economics*, 22, 3–42.

Lui, F. (2007). Comment on external debt, adjustment, and growth. In: T. Ito and A. Rose (eds.), *Fiscal Policy and Management in East Asia*, pp. 221–222. National Bureau of Economic Research: University of Chicago Press.

Manasse, P. and A. Schimmelpfenning (2003). Predicting sovereign debt crises. *University of Bologna, IMF, and New York University Working Paper.*

Manasse, P. and N. Roubini (2005). Rules of thumb for sovereign debt crises. *International Monetary Fund Working Paper 05/42.*

Otani, I. and D. Villanueva (1989). Theoretical aspects of growth in developing countries: external debt dynamics and the role of human capital. *IMF Staff Papers*, 36, 307–342.

Otani, I. and D. Villanueva (1990). Long-term growth in developing countries and its determinants: an empirical analysis. *World Development*, 18, 769–783.

Patillo, C., H. Poirson, and L. Ricci (2004). What are the channels through which external debt affects growth? *International Monetary Fund Working Paper 04/15.*

Phelps, E. (1966). *Golden Rules of Economic Growth.* NY: W.W. Norton & Company.

Ramsey, F. (1928). A mathematical theory of saving. *Economic Journal*, 38, 543–559.

Rebelo, S. (1991). Long-run policy analysis and long-run growth. *Journal of Political Economy*, 99, 500–521.

Reinhart, C., K. Rogoff and M. Savastano (2003). Debt intolerance. *Brookings Papers on Economic Activity.*

Rivera-Batiz, L. and P. Romer (1991). International trade with endogenous technical change. *Working Paper 3594.* Washington: National Bureau of Economic Research.

Romer, P. (1986). Increasing returns and long-run growth. *Journal of Political Economy*, 94, 1002–1037.

Romer, P. (1990). Endogenous technological change. *Journal of Political Economy*, 98, S71–S102.

Solow, R. (1956). A contribution to the theory of economic growth. *The Quarterly Journal of Economics*, 70, 65–94.

Solow, R. (1991). *Policies for Economic Growth.* SAIS: Johns Hopkins University.

Swan, T. (1956). Economic growth and capital accumulation. *Economic Record*, 32, 334–362.

Szpiro, G. (1986). Relative risk aversion around the world. *Economic Letters*, 20, 19–21.

Villanueva, D. (1994, **Chapter 6**). Openness, human development, and fiscal policies: effects on economic growth and speed of adjustment. *IMF Staff Papers*, 41, 1–29.

Villanueva, D. (2003). External debt, capital accumulation, and growth. *Singapore Management University-SESS Discussion Paper Series in Economics and Statistics.*

Villanueva, D. and R. Mariano (2007, **Chapter 9**). External debt, adjustment, and growth. In: T. Ito and A. Rose (eds.) (2007). *Fiscal Policy and Management in East Asia*, pp. 199–221. National Bureau of Economic Research: University of Chicago Press.

Villanueva, D. (2008). *Macroeconomic Policies for Stable Growth.* Singapore: World Scientific.

Villanueva, D. (2020, **Chapter 3**). A modified neoclassical growth model with endogenous labor participation. *Bulletin of Monetary Economics and Banking*, 23, 83–100.

Villanueva, D (2021, **Chapter 4**). Capital and growth. *Bulletin of Monetary Economics and Banking*, 24, 285–312.

Chapter 11

Economic Adjustment and Growth: A Summing Up*

Before presenting the book's last chapter on the case study of an emerging market economy, it would be useful to sum up the previous chapters and briefly discuss the IMF approach to economic adjustment and growth.

As shown in Section 10.3, in an open economy the national income identity shows that total uses of funds equal total sources of funds. Total uses are aggregate consumption C and aggregate gross investment I, including imports of consumer and capital goods. Total sources are (a) output GDP including exported goods and services, and (b) net foreign borrowing (increase in foreign liabilities less increase in foreign assets) plus principal and interest receipts, minus principal and interest payments, plus profits/dividends received, minus profits/dividends paid. As accounting identity, item (b) includes imports of goods and services less exports of goods and services, or the external current account balance, CA.

$$CA = GDP - (C + I)$$

CA is a deficit (−) when $C + I > GDP$, or aggregate demand $(C + I)$ exceeds aggregate supply GDP, the latter given by the aggregate production function. Under these circumstances, a country faces a balance of payments problem. When this magnitude is large

*Written by Delano S. Villanueva.

and persistent and access to net external financing [item (b) above] is limited, the country faces adjustment policy choices including, but not limited to, a depreciation of the exchange rate, cuts in C and I through restrictive fiscal and monetary policies, and needed structural reforms to boost aggregate supply.

Assuming the country is a member of the IMF, she approaches the Fund for financial assistance. She does so under an agreed program of adjustment with policy conditionality. For non-inflation targeting countries, quantitative performance criteria include reductions in the fiscal deficit and in the central bank's net domestic assets, and floors for net international reserves. For inflation targeting countries, the required policy adjustments include an agreed inflation target, reductions in the fiscal deficit, and increases in interest rates.

An IMF program of economic adjustment involves six steps (Mussa and Savastano, 1999): inception, blueprint, negotiation, approval, monitoring, and completion. The adjustment program starts with a formal request by a member country for a Use of Fund Resources (UFR) arrangement (e.g., a stand-by arrangement or SBA). The IMF staff team working on that member country (area department, e.g., Asia and Pacific), along with other concerned IMF departments (Strategy, Policy, and Review; Money and Capital Markets; Fiscal Affairs; Research) prepare a briefing paper outlining recent economic and financial developments, external payments problems, access to international financial markets, and evaluation of the national authorities' policy responses to the nature and size of the balance of payments difficulties. The briefing paper contains the elements of the country's adjustment program that can qualify for use of IMF financial resources with access amounts and phasing. Required policy measures are identified (known as "conditionality"). In countries with a large current account deficit relative to available financing, prior policy actions, such an exchange rate depreciation, may be required.

Following clearance of the briefing paper by IMF management, a Fund mission is dispatched to the member country for about two weeks. The mission is headed by a senior staff from the area department and consists of the desk economist assigned to the member country, and economists from Strategy, Policy, and Review, Monetary and Capital Markets, Fiscal Affairs, and Research departments. An advanced team, except for the mission chief, spends the first week collecting necessary information and documents pertaining to recent economic and financial developments, including estimates of external disequilibrium and macroeconomic imbalances.

At the beginning of the second week, the mission chief arrives for the negotiation conducted *ad referendum.* Upon return to Washington, a staff report on the arrangement is prepared and submitted to management and once approved, sent to the Executive Board for discussion and approval. The first loan disbursement and program monitoring follow Board approval. Subsequent disbursements are usually made over a 1- to 3-year period subject to compliance with numerical and structural performance criteria. The arrangement is deemed completed when the last tranche is disbursed.[1]

The IMF approach to economic adjustment consists of three elements: (1) availability of external financing; (2) implementation of demand-restraining policies; and (3) adoption of structural reforms. In the case of a member country whose monetary policy framework is inflation targeting, the first item is element (b) mentioned in the second paragraph of this chapter. Item (2) refers to restrictive fiscal and monetary policies, including strict adherence to the inflation target. Examples of item (3) are reforms and regulation of key financial institutions (e.g., banking system) and operations or outright privatization of non-financial public enterprises.

The analytics of demand-restraining fiscal and monetary policies can be summed up as follows (see Figure 11.1).[2] A country is initially

---

[1]Renegotiation of the arrangement is triggered when disbursements are halted because of non-fulfillment of the quantitative or structural performance criteria.
[2]See the discussion of the phase diagrams, Figures 7.1 and 7.2 in **Chapter 7**. Figure 11.1 is adapted from Figure 7.2. As in Figure 7.2, the vertical axis measures the observed, expected, and target rates of inflation, while the horizontal axis measures the output gap (*GDP* minus its potential level). The demand-inflation line D is downward-sloping because an increase in inflation triggers a rise in interest rates, dampening aggregate demand and lowering the output gap. The price-adjustment line P is upward-sloping because a higher output gap (excess aggregate demand) results in higher inflation.

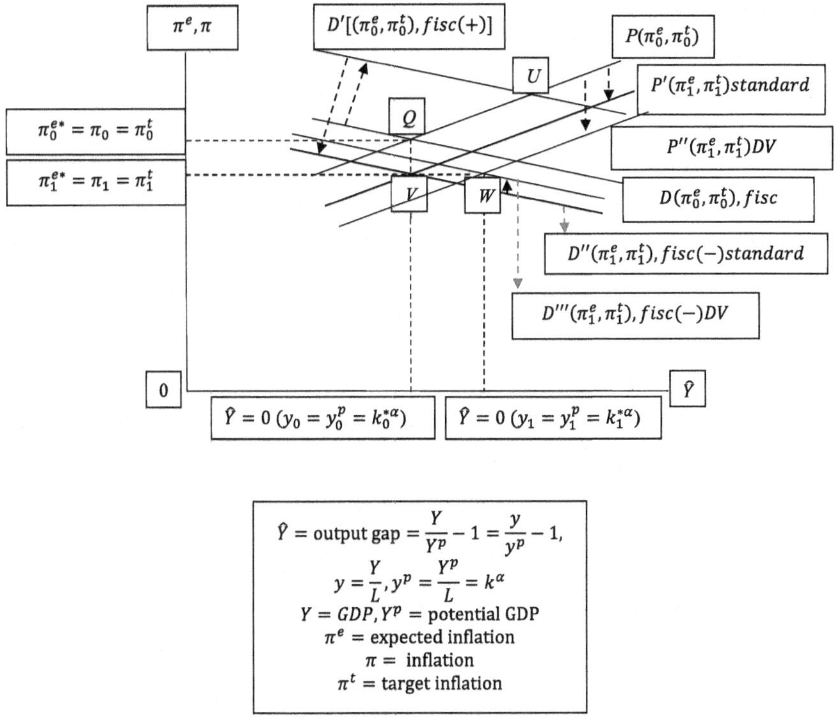

Figure 11.1. Economic adjustment and growth.

in an equilibrium position at point Q, wherein real GDP equals its potential level ($y_0 = y_0^p$), and the external current account is in balance (aggregate demand, $C + I$ = aggregate supply, GDP).[3] Inflation is on target at π_0^t. Suppose that a country's fiscal position has deteriorated rapidly because of burgeoning public sector deficits, shifting the demand-inflation D curve upward to D' and intersecting the price-adjustment P curve at point U. The economy temporarily moves from Q to U. Aggregate demand and inflation rise. The external current account turns into an unsustainable deficit: $(C + I)$ exceeds GDP, the latter fixed by the unchanged capital intensity k_0^* at Q. Inflation exceeds the target rate by a substantial margin,

[3] At Q, the demand-inflation line $D(\pi_0^e, \pi_0^t)$, $fisc$ intersects the price-adjustment line $P(\pi_0^e, \pi_0^t)$.

implying loss of export competitiveness. Owing to the unavailability of external financing of the balance of payments deficit at U and continuous pressure on the exchange rate, the country approaches the IMF for a standby arrangement, hoping that an IMF imprimatur will help unleash foreign credits in addition to IMF resources. The IMF conditionality includes reduced fiscal deficits, a lower target inflation at π_1^t, and a higher central bank policy interest rate.

Upon meeting the IMF performance criteria, the demand-inflation curve shifts downward to $D''(\pi_1^e, \pi_1^t)$, $fisc(-)standard$, and the price-adjustment curve shifts downward to $P(\pi_1^e, \pi_1^t)standard$ the two curves intersecting at V. The external current account is in balance, real GDP is back to its potential level, and inflation is cut to its lower target rate. The adjustment path U-Q-V is in line with existing macroeconomic principles of adjustment and growth. The only effect of monetary policy is to reduce inflation to its lower target rate at V. Full employment output returns to the level produced by the unchanged equilibrium capital intensity k_0^*, in line with rational expectations.

When expected inflation is a mix of adaptive and rational expectations (**Chapter 7**), and labor productivity is a positive function of capital intensity through learning by doing (**Chapters 6** and **10**), real and potential GDP go up (the latter produced by a higher equilibrium capital intensity k_1^*), traced by the movement from V to W, while the rate of inflation is kept at the lower targeted level. The short-run and long-run economic adjustment is traced by the segment U-Q-V-W. The explanation is as follows.

According to modern macroeconomics with rational expectations, the price-adjustment P line shifts downward to $P'(\pi_1^e, \pi_1^t)standard$ corresponding to the lower inflation target. As part of the adjustment process, aggregate demand (via lower fiscal deficits and higher interest rates) falls to y_0, equal to the prevailing potential output at V.[4] At V, inflation equals its lower target rate π_1^t as predicted by modern macroeconomics, with no change in potential

[4]Where the lower demand-inflation curve $D''(\pi_1^e, \pi_1^t)$, $fisc(-)standard$ intersects the lower price-adjustment curve $P'(\pi_1^e, \pi_1^t)standard$.

output ($y_0^p = k_0^{*\alpha}$), which is determined by the production function and prevailing technology. The external current account is in balance.

At W, as postulated and explained by the growth model of Chapter 7, potential output is higher ($y_1^p = k_1^{*\alpha}$) because equilibrium capital intensity is larger owing to a higher investment rate responding to a decline in expected inflation. The latter owes to adaptive inflationary expectations being partly operative (**Chapter 7** cites both empirical and theoretical studies supporting adaptive expectations[5]) — expected inflation goes down when observed inflation decelerates from U to W.[6] Lower expected inflation increases investment, shifting the demand-inflation curve upward from D'' to D'''.

The larger capital stock with embodied advanced technology enhances labor productivity via learning by doing. The higher potential output matches the larger aggregate demand D''' (relative to D'' of the standard model).[7] The larger investment rate means that the warranted rate goes up and matches the higher natural rate at the enhanced capital intensity level. At W, the equilibrium growth rate of per capita output is higher.[8] This growth dynamics is the result of adaptive expectations and learning by doing as described and analyzed, respectively, in **Chapter 7** and **Chapters 6** and **10**. The external current account is similarly in balance with identical lower inflation outcome, but with higher imports and exports.

To sum up, the key difference between the two equilibrium points V and W is that W is associated with *larger* levels of potential output and real income, as well as a *higher* growth rate of per capita output corresponding to a *larger* level of capital intensity associated with higher investments induced by lower expected inflation. The higher

---

[5]Conlisk (1988) had shown that rational expectations need not be the optimal solution to a properly specified optimization problem if the optimization cost is substantial. Adaptive expectations may well be the optimal (least costly) solution as suggested by bounded rationality.

[6]The price-adjustment curve shifts downward to $P''(\pi_1^e, \pi_1^t)DV$, a larger shift (in absolute terms) than the downward shift of the $P'(\pi_1^e, \pi_1^t)$*standard* curve.

[7]$\hat{Y} = 0\,(y_1 = y_1^p = k_1^{*\alpha})$.

[8]The equilibrium growth rate of per capita output $= \lambda + \theta k_1^*$ at W, which is greater than $\lambda + \theta k_0^*$ at V, since $k_1^* > k_0^*$, where $\lambda =$ the rate of exogenous labor-augmenting technical change and $\theta =$ the learning coefficient.

output growth rate owes to *enhanced* learning by doing associated with larger imports of technologically advanced capital goods.

References

Conlisk, J. (1988). Optimization cost. *Journal of Economic Behavior and Organization*, 9, 213–228.

Mussa, M. and M. Savastano (1999). The IMF approach to economic stabilization. *IMF Working Paper 99/104*.

Chapter 12

Stabilization Policies and Structural Reforms: The Philippine Case*

The Philippines is no longer the sick man of East Asia, but the rising tiger. There is macroeconomic stability, and the fiscal situation of the government is sound and improving. The fight against corruption is being waged with determination and it is paying off. Transparency is improving everywhere in the Philippines.

World Bank, 5 February 2013

The Philippines at this moment is one of the economies with stellar performance in ASEAN as well as in the whole world. And in the last five years, the Philippines grew over 5 percent, which is a very rare case in many other countries.

International Monetary Fund, 24 September 2014

After a soft patch in the first half of this year, the Philippines' GDP growth is expected to strengthen in the remainder of 2019 and in 2020, underpinned by government spending catching up with targets, and the recent monetary policy easing.

IMF Article IV Press Release, 18 November 2019

12.1 Introduction

Before it recently emerged as one of Asia's fastest growing economies, the Philippine economy had earlier been characterized by the following salient growth features: 1) uneven and susceptible to boom-bust

*Written by Diwa C. Guinigundo.

cycles; 2) absence of productivity gains; and 3) distorted industrial structure (Kongsamut and Vamvakidis, 2000).

In the 1950s to 1980s, development fluctuated around a low average growth rate and was subject to serious economic imbalances. Consequently, the country lagged behind most of its Asian neighbors, earning the moniker "the sick man of Asia." The poor economic performance culminated in an economic collapse in 1984 and 1985, amid a political turmoil, when the country's gross national product (GNP) contracted by 6.8 percent and 3.8 percent, respectively.

In the early 1990s, the country began to turn things around and exhibited some fundamental improvements. Growth accelerated until the onset of the Asian Financial Crisis (AFC) in 1997–98. While growth eased during this challenging period, the economy managed to avoid a deep recession, unlike many of its Asian neighbors. The economy also proved to be resilient during the Global Financial Crisis (GFC) in 2007–08 as it weathered the external shocks without significant costs to the real economy. The country has since been growing at consistently high levels and has re-emerged as one of what the World Bank once described as Asia's rising tigers. This streak of positive growth has been maintained until the outbreak of the COVID-19 pandemic.

Many attribute this transformation to the painstaking structural reforms and policy adjustments that policymakers were able to institutionalize after the country's economic collapse in the 1980s. A plethora of literature has found significant empirical evidence linking the country's growth with economic policy reforms.

This chapter begins with testimonials from the two major international financial organizations, namely the International Monetary Fund (IMF) and the World Bank, on the Philippines' turnaround from being the laggard in Asia to a very promising emerging economy. It explains in succeeding parts its narrative of relative success in the last 20 years. It looks at how the country's stabilization efforts and structural reforms translated into sound and robust macroeconomic fundamentals as the country completed its various rounds of IMF stabilization programs that also helped put these reforms in place. Section 12.2 discusses the various structural reforms pursued in the Philippines from the 1960s to the present, with focus on the IMF's role in helping catalyze economic reforms in the country. Section 12.3 examines the impact of these reforms on the Philippines' macroeconomic fundamentals, with some focus on the deregulation and liberalization efforts undertaken in the 1990s. Section 12.4 covers the impact of the pandemic and shows the remaining weaknesses in the economy. Section 12.5 puts forward some policy recommendations.

12.2 Structural Reforms in the Philippines and the Role of the IMF

Before its economic collapse in the early 1980s, the country's economic policy environment was mainly inward-looking. According to Sicat (2002), as the country was just transitioning into a fully sovereign state, the 1935 Constitution set the stage for policies geared towards providing new opportunities for Filipino citizens to expand their participation in economic activities. Before then, Spanish and American colonialists were given the priority to own and operate business in the Philippines. This transition naturally led to a more restrictive environment for foreign investors in the Philippines especially with respect to land use, exploitation of natural resources, and movement of foreign capital which proved detrimental to a more dynamic, more open and more competitive growth of the Philippine economy.

12.2.1 *Protectionism in the 1950s to 1980s*

By 1950, protectionism emerged as the dominant theme of the country's economic policies. Import controls were imposed and foreign exchange policy adhered to a fixed exchange regime. This persisted until imbalances in the country's foreign exchange started becoming more apparent due to import controls and fixing the exchange value of the peso (Sicat, 2002). Protectionism was anchored on the belief that restricting imports would lead to the emergence of a local industry that would propel the domestic market. However, this approach, which came to evolve as "import-substitution" strategy, proved to be unsustainable.

The restrictive policy environment contributed to the country's subpar growth. Building from Barro Sala-i-Martin (1995), the Philippines' poor performance relative to its peers can be attributed to its lower degree of openness, low and uneven investment rates and foreign direct investments (FDIs) flowing into the domestic economy. This was evident during the 1960s and 1970s. During this period, the Philippines became the slowest growing economy in Southeast Asia with an annual average per capita GDP growth rate of 2.2 percent, significantly below the regional average of 3.8 percent. The country likewise consistently ran a trade deficit and was always under threat of a balance of payments (BOP) crisis (de Dios *et al.*, 2021).[1]

In 1962 during the Macapagal administration, decontrol of the foreign exchange system started but at the same time protective tariffs were introduced. The consequent devaluation of the peso only provided a temporary relief on the country's BOP position.

According to de Dios *et al.* (2021), the situation persisted during the Marcos regime starting in 1965. While the quota system was abolished during this time, protectionist policies remained in the form of high tariffs on finished products. During this time, fiscal and monetary policies became increasingly expansionary. Government spending surged by 92 percent in 1966–70. For its part, monetary policy was broadly accommodative of economic growth and inflationary pressures during this period, particularly from 1967 onward.

Consequently, structural weaknesses in the domestic economy slowly built up in the form of a large current account deficit, mounting external debt, worsening fiscal balance, declining gross national savings, and a system of cronyism and monopolistic practices, among others (Rodlauer *et al.*, 2000). This accumulation of structural weaknesses persisted until the economy collapsed in the

[1] **Chapter 8** develops and analyzes an open-economy growth model with emphasis on the key role of outward-oriented trade and flexible exchange rate policies to achieve a high growth rate of per capita output. **Chapters 2** and **6** provide empirical support to such a hypothesis.

1980s. The two oil price shocks in 1973 and 1980 also contributed to the inevitable deterioration of the country's economic performance.[2]

12.2.2 *Liberalization in the 1990s to Present: The Role of the IMF*[3]

After reeling from the crisis in the 1980s, public policies shifted and followed more outward-looking and market-oriented directions.[4] Policy reforms were implemented in the broad areas of the macroeconomy, social governance, infrastructure, investments, monetary policy and public finance.

To some extent, the country's stronger implementation of structural reforms was catalyzed by its engagement with the IMF. Among the countries in Asia, the Philippines has had one of the most prolonged engagements with the Fund. From the period 1962 to 2000, the Philippines made use of Fund resources under a total of 23 various financing agreements with the IMF that included Stand-By Arrangements (SBAs) and Extended Fund Facilities (EFFs).

These financial arrangements are invariably predicated with several conditionalities. Conditionalities are commonly viewed as a set of actions that a borrower must implement in order to obtain and continue receiving financial assistance from the Fund. These conditionalities are normally aimed at addressing structural rigidities and external imbalances through appropriate public policy adjustments, establishing safeguards that ensure funds are used only for the country's stabilization purposes.

In the case of the Philippines, conditionalities involved a long menu of structural measures. For instance, as early as the 1970s, its

---

[2]**Chapter 11** shows that such expansionary fiscal policy and accommodative monetary policy, combined with anemic response of output supply owing to structural weaknesses, plus a fixed exchange rate regime, led to persistent external current account deficits and mounting external debt.

[3]**Chapter 11** summarizes the steps and elements involved in IMF economic adjustment programs. **Chapters 1–10** provide a theoretical framework to the IMF approach to economic adjustment and growth.

[4]It should be noted that liberalization measures had their roots earlier in the 1970s; however, the political instability during the time curtailed its progress.

SBA with the Fund included an important component of floating the peso and allowing market forces to determine the country's foreign exchange rate. This was a prelude to the country's major transition to a more flexible exchange rate policy.

In the 1994 EFF, structural conditionalities covered six major areas involving over 40 specific measures. These measures anchored the Philippines' economic adjustments on fiscal consolidation, tax adjustments, and financial sector reforms, among others. Notable reforms supported by this program also included the earlier recommendation of the IMF on the recapitalization of the country's central bank which was institutionalized by Congress through RA 7653 that established an independent central bank. Fiscal consolidation was put in place to manage the country's fiscal deficit. Privatization of the banking, telecommunications, and oil sectors, among others, was also accelerated to open up the economy to market forces and competition to achieve higher levels of economic efficiency and output.

In the last IMF-supported program, the 1998 SBA, structural conditionalities covered eight major areas with more than a hundred specific measures. These included the enhancement of the banking sector through the enactment of the General Banking Law, amendments to the BSP Charter, and banking sector reforms. Measures also led to the rationalization of tax holiday incentives, retail trade liberalization, tax administration reform, and safeguards for local industries against increased imports (Figure 12.1).

These reforms were not silver bullets *per se*. While they were important in attaining the country's macroeconomic stability, there were also some missteps. For instance, despite the 1998 SBA, there were some measures undertaken to safeguard local industries against increased imports but they instead led to further economic distortion and undermined the general direction of liberalization. Nonetheless, these structural adjustments set a precedent to more comprehensive reforms ahead that would help place the country in a stronger and more competitive position.

While some of these reforms were not fully implemented and were challenged in many ways, they would trigger more comprehensive structural reforms years later (Rodlauer, 2000). Other notable reforms included the enactment of the Philippine E-Commerce Act in

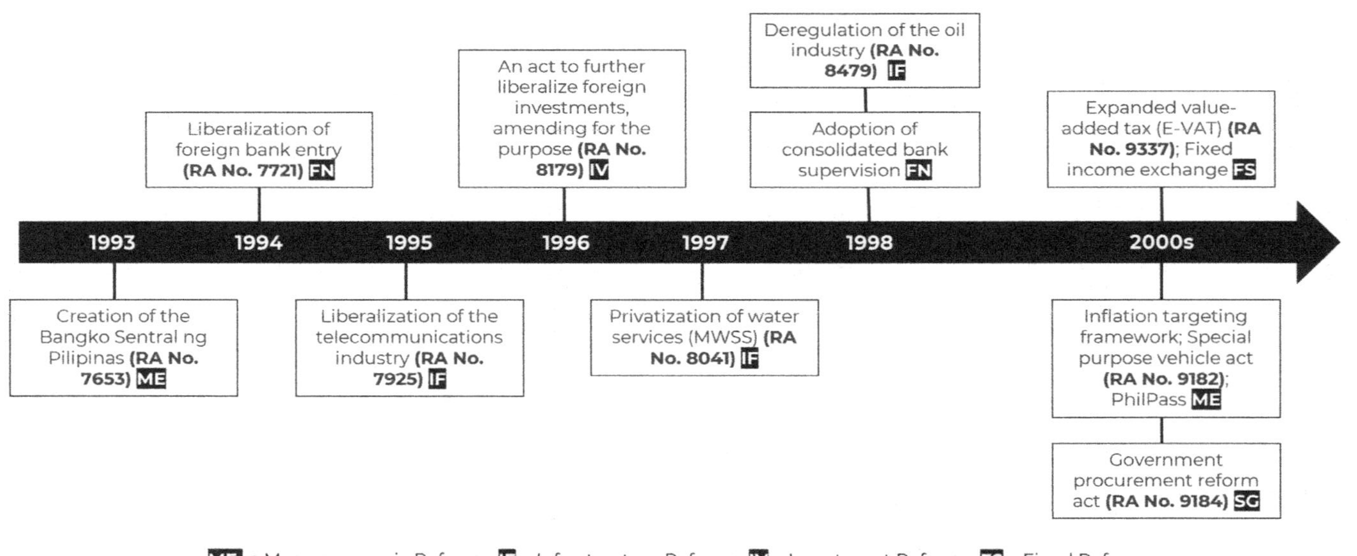

Figure 12.1. Selected structural reforms in the Philippines, 1990s–2000s.

2000 that aimed to facilitate domestic and international transactions and engagements, the shift to inflation targeting framework in 2002, National Payments Systems Act which made the BSP the oversight authority over the national payments system in 2017, and Ease of Doing Business Act in 2018.

More recently, the enactment of Republic Act (RA) 11659 which amended the Public Service Law should boost the inflow of foreign investments in the country (Figure 12.2). The Law streamlines and liberalizes various restrictions on ownership, management, and control of public utilities. This should attract more foreign investments in the areas of telecommunications, railways, expressways, airports, shipping, and power generation and supply. Likewise, the lifting of the open-pit mining, and introduction of terms and conditions to ensure these will be environmentally and socially sustainable, will potentially encourage more investments in the country. Indeed, an enabling legal and regulatory environment is crucial for investments to flourish in the domestic economy.

12.3 The Impact of Reforms on the Philippine Economy

The pursuit of reforms geared towards liberalization and market-oriented policies led to an improvement in the country's macroeconomic fundamentals and ushered in an era of rapid, robust, and sustainable growth. Market-oriented policies likewise provided an adjustment mechanism that helped strengthen the economy to absorb negative shocks.

12.3.1 *Solid Macroeconomic Fundamentals*

Growth started accelerating in 1993 with the observed improvements in productivity and reduced distortions in the industrial structure. The country's average real GDP growth for the period 1993 to 2021 increased to 4.2 percent, compared to its 1981–1992 average of 1.6 percent (Kongsamut and Vamvakidis, 2000). Growth remained broadly stable and positive since then, until the AFC in 1997 which culminated in economic decline in 1998 and the onset of the COVID-19 pandemic which saw growth plummeting in 2020 (Chart 12.1).

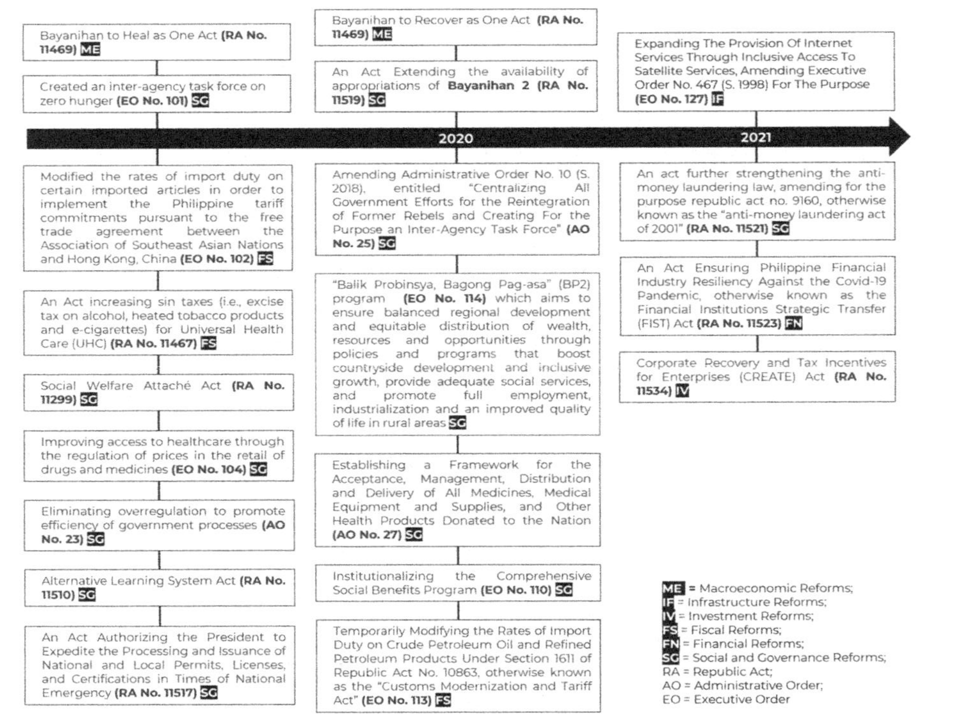

Figure 12.2. Recent structural and policy reforms in the Philippines.

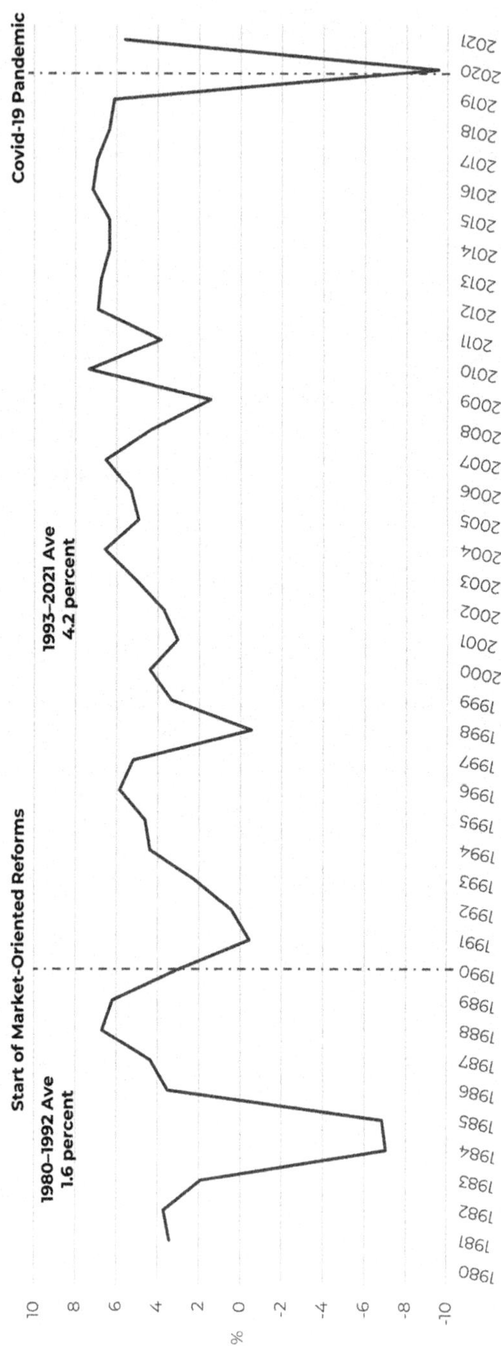

Chart 12.1. Gross Domestic Product (GDP), % growth rate at constant prices, 1980–2021.

Source: Philippines Statistics Authority.

Before the pandemic, the Philippines exhibited robust growth and became one of the fastest growing emerging economies in the region, with average quarterly growth of 6.4 percent from 2010–2019 (Cabote and Fernandez, 2020).

The reforms helped set the stage for higher potential growth due to several positive growth additives. First, total factor productivity (TFP) has been steadily increasing and is even considered to be one of the highest in the Asian region (Chart 12.2). During the period 1993–2001, TFP increased from a range of 0.4 to 0.8 percent, compared to the −0.5 to 0.7 percent range for the years 1989–1992. TFP was highest at 0.8 to 1.8 percent during the 2002–2009 period. However, TFP showed some decline during the years 2017–2019 on account of the unprecedented increase in oil prices spilling over to food and other non-food prices. Inflation in 2018 rose to 5.2 percent from 2.9 percent a year earlier, with the peso-dollar exchange rate rising from an average of P50.40 to P52.66, exports slowing down significantly and capacity utilization losing more than nine percentage points. In 2020–2021, TFP sustained its decline due to the global pandemic. With government attempts to contain the spread of COVID-19, the economy was literally locked down resulting in limited business activities, job losses and generally shorter hours in various economic sectors. Capital formation was weakest in 2020 as it plummeted by over 34 percent.

Second, estimates of the country's incremental capital output ratio (ICOR) have also been declining, indicating greater capacity to utilize its resources more efficiently. ICOR declined from a high of 8.3 during 1989–1992 to 5.5 during 1993–2001 (Chart 12.3).[5] The subsequent deterioration in the ICOR could be traced to the same external shocks that impinged on TFP.

The country's robust and resilient growth was achieved in a generally benign and therefore manageable inflation environment. Price stability emerged as an enabling factor in supporting and

[5]As analyzed in previous chapters, such a productivity increase is mirrored in increases in the warranted and natural rates of growth, capital intensity, and the long-run growth rate of per capita output.

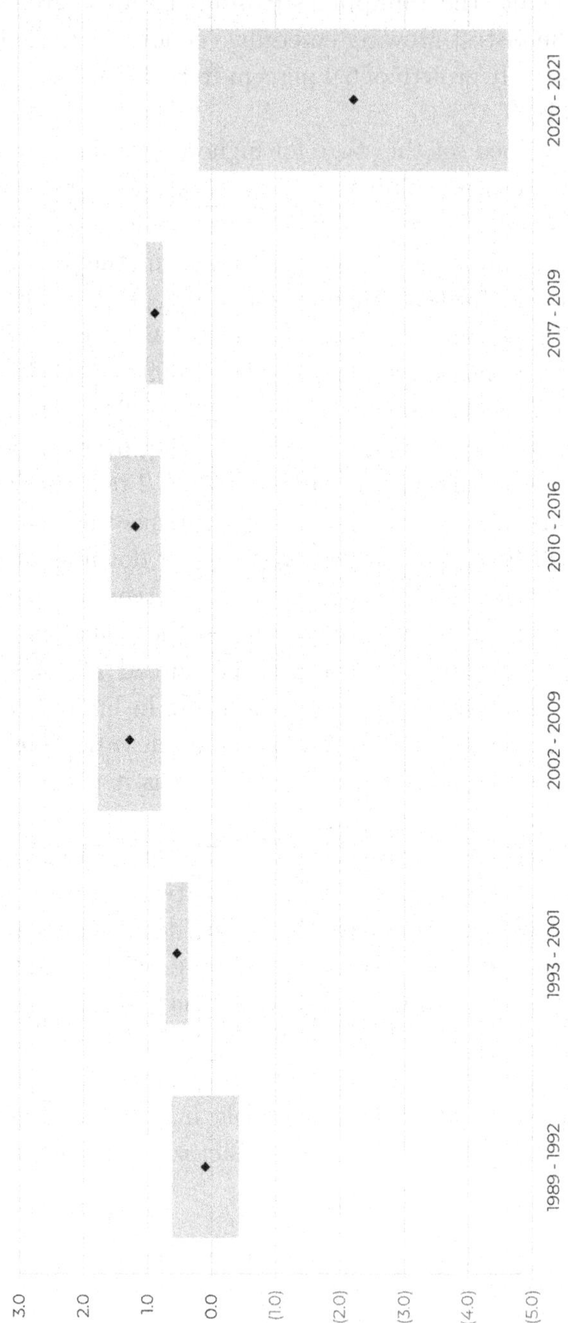

Chart 12.2. Total factor productivity (in percent), 1989–2021.

Source: Bangko Sentral ng Pilipinas.

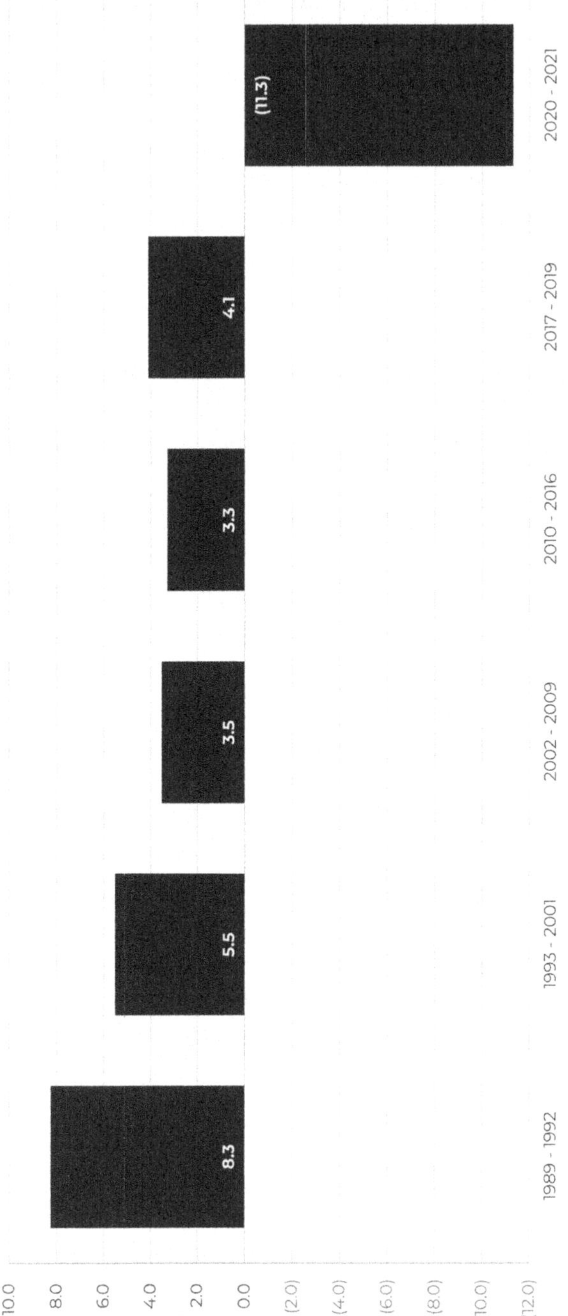

Chart 12.3. Incremental capital output ratio, 1989–2021.

Source: Bangko Sentral ng Pilipinas.

promoting greater economic activity. Since the BSP's shift to an inflation targeting (IT) framework in March 2002, headline inflation has been low and stable relative to those achieved in the 1980s–1990s under monetary aggregate targeting framework. For the period 2002–2021, headline inflation averaged at 3.7 percent (Chart 12.4). Moreover, the BSP was able to keep inflation within target for the years 2009–2014, 2017, and 2019.[6]

The reforms put in place by the BSP along with the banks' commitment to improve their ability to manage operational risks have resulted in significant improvements in the quality of Philippine banks' assets and loan portfolios as well as their strong capital base. Capital Adequacy Ratios (CAR) remained well above the international standard of 8.0 percent. The sound financial system enabled the effective intermediation of funds to productive sectors, thus helping promote economic growth.[7]

The country's external payments position also exhibited marked improvements. The country's S-I gap remained positive from 2003 through 2015, or alternatively, CA position yielded surpluses during this period. But starting 2016, the S-I gap reversed as investments and infrastructure spending expanded relative to savings. This signaled a potential shift to greater reliance on investment-led economic activities to support economic expansion (Chart 12.5).[8]

The positive dividends from the reforms also allowed the country to build up sufficient external buffers. The country's gross international reserves (GIR) grew steadily during the period (Chart 12.6). As of end-2021, GIR stood at US$108.8 billion, providing more than adequate external liquidity buffer.

---

[6]As summed up in **Chapter 7**, the achievement of a low and stable inflation rate under inflation targeting led to a low and stable *expected* rate of inflation that, in turn, encouraged higher investments and permanently higher growth rates of potential and observed *GDP*. For some discussion on the Bangko Sentral ng Pilipinas' implementation of the IT framework, see Guinigundo and Cacnio (2019), pp. 51–61.

[7]As predicted in **Chapter 5** on the role of finance in growth.

[8]The marked improvement in the external current account balance reflects the analysis of Figure 11.1 in **Chapter 11** under the impact of adjustments in fiscal, monetary, and exchange rate policies, as well as adoption of structural reforms.

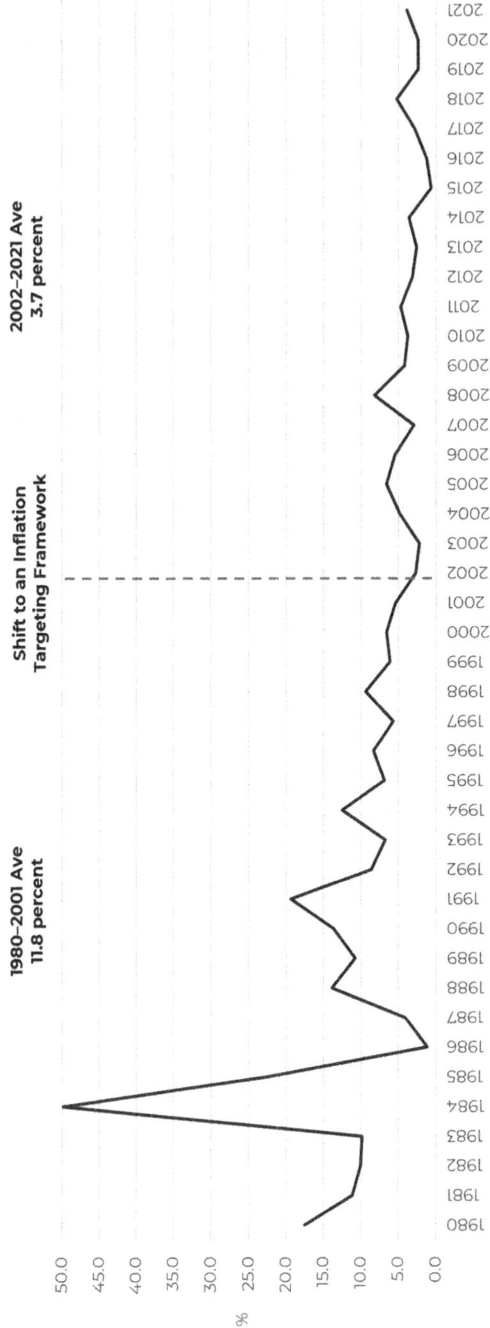

Chart 12.4. Inflation rate, 1980–2021. 2018 = 100.

Source: Philippines Statistics Authority.

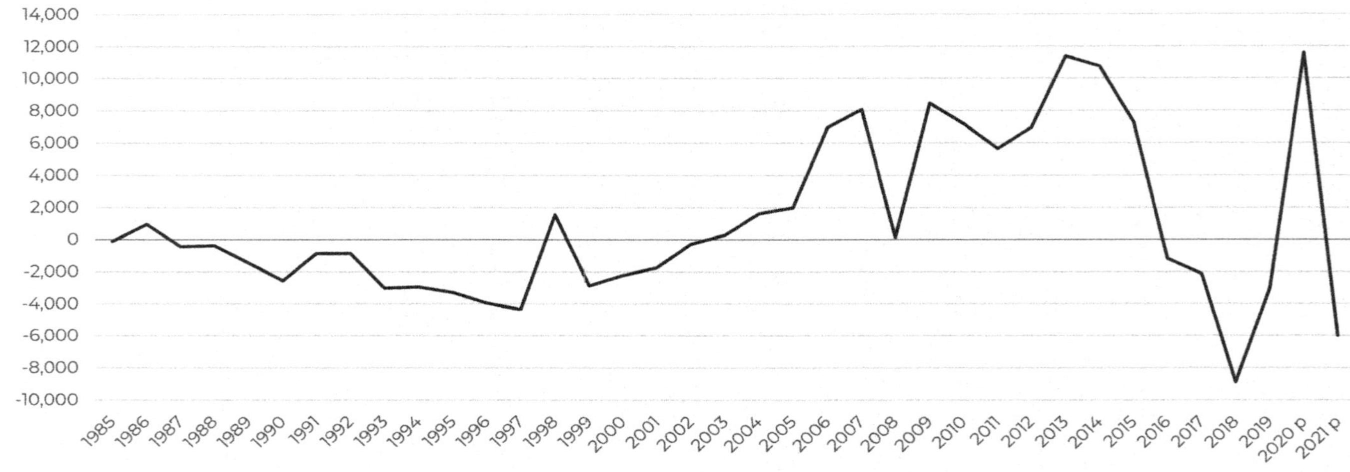

Chart 12.5. Current account balance (in million US dollars), 1985–2021.

Source: Bangko Sentral ng Pilipinas.

Note: 2005-present data are based on the Balance of Payments and International Investment Position Manual, 6th Edition (BPM6); 1999–2004 data are based on the Balance of Payments, 5th Edition (BPM5); and 1985–1998 data are based on BOP old concept/national presentation. p = preliminary.

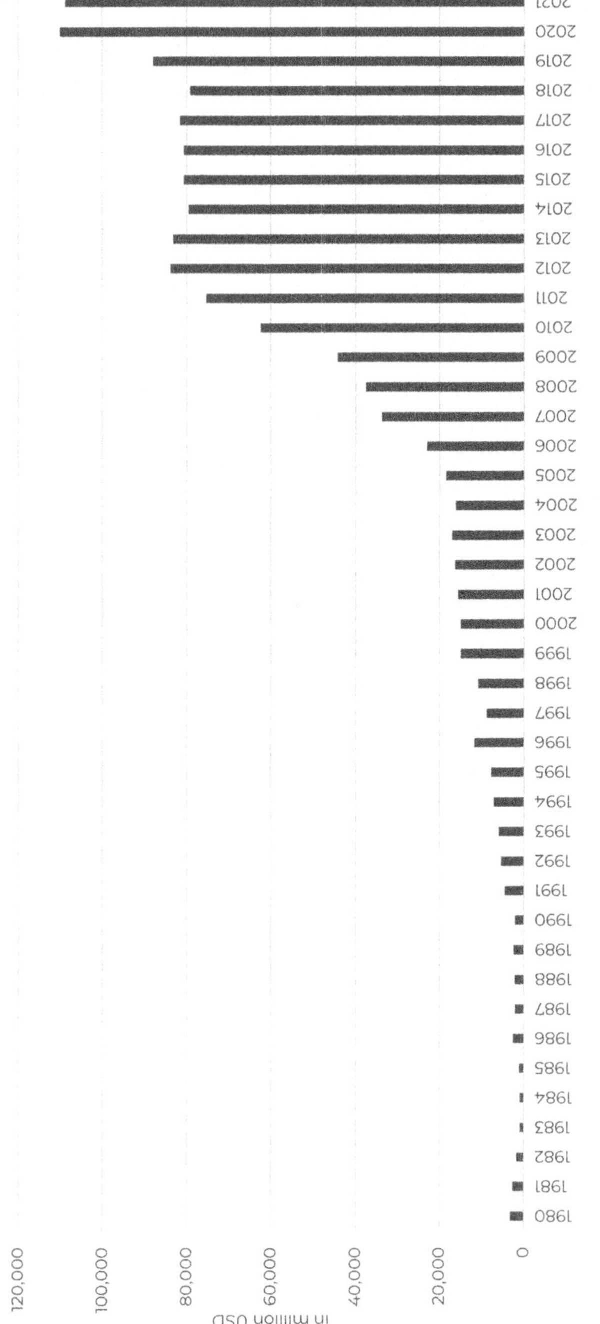

Chart 12.6. Gross international reserves (in million US dollars), 1980–2021.

Source: Bangko Sentral ng Pilipinas.

12.3.2 *Automatic Stabilizer*

The shift towards market-oriented policies has also allowed the domestic economy to be more resilient in absorbing external shocks. For instance, the BSP's shift to a flexible exchange rate regime allowed fluctuations in the peso to act as automatic stabilizer for a small open economy like the Philippines.

Chart 12.7 depicts how flexible exchange rates could perform this role. The horizontal axis refers to output shocks (year-on-year changes in the GDP forecasts for the Philippines by IMF), while the vertical axis refers to percent changes in the nominal peso. In this chart, a negative change in the peso means appreciation and vice versa. The chart shows that when output growth is revised upward, the peso tends to appreciate. Conversely, when output growth is revised downward, the peso tends to depreciate. These adjustments suggest that the peso acts as a buffer for the domestic economy during instances of output shocks.

This is consistent with Obstfeld's (2015) findings that emerging market economies (EMEs) that adopt a flexible exchange rate regime are better positioned to moderate the impact of global financial and monetary economic and financial developments.

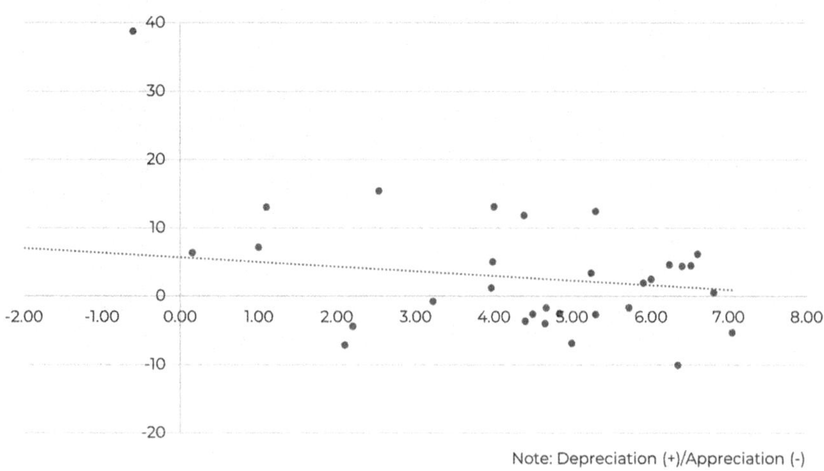

Chart 12.7. Peso-dollar exchange rate.

Sources: Bangko Sentral ng Pilipinas, IMF WEO database.

Table 12.1. ERPT estimates: Philippines, 1990-June 2017.

	Pre-IT (1990–2001)	IT (2002–June 2017)
Short-run ERPT	0.269	0.042
Long-run ERPT	0.547	0.419

At the same time, the transmission from exchange rate movements to domestic inflation has significantly moderated since the BSP transitioned to the flexible inflation targeting (FIT) framework. As Table 12.1 shows, the exchange rate pass through (ERPT) dropped from 0.269 percentage points (ppts) and 0.547 ppts for every P1 depreciation before the adoption of the FIT framework in 2002, to only 0.042 ppts and 0.419 ppts for every P1 depreciation after FIT, in terms of short-term and long-term impact, respectively. The FIT years were also the period during which the Philippines became increasingly drawn into the global value chain through its increased trading links with the US, Japan and China.

Estimating the impulse response of inflation to exchange rate shocks by breaking the FIT years (2002 to first quarter of 2022) into sub-periods before and after the GFC shows lower reading after the GFC (Chart 12.8).

Nonetheless, it is recognized that exchange rate adjustments may not fully insulate economies from external shocks and additional tools are obviously needed.

The conventional wisdom has been that countries face a trilemma and must choose between free capital flows, a fixed exchange rate, and an autonomous monetary policy. However, Rey (2015) argued that because of globalization and the presence of global common factors, governments, instead of a trilemma, actually face a dilemma, or an "irreconcilable duo," where free capital flows may inevitably mean a loss of monetary policy independence. In such a case, it is possible for the country to consider an expanded policy tool kit including complementary macro-prudential measures to help temper any systemic risk buildup. This could reduce procyclical feedback between asset prices or the exchange rate and local credit.

It should also be noted that Fernandez (2015) found sufficient empirical evidence that the US Federal Reserve's monetary policy

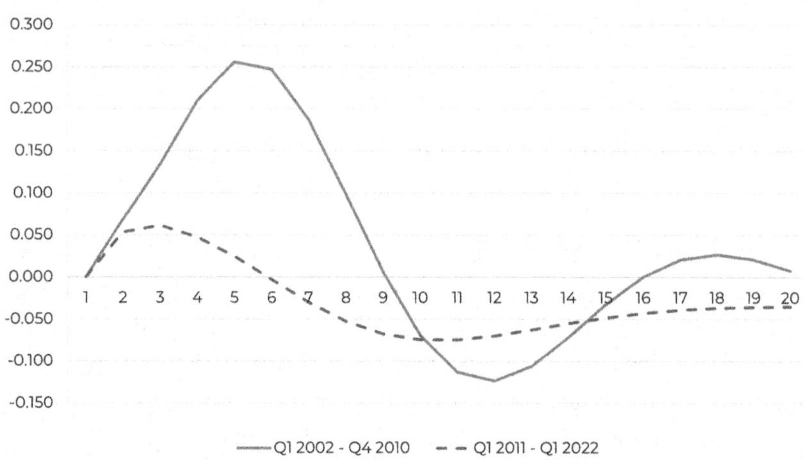

Chart 12.8. Impulse response of inflation to exchange rate shocks, Q1 2002-Q1 2022.

tools, such as its quantitative easing program, significantly contributed to the flow of portfolio capital into the Philippines. Local equity flows were particularly sensitive to US long-term interest rates. With capital flow surges, adjustments in the exchange rates may at times be unable to provide sufficient buffers to external shocks. Against such an operating environment, a more comprehensive and integrated approach in macro stabilization policies is needed.

12.3.3 *Credit Rating Upgrades*

The macroeconomic gains from the economic reforms and liberalization efforts sustained for nearly 30 years have been recognized by international credit ratings. The robust growth and sustainability that the country has enjoyed pre-pandemic has resulted in several credit rating upgrades from major global credit rating agencies (CRAs). These upgrades have moved the long-term sovereign debt status from junk grade to investment grade starting March 2013. These successive recognitions of the country's increasing creditworthiness have undoubtedly cemented the Philippines' status as an excellent investment destination. In fact, the reforms on the country's borrowing programs were so sustainable, CRAs still affirmed the Philippines credit rating even during the pandemic. Chart 12.9 shows how the country's credit default swap spreads have narrowed over the years.

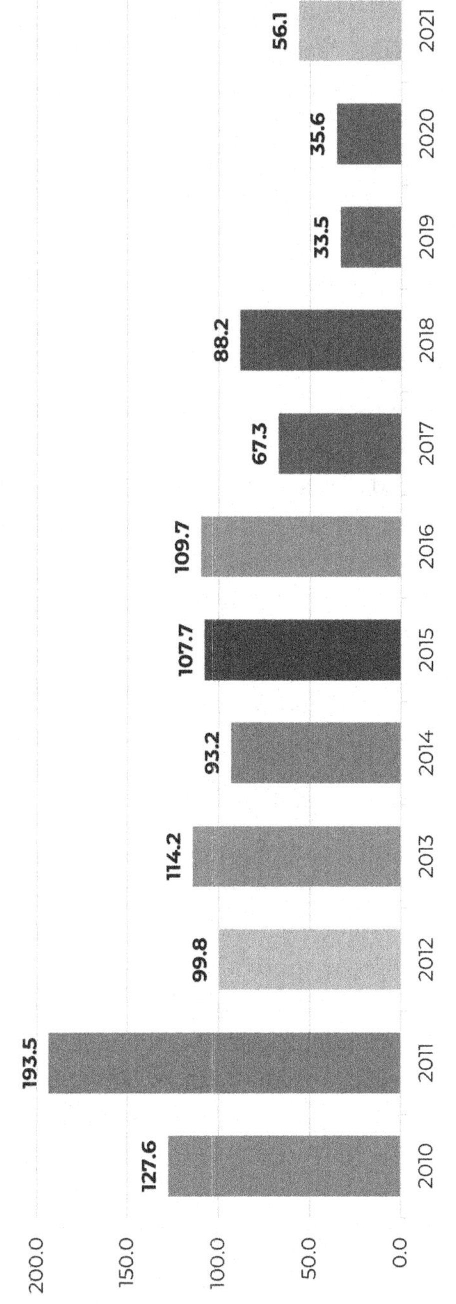

Chart 12.9. Philippine credit default swap.

Source: Bloomberg.

The Washington-based Center for Global Development (CGD) has also recognized the country's gains from its commitment to reforms. In 2014, CGD's "resiliency indicator", which is an overall index of resilience using several determinants such as macroeconomic factors comprising cost and availability of foreign financing and ability to respond to global shocks like fiscal spending and public debt, ranked the Philippines as the most resilient economy among 21 other economies, ahead of South Korea and China (Figure 12.3). This was a significant jump from its 7th place ranking seven years earlier in 2007.

12.4 The Pandemic and Policy Lessons

While the reforms pursued in the past decades have made the country's macroeconomy more robust and resilient, the COVID-19 pandemic has revealed remaining fragilities in the economy and underscored that more adjustments and structural reforms still need to be considered to make the economy more resilient to this type of shocks.

Like most economies, the pandemic and lockdown measures drove the domestic economy into a recession. During the height of the pandemic in Q2 2020, GDP bottomed out at a historic low of −16.9 percent, the lowest recorded growth since 1981. This brought the full-year 2020 GDP to contract by 9.5 percent.

What is inevitable is that the economy has to contend with the risk of the pandemic's lingering effects on the economy, or economic scarring. According to Haldane (2020), the pandemic has shifted relative prices that incentivizes firms to invest in machines instead of people, thereby potentially reducing employment and labor productivity. The shift in relative prices can also lead to asymmetrical preference in employment across sectors. In June 2020, unemployment reached a historic high of 17.6 percent on the back of stringent lockdown measures to contain the transmission of the virus. Labor conditions have improved since then as unemployment rate eased to 6.6 percent in December 2021. However, recovery is asymmetric as some sectors continue to show employment losses particularly in contact-sensitive services such as accommodation, food service activities, transportation and storage.

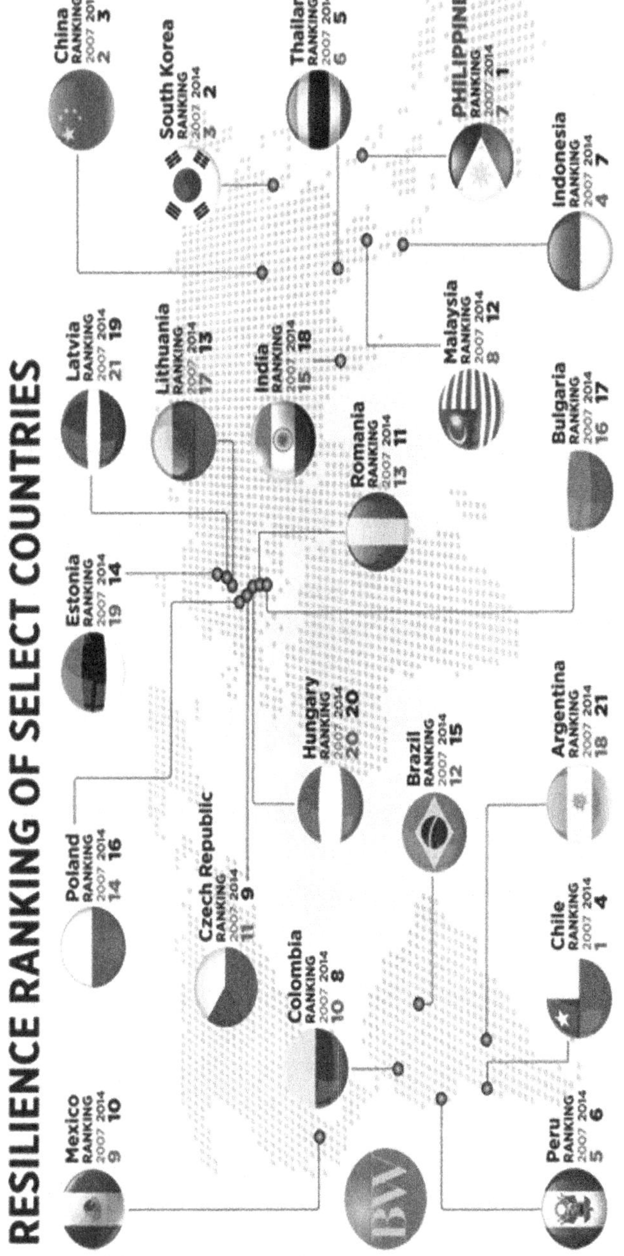

Figure 12.3. Resilience ranking of select countries, 2007 vs 2014.

Source: Center for Global Development.

It cannot be denied that, indeed, a lot of scope for policy adjustments and reforms exists to ensure the economy's track to growth is sustainable.

12.4.1 *Managing Elevated Level of External Debt*

Due to the weakness of public finance during the pandemic, greater reliance on foreign debt was resorted to by many countries including the Philippines. Rising level of indebtedness was unavoidable considering the dual need to spend more due to pandemic management and sustain public spending to ease the immediate impact on the poor and the most vulnerable. With higher spending and weak revenue base, the country's budget deficit more than doubled to 7.6 percent of GDP in 2020 from only 3.4 percent in 2019. But the restrictions to mobility and economic activity further dampened tax and revenue collections. The National Government (NG) had to increase its borrowings to finance programmed expenditures and COVID-19 initiatives. As a result, the NG's outstanding debt-to-GDP ratio rose to 54.6 percent in 2020 from 39.6 percent in 2019 and in 2021, it stood at 60.4 percent (of which 42.1 percent was domestic and 18.3 percent external).

Despite the increase, the government's debt remains manageable as it has preserved the robust structure of its debt profile, a legacy result of its previous encounter with the debt problem in the 1980s. Through its established judicious debt management and favorable credit ratings amid the wave of downgrades globally, the average annual interest rate of government borrowings has continued to decline and financing was secured at longer terms. The NG also expected a rebound in revenue collections through improved tax administration and tax reforms, while the economy gradually recovers. The government programs a downward trend to its fiscal deficit-to-GDP ratio starting in 2022 as it is determined to return quickly to fiscal consolidation. As part of its fiscal consolidation in the medium term, this approach will give some scope to reduce gross borrowings, allowing the debt-to-GDP ratio to stabilize to around 60 percent in the coming years. To minimize external risks, more than two-thirds of the financing requirement of the government will also be continually sourced from the country's very liquid domestic market. Commitment to continue exercising fiscal responsibility is the key to achieve an economic growth that outpaces that of debt over the short to medium term. The goal of the government should be to sustain the pace of economic growth, while strengthening market credibility by keeping the deficit-to-GDP and debt-to-GDP ratios broadly at the median range of the country's neighbors and rating peers around the world.

12.4.2 *Maintaining Monetary and Fiscal Spaces*

The crisis taught the Philippines about the need to maintain the efficacy of macroeconomic stabilization policies by maintaining appropriate policy space. The unprecedented nature of the pandemic prompted both the country's monetary and fiscal authorities to resort to drastic measures. For instance, the BSP implemented several measures to ensure sufficient liquidity in the financial system and complement the NG's policy response. These include the reduction of the policy rate by a cumulative 200 basis points (bps). Likewise, the reserve requirement ratio (RRR) of universal and commercial banks, as well as non-bank financial institutions with quasi-banking functions, was reduced by 200 bps from 14 percent to 12 percent in April 2020.[9] In accordance with its Charter, the BSP also provided bridge financing to the NG and purchased government securities from the secondary market (Dakila, 2021).

On the fiscal side, the NG expanded public spending to mitigate the economic impact of the pandemic but in the process widened the country's budget deficit in 2020. The deficit fell below the full-year program of 9.6 percent, indicating some space for fiscal authorities to continue funding social services and other pump-priming activities. But the NG also increased its borrowings to finance programmed expenditures and COVID-19 mitigation initiatives.

Both of these developments could complicate the conduct of economic policies in the future. First is the issue of potential narrowing policy space that could limit the country's ability to respond to shocks in the future. Second is the concern over formulating an exit strategy as the NG prepares for new economic arrangements towards

[9]The RRR was already previously reduced by 600 bps in 2018–2019.

recovery. The timing of the exit is pivotal because conditions and incentives change. Even the long-term growth path may also change in the post-pandemic world. Thus, the process should neither cause premature withdrawal of support nor give rise to delays in necessary restructuring. Both could be costly.

Efforts in determining the appropriate timing of the exit strategy should be guided by comprehensive economic and financial surveillance. Prompt updating of both the specifications of and assumptions used in the macroeconomic models in policy simulation will be most useful. Early warning systems can also provide additional information on any emerging shocks. Monitoring of leading economic indicators, business and consumer expectations surveys can put more context to emerging data points. Regular monitoring of the financial system and capital markets can validate the emerging trends in the real sector.

In all of these points for consideration, clear, timely and effective communication is key. For instance, it was correct for the BSP to have communicated that the unprecedented measures it implemented in response to the pandemic are time-bound. This minimizes the potential moral hazard risks stemming from such measures. Meanwhile, the NG has likewise started to communicate its fiscal consolidation plan. It is imperative that a prudent and pragmatic approach to ensure long-term fiscal sustainability without undermining short-term economic recovery is achieved. Sharing this with civil society can lead to public ownership of the policy.

However, greater vigilance continues to be imperative in the conduct of monetary policy as the economy tries to navigate its post-pandemic recovery. In particular, the geopolitical tensions between Russia and Ukraine have led to domestic inflationary pressures and increased market uncertainty. In situations where there is potential de-anchoring of inflation expectations, symbolic and tiny increases in nominal interest rates in the immediate future may be necessary to rein in inflation expectations and keep inflation within target.[10] Otherwise, if timing is off, and if what one might call baby steps

[10] A good point made by Charles Goodhart of LSE and Manoj Pradhan of Talking Heads Macroeconomics ("What may happen when central banks wake up to more persistent inflation?", Center for Economic Policy Research, Oct 2021).

were not enough, large and even off-cycle policy rate adjustments are indispensable.

12.4.3 *Adopting Investment-Led Growth Strategy*

The pandemic has underscored the need to further pursue reforms that would allow the economy to shift to a more investment-led growth strategy. One compelling reason for this strategy is what investments can offer to achieve more resilience during periods of economic stress and crisis. Evidence from past crises has revealed that FDIs could potentially be sources of stability and resilience. Alfaro and Chen (2012) found that multinational owned establishments performed better than local competitors on average. In particular, multinational firms showed greater resilience to crises due to their wider global access to production and financial linkages, as well as their multinational network. Similarly, Desai *et al.* (2007) noted that foreign firms perform better than domestic firms during currency crises due to their ability to circumvent financial constraints given their access to parent company's equity.

The role of FDI during recovery also goes beyond financing (OECD, 2020). Multinational firms are generally larger, more research and development intensive, and more productive. They also foster greater cross-border partnerships and collaborations between companies which could facilitate finding long-term business solutions. The last reason follows Jorda *et al.* (2020) who showed that consistent with the neoclassical growth model, capital is destroyed in wars, but not in pandemics. In fact, pandemics could potentially induce relative labor scarcity and/or a shift to greater precautionary savings. These appear to suggest that a growth model centered on investment could be a more viable strategy, especially when recovering from a pandemic.

While significant strides have been made to liberalize the flow of capital to the country, a lot of work areas still need to be explored. Pursuing structural reforms that could further promote investments will help strengthen the Philippines against shocks like the COVID-19 pandemic and insulate it from its health and economic ramifications.

First, there is scope to improve governance and the quality of institutions in the country. Acemoglu and Robinson (2012) argued that inclusive institutions which create incentives for people to innovate, enable productivity growth through education and infrastructure, and maintain peace and order are all essential in creating an environment that is conducive to sustainable growth. In contrast, extractive institutions, or those that cater to oligarchic interests, tend to result in poverty and stagnant growth even in resource-rich economies, like what many African countries experienced. In terms of some metrics, the country's scores in Transparency International's corruption index, the World Economic Forum's global competitiveness, the World Bank's ease of doing business, and International Institute for Management Development (IMD)'s world competitiveness, while showing some improvements, lag behind those of many emerging economies and other Southeast Asian countries in the last few years.[11]

Second, large infrastructure gaps have contributed to the investment bottlenecks in the Philippines. In fact, in the latest IMD's ranking of the Philippines, deterioration was noted in both economic performance and infrastructure development in 2022. More generally, if improvements in the quality of infrastructure services were chalked up, these could have certainly helped cut the cost of doing business, attract more investment, and enhance productivity around the country (IMF, 2020). For instance, Egert *et al.* (2009) employing a Bayesian model averaging of cross-section growth regressions confirmed that infrastructure investment, particularly in telecommunications and the electricity sectors, has robust positive effect on long-term growth due to economies of scale and positive externalities from competition-enhancing effects. However, the authors also noted that the effect varies across countries and sectors over time.

[11]For Transparency International, the Philippines scored 33 out of 100 in 2021 or 117th out of 180 countries covered; World Economic Forum, 61.87 out of 100, or 64th out of 140 countries in 2021; for the World Bank, scored 62.8 out of 100 and ranked 95th out of 190 countries covered in 2019; and International Institute for Management Development, obtained 54.66 out of 100 putting the country at 48th out of 63 economies in 2022.

Lastly, there is also the need to attract investments to the right sector. For instance, there is an urgent need to improve the country's health infrastructure to enhance its preparedness and resilience to pandemic events. Aside from physical infrastructures, Oxford Business Group identified some key sectors where the government should focus on, namely: 1) capacity-building initiatives like scholarship and deployment programs for medical practitioners; 2) improvements in preventive and primary care such as immunizations; and 3) research and innovative health technology.

These recommendations assume greater urgency in the light of the Global Health Security Index (GHSI) for 2021 with the conclusion that "all countries remain dangerously unprepared for future epidemic and pandemic threats, including threats potentially more devastating than COVID-19." Covering areas such as prevention, detection and reporting, rapid response, health systems, commitments to improving national capacity, financing and global norms as well as risk environment, the GHSI ranked the Philippines 57th out of 195 countries with a score of 45.7 out of 100. The Philippines came behind China, Indonesia, Malaysia, Singapore, Japan, South Korea, and Thailand in Asia.

Oni *et al.* (2020) suggested that impact investing could play a vital role in channeling funds to countries that need them most, as well as to the health and health-adjacent sectors. The pandemic offers an opportunity to reevaluate how to pursue innovation and reform of failing systems. This entails integration of knowledge-based systems and a culture of information sharing in responding to crises. For instance, the world could learn from strategies implemented by countries that have successfully controlled and contained the transmission of the COVID-19 virus.

Channeling investments to more sustainable activities is undoubtedly important. The pandemic has underscored the need to take care of the environment. A green and inclusive recovery will significantly enhance the resilience of both economies and societies in the face of the severe recession and accelerating environmental challenges. Introduction of environmental, social, and governance (ESG) considerations in investment decisions is important as they correct for market failure known as tragedy of the commons. ESG forces firms to consider the real cost to the environment and society that their activities impose.

This is especially relevant for the Philippines which is exposed to natural hazards and calamities. These could potentially spill over to the real economy and the financial system. Natural disasters interrupt production activities of firms and households, increasing their financial vulnerability, reducing the value of their assets pledged as collateral for loans, and making debt servicing even more difficult for them.

12.5 Conclusion

To be sure, the Philippine economy has benefited from implementing strategic structural reforms that are geared towards allowing market forces to operate. These reforms placed the economy in a position of strength and flexibility to manage adverse shocks.

In particular, the structural reforms attached to the country's long engagement with the IMF, to some extent, helped catalyze the country's shift towards more outward-looking and market-oriented policies. Most notable of these were the country's establishment of an independent central bank, adoption of a flexible exchange rate policy and adherence to fiscal responsibility.

An independent BSP, as well as its shift to an inflation targeting framework, ushered in a period of low and stable inflation environment, leading to the market's well-anchored inflation expectation. As the growth model suggested in **Chapter 7**, a manageable inflation environment could have potentially led to higher investment, which in turn could have shifted the country's potential output to a higher equilibrium. This is supported by the observed steady increase in the country's TFP and declining ICOR. Even as they were disrupted by the pandemic, there are initial indications that both are beginning to recover. Moreover, the shift to a flexible exchange rate allowed the domestic economy to be more resilient in absorbing external shocks.

These allowed the country to enter the COVID-19 pandemic in a position of strength. Pre-pandemic (2010–2019) GDP growth averaged at above 6 percent. The robust growth of the domestic economy in recent years was achieved in an environment of generally stable inflation and was anchored on purposeful structural reforms. The country's strong track record of prudent policymaking has likewise led to robust external payments position, more than comfortable international reserves, improved external debt metrics, and resilient public finances.

Notwithstanding, the unprecedented nature of the pandemic did not spare the country from the brunt of the stringent lockdowns and restrictions necessary to contain the virus. The pandemic revealed existing weaknesses in the economy and proved that there was still scope to pursue more reforms to keep the economy more agile especially in a post-pandemic operating environment. Implementing reforms that would allow the economy to shift into a more sustainable and resilient growth strategy should be a policy imperative going forward.

The more challenging operating environment, complicated by the presence of global financial cycles, has also underscored the need for a comprehensive and integrated approach to macro-stabilization policies. For instance, flexible exchange rate could act as a first line of defense. The Philippines' experience suggests that the country's flexible exchange rate regime can help absorb some of the pressures arising from external shocks and that it has a built-in mechanism for automatic adjustment in general to deal with external imbalances.

However, in an operating environment where large capital flows could potentially lead to the loss of monetary policy independence, Rey's (2015) irreconcilable duo should point us to the imperative of drawing from an expanded tool kit those measures required to manage the build-up of systemic vulnerabilities over time and reducing procyclical feedback between and among relevant economic variables.

Successfully navigating a complex environment, which was even made more challenging by the pandemic, requires a more coordinated approach to policymaking. The Philippines will be in better stead with its good track record of pursuing policy and structural reforms, building appropriate economic institutions, and moving to market and competitive trade and investment regimes. These elements constitute the ingredients to sustainability and resiliency of economic growth.

PHILIPPINES Selected Economic and Financial Indicators	1995	2000	2005	2010	2015	2020
External Sector						
Current Account Position[1] (in million USD)	−3,297	−2,228	1,990	7,179	7,266	11,578
Current Account Position, as percent of GDP[1]	−4.3	−2.7	1.9	3.4	2.4	3.2
Goods, Net (in million USD)	−8,944	−5,971	−12,146	−16,859	−23,309	−33,775
Exports (in million USD)	17,447	37,347	25,162	36,772	43,197	48,212
Imports (in million USD)	26,391	43,318	37,307	53,631	66,506	81,987
Services, Net (in million USD)	4,765	−1,870	2,148	5,765	5,455	13,866
Exports (in million USD)	14,374	3,377	8,611	17,782	29,065	31,822
Imports (in million USD)	9,609	5,247	6,463	12,017	23,610	17,956
Capital and Financial Account, Net[1, 2] (in million USD)	3,393	3,363	—	—	—	—
Capital Account[1] (in million USD)	—	138	79	88	84	63
Financial Account[1, 3] (in million USD)	—	3,225	1,834	−11,491	2,301	−6,906
of which:						
Foreign Direct Investment, Net[1, 4] (in million USD)	2,944	2,240	1,664	1,070	5,639	6,822
Portfolio Investments, Net[1, 5] (in million USD)	1,485	−553	−1,298	−4,890	5,471	−1,680
Overall BOP (in million USD)	631	−509	2,410	15,243	2,616	16,022
Overseas Filipinos' Remittances						
Personal Remittances (in million USD)	—	—	13,095	20,563	28,308	33,194
Cash Remittances (in million USD)	3,869	6,050	10,689	18,763	25,607	29,903
External Debt (in million USD)	37,871	51,358	61,555	73,594	77,474	98,488
External Debt, as percent of GDP	44.7	61.4	57.3	35.3	25.3	27.2
Public Finance[6]						
Revenues (in million PHP)	361,220	514,762	816,159	1,207,926	2,108,956	2,855,959
Revenues, as percent of GDP	16.6	13.9	13.8	12.9	15.1	15.9
Expenditures (in million PHP)	350,146	648,974	962,937	1,522,384	2,230,645	4,227,406
Expenditures, as percent of GDP	16.1	17.6	16.3	16.2	16.0	23.5
Fiscal Position (in million PHP)[7]	11,074	−134,212	−146,778	−314,458	−121,689	−1,371,447
Fiscal Position, as percent of GDP	0.5	−3.6	−2.5	−3.3	−0.9	−7.6

(*Continued*)

PHILIPPINES Selected Economic and Financial Indicators	1995	2000	2005	2010	2015	2020
Total Outstanding Debt (in million PHP)	1,158,622	2,166,710	3,888,231	4,718,171	5,954,537	9,795,006
Total Outstanding Debt, as percent of GDP	53.2	58.6	65.7	50.2	42.7	54.6
Domestic Debt (in million PHP)	718,395	1,068,200	2,164,293	2,718,202	3,884,380	6,694,687
Domestic Debt, as percent of GDP	33.0	28.9	36.6	28.9	27.9	37.3
External Debt (in million PHP)	440,227	1,098,510	1,723,938	1,999,969	2,070,157	3,100,319
External Debt, as percent of GDP	20.2	29.7	29.1	21.3	14.8	17.3
Output[8]						
Gross Domestic Product, at constant 2018 prices (in million USD)	110,999	132,647	166,618	212,373	284,666	332,829
Growth rate	4.6	4.4	4.9	7.3	6.3	−9.6
Gross National Income, at constant 2018 prices (in million USD)	—	145,726	183,350	237,100	317,543	358,278
Growth rate	—	—	5.3	7.1	6.1	−11.4
Gross Domestic Product, at constant 2018 prices (in million PHP)	5,845,376	6,985,383	8,774,325	11,183,861	14,990,907	17,527,234
Growth rate	4.6	4.4	4.9	7.3	6.3	−9.6
Gross National Income, at constant 2018 prices (in million PHP)	—	7,674,162	9,655,472	12,486,043	16,722,293	18,867,410
Growth rate	—	—	5.3	7.1	6.1	−11.4
Labor Market[8]						
Employment	90.5	88.8	92.2	92.7	93.7[a]	89.7[p]
Underemployment	20.0	21.7	21.0	18.8	18.5[a]	16.2[p]
Unemployment	9.5	11.2	7.8	7.4	6.3[a]	10.3[p]

(Continued)

Prices[8]						
Inflation Rates (2018 = 100)	6.8	6.6	6.6	3.8	0.7	2.4

[−] not available.
[1] Data from 2005 to present are based on the Balance of Payments and International Investment Position Manual, 6th Edition (BPM6); data for 2005 are based on the Balance of Payments Manual, 5th Edition (BPM5); data for 1995 are based on the BOP old concept/national presentation.
[2] The balances of the capital and financial accounts are not added together in the BPM6 presentation. Based on BPM6 in principle, the balance on the sum of the current and capital accounts is equal to the balance on the financial account. Likewise, the current account balance is equal to the balance on the financial account less the balance on the capital account.
[3] In BPM6 (2005–2020), a positive (negative) balance in the financial account indicates net outflows (inflows) or net lending to (borrowing from) the rest of the world. The financial account balance is derived by deducting the residents' net incurrence of liabilities from their net acquisition of financial assets. By contrast, in BPM5 (2000), a positive (negative) balance indicates net inflows (outflows).
[4] Refers to non-residents' net direct investments in the country (liability side of direct investments); a positive balance denotes net inflows.
[5] Refers to the net balance of residents' portfolio investments abroad (asset side) and non-residents' investments in the country (liability side). In BPM6 (2005–2020), a positive (negative) net balance indicates net outflows (inflows). In BPM5 (2000), a positive (negative) net balance indicates net inflows (outflows).
[6] Source: Bureau of the Treasury and Philippine Statistics Authority.
[7] Refers to the National Government Surplus (+) / Deficit (−) sourced from the Bureau of the Treasury.
[8] Source: Philippine Statistics Authority (PSA).
[a] Calculation of estimates excludes data from the entire Region VIII.
[p] Preliminary.
Source: BSP Estimates.

References

Acemoglu, D. and J. Robinson (2012). *The Origins of Power, Prosperity, and Poverty: Why Nations Fail.* Crown Business.

Alfaro, L. and M. Chen (2010). Surviving the global financial crisis: foreign direct investment and establishment performance. *Harvard Business School Working Paper No. 10–110.*

Ari, I. and M. Koc (2018). Economic growth, public and private investments: a comparative study of China and the United States. *Sustainability*, 10(11), 3901.

Barro, R. and X. Sala-i-Martin (1995). *Economic Growth.* NY: McGraw-Hill.

Cabote, N. and J. Fernandez (2020). The distributional impact of monetary policy: evidence from the Philippines. *SEACEN Research Paper.*

Dakila, F. (2020). *Concluding Chapter of BSP Unbound: Central Banking and the COVID-19 Pandemic in the Philippines.* Manila: Bangko Sentral ng Pilipinas.

De Dios *et al.* (2021). Martial law and the Philippine economy. *UP School of Economics Discussion Paper.*

Desai, M. *et al.* (2007). Multinational and local firms' response to currency depreciations. *The Review of Financial Studies*, 21(6), 2857–2888.

Egert, B. *et al.* (2009). Infrastructure and growth: empirical evidence, *CESifo Working Paper No. 2700.*

Fernandez, J. (2015). Quantitative easing and Philippine capital inflows: the role of US long term interest rates. *Bangko Sentral Review.*

Guinigundo, D. and F. Cacnio (2019). Pursuing the cause of monetary stability in the Philippines. In: *The Story of Philippine Central Banking: Stability and Strength at Seventy*, pp. 30–75.

Haldane, A. (2020). Is home working good for you?. Speech delivered during the *Engaging Business Summit and Autumn Lecture*, 14 October 2020.

International Monetary Fund (2020). The Philippines a good time to expand the infrastructure push. *IMF Country Focus,* 6 February 2020.

Jorda, O. *et al.* (2020). Longer-run economic consequences of pandemic. *Federal Reserve Bank of San Francisco Working Paper 2020–09.* https://doi.org/10.24148/wp2020-09.

Koenig, E. (2020). Monetary policy in time of pandemic. *Dallas Fed Economics.* Federal Reserve Bank of Dallas, 16 April 2020.

Kongsamut, P. and A. Vamvakidis (2000). Chapter 2 of Philippines: towards sustainable and rapid growth. *IMF Occasional Paper 187.*

Obstfeld, M. (2015). Trilemmas and tradeoffs: living with financial globalization. In: C Raddatz, D Saravia and J Ventura (eds.), *Global Liquidity, Spillovers to Emerging Markets and Policy Responses*, Chapter 2, 013-078: Central Bank of Chile.

OECD (2020). Foreign direct investment flows in the time of COVID-19. *OECD Policy Responses to Coronavirus (COVID-19)*, 4 May 2020.

Oni, T. *et al.* (2020). *Impact Investment's Pandemic Challenge*, Project Syndicate 24 April. https://www.project-syndicate.org/commentary/covid19-impact-investment-to-improve-global-public-health-by-tolullah-oni-et-al-2020-04.

Rey, H. (2015). Dilemma not trilemma: the global financial cycle and monetary policy independence. *NBER Working Paper 21162.*

Rodlauer, M. *et al.* (2000). Philippines: toward sustainable and rapid growth: recent developments and agenda. *IMF Occasional Paper 187.*

Sicat, G. (2002). Political economy of Philippine economic reforms. *UPSE Discussion Paper No. 0207.*

Index

Printed in the United States
by Baker & Taylor Publisher Services